TRUST
After
TRAUMA

. . . .

A Guide to Relationships for Survivors and Those Who Love Them

. . . .

Aphrodite Matsakis, Ph.D

New Harbinger Publications

Publisher's Note

This publication is designed to provide accurate and authoritative information in regard to the subject matter covered. It is sold with the understanding that the publisher is not engaged in rendering psychological, financial, legal, or other professional services. If expert assistance or counseling is needed, the services of a competent professional should be sought.

Distributed in Canada by Raincoast Books.

Copyright © 1998 by   Aphrodite Matsakis
New Harbinger Publications, Inc.
5674 Shattuck Avenue
Oakland, CA 94609

Cover design by Lightbourne Images, © 1997
Edited by Kayla Sussell
Text design by Tracy Marie Powell
Author photo by Bryan Payne

Library of Congress Catalog Card Number: 97-75470
ISBN 1-57224-101-2 Paperback

New Harbinger Publications' Web site address: www.newharbinger.com

05   04

15   14   13   12   11   10

Acknowledgments

I would like to acknowledge both Kayla Sussell for her excellent editorial revisions, and the staff at New Harbinger Publications for their support during the writing of this book. I would also like to thank Susan Stutman, M.S.W., Peter Valerio, M.A., C.P.C. and Patience Mason, author of *Recovering from the War,* for their excellent insights into the relationship struggles of trauma survivors.

Most of all, however, I would like to thank the trauma survivors who have trusted me enough to share their pain with me. They have served as models of inspiration in their efforts to bear what for most people would be unbearable emotional pain and anxiety, often accompanied by significant physical pain, as well. Despite their many hardships, most of the trauma survivors described in this book have striven to contribute to their families, friends, and communities and have often succeeded in making a positive difference in the lives of others.

This book is dedicated to my two daughters, Theodora and Magdalena, and to my clients, both dead and alive, who have suffered as a result of human cruelty, human error, or tragic events beyond their control. It is they who have helped teach me the true meaning of courage, perseverance, love, and loyalty.

Contents

Introduction

Trust After Trauma—
A Guide to Relationships
for Trauma Survivors and
Those Who Love Them

The Private World of Pain

> In my private world of pain
> The past, it lives again
> And I cannot make it go away
> No matter what I do or say.
>
> —Jack, a trauma survivor

This book is about trauma and relationships, about how being traumatized as the result of violence has strained your existing relationships and made it difficult for you to feel close to others. The violence you experienced may have resulted from any number of trauma-producing events. For example, there may have been violence in your family, such as sexual or physical abuse, or you may have lost a loved one to homicide or suicide, or to a vehicular disaster. You may work as a police officer, firefighter, or medical-crisis professional where dealing with the results of violence is an everyday part of your job. The violence that led to your trauma could have been caused by a natural event, such as a flood or an earthquake, or have had a political cause, such as war. Modern life, unfortunately, does not lack for trauma-producing events. (See appendix B for a more expanded definition of traumatic situations.)

But this book does more than simply explain how having been traumatized can make it so hard to relate to others. It can also help you learn, step-by-step, how to slowly reconnect with others, not as you did before you were traumatized, but as you are now, with real limits and real trauma-related reactions which, until now, have severely hampered your ability to enjoy the company of others. Many survivors feel irrevocably different from others—deficient, undesirable, and permanently scarred because of the trauma. Some are certain their trauma "shows," even though there are no physical scars.

Hence, even when trauma survivors are with others, they may feel alone; sometimes they feel even lonelier than when truly alone. Through no fault of their own, many trauma survivors feel condemned to a life of emotional numbness, loneliness, or superficial relationships. Although they may be engaged in some relationships, they *feel* as if they live on the fringes of their family and society. They may resent the fact that their traumatic experiences robbed them not only of their peace of mind, physical health, and years of life, but also of the ability to be social and to initiate and sustain an intimate relationship.

Quite often trauma survivors develop symptoms of post-traumatic stress disorder (PTSD), clinical depression, panic disorder, or other post-traumatic problems that can interrupt or limit their abilities to be productive and to develop and maintain close human ties. For many survivors, their PTSD or other trauma-related symptoms are just another source of shame and stigma and another reason to be angry at the past or at life itself and to withdraw from and stay away from other people.

This book will help you to understand how trauma can damage a person's ability to relate to others; for example, why trauma survivors so often feel alienated from, furious at, or suspicious of other people. It will help you understand why they so often choose isolation because of their fear that being with people will trigger rage, depression, or despair. To avoid the possibility of such emotional pain, many trauma survivors choose to be alone or to restrict their relationships to a few select persons. Dinner invitations are turned down; movie dates are canceled; and family gatherings, even holiday parties, are avoided, or attended with great trepidation. For some survivors, problems in coping with people make it difficult to keep a job, or do what it takes to get a promotion. Their small emotional world may feel safe to them, but it can also feel like a trap.

On the other hand, there are some trauma survivors who don't feel comfortable unless they are surrounded by others or engaged in an intimate relationship. Despite the physical presence of others, however, they may still feel intensely alone because they are constantly on guard and don't feel free to be their true selves. A pervasive sense of doom, insecurity, and mistrust haunts their relationships, transforming times of comfort or pleasure into times of anxiety and tension.

For some trauma survivors, the major problem is developing the capacity to be close to others. For other survivors, especially women, the ability and desire to form attachments to others are there, but the issue is with whom and under what conditions. Can a woman who has been terrorized in an intimate relationship, or by wartime circumstances, learn to select friends, co-workers, and intimate partners who won't revictimize her? Can she learn to negotiate in relationships to have her needs met and her boundaries respected?

Is This Book for You?

This book is for trauma survivors who have already completed some work in understanding their trauma either in therapy or a recovery program. It is not for persons who have never dealt with their past, or for persons who are still actively abusing substances, such as alcohol or drugs, or whose eating disorder is still controlling their lives.

If your alcohol, drug, food, gambling, or sexual addiction is the focus of your life, then you need to seek help to gain some control over your symptoms before you can profit from this book. While it is not necessary to be *totally* free of an addiction, it is necessary to be in a recovery program and have the symptom under *some* control; otherwise, realistically, you will not have the time and energy to pay attention to your relationships. This book is also not suitable for persons suffering from multiple personality disorder, unless it is used under the direction of a trained mental health professional.

Who Is a Trauma Survivor?

Trauma survivors are men and women who, at one or at many points in their lives, were rendered helpless and trapped in situations of great danger. A traumatic incident is one in which there is a real potential for loss of life or serious injury to one's self or others. Not everyone who is exposed to a traumatic situation develops psychological difficulties as a result, but many people develop some form of stress reaction. The symptoms may lift after several weeks if the trauma does not reoccur again and if there is ample support available to the victim. However, when someone is repeatedly traumatized without any effective treatment or assistance or when the traumatic stressor is massive, such as losing one's entire family in a car accident or being raped by a family member, it is highly likely that the victim will suffer psychological damage.

Some people undergo several traumas before developing symptoms. As Dr. Bessel van der Kolk (1996) explains, one particular traumatic incident can "activate other, long-forgotten memories of previous traumas and create a 'domino effect.' A person who was not previously bothered by intrusive and distressing memories may, after exposure to yet another traumatic event, develop such memories of earlier experiences" (van der Kolk 1996, 9). Each exposure to traumatic stress tends to make people more sensitive to the next traumatic incident, not more resilient (James 1994).

For example, a nurse on a burn unit who has seen many suffering people may not develop stress reactions after the first death on her ward, but after the thirty-fifth. At that time, the nurse may be flooded with images not only of the thirty-fifth death, but of many of the previous deaths. Or an adult who is the survivor of child abuse develops symptoms of post-traumatic stress disorder after being mugged, at which time memories surface not only of the mugging, but of the abuse suffered as a child.

Two Case Histories: Claire and Don

The following two case histories illustrate how trauma can damage a person's ability to relate intimately with others. They also describe how the effects of trauma can be counteracted.

Claire was sexually abused by her uncle for ten years, from the age of seven until she was seventeen. Then she married a man who maltreated her in many ways. After finally leaving her husband, she abused food and alcohol to manage her feelings, because she knew no better way. One day, however, she decided enough was enough and she sought help. Getting in touch with her traumatic memories and her long-suppressed feelings was frightening and excruciatingly painful. However, as the result of her therapeutic efforts, she became sober, lost a hundred pounds, graduated from college, and began to feel ready to love again.

But each time she started to be close to a man, he triggered memories of her abusive uncle and her brutish husband.

What should she do? Tell her boyfriend about her past and risk his viewing her as a "psycho" and leaving her? Or say nothing, and then go numb, or ballistic?

A few times when she described details about her past, men did reject her. One former boyfriend became so sickened by Claire's story that he vomited. Another became angry at Claire for "allowing" herself to be abused. These men were not therapists and in their minds they truly believed that a seven-year-old could do battle against a manipulative, emotionally powerful favorite uncle and that a seventeen-year-old whose self-esteem had been trodden on most of her life could see through an exploitative older man.

Such reactions to her self-disclosures caused Claire so much shame, and anger, she decided never to talk about her past again. But she had to. How could she really get close to a man without telling him something about her history? Besides, when she tried to have sex, sometimes her boyfriend did things that were not truly hurtful, but which distressed her because they reminded her of the sexual abuse she had suffered in both her childhood and her marriage. Then she would shut down, emotionally and sexually, and the romantic evening would be a "flop."

Claire knew that if she didn't explain her shutdown, then her boyfriend might feel frustrated, inadequate, and hurt. But if she did explain, she worried he would judge her as inadequate and ultimately reject her. How could she say enough to ease the situation without overwhelming or alienating her partner? At the same time, she wondered why she should even bother trying to relate to a "civilian." "Civilians" is what Claire called people who had never been traumatized.

"They're in another world. They don't have a clue what it's like to have PTSD, depression, anxiety attacks, and fight an addiction. Why should I bother with those Pollyanna types anyway? They'll never accept me and I can't stand them anyway," Claire would say. But she still wanted to have relationships with people other than her therapist, members of her support group, and a few special friends.

Claire was furious! She wanted to be free of her past. She couldn't erase the past, but in the present she wasn't out of control of her own life, as she had been in the past when others had dominated her. During her years of traumatization, most of the choices she had were "all or nothing" choices because she was in life-or-death situations. Either she complied with her abuser, or he hurt her. There was no room for negotiation. Either she obeyed or rebelled. Either way, she paid a heavy price.

In therapy, she learned that she had some choices. For example, there were more choices than saying nothing or telling everything about her past. If she wanted, she could describe just a little bit of her past, see how her partner reacted, and more importantly, see how *she* felt, before deciding to share any more. She learned that she could also let her sexual or other preferences be known without having to explain why she had these preferences.

Dan, a police officer, had learned from both his father and the police force that "real men" did not talk about their feelings or admit to any kind of weakness. Despite having been traumatized as a police officer for many years, Dan believed the myth that policemen, like rescue workers and other types of emergency personnel, become so accustomed to death that they accept it easily without feeling any emotions. For many years, Dan thought that sleepless nights, nightmares, migraine headaches, severe heartburn, and stomach cramps were a "normal" part of life. When these symptoms led to difficulties on the job, Dan finally went for counseling.

He was ridiculed on the job for seeing a therapist, but he did not care. He realized that he was fighting for his sanity and his marriage.

His wife was tired of sleeping alone, going to family gatherings without her husband, and having to function as if she were a single parent.

Like Claire, Dan looked down on "civilians" while also longing to be like them. Also like Claire, he found intimacy with the opposite sex difficult and he was constantly trying to find ways to cover up his anxieties about intimacy. Unfortunately his wife's hair was the same color as the hair of the first person he had killed as a police officer in the line of duty, that unforgettable "first kill." And when his wife disrobed, memories of naked female corpses flooded his consciousness.

Dan didn't want to tell his wife about these memories, but he had to do something in order to reduce their power over him. In therapy he learned that talking to his wife as they went to bed helped to ground him in the present and diverted his attention from the old memories. He didn't even have to explain to his wife why he wanted to talk before they made love. He simply said that he would really like it if they could spend some time talking or watching TV together before being intimate. That way he was spared the heartache of having to talk about a past he was trying to put behind him while at the same time focusing on his wife. The old memories didn't go away, but they didn't take over the bedroom either.

Healing from Trauma

Post-traumatic stress disorder (PTSD) is one possible reaction to trauma, but it is not the only one. Throughout history, people have reacted to the tragedies in their lives by falling victim to clinical depression, somatization, and any number of other dissociative disorders. (See appendix B for a brief description of PTSD, clinical depression, somatization, and dissociation.) As Dr. van der Kolk explains, "The diagnosis of PTSD alone never fully captures the totality of people's suffering" (van der Kolk 1996, 7). Furthermore, "Focusing solely on PTSD to describe what victims suffer does not do justice to the complexity of what ails them" (van der Kolk 1996, 16). The same observations hold true for depression, somatization, and any number of other reactions people have to traumatic stress. No diagnosis can capture the range and depth of suffering or the specific way that trauma can affect a person's life.

In her 1992 landmark book, *Trauma and Recovery*, Judith Herman writes that the first stage in healing from trauma involves making your world as safe as possible. This means ending abusive or exploitative relationships and situations; it also means learning to feel safe within yourself by learning how to control your nightmares, intrusive thoughts, flashbacks, insomnia, depression, or any addiction. Feeling safe within yourself also means learning to tolerate strong feelings, such as rage, grief, and anxiety, without being destructive towards yourself or others.

Only when you've established a certain degree of internal and external safety can you then safely proceed to the second stage of healing, which involves remembering the trauma and feeling the feelings associated with the trauma. The major feelings that need to be dealt with are anger, shame, powerlessness, anxiety, and grief. During this second stage of healing, you will begin to identify your many losses and, as much as you can, to mourn.

The third stage in healing from trauma involves re-establishing human ties. When your life is dominated by memories of the trauma, or by an addiction that serves to help numb you to the effects of the trauma, you don't have much time or energy to devote to relationships. Yet problems with your family life, your friendships, or love life may have caused you to turn to alcohol, drugs, food, gambling, or sex as a substitute for meaningful human contact. When you have some understanding of your trauma and some control over your symptoms, including any addictions, you will be ready to begin to reestablish some old relationships and even consider building new ones.

Ideally, using this book is part of your ongoing therapeutic program, either with a trained professional or with a self-help or other recovery program. As you continue to do therapeutic work on your trauma, your increased awareness of its impact on your inner life can only help you in your goal of improving your relationships. The greater your commitment toward some trauma-processing work either with a therapist, a support group, or a recovery program, the more you will benefit from this book.

If you have yet to begin on your quest for self-awareness, several self-help books and other kinds of information are available (see appendix A).

Family, Friends, and Partners

This book is also for family members, friends, and the significant others of trauma survivors who are frustrated in their efforts to sustain and deepen a relationship with someone who has been traumatized. All too often intimates, friends, children, parents, siblings, and other loved ones try their best to be supportive, only to be told they "don't understand" or that their way of helping is "no help at all." They want to help, or at least "to be there," for the one they love, but they feel helpless and confused about what to do. Despite their good intentions, family members and friends frequently find themselves subjected to the survivor's anger, or to an icy, cold emotional distance.

If you have tried to connect emotionally with a trauma survivor, you've probably found that what "works" with others, doesn't always "work" with the survivor. You try to be as understanding as possible, but you don't know how to fit into your loved one's life in a way that works for both of you. You can see that he—or she—is tormented and you want to reach out, but you do not, and should not, have to shoulder all of the survivor's pain or needs. Neither should you be treated like a second-class citizen simply because you were not traumatized and cannot understand what your loved one is going through the way that a fellow survivor or a therapist would understand.

For the family members and loved ones of trauma survivors, this book provides information and some guidelines on how to cope with a most complex and demanding challenge: having a relationship with someone who has been traumatized in a way that respects the effects of the trauma, but also respects your needs and dignity too. (Appendix A lists books on trauma that may assist you in learning more about your loved one.)

Changing Your Life

Many trauma survivors ask, "Will I ever be able to have a 'normal' relationship?" The bad news is that the trauma happened and that it did damage you in many ways, including your ability to relate to others or to select and sustain safe relationships. The good news is that even if you have been traumatized, you don't need to spend the rest of your life in an emotional prison or in oppressive relationships. You can begin to climb out of the emotional barriers that the trauma created and learn how to create a more loving, caring world for yourself *one step at a time* by slowly improving your relationships or by learning to structure them so you can be comfortable. Even though right now you may think it is impossible, you *can* overcome some of the serious obstacles that the trauma imposed on your life. You *can* learn to create and sustain healthy and rewarding relationships and shape them so that they won't become reincarnations of previous abusive relationships.

You may never be as free and easy within your relationships as you might have been had your life not been tragically disrupted. But you don't have to live in a prison of isolation or in an emotional desert either. Neither do you have to tolerate relationships where you feel you can't speak up or exert any control. The joys and satisfactions of sharing with others, in a way that's manageable for you, are not forever out of reach. Just as seeking out a therapist or support group can teach you that you need not suffer alone all the time, this book can show you that you need not live out your life in loneliness.

If you were an abused or neglected child, no current relationship can make up for the parenting that you lost. If you were a battered wife, no current relationship can totally undo the damage inflicted on your heart and body by your abusive husband. If you are a combat veteran or a survivor of a loved one's suicide or homicide, all the re-lationships in the world cannot bring back the precious person or persons who were lost. But isolating yourself or limiting your interactions to small talk won't heal your scars or bring back your dead either.

This book is about what is going on in your emotional life now—today. It is based on the belief that although relationships have their limits (especially in terms of making up for what was lost) authentic communication, along with affection and caring, can make the terrors of the past more bearable. Furthermore, involvement with others can provide you with reasons to go on living during those times when just staying alive is such a struggle. Whereas during your trauma, detaching from others and not trusting them may have saved your life, in the present, forming safe relationships is a life-preserving strategy (Harvey 1995). No matter how "safe" staying alone or keeping to yourself may seem, self-imposed isolation can be very lonely and can create a hunger for human companionship that all the televisions, VCRs, computers, and books in the world cannot satisfy.

If you feel ready to end your isolation but are fearful and wary of taking steps toward others, then this book is for you. Its aim is to help you understand how the trauma affected your relationships and to guide you in taking constructive steps toward improving your human ties, within the limits imposed upon you by your history. Neither this book, nor any other, can remove your trauma symptoms completely. But knowledge is power and the more you know about trauma and how it affects you and your relationships, the greater the chance that you can enjoy a richer life.

How to Use This Workbook

Read this book slowly and work on the written exercises at your own pace. Set a time limit on the amount of writing you do. Try not to write more than thirty minutes at one time. There may be occasions when you want to write more. Feel free to do so, but observe the following cautions and stop at the first sign of becoming overwhelmed, anxious, or "tuned out."

The Value of Writing About Painful Experiences

Research has shown that writing about painful experiences can be very helpful. Like being in group therapy, writing can help to boost your immune system and keep your body healthy (Pearlman 1994). Writing, like any form of expression, can be a healing activity. Writing about troubling experiences and the troubling aspects of your relationships helps you to see them more clearly and gives you a sense of mastery over your experiences. Once you put something down on paper, you may make connections you were not previously aware of and you may get in touch with feelings you haven't experienced before. You may start to grieve for losses that you haven't grieved for previously because you may become newly aware of those losses. Such grieving is painful in the short run, but it can be very healing in the long run because unresolved grief is an obstacle to emotional growth. Also, getting in touch with your losses may be the beginning of being able to make plans and decisions for your future.

Cautions

You will need to monitor your reactions to this book, because even though you may have processed some of your trauma in therapy, some parts may cause traumatic memories or reactions of which you were not aware to rise to the surface of your consciousness. Readers who have been repeatedly traumatized must be especially cautious, since some traumatic memories that are still buried may be triggered into awareness by the material. Should this occur, it is highly recommended that you seek professional help.

If, during your reading of this book or at any other time during the healing process, you experience any of the following reactions, seek professional help immediately and do *not* continue reading without first consulting your physician or counselor. (The following material is adapted from *I Can't Get Over It* (Matsakis 1996).)

- Hyperventilation, uncontrollable shaking, or irregular heartbeat

- Feelings that you are losing touch with reality, even temporarily; for instance, having hallucinations or extremely vivid flashbacks of certain traumatic events

- Feeling disoriented, "spaced out," unreal, or as if you might be losing control

- Extreme nausea, diarrhea, hemorrhaging, or other physical problems, including intense, new or unexplained pains, or an increase in symptoms of a preexisting medical problem; for example, erratic blood sugar levels if you are diabetic or wheezing if you are an asthmatic

- Self-mutilation or the desire to self-mutilate

- Self-destructive behavior such as alcohol or drug abuse, self-induced vomiting, or compulsive gambling or overspending

- Suicidal or homicidal thoughts

- Memory problems

Call for help if you are experiencing so much emotional pain, anxiety or anger that you fear you will die. Mild anxiety is to be expected, but extreme anxiety or despair needs professional attention as soon as possible. If you are unable to contact a mental health professional, and are truly frightened, go to the emergency room of a local hospital. Meanwhile, do the following:

- Stop reading this book (or whatever healing work you are engaged in) and focus on something else

- Talk to someone right away

- Touch something tangible

- Find someone to be with and avoid isolating yourself

- Do not take alcohol, drugs, or other mood-altering substances

- If you are angry, try expressing it safely, e.g., talking to a trusted friend, punching a pillow, or tearing up a telephone directory

- Do something pleasurable and relaxing, i.e., take a hot bath, go for a long walk, listen to favorite music, pet the cat

Even if you feel certain you do not need professional help, if you experience any of the reactions listed above, take a break from reading this book, and follow one of the listed suggestions. Keep in mind that having a strong reaction to thinking about the trauma, even in the context of its effects on your relationships, does not make your work a "failure." Developing symptoms as a result of reading this book or being in therapy does not reflect either an inability to heal or a hidden unwillingness to heal.

Instead, your reactions probably reflect the degree of traumatization you endured, which was not under your control. Your reactions have nothing to do with your strength of character or your intelligence. If you need to stop at any time and take a breather, whether that is for one day or several weeks, you can always come back later and examine the past.

Note, however, that there are some people who have been so severely traumatized that they may be better off not thinking about their pasts. The memories of some family abuse survivors, combat veterans, victims of torture, prisoners of war, and concentration camp survivors may be better left buried. If you fall into one of these categories, or find that the reactions listed above occur so frequently and intensely that the "healing" process is making your life unlivable, you should concentrate your efforts toward finding relief from your symptoms, rather than trying to understand the trauma or improve your relationships.

This book is not for persons suffering from multiple-personality disorder. If you suffer from panic disorder, clinical depression, manic-depressive illness, or another major psychiatric problem in addition to a post-trauma reaction, you need to be under the care of a trained professional.

It is also beyond this book's scope to offer guidance to survivors of family violence or sexual assault for confronting their abusers. The issue of confronting an abusive family member or another assailant is one that needs careful consideration and planning. Books for the layperson, such as *The Courage to Heal Workbook* (1990) by Laura Davis and books for professionals, such as *Healing the Incest Wound: Adult Survivors in Therapy* (1988) by Christine Courtois and similar materials should be consulted in deciding whether or not or how to confront an abuser.

Questionnaires and Exercises: Keeping a Journal

Working through this book is a *process*. This means that you will reread, reevaluate, and expand on your work as you go along. For that reason, you need to keep a journal that consists of all the writing you do in completing the exercises. You may already keep a personal diary, or you may decide to begin one after you have begun to heal, but right now all you need to do is make a separate "relationship healing" journal for the work you will do with this book.

Many chapters include either questionnaires or written exercises. The more honest and complete you are in completing these exercises, the more you will learn about yourself and the more you can help yourself to change and heal. I recommend that you buy a three-ring binder, some dividers, and some loose-leaf paper. Since you will be asked to go back, reread, and add to the writing you have done for previous exercises, using a loose-leaf notebook will enable you to add sheets as necessary. You will also be asked to write on a number of specific relationships and topics, such as feeling betrayed or becoming numb. The dividers will make each topic distinct and easy to find later on.

A number of exercises have been provided with blank lines for you to begin the exercises while you are still reading. It is highly recommended, however, that you transfer your answers to the pages in your three-ring binder, both for the additional space to write complete answers and for the ease of finding them for review.

As you work through this book, you need to keep several things in mind. Despite considerable recent interest and research on the effects of trauma on human beings, historically, professional interest in the area of trauma has been relatively sparse compared to the study of other problems. Consequently, our knowledge of the effects of overwhelming stress on human beings is limited, and sometimes the results of research studies are conflicting.

Research on the effects of trauma on relationships is even more limited, except for studies that show that early childhood trauma causes problems in bonding with others and that adolescent and adult trauma can seriously impair a person's ability to trust and be close to others.

There have been a few studies on couples and family therapy with trauma survivors, but no studies on friendships or work relationships. Most of the suggestions in this book are based on clinical experience, in combination with existing research. Some of the material in this book has been adapted from *I Can't Get Over It* (Matsakis 1996).

Because a relationship depends on the interaction between two persons there are no guarantees that any of the suggestions made here will transform your relationships. If there is any guarantee, it is that you can help to change yourself to exert more control over how you act and what you say and do in a relationship. The response of the other person is not under your control, but you can do your best to communicate clearly and to protect yourself from being triggered into anger, grief, or depression by a relationship.

Remember, however, that this book is only a beginning guide for improving the quality of your relationships. No self-help book, regardless of its value, is a substitute for individual, couples, or family counseling or some other form of in-depth help. You probably will need the assistance of caring friends, other survivors, and qualified professionals in your efforts to reconnect with others and to understand and meet the challenges the trauma has thrust upon you.

Some of the writing exercises and suggestions may be helpful; others may not. What helps one person may not help another. If a particular writing exercise does not apply to you or doesn't offer you insight or relief, this does not mean that you do not have the "right answer" or that you aren't trying hard enough.

References

Courtois, Christine. 1988. *Healing the Incest Wound: Adult Survivors in Therapy*. New York: W. W. Norton.

Davis, Laura. 1990. *The Courage to Heal Workbook*. New York: Harper and Row.

Harvey, Claire. 1995. "Stories of Resiliency in Trauma Survivors." Audiotape 951STSS of lecture presented at the Annual Conference of the International Society for Traumatic Stress Studies. Boston. November.

Herman, Judith. 1992. *Trauma and Recovery*. New York: Basic Books.

James, Beverly. 1994. "Trauma in Infants, Children and Adolescents: Context and Connectedness." Audiotape 96ISTSS-1 of lecture presented at the 12th Annual Meeting of the International Society for Traumatic Stress. San Francisco. November.

Matsakis, Aphrodite. 1996. *I Can't Get Over It*, Second Edition. Oakland, CA: New Harbinger Publications.

Pearlman, Laura. 1994. "Trauma and the Fulfillment of Human Potential." Audiotape of lecture presented at the 12th Annual Meeting of the International Society for Traumatic Stress. San Francisco. November.

van der Kolk, B. 1996. "The Black Hole of Trauma." In *Traumatic Stress; Effects of Overwhelming Experience on Mind, Body and Society.* Eds. B. A. van der Kolk, A. McFarlane, and L. Weisaeth. New York: The Guilford Press.

1

Taking an Inventory of Your Relationships

Those of you who have been in twelve-step programs such as Alcohol Anonymous (AA), Narcotics Anonymous (NA), Overeaters Anonymous (OA), or Al-Anon may be familiar with the fourth step, to take a "fearless and searching" moral inventory of yourself. Usually this step consists of making a list of those persons whom you think that you may have hurt, either intentionally or unintentionally, during your days of drinking, drugging, overeating, or starving yourself, as a result of the fears and anxieties that underlay your substance abuse.

One of the persons who should definitely be on that list of injured parties is you yourself. When trauma survivors work on the fourth step and remember to include themselves on that list, they often come to see how they let themselves down, injured themselves, or allowed others to take advantage of them. For many trauma survivors, this pattern of allowing themselves to be victimized had its origin in their being abused as children or in their being trapped in aversive circumstances where they had little or no control. (See chapter 12, "Revictimization and Reenactment," for a discussion of the reasons why someone who has been emotionally, physically, or sexually battered is vulnerable to being revictimized.)

In this chapter, you are going to be asked to write something similar to the fourth step of a twelve-step program, but there will be no moral judgments involved, and the entire focus will be on your relationships. Basically, you will be asked to take a relationship inventory: to take a close look at your relationships; to examine your relationship problems prior to your trauma, during your trauma, and today.

At first, this task may seem overwhelming, but you will be asked to focus on only a few relationships at a time and you will be guided in completing the task one step at a time. It is essential to take such an inventory because until you know the specific nature of your relationship issues, you cannot begin to address them.

Not every trauma survivor is the same. Even people who have endured similar kinds of hells may have radically different relationship issues because each person's experiences are unique in that each person had a life and relationships before the trauma took place. It is important to have a mental picture or "map" of the relationships and relationship needs you had prior to your trauma so that you can better assess how the trauma affected them; and then you can begin to think about the relationships you want to work on and in what kinds of ways. The purpose of requiring you to think about your relationships prior to, during, and after your trauma is that you can begin to make associations between how your relationships at these different stages of your life might, or might not, be connected.

As you read this book, you will become better able to answer the questions below. When you begin to answer the questions, leave plenty of space after each response in case you decide to come back and review your answers later and to write some more.

You will take a close look at your relationships during three periods of time: before the trauma, during the trauma, and after the trauma. Those of you who have been traumatized since early childhood may not be able to identify any "pre-trauma" relationships since your first memories may be of abuse. Also, for those of you who have been repeatedly traumatized, the idea of looking back to a period of time when there was no trauma may seem like a bad joke. If your earliest memories are traumatic or your life has been a series of traumatizations, then either skip the section on pre-trauma relationships or write about any nonabusive relationship you had during that period. For example, you could write about someone who treated you in a caring way, or someone who was not involved in the trauma but with whom you had a good relationship, such as a school friend or a neighbor.

Your Relationship Inventory

In our lives we have many different kinds of relationships that function on many different levels. We have family relationships, friendships (from casual acquaintances to lifelong "buddies"), romantic/sexual relationships, school and work relationships, and special purpose relationships, such as people we play basketball with or salespeople we see regularly. You can choose from any of these categories of relationships to answer the following questions.

Pre-Trauma Relationships

Prior to the trauma, what were the important relationships in your life? Although there may be several, pick only three. For example, you could pick your relationship with a parent or a caretaker, a sibling, friend, teacher, neighbor, or even someone who would abuse you in the future.

It may be there are more than three people you remember as being important to you. You can list their names, too, and at a future point in time come back and write about your relationships with them, if you choose to do so. But for the time being, pick only three relationships that mattered to you, either positively or negatively, and answer the following questions for each of these relationships:

1. For each relationship, list five adjectives that best describe that relationship.

2. For each adjective, write down a memory that supports the adjective. For example, suppose you chose to write about your grandmother and one of the adjectives you selected was "spiritual." A memory that would support the idea that you and your grandmother had a spiritual relationship would be that of praying with her or of her reading spiritual materials to you at bedtime.

3. What aspects of each relationship did you enjoy? What aspects did you not enjoy?

4. How did you feel when you were with this person?

5. Did you trust this person? Why or why not? Did you trust him or her completely or only in some areas? How did you decide he or she was trustworthy or trustworthy only in some areas, but not others?

6. What did this person do for you? What needs of yours did he or she fulfill? What needs of yours did he or she leave unsatisfied?

7. How did this person respond to you during or after your trauma? How did you want him/her to respond to you?

   If this person was not alive or was not present during or after the trauma, this question may not apply. Instead, consider this question: If this person had still been alive or present during or after your trauma, how might you have wanted him/her to relate to you?

8. If this person is still in your life today, write three or four sentences about how the trauma has affected your relationship with him/her? Do you wish your relationship with this person was different? If so, how?

9. Now, take a moment to reflect on the feelings you had while writing about this person. What were the various feelings you experienced? For example, did you feel love, anger, longing, confusion, self-hate, sexual desire, sexual repulsion, disgust, a desire for revenge, or a desire for forgiveness? If you can't identify any feelings, you need to ask yourself if this was a truly neutral relationship emotionally,

or whether your feelings are still so powerful or surrounded by taboos that you need to not remember or feel them. Perhaps you unconsciously believe that you might be (or would have been) punished for admitting what your feelings are. If necessary, you may need to consult a therapist to help you identify your feelings.

10. If you were able to identify your feelings, ask yourself if those feelings match your descriptions of the relationship. For example, if you wrote about a series of happy times with the person, and then you noted that you "still hated" him or her, how do you account for this discrepancy? Similarly, if you listed some abusive memories with that person, and then, in describing your feelings, you did not indicate that you felt any anger or other negative feelings toward that person, how can you explain the discrepancy? Once again, you may need to consult a therapist if you cannot make headway with this question in regard to any discrepancies between what happened and how you feel.

After you have answered the ten questions above for three relationships you had prior to your trauma, answer the following questions to the best of your ability.

1. Looking back over these three relationships, do you see yourself as having certain relationship difficulties prior to the trauma? Some common relationship problems that all people, not only trauma survivors, tend to experience are

   (a) difficulties expressing their feelings,

   (b) saying "no" to requests, and

   (c) allowing fear of abandonment and/or rejection to determine their behavior.

2. Looking back over these three relationships, what do you see as having made these relationships "work" for you? What did these people do (or not do) that made you feel comfortable with him/or her? What did these people do (or not do) that made you feel frustrated or uncomfortable?

3. Which of your needs were met in this relationship and which were not?

4. Did you ever do anything to make this relationship better, or, alternatively, to hurt it? How do you feel about your behavior today?

Relationships During the Trauma

If you have had many traumatic experiences, pick only *one* experience to write about now. Later on, after you work through this book, you may decide to write about your relationships during other traumatic episodes.

Looking back over a particular traumatic episode, select three relationships that were important to you, either in a positive or a negative way. For each of these three relationships, list five adjectives that best describe the relationship and provide memories that explain the adjectives you have chosen. Then answer the following questions:

1. How did the relationship affect you during your trauma? Did it help you in any way? Did it harm you in any way?

2. Do you wish this person had acted differently during your trauma? If so, how?

3. How do you feel about this relationship as you think about it? Angry? Sad? Afraid? Happy?

4. Did your relationship with this person during your trauma affect any of your current family, work, community, or love relationships? If so, how?

5. As you did with the previous set of questions regarding pre-trauma relationships, take a moment to reflect on the feelings that you experienced while you were writing down your memories about this relationship. What were those feelings? Are you having trouble identifying what your feelings were? If this is so, why?

6. Do the feelings you identify for each relationship match the descriptions of the relationships? If there is a major discrepancy between what happened and what you feel, why might this be the case? Once again, you may need to consult a therapist to help you understand the difference between what happened and what you might expect to feel about what happened.

Post-Trauma Relationships

Identify three relationships that are important to you in your life *today* and, once again, list five adjectives that best describe each relationship. Then provide memories that illustrate the adjectives you have chosen and answer the following questions for each relationship:

1. Which aspects of this relationship are positive for you and which are not?

2. What is it about this person that causes you to trust, or not trust, him or her? Are there ways in which he or she is trustworthy and other ways in which he or she is not?

3. Which of your needs are met in this relationship? Which of your needs do you wish he or she would meet that are not being met? Why do you think these needs are not being met?

4. What needs do you fulfill for this person? Which of his or her needs are you unable or unwilling to meet? Why do you think you cannot or will not meet these needs?

5. Suppose you had never been traumatized, what do you think your relationship with this person would be like?

6. How do you think the trauma and its aftermath affect your relationship with this person? How much do any feelings caused by the trauma, e.g., survivor guilt, feelings of unworthiness, shame, anger, mistrust of others, and so forth affect your relationship with this person?

7. How would you like this relationship to be different? Is it possible to discuss your concerns with this person? If not, why not?

8. What prevents you from taking action to improve this relationship?

9. What feelings did you have while writing about your relationship with this person and what are your wishes for the future of your relationship with this person?

10. Do the feelings you identified match the descriptions of the relationship and your hopes for the future of that relationship? If there is a major discrepancy between the current status of the relationship, the way you currently feel, and your future hopes, why might this be the case? Once again, you may need to consult a therapist to help you understand this important aspect of your life: the difference between what happened, what is, what might be, and what you might expect to feel about what happened.

Congratulations. You've just done a lot of work in examining your relationships. As you continue on, hopefully, you will gain new insights into your relationship needs and patterns and learn more about how your having been traumatized has affected your relationship needs and patterns.

2

Exile: Feeling Like Frankenstein

The Strange Woman

"You're a little strange," said he
He, who lived so comfortably.

But can I help it?
I was hurt
And can I help it
I was used?

Dear Sir,
I have news for you.
If you had had my life
You'd be a little strange
Too.

—Betty, a trauma survivor

Frankenstein! The name immediately conjures up the image of the hideous monster we've all seen in the movies. However, Frankenstein isn't the name of the monster but of the monster's creator, Dr. Frankenstein. The original Frankenstein in Mary Shelley's book, *Frankenstein*, was an ambitious, well-intentioned scientist who wanted to create life in the laboratory. Using all of his ingenuity and knowledge he created a living being by combining different body parts from long dead corpses. His original purpose was to create a human being of superior intellect, beauty, and moral character. Instead, he created a repulsive beast.

Not knowing what to do when his experiment went awry, Dr. Frankenstein threw the beast out of his home, hoping that it would die. But the beast didn't die. Instead, he wandered throughout the world, homeless, hungry, unloved, and lonely. When he approached people, they shunned him, called him vile names, and beat him. At one point, the beast realized that, because of his looks, he would never become a part of society. He understood that he would be forever lonely. It was his rage over his loneliness and his abandonment by his creator, Dr. Frankenstein, that turned the ugly, but benevolent, beast into a blood-thirsty monster.

The beast Dr. Frankenstein created may have been horrible to look at, but he had human intelligence, senses, and emotions. Like abused children, he was emotionally and physically neglected and, later on, beaten and verbally abused. The monster Dr. Frankenstein created did not become a monster until he was exiled and denigrated. When he realized that he would be forever exiled from society and deprived of human love and companionship, he became so full of hate that he became a killer. Yet he wasn't born to be a murderer. "I was benevolent and good," the monster told Dr. Frankenstein, "Misery made me a fiend" (Shelley 1965, 139).

Several times, the monster tracked down his "father," Dr. Frankenstein, and begged the doctor to love, accept, and help him. "I am alone, miserably alone," the monster wept. But to no avail. Dr. Frankenstein abhorred him and threatened to kill him (Shelley 1965, 95).

"I expected this reception," said the monster. "All men hate the wretched; how then, must I be hated, who am miserable beyond all living things! Yet you, my creator, detest and spurn me, thy creature" (Shelley 1965, 95).

How many formerly abused persons feel like Dr. Frankenstein's beast, abandoned and mistreated by the very people who are supposed to love and care for them? And how many trauma survivors feel like the monster, unwelcome, and perceived as so misshapen, deformed, and ugly, that nobody wants them?

The beast didn't ask to be created, just as people who have been traumatized didn't ask to be traumatized. The beast could have coped with his ugliness, if only a few people could have accepted him and at least one person could have been close to him. But what he could not tolerate (and what many trauma survivors cannot tolerate) is being, or feeling, forever exiled from their fellow humans.

Exile

To the ancient Greeks, exile was worse than death. Common criminals were flogged, imprisoned, or even executed, but those who committed the most heinous of crimes were punished with what was considered the most supreme form of torture—banishment from the community. To be exiled is to be removed from everything one loves—family, friends, love relationships, and community—and no longer allowed to function as a member of a family, a worker, or a citizen. Without a place in society and deprived of all of his/her former relationships, the exile begins to feel like a thing, a nonperson. He or she is completely dehumanized, because without a purposeful role in society and without emotional connection to others, people do come to feel more like objects than living human beings.

Even though most trauma survivors are not formally exiled from society, they can feel like outcasts, banished from "normal" human society. In the movie, "Born on the Fourth of July," a crippled combat veteran is pulled out of his wheelchair by his fellow Americans and severely beaten. This event really happened and it has happened to other war-wounded veterans in wheelchairs, too, because combat veterans became the scapegoats for the nation's ambivalent feelings about the Vietnam War. In homes where there is incest or physical abuse, it is not uncommon for the victim to be treated by neighbors, friends, and relatives, and even some health care professionals, as if he or she is the "bad" one who should be shunned and punished.

Why is this so? How does it happen that being traumatized and surviving the threat of death inherent in the trauma can so often lead to a form of living death, that of feeling like an exile, or refugee, in one's own land?

Survivors also can feel like "exiles" because frequently they have difficulty participating in, much less enjoying, the social gatherings, family events, and community celebrations that most people take for granted. Events involving a crowd can make some survivors feel claustrophobic or paranoid. The noises and uncontrolled movements of a large group of people can resemble the chaotic nature of the trauma, and send the survivor into a tailspin of physiological overstimulation, or a form of panic. (See chapter 4, which addresses the biological aspects of PTSD in detail.)

A person's trauma may permanently change the meaning of particular events. For example, although many people consider the Fourth of July a time for celebrating, when the fireworks go off, the combat veteran may see body parts—not pretty colors. While he may feel as patriotic as the next person, the Fourth of July may fill him not with patriotic feelings, but with panic at his own mortality. He was on the front lines for his country, but on the Fourth of July he might hide in his home with his earplugs in and the curtains drawn, because the sight and sound of fireworks remind him of the hell of war.

There would be nothing "wrong" with this reaction, except that he might like to be a part of his family's Fourth of July barbecue and he might like to attend the Fourth of July parade with his girlfriend and he might like to feel as if he were a member of his community. Ironically, a veteran can feel like an "exile" from a holiday for whose meaning he was willing to risk his life.

The winter holidays are a joyous time for most people. Yet a firefighter may not see chestnuts roasting in an open fire but the burnt bodies he pulled out of a blazing building. The incest survivor may remember being raped under the Christmas tree and have no wish to go home for the holidays. The problem is, however, that she may have no other place to go that feels like "home." Through no choice of her own she feels orphaned at the time of the year that families traditionally gather together and celebrate their togetherness. Emotionally, she is an exile. On Mother's Day or Father's Day, persons who were abused by their parents also can feel like emotional exiles.

Gay or lesbian trauma survivors especially can feel ostracized because they may be separated from their families of origin or their children due to their sexual orientation. Their feelings of being "different" because of their traumatic histories are only heightened by the outcast status of homosexuals in our society.

In most cases trauma survivors are not formally exiled from their families of origins, their jobs, or their communities. But the unstated rule for belonging is that the trauma must not be mentioned. Most people don't want to hear about your trauma because if they really listened and understood the kind of horror you have been through, they might feel hurt the way that you do. Think about how badly you hurt sometimes because of your trauma. Haven't you gone to great lengths sometimes not to feel that pain? When you think about it this way, it's somewhat easier to understand those who do not want to hear your story, or those who need to discount your experiences.

Some people may be afraid that if they listened to you and understood the horrible struggles you have endured, they might not be able to function, or that they might have to rethink their concepts of the meaning of life, the nature of humanity, and other ideas on which they base their sense of security. As a result, people who have been traumatized are required to act as if their trauma had never happened, or if it did, it was not that important and, in any case, it is over now and need not be remembered—and certainly not discussed. Don't "dwell in the past" the trauma survivor is told, directly or indirectly. This "no talk" rule is in effect especially during times of family celebrations.

Blaming the Victim:
Natural Catastrophes
Versus Man-Made Traumas

Trauma survivors can be divided into two major groups: those who suffer as the result of natural catastrophes, such as earthquakes, hurricanes, or floods, and those who suffer as the result of man-made catastrophes, such as wars, domestic violence, or criminal assault. In general, natural catastrophes are seen as "acts of God" or as events clearly outside the realm of individual control. Hence, natural catastrophe survivors are rarely blamed for their trauma. Some vehicular accidents and technological disasters are also seen as the result of blind luck, rather than due to an individual's actions or character, and survivors of these kinds of events, such as airline crashes, are rarely blamed for their misfortunes. However, this is not always the case. Some hurricane survivors have been blamed for living in areas with histories of tropical storms and some earthquake survivors have been blamed for residing in areas known to be earthquake prone. Even some airline accident survivors have been blamed for flying.

However, the persons most blamed for their miseries are those who were involved in man-made disasters, just as Frankenstein's monster was blamed for his ugliness. This tendency to blame the victim is especially strong if the victim is already culturally devalued; for example, if the victim is a woman, a child, or a member of certain social or ethnic groups that are considered inferior. Survivors of suicide or homicide are often indirectly blamed for their loved ones' deaths, even if they were models of love and devotion to the individuals who died.

In the past, soldiers who suffered from combat trauma were frequently seen as cowards or traitors and were punished; some were executed. Even today, veterans with post-traumatic stress disorder are viewed by some as "weaklings" or "cry babies." Similarly, abused women have been viewed as psychological derelicts who "permit" the abuse and who, at times, even encourage it.

Prior to the 1960s, many mental health professionals blamed child abuse victims for the abuse they had suffered (Bender and Blau 1937; Freud 1933; Hoffman and Dodd 1975; Quina-Holland 1979). In this literature, young children were described as "seductive" and as having intense unconscious sexual fantasies that caused adults to rape them. Recipients of physical abuse were judged as "provoking" or as "deserving" of abuse because of certain personality traits or behaviors (which, in retrospect, the abuse may have created).

Not all professionals held such biases and certainly such biases are not as widely held today as they once were. Nevertheless, these blame-the-victim biases in the medical and mental health community reflected and, to the extent that they still exist, continue to reflect antivictim biases in the community at large. Current popular opinion still tends to blame victims of domestic violence and sexual assault for their own victimization.

When victims are not accused of creating their own pain, they are often accused of exaggerating their sufferings for purposes of compensation, or sympathy, or as an excuse to avoid responsibility. A century or so ago, for example, survivors of railroad accidents who filed for compensation were seen as imagining or magnifying their complaints for financial gain. Today, survivors of vehicular accidents may encounter the same accusation.

Even the Jews and other persecuted groups who died in the Nazi concentration camps have been blamed for their own destruction. "They should have known the Nazis wanted to destroy them and fled to safer countries. They should have organized a resistance and fought. If they had known better and done more, they might be alive today," such arguments hold.

The historical record shows that many Jews did flee and many more tried to, but were prevented. When they could, they also resisted. Most, however, were so terrorized, brutalized, impoverished, or starved by their enemies that they were unable to defend themselves.

Yet even when presented with historical evidence, there are people who insist that the victims of the concentration camps were responsible for their own deaths (Dawidowicz 1975; Herman 1992). This example of blaming the Jews for the Holocaust is extreme, but it serves to illustrate clearly the phenomenon of "blaming the victim." Fortunately, this attitude about the Holocaust is not widely held; but the fact that it even exists illustrates the extent to which victims, even the most obvious of victims, can be blamed for their own pain.

How is it that the "blame-the-victim" attitude can be so strong, as to defy all reason, evidence, and compassion? Why are victims so often despised and discredited?

One reason is that the very existence of trauma survivors challenges people's belief that they can control their own lives. As human beings, we need to believe that if we are strong enough, careful enough, or smart enough, we can make our world safe and happy. Our need to structure our lives so they can be as rewarding and secure as possible would be more realistic if we took into account the possibility of tragic events outside of our control. However, some people cannot deal with the prospect that they or their loved ones can be hurt or killed. The very thought is so terrifying that they would rather blame the victim than face the reality of trauma in everyday life.

The "Just World" Philosophy

The "just world" philosophy contributes to the blame-the-victim attitude. This philosophy pervades our society. According to this philosophy, the world is basically fair and people "deserve what they get and get what they deserve." The fundamental assumption of this essentially Western perspective on life is that if you are sufficiently careful, intelligent, moral, and competent, you can avoid misfortune. This fairy tale perspective is promoted in many popular books, movies, magazines, and some newspapers. Thus, people who suffer trauma are somehow to blame for their fate. Even if the victims aren't directly blamed, they are seen as somehow causing their victimization by being inherently weak or ineffectual.

The more accurate and certainly more sympathetic attitude toward survivors is summed up in these sentences: "If it can happen to him or her, it can happen to me. Life can be dangerous and unfair. Sometimes good capable people get hurt for no reason at all." However, people who try to avoid thinking about the possibility that they could be the next one to suffer might think instead, "What's wrong with this person? What did he or she do to cause this to happen?" When others can blame the victim, then they believe they can shield themselves from the real possibility that they too are but one collision away from a life of ongoing pain and disability.

According to van der Kolk and McFarlane (1996) having one's trauma validated by others is critical in treating PTSD. Yet, when the "psychological needs of victims and the needs of their social network conflict," such validation may be impossible. This is especially the case when the "meaning of the trauma is secret, forbidden or unacceptable (as in intrafamilial abuse or government-sanctioned violence)" or when the victim's persistent symptoms and disability impose major burdens on others (van der Kolk and McFarlane, 1996, 25).

Another reason that trauma survivors are often avoided is that many people don't know what to say to someone who has been traumatized. They may be afraid of saying the wrong thing and making the trauma survivor even unhappier or angrier, or they may simply not know how to talk about feelings. Or they may have a superstitious belief that trauma is contagious. On some primitive level some people think that if they are near a suicide survivor, car-accident survivor, or survivor of any other kind of tragedy, then that tragedy will happen to them, too. So they stay away.

Sometimes those who have never been hurt may have difficulty understanding and being sympathetic with those who have. "He jests at scars who never felt a wound," Shakespeare's Romeo tells his friends as they mock his sorrows (Romeo and Juliet, Act II, Scene 1). Also, people who have never confronted human tragedy are sometimes unable to comprehend the lives of those who have or those who work in occupations that involve dealing with human suffering or mass casualties. Simply put, some people have not had to face the negatives in life. Therefore, it is natural for them to ignore the fact that sadness, injustice, and loss are just as much a part of life as joy and goodness. When such individuals confront a trauma survivor, they may be at a loss as to how to react or they may reject or disparage the survivor because that individual represents those parts of life they have chosen to deny or that frighten them.

On the other hand, it also happens that sometimes trauma survivors are rejected or disparaged by other survivors—those who have chosen to deny or repress their own trauma and have not yet dealt with their losses and anger, and may not even be aware of them. This is the result of emotional numbing, a major symptom of PTSD. When trauma survivors who have not dealt with their traumatic pasts see someone who is obviously suffering, they may choose to stay numb to protect themselves from feeling. Thus, they may block out the trauma survivor to leave their own denial system intact. Also, it is much easier to be angry or to look down on the victim for what he or she supposedly "did" to "cause" the trauma than to share the burden of the victim's pain.

Often, when someone is traumatized, there may be a predictable initial rush of empathy and support. For example, if you were raped, or injured in a war or in an airplane accident, or if someone in your family committed suicide or was murdered, people will, at least initially, rush to your aid and shower you with support. But, just as predictably, a short time later they may expect you to "get over it."

As psychologist Jeffrey Jay (1994) points out, the message of the community to the trauma survivor is: "Forget the past. Come back to the family and the community where we have our beliefs and assumptions about how life is basically good and fair." As Jay stresses, this message is not necessarily a bad one. It invites the trauma survivor back into the family or community fold. Most people don't understand that it can take years to get over even an expected death, such as the death of an ill, aged parent. Obviously, more time is required when the death, or the loss, is completely unexpected.

But the truly traumatized can't go back without doing a lot of healing. They have been irrevocably changed. Unless they deny the trauma and push it out of their awareness, they cannot return to their pre-trauma selves because usually their previous assumptions about life have been shattered. They have been to another world, a world of terror and horror. Their family's and community's assumptions about life, that is, the "just world" philosophy, no longer make sense.

The Shattering of Assumptions

As psychologists Janoff Bulman and Frieze (1983) point out, victims are usually forced to reconsider at least three assumptions about themselves:

1. They are personally invulnerable,

2. The world is orderly and meaningful, and

3. They are good and strong people.

People who haven't been traumatized may also come to question these assumptions if they know trauma survivors or if they have studied history or psychology, but they are not forced to question the basic truth of these assumptions in the same way that trauma survivors must.

Similarly, all people are forced to confront the fact of their mortality; that they will someday die. Most people deal with this issue in mid-life, when they begin to see signs of their own aging or face the deaths of their parents or grandparents. Trauma survivors, however, are forced to confront the fact of their mortality at the time of the trauma, regardless of their age. They have a heightened sense of the fundamental fragility of life which, although it can empower them to try to make the most out of life, can also be frightening and overwhelming not only to themselves, but also to others who, quite understandably, prefer to avoid confronting the inevitability of their own deaths.

The Loss of Invulnerability

"It can't happen to me," you may have thought. But it did happen to you, therefore you may no longer feel the world is a safe place. At the very least, you probably feel less safe than you did before the trauma. And because you were traumatized once, even if others assure you that it can't happen again, you know that it could and fear that it will. These feelings of vulnerability indicate two symptoms of PTSD:

1. A sense of doom or an expectation of a foreshortened future, and

2. An intense fear that the trauma will repeat itself.

The Loss of an Orderly World

The just world philosophy cannot explain what happened to you. You used to think that if you were careful, honest, and good, you could avoid disaster. But the trauma taught you that all your best efforts could not prevent the worst from happening. Perhaps you saw others who were also innocent die or be unfairly injured. So, while you would like to believe that the world is orderly, and that good is rewarded and evil is punished, you had experiences that contradict these beliefs. If you were punished precisely because you were trying to be a good and competent person, it is even harder for you to hold to the just world philosophy.

The Loss of a Positive Self-Image

One of the most profound losses trauma survivors experience is the loss of a positive self-image. This loss affects their ability to excel at work and to relate to others; for, as so often happens, no matter how much someone else may assure you that you are valuable and lovable, if you've been deeply traumatized, you have trouble believing it. Like men and women who have been exiled from their communities for committing an unforgivable crime or carrying a deadly communicable illness, a part of you feels "bad," scarred, diseased, or otherwise unacceptable.

You might even feel ugly—as ugly as Dr. Frankenstein's monster, regardless of how attractive you really are. It is an established fact that women with histories of sexual abuse often feel "ugly" and undesirable even when they are models of feminine beauty. They believe they look ugly on the outside, because they feel ugly on the inside, or because ugly things have happened to them. Not just sexual trauma survivors, but other kinds of trauma survivors, describe themselves as feeling "ugly"—like monsters. They may talk about their facial features and other physical attributes, but in reality they are referring to the ugly feelings they harbor inside of themselves; feelings like shame, self-hate, jealousy, and the desire for revenge.

Like Frankenstein's monster, they may have thoughts of harming those who hurt them or caused their pain. Also like Frankenstein's monster, they may want to kill their "ugly deformed selves"—to stop the pain. In most of society, such destructive thoughts are taboo, hence the trauma survivor suffers not only from the destructive thoughts and feelings, but also from the guilt and shame associated with harboring such ideas and impulses. In the words of one trauma survivor, "It's no fun to be mad all the time. It takes everything out of you. I hate being so angry, but I can't help it either. If people hadn't treated me so badly, I wouldn't be so mad. Then I get angry with myself for being so mad. It's a vicious cycle."

A trauma survivor can truly come to feel like a monster because of the monstrous feelings within, even though, like Frankenstein's beast, these resentments are the result of being rejected and treated as an outcast. In our Judeo-Christian culture, having such intense negative feelings is not usually considered part of a "good person's" makeup. Thus, when homicide survivors fantasize about torturing the murderers of their loved ones, when formerly abused persons take pleasure in planning exquisite forms of cruelty for their former abusers, or when crime victims engage in violent revenge fantasies, they don't feel like good, attractive people: they feel like "bad, ugly" ones.

The intensity of your anger and resentment can destroy any previous concept you had of yourself as a "good" person. Trauma can also destroy your illusions about your strength, self-sufficiency, and competence. You have confronted your personal limits and the limits of human intelligence, action, and love in ways that only your fellow trauma survivors can understand. Your co-worker who has been lucky enough never to have lost a dear one or to have known a personal defeat does not know the way that you know what it's like to stand helplessly by as someone dies. That co-worker does not know what it's like to be trapped in an abusive relationship whose power has permeated every aspect of his or her inner being. That co-worker does not know what it's like to be subject to unpredictable anxiety attacks in the middle of the day or night. Because of your suffering, you may have had times when you felt as though you were "losing your mind" or feared you were "losing control" of yourself. These fears may have propelled you to seek help.

However, in our society, which worships self-sufficiency and happiness, admitting that you are unhappy and need help is a "no-no"—a sign of weakness. Few believe the Buddhist maxim that "life is suffering" and even fewer adopt the philosophy that "suffering is the beginning of wisdom." In mainstream USA, shame and stigma are associated with going to a therapist or a support group, although in a few small circles therapy has begun to be acceptable.

Despite increased acceptance of the need for psychological services, old attitudes die hard. Many survivors do not feel "safe" disclosing the fact that they have sought help or are in therapy or a recovery program. Few veterans, for example, want to be identified as a veteran with "problems." Trauma survivors often fear that their partners or friends will reject them if they learn the truth.

Trauma survivors often feel "different" from others and, in many ways, they are. But the problem is not that the trauma changes a person's emotions and biochemistry (see chapter 4), but in how these changes are viewed. Often the emotional and physiological consequences of having been traumatized are seen in a negative light—as signs of deficiency, incompetence, or moral or personal weakness. But where is the evidence for this?

Some traumatic reactions and PTSD symptoms can be dangerous, for example, dissociating while driving. Still other symptoms can impose limits on the survivor's activities, for example, the inability to sleep. But many symptoms are relatively benign, for example, overprotectiveness and hypervigilance. They can be seen as survivor skills that effectively helped the individual to survive the trauma, but they are not as useful in nontraumatic situations.

Think about it. Is there something inherently "wrong" or "immoral" about the startle response, or being hypervigilant, or "on guard?" If a combat veteran startles when he hears a car backfire or a helicopter fly overhead, if an armed robbery survivor checks the locks on the door four times before going to bed, if a car-accident survivor breaks into a cold sweat when another driver runs a red light, or a sexual assault survivor carefully screens her dates for signs of violent or sadistic tendencies, are these people showing signs of mental retardation?

Probably not. Each symptom needs to be examined separately, with an eye to its possible negative and positive consequences in the survivor's life. However, such distinctions are rarely made between symptoms, either by the survivors themselves, or their families, unless they have been educated about trauma and PTSD. The tendency is to view all symptoms as signs of "craziness" and as cause for shame. As a result, survivors can feel stigmatized, like outcasts in their homes and communities, even though they committed no crime worthy of exile.

Contributing to the trauma survivor's low self-esteem is society's "blame-the-victim" attitude, the just world philosophy, and the general lack of information about trauma and its effects. If everyone knew as much about post-traumatic stress disorder and depression as they do about the common cold, the trauma survivor would live in a much more supportive emotional world. But, of course, such is not the case.

The fact that trauma survivors all too often internalize society's "blame the victim" and other such negative views is as damaging as the negative attitudes they receive from others. Hence, the incest survivor may not only be seen by others as "damaged goods"—she or he believes that, too. The emergency room nurse who is suffering from burnout and other traumatic reactions may not only be seen by others as incompetent—she judges herself in the same fashion. The suicide survivor senses the condemnation of others, which only heightens the guilt already felt regarding the suicide attempt. In some cases, others' negative judgments are subtle, in other cases, blatant; but in all cases the problem is not just that others may denigrate the trauma survivor, but that the trauma survivor *internalizes* the condemnation.

Another, equally powerful, reason that trauma survivors tend to blame and criticize themselves is their need to feel in control of their lives and to believe the world is safe and fair. If you were a small child and had a choice between believing that your parents were incapable or unwilling to take care of you, or that you were "bad," which would *you*, prefer to believe?

If you believe that your parents are unable or unwilling to take care of you, then you have no hope of ever being protected or nurtured. However, if you believe *you* are "bad," then there is some hope. The hope is that if you become "supergood," for example, by overachieving, or "superbad," perhaps by destroying property, then you have at least some chance that your parents will pay attention to you. But if you decide that the problem is in your parents, and not in you, then the situation is bleak indeed; for then there is no way to get the love, protection, and attention you need.

Similarly, a soldier would prefer to think that his combat trauma is the result of his inadequacies rather than to fully acknowledge and appreciate the magnitude of the horror of war. Parents who have lost a child to murder or suicide may find it easier to blame themselves for their child's death than to face the extremely anxiety-provoking knowledge that the stresses of modern life can overwhelm even the best of parents, or that the rule of the jungle, not the rule of law, reigns in some parts of our society.

Self-Esteem and Trauma

Post-traumatic stress reactions, depression, and other aftereffects of trauma can cause the loss of self-esteem. If the trauma survivor also spent years abusing drugs, alcohol, or food, then most likely during those years, the survivor's educational, economic, and social development suffered. When survivors complete substance-abuse recovery programs and they begin to make emotional, social, and vocational progress, they become aware of the opportunities they lost due to the trauma and the years in addiction and denial that followed. This awareness of what might have been accomplished had not the time been spent time drinking, drugging, compulsively overeating, or bingeing and purging is extremely painful and can lead to feelings of extremely low self-esteem.

"I look at my cousin who is my age. He has a wife, a house, and a car. What do I have? Nothing and I'm just beginning to know myself," says Larry, age forty. Larry abused alcohol and drugs for twenty years before discovering that the root cause of his addiction was sexual abuse when he was a child. He's been clean and sober for five years, but he is still struggling to strengthen both his self-esteem and his ability to concentrate on goals that are important to him.

"I wasted my youth running from the abuse. Now that I've woken up I find I'm way behind my friends and relatives who weren't abused. That makes me feel bad about myself. Here I am, at forty, going to college. I should have done that when I was young like everyone else. I should have gotten married, too. Instead I got my Ph.D. in booze and married the bottle. Now I'm paying, big time."

Shame

Larry feels ashamed. His therapist's statement that it is his abusers who should be ashamed, not he, doesn't help. But Larry's shame runs deeper than not having the social and financial status of his peers. The first and deepest level of shame originates when you are abused or ordered about, even if you have no choice but to accept it. This is the shame of being denigrated. The resulting humiliation is so deep that it requires a great deal of therapy to alleviate it. Not only sexual assault survivors, but survivors of other kinds of trauma also experience the shame and humiliation of being exploited, although such shame tends to be strongest in survivors of family abuse because of the intimate nature of their relationship with the abuser.

A second level of shame is caused by having to violate one's ethical code, which may be required in order to survive. As Dr. Herman points out in her book, *Trauma and Recovery* (1992), captivity is a precondition for trauma. In other words, to be traumatized, you have to be trapped in a situation where there is no way out or where all the ways out are very difficult or morally undesirable.

Even in captivity a person can retain some pride if he/she can act according to internal moral standards. Too often, however, the perpetrator, whether it be an abusive relative or a corrupt superior, demands that the victim betray his/her moral standards. At this point, the victim ceases to be only a victim and becomes an unwilling accomplice to the abuse, a perpetrator; thus compounding the guilt, shame, and confusion.

For example, it is not uncommon for abused children to be coerced into abusing other children or animals or into committing illegal or immoral acts (Herman 1992). Similarly, battered women are forced to witness the abuse of their children or to engage in prostitution, drug dealing, theft and other forms of crime to appease their batterers. Concentration camp survivors were forced to passively witness their loved ones being tortured or murdered. Individuals involved in vehicular accidents or subject to political terrorism have had to lie to protect loved ones, or themselves. Rescue workers and medical staff involved in trauma work are sometimes compelled to keep silent about questionable procedures to save their jobs or the lives of others.

Often, individuals who are harassed on the job are not only emotionally undermined, but also maliciously placed in double bind situations, where they are asked to participate in actions that are contrary to company or office policy. If they don't comply, their superior, who is harassing them, will punish them. If they do comply, that superior could charge them with unethical conduct or violation of procedures. In *Uncle Tom's Cabin* by Harriet Beecher Stowe (1866), Uncle Tom, a slave, is subject to numerous life-threatening incidents and constant physical and verbal abuse. But when he is asked to whip and torture fellow slaves, he refuses. He tells his owner that he will do everything he's asked to do, except violate certain Biblical principles. Even when threatened with death, Uncle Tom refuses to yield to the slaveholder's command to hurt other slaves.

Uncle Tom loses his life because he refuses to give up his moral principles. Few of us, however, can be as heroic as he was. If you were as heroic, you might not be alive. Most people, when threatened with death or severe injury, will compromise their moral values because they are adhering to other moral values—staying alive or saving others from harm. But that does not mean that there is no remorse when the trauma ends.

The point is, if you've been traumatized, there is probably some part of the trauma about which you may feel guilty. Therefore, when others criticize you or look down on you for your post-traumatic stress reactions or other stress symptoms, you may feel you deserve their contempt. Because of your guilt and shame, you may feel permanently stained and forever cut off from the rest of humanity. Even if you were not forced to violate your own moral standards, there certainly may be some aspect of what you thought, felt, or did, that is open to scrutiny or condemnation. Is it possible to go through a trauma, or any aspect of life, "perfectly"—having what you and others would consider to be the "right" thoughts, feelings, and actions? Even a woman raped at knife point by a stranger who came in through the bedroom window might blame herself in some way, perhaps by viewing the rape as "punishment" or "retribution" for a misdeed that she had committed in the past. (Individuals who have no self-blame or guilt about the trauma usually do not develop symptoms.)

One definition of trauma is that it is an experience that overwhelms the individual's natural coping abilities. As Freud (1933) saw it, trauma creates so much anxiety that a traumatized person is forever doomed to discharge that anxiety through nightmares and other sleep disorders, obsessions, compulsions, and other anxiety-related behavior and thought patterns. Yet another view of trauma is that it is a situation where all the choices are morally or otherwise unacceptable. Such a situation is bound to breed guilt and low self-esteem.

A man who was a commanding officer in the Second World War explains it this way: "No matter how much I thought about what kind of moves to make, men were lost. Were there a thousand ways to execute a particular mission? Yes. Was there any way to know in advance which particular plan would be the least costly in terms of losing lives? No. Did I always lose some of my men? Yes. Will I ever know if the choices I made were the best? No. So how do you expect me to sleep, and how do you expect me to ever take responsibility for anything again without shaking in my boots?"

This veteran has trouble completing the chores he has agreed to do for his wife. His wife interprets his behavior as his not caring about her, which leads to endless arguments and reinforces the veteran's feelings of being a "failure." "If I lost men on the mission, the mission was a failure to me, even if the objective was reached. Now if I forget to go the cleaners as I promised my wife I would do, I feel like a failure as a husband. There's a vast difference between forgetting to go to the cleaners and seeing a dozen of your men die before your eyes. But the feeling is the same: I'm a no-good worthless person because if I only had made the right choices and acted in the right way, I wouldn't have let anyone down or been responsible for anyone's unhappiness."

Exile, Self-Esteem, and Shame

When trauma survivors are received back into their families and communities with open arms, the effects of the trauma can be greatly minimized. Numerous studies show that social support is a critical factor in preventing short-term traumatic reactions from becoming long-term serious conditions (Herman 1992; van der Kolk 1996). However, when trauma survivors are treated like exiles, the negative effects of the trauma are compounded and the trauma survivor must deal with an additional set of problems: the rejection, disbelief, and, sometimes, hostility of other people. Many times it is difficult to distinguish the effects of the trauma from the effects of being stigmatized, mistreated, and "exiled" by important others because of the trauma.

In a society that values happiness, self-confidence, and self-control, trauma survivors find themselves in the position of outsiders because they have known misery, their self-confidence has been eroded, and they have trouble controlling their traumatized reactions. The loss of self-esteem is the result of the following combined factors:

- the stigma associated with being involved in certain kinds of trauma (especially sexual and physical abuse)

- the stigma associated with having certain symptoms of traumatic reaction, such as PTSD or clinical depression

- the guilt and shame from harboring angry and vengeful thoughts

- the humiliations endured during the trauma

- the loss of self-respect that can occur when, under coercion, a person is forced to violate his or her moral standards or betray others in order to survive

- the internalization of society's blame-the-victim attitude by the victim

- the victim's need to feel in control

- the loss of the ability to enjoy certain social and cultural events because they trigger memories of the trauma

- the mental illness label

- the general requirement by society that survivors not talk about the trauma and "get over it" quickly

- the recognition of the emotional, financial, and vocational toll the trauma has taken, especially if years of life were sacrificed to an addiction

Exile and Secondary Wounding

If you feel you've been exiled from or "cast out" by certain family members, or by certain social groups or people, the exercises that follow are geared toward helping you identify those persons and to examine the causes of your feelings of exile. There may also be ways in which you exile, or exclude, yourself.

Many feelings of rejection stem from what is called secondary wounding. *Secondary wounding* occurs when the people, institutions, caregivers, and others to whom the trauma survivor turns for emotional, legal, financial, medical or other assistance respond in a way that further injures the survivor. Basically, there are six kinds of secondary wounding experiences. They are as follows: Denial and disbelief, discounting, blaming the victim, ignorance, generalization, and cruelty.

Denial and Disbelief

When people respond to you with statements like "You're exaggerating," "That could never happen," or simply, "I don't believe it," they are denying the reality of your trauma. "Nobody could survive all that," or "Are you sure you aren't imagining some of this?" or "I never heard of anything like that," are also statements of denial.

Perpetrators, whether they be family abusers, criminals, or political groups are often the first to deny their victims the reality of their experience. "Stop punching me," says the victim. "I'm not punching you. You're punching yourself," says the abuser. "Please don't rape me," says the victim. "I'm not raping you," says the rapist.

Governments, institutions, and other organized groups practice denial also. "See those Marines down there. They're bleeding to death. Let's send this helicopter down to help them," says a helicopter co-pilot. "There's no men down there," says the crew chief, who doesn't want to risk his life, or the aircraft. In the early 1900s, millions of Armenians were killed by the Turkish government. Despite eyewitness accounts and numerous photographs of the genocide, to this day Turkish officials deny that the Armenian Genocide ever took place. There are even groups who argue that the Holocaust didn't happen, or that the Jews "exaggerate" the numbers of those who died, or the sufferings of those who survived (Dawidowicz 1975). These are sociopolitical forms of denial.

Discounting

With denial, people do not believe your story. When you are being discounted, people do not deny that the traumatic event occurred; however, they minimize its effect on you or the magnitude of the event. Here is an example of discounting.

Joellen was in an automobile accident that left her with chronic backaches and headaches. She had to quit her job as a nurse and stay home. Her self-esteem as a working professional was ruined and her family suffered financially because of the loss of her income. When she became clinically depressed, a doctor told her, "How could one little car accident have affected you that much? What's a little back pain and headache? You could work if you wanted to, if you were willing to suffer a little. You weren't even scratched. Just think, you and your children could have been killed."

If the doctor had been supportive and not engaged in active discounting he could have said, "This accident robbed you of a profession that you loved. It must be terrible for a woman who was such an active wife, mother, and professional to be relegated to the status of a semi-invalid. You may have survived the accident, but parts of your life were destroyed and will never be the same. This is truly a sad situation."

Blaming the Victim

The blame-the-victim attitude and the just world philosophy were described previously, but here is an additional example of blaming the victim:

As a young man, Richard worked on an aircraft carrier in a war zone. Over time, the smell of diesel fuel became associated with airplane crashes and with burning, dying airmen. Years later, as a civilian, Richard got stuck in a traffic jam one day. He inhaled some diesel fuel fumes from the bus in front of him, had a wartime flashback, and drove into a tree, crushing his hands. After he finished his military service he had become a dentist. But after his accident he could no longer practice dentistry because of his injured hands.

"Serves you right," said a cousin, when Richard described the accident to him. "I told you not to join the military. Bright man like you, wasting his talents in the armed forces."

A more supportive response would have been, " I can't say I know how you feel, since I've been fortunate enough to have never been in a serious car accident. But I know how awful it is when I have severe arthritis in my hands and I can't do my work. I feel for you. It isn't fair that this happened. First, you served your country and, until the accident, you were serving people as a dentist. It just isn't fair. You didn't deserve this to happen to you."

Ignorance

Ignorance of trauma plays a major role in secondary wounding experiences. If people have not experienced trauma themselves, or have not learned about it in other ways, they often do not know what to say or how to respond to a trauma survivor. Also, as mentioned previously, the fact that you were victimized may threaten other people's belief in the just world philosophy and their defenses against the idea that they could also be victimized.

The following example illustrates a secondary wounding experience caused by ignorance.

"Brenda, I'm sorry I can't make it to your baby shower. Ever since I lost my baby because of the assault, I try to avoid anything related to babies. But your gift is in the mail and I'm sending flowers, too."

"You're crazy," Brenda replied. "You should be thinking of me, not yourself."

Brenda could have said, "What happened to you was horrible. I don't know what I'd do if someone attacked me and I lost my baby. I wish you could be with me at the shower, but I wouldn't dream of subjecting you to an event that would cause you more pain than you already have. If I were in your place, I'd never go to a baby shower again."

Generalization

One of the social consequences of being victimized is being labeled as a victim. Once you are so labeled, others have a tendency to interpret most, if not all, of your actions in terms of that label. For example, if you are blind, you may be assumed to be also deaf or retarded. Furthermore, once you are labeled, it is difficult to escape from the label. It may also be assumed that because you suffered some ill effects from your trauma those effects are irreversible, and you will be permanently damaged by them. Consider this example:

Berneice had been sexually assaulted by a stranger. Upon her return to work as a department manager, her supervisor asked her to serve as a receptionist instead. The supervisor assumed that, because Berneice had taken a few days off work to rest after the assault and had also attended a six-week rape crisis group, she would be unable to function in her former position. The logical (and far more supportive) approach the supervisor could have taken would have been to wait and see whether Berneice could continue to handle the job before demoting her.

Cruelty

Almost all secondary wounding experiences *feel* cruel. Therefore, it is frequently difficult to determine whether the person involved is trying to cause pain or whether the pain that person is causing is the result of ignorance, generalization, or the need to blame the victim to avoid facing his or her own sympathetic anguish. Sometimes, though, real cruelty is mixed in with the other processes such as generalization.

✍ *Exercise: Identifying Your Secondary Wounding Experiences*

In your journal, list as many instances as you can remember of feeling or being exiled as a result of your trauma. Also list as many secondary wounding experiences as you can recall, including any current ones. List one experience to a page. You will need space for analyzing and commenting on each experience.

Sample: When I told my friend it had been ten years since my son was murdered, she said to me "That's a long time ago. Why do you dwell on it?" She was discounting my pain from ignorance. I felt disappointed that she couldn't comfort me and irritated that she couldn't be more understanding.

When you have finished creating your list, review each page and categorize each experience as denial or disbelief, discounting, generalization, victim-blaming, ignorance, or cruelty. Include as many labels as apply; for example, a single experience may contain elements of ignorance, cruelty, and blaming the victim.

After you have completed labeling each experience, identify your emotional responses. Did you experience irritation, anger, rage, sorrow, disappointment, disgust, a desire to retaliate, or any other feeling? Did you have no feeling at all? On each page, list as many emotional responses as apply.

Now, take some time to reflect on the process you have just worked through. Were you surprised at how many secondary wounding experiences you have endured? Did labeling the experiences help ease the pain or did it make you sadder or more furious?

Did any of the secondary wounding experiences ignore your anger, lower your self-esteem, or cause you to feel hopeless or helpless? In your journal, write more about those particular experiences.

It is likely that you will never feel neutral either in the midst of a secondary wounding experience, or when you are remembering it. If you are aware enough to really feel your feelings, you are going to feel angry, sad, powerless, betrayed, and many other strong emotions. However, once these feelings are faced, their intensity may lessen and your negative feelings may become more manageable. Also, having these feelings does not mean that you are hopelessly bound to the past and will never be able to relate to others again.

Exercise: Secondary Wounding and Your Relationships Today

In your journal, do some writing on how your secondary wounding experiences are still affecting your relationships. More specifically, for each experience, consider whether or not that experience had the following effects:

1. Did it alter your views about your social, vocational, and other abilities? If so, how?

2. Did it affect your family life, friendships, or other close relationships? If so, how?

   Write as many details as you can about how it affected the important relationships in your life.

3. Did it alter your ability to participate in groups or belong to associations? Did it affect your attitude towards the general public? If so, how?

4. Now, read what you've written and ask yourself, "How much power do I want to give this secondary wounding experience in my life today? Are there lessons and attitudes I learned during this experience that I want to keep? Are there attitudes I learned about that are not helpful to me today?"

Self-Esteem Issues for Trauma Survivors

It is beyond the scope of this book to address the many and complex self-esteem issues that a trauma can create. However, the following exercises will address how your trauma-related feelings about yourself affect your relationships.

When you reviewed your secondary wounding experiences and the kinds of social situations and relationships from which you feel exiled, you probably realized that, to some extent, you have decided to exile yourself from certain social situations or relationships because they are too painful for you. This statement is not intended to "blame the victim"—you—for your legitimate need to avoid interpersonal and/or social situations that set off PTSD triggers or that cause you severe emotional stress. Rather, the statement is made to help you begin to examine any fears you might have about being viewed by others as deficient or inadequate.

The problem with the monster in Frankenstein was that he was ugly—in other words, his trauma showed. Do you feel "ugly"—as if your trauma also "shows"?

Exercise: Do You Feel That Your Trauma "Shows"?

In your journal, respond to the questions below. Take a few minutes to think about each question before you begin to write. If you can, visualize yourself in a social situation with others and try to identify what you are saying, what you are doing, and how you are feeling. Pay particular attention to any anxieties or fears that you might experience and to how those anxieties and fears influence your feelings, your behavior toward others, and your decision about how long to stay in that situation.

Which of the feelings, thoughts, and anxieties you visualized are related to your trauma?

In the questions below, you are asked to write about the parts of your body or physical aspects of yourself that you deeply wish were different from the way they really are. As you answer each question, be as honest as possible, no matter how painful that might be. Remember, you do not have to share what you write with anyone, ever.

You are writing about yourself, for yourself. The more you know about how you honestly feel (and not how you or others think you "should" feel), the greater the odds are that you will be able to manage your feelings so that you will have more choices in your life. You may even come to view yourself in a new, improved light.

Try to write at least a six-sentence paragraph for each question and make that paragraph as detailed and as truthful as possible. If you can write more than one paragraph, do so. However, pay attention so that you do not become overwhelmed, as discussed in the Cautions section of the Introduction.

To begin this exercise, you may use the following lines to list those parts of your physical self that you do not like or wish were different, but be sure to use your journal to answer the questions.

I don't like the following parts of my body:

_____   _____

_____   _____

_____   _____

_____   _____

1. Are there parts of your face, body, or physical self that reveal or symbolize the trauma and its effects to you; for example, the need to take medication or the tendency to sweat during anxiety attacks? Do you feel these parts are "ugly," misshapen, deformed, deficient, or socially undesirable? If so, why? Are any of these reasons related to your trauma?

   Remember that the physical effects of trauma include more than injuries, scars, and the physical manifestations of extreme emotional stress, such as the need to take medication, or stress-related medical problems like bronchitis, asthma, headaches, or backaches.

   Try to be as objective as possible in answering these questions. This may be difficult since trauma survivors who are down on themselves or who suffer from clinical depression can easily exaggerate their physical imperfections. For example, what you would say about yourself if you saw yourself in a movie or a studio photograph?

2. Do you think others can "see" those parts? If so, what do they see and how do they feel about what they see? Make a list of comments people have actually made to you about the specific physical part that you are concerned about, then ask yourself the following questions: How accurate was this person in his or her assessment? Was it an offhand comment or a seriously thought-out observation? What might have been that person's reason for saying what was said to you other than giving you objective feedback? For example, was a statement about your physical feature used as a cover to vent anger or disappointment about something else? Is it possible that person was just having a hard day? If so, could that have affected the accuracy of the statement about the physical part you are so concerned about?

3. For each aspect of your physical self you are writing about, make a list of what you fear people will see or what you fear they will think when they see this part of you.

4. For each aspect of your physical self, consider how the feedback you've received and your fears about how people see you may have caused you to avoid certain social situations or relationships. How has the physical reality of any injuries or scars from your trauma, or your fears about how these physical aspects are received, influenced or controlled your relationships?

A part of the body that physically reveals the effects of an eating disorder or an addiction may become the focus of the survivor's attention and a reason to avoid social contact. People who developed eating disorders, such as compulsive overeating, bulimia, or anorexia or those who became addicted to alcohol or drugs, as a way of coping with their trauma may have parts of their bodies that bear the evidence of the eating disorder or substance abuse. Prolonged alcohol abuse can cause the collagen of the skin to break down, which causes premature wrinkling. Thus, a thirty-year-old survivor may look ten or twenty years older and avoid social gatherings because of "looking old."

The problem is not just that the physical effects of the addiction may be evident but that this physical evidence of the past becomes magnified in the survivor's mind because it is associated with very painful, hopeless times that the survivor would rather forget. Then, too, when the survivor was using, he or she may have led an isolated life in order to pursue the addiction. Even when the addiction has been vanquished, the isolation may persist because of the scars it left in its wake.

Prolonged alcohol and substance abuse also can cause health problems, such as cirrhosis of the liver and other internal disorders. Nobody can see these problems, but survivors sometimes feel as if they "show" and that they will have to talk about these problems with others they meet, even though such discussions are seldom necessary. The survivor may also feel intense shame about a medical or dental problem that is the result of the lack of personal hygiene, such as bad teeth.

John S., a policeman with PTSD due to years of exposure to death and dying, is a recovering alcoholic. He also suffers from liver damage due to his years of drinking. In his recovery program, John learned that he turned to alcohol to manage a wide range of feelings. There were two pivotal incidents that transformed him from being a moderate drinker into an alcoholic. One involved his accidental shooting of an innocent person; the other involved his abandonment of a fellow police officer to save his own life.

In John's mind the guilt and shame he feels about these two incidents are closely associated with his alcoholic history and his current liver damage. Except for his family and some friends also in recovery, however, very few people know about John's history of alcoholism. Even fewer know about his liver damage, and no one except John's therapist, knows about the person he accidentally killed or the fellow officer he abandoned. Yet John avoids most social situations because he is afraid that if someone asks after his health, that person will automatically sense that he has a diseased liver and intuit the shameful deeds that John associates with his liver problem.

Even if John told people about his liver problem, most people would not connect the physical problem with the traumatic actions that cause John so much anguish. But his medical condition causes him to feel like a monster.

Fighting the Power of the Past

You can begin to fight the power of the past, as symbolized by your negative feelings about parts of yourself. Notice the word "begin" because it takes practice to overcome the past. After all, you've felt "ugly" or undesirable for quite some time. You are going to have to "fight" with the only weapon you have—your own mind. If you decide to fight the strong tendency to use your past to control your future, the full range and depth of your feelings about your past must first be acknowledged and confronted.

Exercise: Writing a Letter to the Parts of Your Body That You Hate

In the previous exercises, you identified various parts of your physical self that either symbolized your trauma or caused you to withdraw or isolate from others because that part made you feel "ugly." In some instances you may even have mixed feelings about the part—both love and hate. That should not interfere with doing this exercise because you can address both sets of feelings when you are writing to that part.

In the following exercises, you will first write a letter to those parts of yourself that symbolize the trauma—write a separate letter for each part if there are several. You will tell that part of yourself how you feel about it. Write down all of the reasons you hate and despise that part of your body. Take all the time you need to write this letter. It's OK if it takes several hours or even several days.

Then, when you have exhausted all of the negative feelings you have for that part, see if you can't come up with a positive spin. See whether you have any positive feelings for that part, and if you do, write those down, too. In the exercise after this one, you will be asked to write a letter to those parts of yourself that you love and admire that may or may not be associated with your trauma.

Examples of how two very different survivors dealt with this issue are provided below:

Eileen was a childhood sexual abuse survivor who felt that she was "ugly" because of her small breasts. All of her social interactions, not only those with men, were affected by her belief that her small breasts revealed to the world what an immature, unlovable person she was. She would go to parties and after a while her anxiety that everyone was looking at her breasts would begin. Within an hour or two, the anxiety would overwhelm her and she would have to leave. To complete this exercise, Eileen wrote the following:

"My breasts are small and undeveloped because when I was a child I was sexually abused by my uncle. He told me that I'd have big breasts like my mother when I grew up, so I think, unconsciously, I must have stopped my breasts from growing. But sometimes I think it was my eating disorder that messed them up. When I was a teenager, I'd starve myself, get real thin, and then gain fifty pounds. Then, the following year I'd starve myself and binge my way up and gain seventy pounds! This went on for years. By the time I got help and stopped the binge-starve cycle, my breasts had been inflated and deflated so many times that now they are like empty balloons. They just don't look normal.

"Nobody has ever said anything bad about my breasts to me and, if I have to be objective, I guess they really aren't that ugly. But I feel they are and I'm so ashamed because I think they broadcast to the world—'Look at this woman here. Not only did she allow herself to be raped and mauled and covered with an awful man's sperm, but she developed a disgusting eating disorder and ruined her body by stuffing it and starving it. Not only was she a whore, she was also a weakling who couldn't handle the abuse and became a food junkie.

"Nobody knows I stole money to buy the food I needed for my binges. But when people look at my breasts, I think they see all of it—the abuse, the eating disorder, the stealing. My head knows this isn't so, but emotionally that's how it feels, and that feeling makes it impossible for me to relax around others. It makes me want to hide—forever."

After Eileen finished writing down all the grief, anger, and sorrow that she felt about her breasts, she wrote the following:

"Dear Breasts. I'm sorry I hate you so much. You never did anything wrong. You might have been better looking if I hadn't been abused, and then hurt myself the way I did. But I couldn't help being abused. I didn't ask for it. I was just a little girl and didn't know what was going on and there was no one to help me. The only friend I had was food, so I became a food addict. I have to forgive myself for that, which isn't easy.

But, I guess I could have done worse things than be a food addict. The only person I was hurting was me—I never hurt anyone else.

"Breasts, why am I blaming you for my problems, when the problem was the person who hurt me and the people around who allowed it? I should be proud of you—you are me. I can't let my uncle or anyone else to continue to hurt me by making me ashamed of how I look and causing me to run away from people who are nice to me now and want to be with me.

"Dear Breasts, If I could learn to love you, I could learn to love myself, all of myself. If I could learn to love you, then I could socialize with others and be happy, instead of staying by myself to hide you."

Here is the second example of how a relatively small physical imperfection can create a large problem: Karl, a car-accident survivor, has a scar on his neck from the surgery that was needed to save his life after his accident. The scar is barely noticeable but Karl is aware of it all the time. Karl suffered some minor head injuries in the accident, which made it impossible for him to continue in his profession as an accountant. Although he was still able to work, he had to take an easier and less remunerative job. Ultimately, the scar on his neck came to symbolize his financial problems, his wife's leaving him, and his problems in finding a new intimate relationship. Objectively, the scar is only two-inches long, but it consumes all of Karl's attention because it signifies the emotional and vocational disruptions his accident caused.

When Karl wrote a letter to his scar, he described how the scar symbolized all of the unpleasant changes in his life. But when he finished listing his grievances and venting his anger, he also told his scar that he was grateful to be alive—that he understood the scar also symbolized the success of the surgery that had saved his life. He told his scar that he was glad to be alive. He finished his letter with an affirmation that he would try to concentrate on how glad he was to be alive.

Karl and Eileen are lucky. Their trauma-related scars don't really attract attention. Survivors who have very large visible injuries from the trauma, and survivors who hurt themselves by gaining large amounts of weight, or by cutting themselves must deal not only with their own feelings about their "battle scars" but also with the reactions of others. If you have trauma-related scars or physical changes that actually do show, be sure to address in your journal entry what it feels like to have those aspects of your physical self noticed by others. This should include not only permanent physical manifestations caused by the trauma, but temporary ones, such as the sweating or hyperventilation that can accompany nightmares or anxiety attacks.

Now, write a letter in your journal addressed to the part or parts of yourself that you believe make you seem ugly or monsterlike to yourself or to the others. If you have difficulties with the idea of writing such a personal statement, reread the two examples given above. They may help you to loosen up and let go of your inhibitions Remember, the writing is for your eyes only. You need not show anything you write to anyone.

✍ Exercise: Acknowledging the Parts of Your Body That You Love

In the previous exercise you wrote a letter to those parts of yourself that you associate with the trauma that cause you to withdraw socially because they make you feel different or inferior. In this exercise you are going to identify those aspects of your physical self that you love, admire, or otherwise make you feel proud of yourself. These parts of your physical self may or may not be related to your trauma.

As you respond to the following questions be as detailed and as honest as possible. You are writing only for yourself, no one else. If you keep your writing private, there will be no one to criticize you for being vain, egotistical, self-centered, or anything else.

The physical parts of you that you love are as important as those parts of you that you despise. To look only at the parts that you loathe would be as incomplete a picture of the truth as to look only at the parts that you admire. For example, Eileen, the survivor of childhood sexual abuse who struggled with negative feelings about her breasts, really liked her beautiful hair, and Karl, the car-accident survivor with the troublesome scar, was very proud of his shapely, muscled, very strong legs.

On the lines provided below, list four parts of your physical self that you love or admire.

1. _____
2. _____
3. _____
4. _____

Now write at least a six-sentence paragraph for each physical part of yourself that you love or admire. Use a separate sheet of paper in your journal for each part because you may decide to write some more later.

To complete this exercise, Eileen wrote the following:

"My hair is naturally curly and very shiny. I always liked my hair, even when I was a very small child before the abuse. Even during the abuse I remember brushing my hair and telling myself, 'This part of me is still pretty and he can't take it away from me. Even if he cuts my hair off, to be mean to me, it will grow back as beautiful as ever.' To this day I get compliments on my hair and I enjoy the attention. I don't feel guilty about liking the compliments. After all the emotional and physical pain I've been through and all the self-esteem issues I've had to deal with, don't I deserve to feel good about some part of me?"

To complete this exercise, Karl wrote the following:

"You were born with weak, spindly legs but you worked hard at the gym to build up their strength and endurance. They look good and you know it. Why just last week a guy at the gym wished his legs looked as good and were as strong as yours are. And remember that time you saved that child by being able to run fast enough to pull him to safety? Your legs not only have sex appeal, they help to save lives. Come to think of it, how come you spend more time thinking about your tiny scar than you do about your legs, which take up almost half of your body?"

Healing Self-Statements

If you completed the written exercises above, you should now have a fairly clear picture of how and why you feel like a social outcast or "ugly." You can now use this knowledge to help yourself when you are with others and the critical, condemning voice within rises and makes you want to run and hide or lash out at the smallest provocation.

There is a critical moment in social interactions, or job situations, when you can feel the anxiety start. There is a moment when it just begins but hasn't taken you over yet. If you can catch yourself as the panic, self-hate, rage, and grief begin to rise, and before they flood your mind and you can no longer think straight, then you have a chance of enduring that stressful moment when you feel like Frankenstein's monster and you will still have some choice about what to do next.

You may still choose to leave or lash out; but if you can begin to work on your attitude, just a little, by repeating healing self-statements to yourself, you may be able to calm yourself, and the more you can calm yourself, the more you will be able to look at your choices and the more choices will become available to you.

If, however, you go into a state of hyperarousal (pain, anger, self-hate) or a state of numbing, your choices will be very limited. You will get so "hyper" all your feelings will get mixed up. The terror, anger, and grief will all combine and overwhelm you. In such a hyperaroused state you can't distinguish fear from anger, or grief from panic, but you can discern that you can't think properly or make good choices, which will create even more panic and anger. At this point, you may decide to exit the situation physically, by leaving, or emotionally, by going numb, dissociating, "tuning out" or entering an altered state of consciousness. Whether you are "hyper" or "numb," your choices are limited. The purpose of creating healing self-statements is to increase the range of your choices.

The first step is to create healing self-statements. Whenever you are with others, except for a trusted few, you must prepare yourself to be assaulted by both the secondary wounding comments of others and the secondary wounding comments you have internalized. In a previous exercise, you were asked to review your secondary wounding experiences in terms of whether they involved a specific form of secondary wounding, e.g., ignorance, cruelty, etc. The purpose of that exercise was to help you see that the others' harmful behaviors and comments originated with *their* mistaken notions and motives, not with *your* failures as a human being. Hopefully, seeing those wounding behaviors from this broader perspective gave you some protection from the pain and helped lessen your natural tendency to internalize others' critical comments.

The next task, that of combating *internalized* self-criticism, is very difficult. You may want to ask others, including a trained therapist, to help you develop healing self-statements for each of the parts of yourself that you feel are undesirable ("ugly") and that stand in the way of your social life and intimate relationships. What are you going to say to the unsympathetic, cruel, and ignorant critic who tends to overgeneralize and blame the victim who doesn't live next door, but inside your own head? When Eileen is at a party and she becomes aware that she is obsessing about her "ugly" breasts and is thinking about leaving, what healing self-statements does she tell herself? Below are some self-statements that she has found helpful.

Eileen's Healing Self-Statements

"I'm getting that anxious feeling again, like everyone is looking at me and knows I was a slut, a pig, and thief. Now wait a minute, I wasn't a slut. I was forced into the abuse. And, yes, maybe I did eat like a pig, but I was trying to save my life the only way I knew how. And yes, I did steal and that was wrong, but I did pay back the people I stole from and I don't steal anymore. And yes, people are looking at me, but the truth is, they can't see through me. Maybe a few of them have X-ray eyes and know I have a deformed chest, but are they going to hate me for that? Do I hate people who have scars or ugly parts or who are missing an arm or a leg? Would I reject someone because they went through what I went through? Do I hate or look down on others in my abuse support group because they were abused? No. So why should I hate myself?

"My healing self-statements are: I am a good person. I was abused and it wasn't my fault. I can't help having bad feelings about myself, but I'm not going to let those bad feelings from the past totally control and ruin my life today. What is my goal in being here today? How can

I achieve that goal? I need to stop focusing on what I think others think and concentrate on what I have to bring to this situation, and what I'd like to receive from it.

"And I'm not going to beat myself up for overreacting and being so paranoid either. After all I've been through, I'm entitled to be paranoid. But I'm also entitled to get the most out of the situation I am in now. If I have to say it a million times, I will: It doesn't matter if my breasts are all messed up. Nobody is really looking and nobody really cares."

Karl's Healing Self-Statements

Karl wrote the following healing self-statements about his scar:

"It wasn't my fault I was in that car accident. It *will* be my fault, however, if I let this tiny scar disrupt my attempts to relate to others and do well on the job. I can't help my feelings of inferiority, but I can help my behavior. How would I be acting if I didn't have this scar? Can I try to act like that? Can I "act as if'" not for the sake of others, but for my own sake?

"I was cheated out of a good marriage and job. I don't want to cheat myself out of what I can accomplish, socially and vocationally. Even though I'm preoccupied with this one little part of my body because it symbolizes all the hell I've been through, I'm going to act as if the scar is invisible and think of what I need to do to have a good time or to get the job done and of what I can contribute here today.

"I want to get absorbed in what's going on now, rather than what happened in the past. To help myself, I'm going to repeat my healing self-statements: Having this scar doesn't mean I'm a failure. It only means I have a scar. It isn't a death sentence; it's the natural result of what happens to people in today's society who are in car accidents. It doesn't mean I'm intellectually or emotionally inferior to others. It just means one-square inch of me looks different from other people. I have something to offer here, too. It's up to me to contribute the good that I can. Holding back what I have to offer isn't going to give me back what I lost. Punishing the people here by withholding my talents isn't going to hurt the people I really would like to hurt—those who caused the accident and the woman who left me when I needed her most. No, trying to hurt these people is only going to hurt me further."

✍ Exercise: Writing Healing Self-Statements

1. The first step involves looking at your trauma in a neutral, non-self-blaming way by putting what you did, felt, or thought in the context of the real options that were available to you during the

trauma. If you have not completed any trauma-processing work on your own, with a therapist, or a recovery group, most likely you will need assistance to complete this exercise. If you have yet to begin any trauma-processing work, you may need to start that process and return later to this exercise.

Sample:

- I feel ashamed of (or guilty about) _____ because it reminds me of how I wasn't able to help those in trouble around me. But it wasn't my fault that the _____ happened or that there was so much going on that I wasn't as efficient as I could have been under calmer conditions. It's not my fault I wasn't superhuman, all-knowing, or all-powerful. I did the best I could under very difficult circumstances.

- I feel ashamed of my ugly _____ (or, I feel others will notice _____ and reject me) because it reminds me of how out-of-control I was. But it wasn't my fault I was out-of-control. I was a child who needed love and security and I tried to find it in alcohol, drugs, or food. It was not the best choice, but I didn't know better and there was no one to guide me and I didn't know how to ask for help.

2. As you progress in healing, you will feel less guilty, ashamed, and deficient. However, until the day when the trauma is in the background, rather than the forefront of your life, to help yourself feel more confident around others, you must acknowledge whatever guilt, shame, or other trauma-related feelings you have, and not beat yourself up over them. For example:

   Sample:

   - Even though I know I shouldn't feel as guilty, angry, or ashamed as I do, I can't erase all the guilt and shame. But I can decide not to let the guilt, shame, anger, and other bad feelings from the past totally determine what I can do right now.

3. Identify what it is that you want to gain out of the situation.

   Sample:

   - "Whenever I go to a meeting, I think about how I'm going to say something that will make me look foolish or weak. But I need to ask for what I want to get out of the meeting instead of worrying about what others will think. I'm at this meeting because I want a sponsor or the phone number of someone to add to my list of support friends. I'm at this meeting to gain some hope and to see my problems in a new light. Let me focus on those things, not on what others might think about the parts of my trauma that I think 'show.'"

4. Identify the strengths or contributions you can make to the situation. What do you feel good about?

   Sample:

   • "There are parts of me that make me feel different—like I was an outcast. But I also am very strong. After all, I am a survivor. I have intelligence and humor and other positive qualities to contribute to this situation. How I can I participate in a positive way? How can I make a difference here today?"

5. Give yourself credit for being able and willing to do what you can to break the bondage of the past.

   You may never be totally free of traumatic reactions to social and other types of interpersonal situations If you hold that kind of freedom as a standard for "success," you aren't being fair to yourself. It may be impossible to ever react to others as if you hadn't been through what you have been through. Some of the ways you react socially or interpersonally may be permanent. But if you use your coping skills, whether they be writing and practicing healing self-statements, talking to supportive others, or other coping skills, such as relaxation, you are doing what you can to make your life better. You may never be as relaxed or self-confident as you would like to be, but if you make the effort to manage your reactions so you can be more positive and participate more fully, you must honor yourself for your efforts. To the best of your ability, you will have exerted some healing power over your past.

   Carry your written self-statements with you when you go out. If you anticipate a problem, read your self-statements before you enter a social or intimate situation. Once there, if you need to leave and go off to reread them, do so. Your goal is to put up the best fight you can against allowing trauma-related fears and feelings dominate your life today.

   That's all you can ask of yourself: To put up a good fight. If your goal is to attend a family gathering, a friend's birthday party, an office social event, or some other function, reciting your healing self-statements may help you decide to attend, and once there, to stay a little longer than you usually would. If the anxiety or other negative feelings become too great, then you may need to take care of yourself and leave to be alone. But if each time you go out you can tolerate a little more tension and turn to yourself for soothing, self-healing comfort, you may find that you can slowly extend the amount of time you spend with others and increase your chances of enjoying it.

   Keep in mind that if you need to read your self-statements to yourself many times, that doesn't mean you will have to read them to yourself forever. Eventually you will memorize them, internalize them, and they will become part of you. But it is up to you do the initial work of reading and rereading, stating and restating them. The critic who lives in your head has had a lot of practice putting you down. Your new healing voice can't even begin to overcome the power of the critic unless it is given a chance to practice, and equal time.

If you are in an intimate relationship or close to particular family members and friends, you can let them know that you have some "soft spots" that you would rather they not make comments about. You don't have to tell them why you are sensitive about certain parts of yourself. All you have to say is "I am very sensitive about _____ . It would help me out if you would please not talk about _____ ." If your request is not respected, then you may need to reconsider the person's reasons for not respecting your needs and reconsider the relationship.

If you find that you cannot compose self-statements or cannot practice them or other coping skills, then it is critical that you find out why you can't do so. What beliefs or fears stand in the way of you taking action against the trauma-related feelings and memories that limit your life today? This is a major issue and it is beyond the scope of this book. If you have reached such a stumbling block in your ability to carry out the above exercises, this may mean you need to do more trauma-processing work with a recovery group or a trauma therapist.

References

Bender, L. and A. Blau. 1937. "The Reaction of Children to Sexual Relations with Adults." *American Journal of Orthopsychiatry* 7:500–506.

Dawidowicz, Lucy. 1975. *The War Against the Jews*. London: Weidenfeld and Nicolson.

Freud, Sigmund. 1933. "Lecture 33. Psychology of Women." In *New Introductory Lectures on Psychoanalysis*. New York: W. W. Norton.

Herman, Judith. 1992. *Trauma and Recovery*. New York: Basic Books.

Hoffman, S. L. and T. L. Dodd. 1975. "Attribution of Responsibility to an Accused Rapist as a Function of Characteristics of the Victim and of the Subject." Paper presented at the Annual Meeting of the Southeastern Psychological Association, Atlanta, GA. March.

Janoff Bulman, R. and Irene Frieze. 1983. "A Theoretical Perspective for Understanding Reactions to Victimization." *Journal of Social Issues* 39:2 (May).

Jay, Jeffrey. 1994. "Spiritual Perspectives on the Occurrence of Trauma." Audiotape 94ISTSS-3. of lecture presented at the Tenth Annual Meeting of the International Society for Traumatic Stress Studies. Chicago. November.

Shelly, Mary. 1965." *Frankenstein*. New York: Signet Classic, Penguin Books.

Stowe, Harriet Beecher, 1866. *Uncle Tom's Cabin*. New York: Signet Classic, Penguin Books.

Quina-Holland. 1979. "Long-term Psychological Consequences of Sexual Assault." In *Concepts of Human Sexuality for Health Professionals*. F. E. Schmitt, E. Kerfoot, and P. Grinager Eds. New York: Appleton-Century-Crofts.

van der Kolk, Bessel and Alexander McFarlane. Eds. 1996. *Traumatic Stress: The Effects of Overwhelming Experience on Mind, Body, and Society*. New York: Guilford Press.

3

Trust

"The only people I trust are my dogs. With animals, there are no games, no hidden agendas. When they're happy, they're happy for real. They aren't pretending to be happy to get something out of me. When they're mad, they show it. I don't have to wonder what they're really thinking and feeling. It's all out there, plain as day.

"But with people, you never know what's up and when you need them, they aren't there. The dogs are a different story. The minute I feel bad or hurt, they're right by my side, loyal to the end," says Paul, a trauma survivor.

Like his beloved pets, Paul, too, is loyal to the end. Despite Paul's statement that he trusts "no one," he does, in fact, trust a small circle of people—his children, his mother, one of his sisters, and a fellow trauma survivor. Not only does he trust these people, he's committed to them one-hundred percent. He showers upon them all the protection and care he never got during his trauma and there is little he wouldn't do for any of them.

His view toward the rest of the world, however, is one of almost absolute mistrust. Whereas he would give his sister a thousand dollars with hardly a moment's thought, he goes through major mental calculations when someone else asks to borrow change for a local phone call. Is this person "using" him or "setting him up"? Paul wonders. Automatically, Paul is "on guard"—waiting for the person to make the next dangerous move.

To the nontraumatized, Paul looks "crazy." But Paul isn't crazy. The way he trusts some people and distrusts others makes perfect sense in terms of the trauma he experienced. The way he acts saved his life during the trauma and all he is doing now is, once again, trying to protect himself and his own.

Man-Made Versus Natural Catastrophes

According to the *DSM-III-R* (1987), survivors of man-made catastrophes suffer from longer and more intense PTSD than survivors of natural catastrophes. Because, it is argued, natural catastrophes can be explained away as acts of God or bad luck, natural catastrophe survivors are less likely to lose their trust in other human beings and in society than are the survivors of man-made catastrophes.

However, in many cases, the sufferings caused by natural disasters involve one or more significant errors or betrayals, either by individuals or institutions. For example, in the case of the 1972 Buffalo Creek Flood in West Virginia, survivors did not blame excess rain or the hand of God for causing the dam to break. Instead, many held the Pittston Coal Company's failure to build an adequate slag pile responsible (Jacob 1985; Green et al. 1990).

Similarly, survivors of the massive fire at the 1977 Beverly Hills Supper Club outside of Cincinnati, Ohio did not blame fate but faulty wiring for the disaster. Or, as in the case of the tornadoes that hit northeastern South Carolina in 1984, those that hit Andover, Kansas in 1991, and other recent tornadoes, either the tornado-warning equipment did not function properly or the tornado-warning system failed to operate as intended (Jacob 1985; Madakasira and O'Brien 1987; *Washington Post*, 30 April 1991).

Natural catastrophe survivors may also feel betrayed or let down by rescue operations and other services. For example, they may have to face long lines, delays, and considerable red tape before they receive promised compensation for their losses. And, in many cases, when the promised compensation appears, it is not adequate to cover the losses suffered.

In addition, since it is difficult to be angry at "nature" in the form of hurricanes, floods, or tornadoes, there is a tendency to place some of the anger that should be directed at the natural catastrophe onto human beings who were involved in the catastrophe. Last, but not least, whenever there is a natural catastrophe, usually there is an upsurge in crime and family violence. Survivors of floods and hurricanes must contend not only with disastrous physical forces, but also with looting and physical assault by strangers, and increased family violence, including both wife-abuse and child-abuse. In sum, from the survivor's point of view, there are few purely natural disasters. Consequently, natural trauma survivors may have more in common with survivors of man-made catastrophes than is often thought.

Survivors of natural disasters do in fact differ from other survivors, however, especially abuse survivors, in that they tend to be less stigmatized. Natural catastrophe survivors are in general spared the blame-the-victim attitudes that frequently afflict survivors of man-made catastrophes.

For example, in many cases, rape, incest, and victims of other types of abuse are blamed for either provoking the abuse, or for accepting it—as if it had been their choice. Furthermore, survivors of man-made catastrophes are much more likely to be seen by others as lacking in strength, caution, intelligence, or moral integrity. The message they are given is, "What happened is your own fault. If you had been more careful, less stupid, more righteous, etc., it wouldn't have happened to you."

Trauma and the Loss of Trust

Trauma is about loss, and one of the first casualties of having been traumatized is the capacity to trust, especially if your trauma truly involved human evil or error. Trauma survivors not only lose trust in some of the basic premises that keep people functioning (such as the assumptions of personal invulnerability and that the world is just and fair) but they can also lose trust in people, including themselves.

"To trust, or not to trust?" is the question trauma survivors ask most frequently.

"I want to trust, but I know better," is the usual reply.

If you've been traumatized, you probably have good reason not to trust others. Your list of personal betrayals may be extensive, and quite devastating. If you trusted others during your trauma and they let you down, their failures to do as they had promised didn't result in the mere loss of a few dollars or a few hours of your time. Their failures may have put your life at risk, damaged you permanently, or cost the lives or health of others.

There is another side to this coin; however, the tendency to automatically and completely trust others. Thus, some combat veterans instantaneously trust another combat veteran, without taking time to find out if they are indeed reliable. While in combat, a soldier could safely assume that members of his unit would treat him like family. Back in civilian life, the code of "your blood is my blood" may no longer operate. Trusting another soldier may have saved a soldier's life on the front lines; however, trusting all fellow soldiers implicitly might cause problems back home under nontraumatic situations.

Similarly, there are some family violence and sexual assault survivors who trust others quickly. Because those who abuse family members or persons with less power than themselves often take advantage of the implicit trust that exists within a family or other nurturing context (e.g., day care or church), the victim may still retain the attitude of trust, despite evidence to the contrary. This is especially the case among survivors who were traumatized early in life and whose childhood innocence and trust were ruthlessly manipulated by abusive persons. (The issue of revictimization of family violence and sexual assault survivors and the reasons why these survivors will sometimes "overtrust" others will be addressed more fully in chapter 12 on revictimization.)

Without adequate help, there is a tendency for traumatized persons to stay "stuck" in the mind-set of extreme distrust (or, less likely, extreme trust) that existed at the time of the trauma. When such mind-sets are rigidly held in nontraumatic conditions and do not take into account current reality, they can cause numerous problems both in daily living and relationships.

When It's Safer to Not Trust than to Trust

Not all traumas are alike, but during some traumas, it makes sense to divide people into two groups and two groups only: friends and enemies. In the midst of a trauma, friends are those you trust with everything including your life, and enemies are those you trust with nothing. Although there might be some people you aren't sure about or those who are trustworthy in some matters but not others, when you are living through a trauma, these kinds of fuzzy categories are useless. Hence, if someone is of questionable reliability, sheer survival may demand that person be seen as an "enemy." One of the most difficult problems trauma survivors have is learning how to adapt this all-or-nothing kind of thinking, that may have served them so well during their trauma, to nontraumatic, everyday kinds of situations.

For example, in some criminal assaults or war situations, there may be some people on the scene who aren't clearly identified enemies, but haven't declared themselves as friends either. However, the person being attacked, the soldier, or the refugee must quickly identify and categorize these others as "friend" or "foe" or risk injury or death. In such situations it is generally deemed safer to not trust unfamiliar persons than to trust them.

People who are being traumatized also tend to assume that it is safer to anticipate the worst rather than hope for the best. For example, in families where there is abuse, the violent family member is not violent all of the time. Nevertheless, there is more self-protection when family members assume that there will be violence, rather than hoping for peace and quiet. It is prudent for potential victims to be on the lookout for signs of impending assault, and upon on seeing one or two indications that assault is imminent, assume it is going to happen, and try to avoid or be prepared for it, rather than to be caught "off-guard." Similarly, persons who live in violent neighborhoods are far better off expecting to be criminally assaulted and taking whatever precautions are possible than assuming they live in a safe zone.

For trauma survivors, this fear of imminent danger often persists in post-trauma relationships that are not dangerous. A "pervasive sense of doom" is part of post-traumatic stress disorder and is related to depression, another common reaction to trauma. While expecting the worst makes perfect sense given the trauma survivor's experiences, friends and family members of trauma survivors may label the survivor as "cynical," "paranoid," or "too negative," and find the survivor's attitude oppressively burdensome.

Quick Decisions Versus Fact-Finding Missions

Under traumatic conditions, decisions about trustworthiness have to be made fast. There is no time to make extensive inquiries or to go into complex analyses of each person's personality. In contrast, in ordinary, everyday life, most thinking adults take time to decide if someone is trustworthy or not.

They gather data about the person and on the basis of that data, make hypotheses or guesses about how trustworthy that person might be. Then, they test their hypotheses or guesses, and revise their opinion, accordingly. They learn about a person's history and behavior, observing that person's behavior not just once, but many times, and not just in one situation, but in a variety of situations, especially when that individual is challenged or under stress.

Once all this information is put together, the thinking adult draws some tentative conclusions about the person's character and then waits to see if the conclusions are accurate or not. Although no amount of information can predict something as unpredictable and capable of change as human character, this factual approach is the most reliable way to assess character that we have. In fact, it is also the *only* method available to us humans who do not have the power to read minds or predict the future.

Under the conditions of a traumatic situation, this approach of data-gathering, hypothesis making, and testing is an impossible luxury. Information about the person may not be available and there is certainly no time to make hypotheses and test them. Decisions must be made quickly, with whatever information is available, often relying on first impressions and "gut feelings."

Global Versus Partial Trust

Under traumatic conditions, one usually trusts, or mistrusts, absolutely, one-hundred percent. During the trauma, you may have trusted someone with everything you had—your possessions, your secrets, your very life—because the situation was potentially life threatening. For example, an abused wife planning to leave her violent husband trusts a woman friend with all of her escape plans. She might also give her friend financial papers for safekeeping, as well as items of sentimental value, lest the abuser find out about her plan to leave. This is called *global trust*, because the abused wife trusts her friend with everything—her physical safety, emotional well-being, and financial assets.

In everyday life, as a rule, we extend *partial trust* to others. Generally we do not need to trust someone with everything because everything is not at stake, as it is during a trauma. We trust partially. In deciding whether to trust someone or not, the question is not whether to trust that person entirely or not at all. Rather, the question is how much to trust that person and with what and under what conditions. We try to distinguish differences between those areas in which that person might be trustworthy, from the areas in which that person might not be untrustworthy, from the areas in which it is difficult or impossible to tell with the existing information we have.

In ordinary life, instead of black and white, there are shades of gray. For example, you might trust someone to return a loan of forty dollars but not of one-hundred dollars, or you might trust that a friend will meet you for dinner, but not trust him or her with your car or with the keys to your home. You might trust your supervisor to stick to the regulations and not make up capricious rules to harass you, but not share personal information with that supervisor because you have evidence that he or she is more loyal to management than to employees. These are examples of partial trust, which characterizes most nontraumatic relationships. You don't trust your supervisor as much as you might your best friend, but neither have you branded him or her as "totally untrustworthy" in every area of life either.

If you usually take some time to decide whether or not to trust someone, if you do not automatically classify the people in your life as either "friends" or "foes" with no in-between categories, and if you can make distinctions between what you can trust those people with and what you can't, you probably don't need to read this chapter. If, however, you tend to trust "too much" or "too little," make snap decisions about another person's trustworthiness, and find that your lack of trust is causing major relationship problems, then you need to read on.

Caution: If you are a victim of family violence, the exercises in this chapter are only partially helpful for dealing with your abuser and with your other family members. Families in which there is violence, sexual abuse, or other forms of exploitation are extremely complex. Although the following exercises might help you to examine your relationship with your family, there are family-specific, hurtful issues present in all families that are not addressed in this chapter and can be addressed only with a therapist.

If you are trying to decide whether to trust a family member who has a vested interest in denying or not understanding the negative events in your family, the following exercises should *not* be used as the sole basis for your decision. The other kinds of powerful dynamics, often contradictory, that exist in dysfunctional families need to be taken into account with the guidance and support of a professional trained in family violence, family dynamics, and trauma.

The Process of Trusting

Trusting others is a process. It is impossible for you to know whether someone is trustworthy or not and in what ways, immediately. It takes time and experience, as well as a sharp eye and a well-developed intuitive sense. If you tend to mistrust others instantly, this is to be expected. If you've been traumatized and you trust everyone right away, something is amiss, for to trust so readily means you have discarded all that you learned about human vulnerability during the trauma.

Initial mistrust is normal, and not necessarily harmful. What is harmful is when

- you maintain a stance of total mistrust despite evidence to the contrary

- you are not willing to try to learn more about the other person to verify whether your "gut feeling" is correct, or

- you are not willing to give the other person a chance to earn your trust.

It makes as little sense to distrust everyone in every matter as it does to trust everyone in every way no matter what they say or do. Your trust in another person must be grounded in reality: in concrete observations about that person's actions, not in a stereotype derived from the past. If you have a "gut feeling" about someone, do not disregard it. Use it as a starting point for your assessment of that person. Sometimes, traumatized people develop a "sixth sense" about who is potentially violent. Just as seasoned police officers can sense when someone is carrying a weapon, formerly abused persons can sense anger and intuit whether someone is capable of out-of-control rage. Abused and neglected children have been described as "mind readers" who can sense what the abusive adult wants before the demand is stated. Like traumatized adults, traumatized children can "smell" danger in the same way that some animals can "smell" predators they do not see.

Your "sixth sense" is valuable. It provides you priceless information and the kind of wisdom that doesn't come from books, but from suffering. Your trauma may have given you both hard facts and intuitive insights into human frailty and human cruelty and the inadequacies, contradictions, and corruptions that exist in human institutions. You need to retain all those hard-won insights, but you don't want your information bank to be limited to them either. If you really want to be safe, you'll need to take into account every single bit of input you can find, from your past and present, from the observations and experiences of others, and from direct knowledge of who and with what kind of situation you are dealing.

The challenge for trauma survivors is always the same: to not view present-day events as replays of the past trauma (except when they are). If you are grappling with the issue of trust in your relationships, the following exercises are designed to help you differentiate the past from the present and to use what you learned about human nature during your trauma to make solidly based decisions about trusting the people in your present life.

It is beyond of the scope of this book to address trust issues for those who have been diagnosed as suffering from paranoia, paranoid schizophrenia, or other kinds of paranoid disorders. If you suffer from paranoia, you will need to consult a psychiatrist or professional therapist. The exercises in this book are insufficient to help you ground yourself in reality. Professional help is mandatory.

An Inventory of Past Betrayals

In chapter 1, you completed a relationship inventory where you examined three relationships during three time periods: pre-trauma, during the trauma, and post-trauma. Reread your journal entries, where you've listed specific persons and described the memories and feelings you associate with them. Note which among these relationship involved a betrayal of trust. In the following exercise, you will make a list of the persons who betrayed your trust and describe how they betrayed you and what the consequences were. There is power in identifying and naming those who betrayed you.

✍ *Exercise: Identifying Past Betrayals*

Complete the following sentence for three relationships from your past that involve betrayal. (You can always write about more than three persons if you choose to, and you can do as much writing as you like about as many relationships as you wish.) Be alert for signs of becoming overwhelmed as described in the Cautions section of the Introduction. In addition, remember to use three separate sheets of paper, one for each relationship.

Use the following sentence as a model:

I was betrayed by _____ and *as a result*, I _____ .

Example A: (Rape Survivor, Car-Accident Survivor, Homicide Survivor, Assault Survivor)

"*I was betrayed by* Mrs. Z. who lied at my court hearing. Her lies influenced the judge to give my assailant a more lenient sentence.

As a result, I was publicly humiliated and discredited and made to feel like the crimes committed against me were not that important. My self-esteem has never been the same since."

Example B: (Combat Veteran, Police Officer, Rescue Squad or Emergency Room Worker)

"*I was betrayed by* my superior who promised to send me needed help and failed to do so. I waited and waited until I finally had to (kill a civilian to get the food I needed so my men and I wouldn't starve to death; let the suspect get away rather than take a chance that he'd kill a fellow officer; perform the medical procedure without proper equipment and the patient died).

As a result, I've suffered from intense guilt ever since."

Example C: (Family Violence Survivor)

"*I was betrayed by* my mother/father/sister/brother/cousin/aunt/uncle/lover/spouse who not only physically/sexually abused me, but also stole money from my bank account.

As a result, I have to work overtime to make ends meet, which exhausts me and allows me very little time to start a new life."

✍ *Identifying Trust Issues in the Present*

Are there any connections between the ways you were betrayed before or during your trauma and the difficulties you have trusting others in the present? Can you identify any relationships in the present where you have trust issues that originated in the trauma or in secondary wounding experiences?

Use the following sentence as a model:

Because I was betrayed by _____ , who did the following _____ , I now distrust _____ and have strong reactions when someone does _____ .

Example A: (Rape Survivor, Car-Accident Survivor, Homicide Survivor, Assault Survivor)

"Because of Mrs. Z's lies, I can't stand any form of lying, even slight exaggerations. When one of my co-workers tells white lies about her supervisor, I start suspecting that she will make up stories against me and cause me trouble on the job. Now, no matter what she says, even 'hello,' I fly into a rage because it reminds me of how Mrs. Z lied on the witness stand."

Example B: (Combat Veteran, Police Officer, Rescue Squad, or Emergency Room Worker)

"When someone is supposed to send me help and they don't, it reminds me of (my commanding officer failing to provide food or reinforcements, the team leader not providing needed equipment) and the suffering that followed. So today, when someone delays completing a task, whether it be my child or my co-worker, I feel as if something terrible is going to happen.

My fear and anger get really intense when that person is someone in charge, like a doctor or therapist. If they don't do as they promised, I start hating them the way I hated my (commanding officer, team leader, etc.) and thinking that they are as corrupt and uncaring as he was. I can't stand people in authority who don't do their job and don't do it right, which is why I have job problems."

Example C: (Family Abuse Survivor)

"Because the family member who robbed me was a male/female, I don't trust men/women, no matter who they are. I do not trust _____ or _____ or _____ because he/she is a man/woman. I also break into a sweat and start hyperventilating whenever a cashier shortchanges me and I never go back to that store."

Five Steps for Assessing Trustworthiness

The steps involved in assessing someone's trustworthiness are as follows:

1. Gathering information (include your "sixth sense" or "gut reaction" as references)

2. Forming an opinion (hypotheses, guesses) about that person

3. Testing that opinion or watching to see whether your opinion matches the person's behavior in real life

4. Revising your hypotheses or guesses as a result of the new information; and

5. Repeating the process as necessary.

The process of assessing trustworthiness is similar to dating. On your first date with someone, you form an opinion based on what happens on the date, as well as on other information you may have heard about that person. On a first date you might "fall in love" or decide never to see him/her again. Or, more typically, you won't be sure of how you feel about the person, because you don't know enough and you may decide to go out with him/her a few more times to find out what you need to know.

There's nothing "wrong" with "falling in love" on the first date, but it would not be wise to use one date, or two, or even ten, as the basis for deciding to marry him/her. Similarly, using just a small amount of information or a few limited experiences with someone to decide whether that person is trustworthy (and in what areas) is insufficient data, unless, of course, that information or experience is so extremely negative that there is little question as to this person's character.

As you complete the next set of exercises, bear in mind that no matter how many written exercises you complete, there are no guarantees in life. You can amass a huge amount of information that someone is trustworthy (or not), and then that person can turn around and surprise you. Nevertheless, the fact remains that the only secure bases for such decisions are the information you have, the information you can acquire, and your "gut feeling" or "sixth sense."

But if your "gut feeling" is always the same message, that is, "Don't trust," with nearly every person you meet, that "gut feeling" probably is responding more to what happened during your trauma than to what is happening today. If you are working in a hostile environment, living in a dangerous neighborhood or violent home, or dwelling under conditions of political terror or war, then the message "Don't trust" is clearly useful. But this means you are *still* living in a traumatic situation and are not ready to deal with post-traumatic stress yet.

If you are living in a nontraumatic situation, the likelihood is strong that your reality is mixed: There are people who shouldn't be trusted with very much at all; people who can be trusted only in particular ways; and people who are generally trustworthy. If your "trust sensor" is always set at "Don't trust," you may not be reading your environment correctly. What used to be a lifesaver, i.e., not trusting, may turn into an obstacle in both your work and personal relationships.

✍ *Exercise: Assessing Trustworthiness*

In a previous exercise, you identified three persons who betrayed you in the past and the ways in which those three betrayals affected your current relationships. In the following exercise, you are asked to do something more complicated: to assess the trustworthiness of three persons from your present-day life, given the information you currently have.

Consider the following questions: Do you mistrust this person totally, or do you trust him/or her in some areas, but not others? What evidence do you have that it is safe to trust the person in these areas? What evidence do you have to the contrary? What else would you need to know to put your trust in this person in the areas you specified? Is it possible to find out this information? For example, are there other people you can talk to about this person? Are there written records you can examine? Are there questions you can ask this person? Is there a safe way to "test" whether your evaluation of this person is accurate?

Your writing about each relationship should address each of the following categories:

Initial Impressions

Check and complete as many items as apply:

I do not trust _____ in the following
areas _____ .

I do trust _____ in the following
areas _____ .

I don't trust _____ in any way.

I trust _____ totally.

Assessing Trustworthiness: Analyzing Initial Impressions and Information

I have seen, heard, and sensed the following about this person. In
the past, this person has _____ , _____ , and _____ .
At this point in time, the following information indicates this person
might be trustworthy because _____ . At this point in time, the
following information indicates this person is not trustworthy because
_____ . At this point in time, most of the information suggests
_____ about this person's trustworthiness.

I trust this person in the areas of _____ and _____
and _____ because _____ . In order to be more certain
about my trust, I need to find out _____ .

I do not trust this person in the following areas _____ .
The reasons I don't trust this person in these areas is because I have
seen, heard, and sensed the following about this person _____
_____ . In the past this person
has _____ .

Areas of Uncertainty

I am not sure whether or not to trust _____ in the following
areas _____ , _____ , _____ , and _____ .
The reasons I might trust are _____ . The reasons I have to be
cautious are _____ . What I need to know to make a good
decision is _____ . I can find out some of what I need to
know by taking the following steps: _____ . Some areas I
might never be sure about are _____ .

Obtaining Additional Information and Checking Out Reality

With whom can I talk to obtain more information about this person? Is there someone whose opinion I respect with whom I can check
my perceptions and who can help me sort out the information I do
have about this person?

Hypothesis Testing: Devising Experiments to Test Someone: Taking Small Manageable Chances to Find Out More Information

Is there a safe, doable experiment I can devise to test whether this person is caring and trustworthy or to test other thoughts I have about him/her? Is there some small step I can take toward trusting that person that will not be too costly to me and that will help me to judge that person's trustworthiness? What small step might that be? What's the worst thing that can happen if I take this small step? Can I handle the worst thing that might happen? If taking this small step seems extremely risky, then why am I even contemplating it?

Revising Your Hypotheses or Thoughts About Someone

Assuming you have taken that small chance and observed that person's reaction, what did you learn about him/her? How does this change your previous evaluation of this person? Can you take another small step toward trusting him/her or did the information you obtained show you that you need to be cautious?

If this person disappointed you, does this mean that he/she is not to be trusted at all or that there are additional areas where this person isn't to be trusted? If so, what are these areas?

If you learned that this person could be trusted just a little more, does it make sense to take another small step toward trusting him/her a little more and seeing what happens?

With whom can you talk to help you analyze and sort out what you learned about this person?

Revised Current Impressions

Check and complete as many items as apply. Then, compare your current assessment of the person under consideration with your initial assessment. Congratulations on having taken the time and effort to think through issues of trust with this relationship. How do you feel having completed all of this work? Hopefully, you will feel that you now have a little more control in the relationship.

I do not trust _____ in the following areas _____ .

I do trust _____ in the following areas _____ .

I don't trust _____ in any way.

I trust _____ totally.

I am still uncertain about the following with respect to this person _____ . I still need to find out _____ . The steps I need to take to find out what I need to know are _____ , _____ , and _____ .

Generalization and Overgeneralization

Your "trust sensor" (or "don't trust" sensor) exists to protect you. And the lessons it learned during your trauma it learned very well, perhaps, permanently. There is reason to believe that traumatic memories are stored physiologically in a way that makes them stronger and more powerful than ordinary memories. This has great survival value. (Chapter 4 will explain this physiological process in greater detail.)

When your life (or the lives of others) is at stake, you learn survival skills quickly, and you learn them well (unless you develop amnesia about the trauma). In contrast, skills that you learned to solve other less serious problems may not be as well remembered. For example, prisoners of war for whom the only means of communication with fellow prisoners was the Morse code learned that code faster, and more permanently, than those who learned it for a routine job, or for sport. The following story illustrates this point.

Imagine you are a primitive hunter roaming through the jungle in search of prey. You pay no attention to a certain plant that grows in abundance near the marshy swamps, until one day you make camp near a swamp, and a group of crocodiles attack and eat several members of your hunting party.

Suddenly you remember that just before the crocodiles attacked, you were looking at a plant growing near the edges of the swamp. In your mind, the vivid color of the leaves of that plant becomes permanently associated with the attack and forms an indelible memory. Every time you see those plants you think "danger." Every time you go near a swamp, even a swamp where there are people happily catching frogs, turtles, and other wildlife, you look for that plant—and for crocodiles. Even if the people catching frogs and turtles laughingly assure you that there are no crocodiles there, you can't totally believe them. If you pass by a hundred swamps where there are no crocodiles, whenever you see either a swamp or that particular plant, you watch out for crocodiles.

Your caution makes perfect sense. After what you saw, you *should* be on the lookout for crocodiles. If you were a hunter who didn't make a permanent association between that plant and swamps fraught with danger, you would be the hunter who didn't make it. The hunter who ignored the lesson of the first crocodile he met was probably the hunter who, somewhere along the way, got eaten by a crocodile.

This particular hunter generalized his fear of one swamp to all swamps. He also generalized his fear of swamps to fear of the plant that grew near swamps. Even though the plant in itself was not dangerous, it became associated with danger.

Life would be relatively simple if the hunter could go through his life avoiding all swamps and their associated plants, but a day will come when he has to cross a swamp to escape a wild animal. In order to save himself, he will have to cross the swamp, which means facing something else that he feels is dangerous: swamps and the plants that grow around them. This puts the hunter into a double-bind situation. If he tries to protect himself from one danger, the wild animal, he will have to confront other dangers—swamps and their accompanying plants.

Another time he might be hungry, but the only food available is near a plant that looks like the plants he associates with the crocodiles that ate his fellow hunters. There is no swamp near by, hence there could be no crocodiles hiding and waiting to attack. But since the plants are around, the hunter is still afraid. Once again he is in a double bind. On the one hand he is hungry and needs food. On the other hand, the only food available, the plant, is associated with fear.

This is the situation trauma in which survivors find themselves. If they could avoid people, places, and things that they mistrust or associate with their trauma, stay safe from all other dangers, and still pursue their goals, their lives would not be so difficult. But, like the hunter who must hunt along the edges of a swamp that fills him with fear or face another loss, like losing the game he is tracking, trauma survivors often feel "trapped." They feel trapped between their survival-based distrust of a particular person and another need, perhaps a life-enhancing need, such as achieving a much desired goal.

During her incarceration in a concentration camp, Mrs. Jones learned to fear men in uniforms because they were murderous brutes. In the camps, she was always "on alert" when men in uniform passed by and she found ways to avoid their notice. It is more than fifty years since she was freed from the concentration camp, but her fears persist. She refuses to answer the door to any man in a uniform including mailmen, repair persons, and police officers. As a result, she doesn't receive important mail, her appliances go unserviced, and she refuses to evacuate the building during bomb scares or fire drills.

Despite her numerous medical problems, Mrs. Jones refuses to visit a doctor, because in the concentration camps doctors performed sadistic experiments on the prisoners. Mrs. Jones' fears may seem extreme, but they only reflect the severity of her trauma. Her fears were legitimate in the past but she has (understandably) overgeneralized them. Not only is she trapped by her fears, she has also entrapped her daughter, who mediates between her mother and the outside world. Her daughter understands her mother's fears, but in trying to handle her mother's life, as well as her own, the daughter is developing stress symptoms too. The daughter desperately needs to set limits on what her mother asks of her, yet she feels enormous guilt about doing so because of her mother's genuine need and because, after all, her mother was the victim of a cruel fate and much of the rest of the family died in the camps.

Mrs. Jones's example may seem extreme, but it illustrates the kind of entrapment that can result from overgeneralization, the tendency to generalize from the trauma situation to everyday life, just as the primitive hunter does. If the hunter could distinguish the swamp from the plant, he would have more choices. If Mrs. Jones could learn some ways to differentiate between dangerous men in uniform from safe persons in uniform, she would have more choices. There would always be the risk of making a wrong choice and opening her door to a dangerous person, but she is not risk-free now. Her behavior is causing her daughter so much stress that the daughter may become alienated from her, or she might become ill and unable to take care of her mother. Then Mrs. Jones would have no one to help her and would suffer greatly as a result.

Like Mrs. Jones, if you can learn to distinguish true danger from the symbolic meanings you attach to the characteristics of people you associate with mistrust and betrayal (which are probably not dangerous in themselves), you, too, would have more choices. For example, assume that during your trauma, you, like Mrs. Jones, were betrayed by a member of the medical profession. As a result, you universally distrust all medical persons. Inevitably, there will come a day when you need a doctor. Your guiding principle of "Don't trust doctors" will put you in a terrible bind. Either you won't get the medical attention you need, or you will put yourself in a relationship with someone you don't trust. To help yourself, you need to expand your rule of "don't trust doctors," by examining what is about the doctor (or doctors) who betrayed you that caused the betrayal.

What you need to do is identify the true danger. The hunter is afraid of the plant because it is associated with the swamp that hid the crocodiles, but the plant isn't the danger. The crocodiles are. With respect to the example of doctors, what was it about them that caused you to mistrust them? What caused those people to betray you? The fact that they were members of a certain profession, or that they were dishonest, corrupt, racist, sexist, or sadistic? Did any of them have an untreated mental health problem, such as substance abuse, clinical depression, or perhaps even post-traumatic stress disorder?

Determining True Danger

How can you determine whether a doctor is not only competent professionally, but also fair and ethical?

Some of the ways to begin are to make inquiries among friends; ask the doctor for the names of three patients as references; check out library resources on these professionals' backgrounds and on the status of their licensure. There are three volumes in the reference sections of many libraries that provide information on doctors:

1. *Directory of Physicians in the United States.* 1996. Published by the American Medical Association, Chicago, Illinois.

2. *The Official A.B.M.S. (American Board of Medical Specialists) Directory of Board-Certified Medical Specialists.* 1996. Published by the Marquis Who's Who, New Providence, New Jersey. This book also lists the credentials of all the physicians in the United States.

3. *13,012 Questionable Doctors Disciplined by States or the Federal Government.* 1996. Published by Public Citizens, Washington, D. C.

Call your local library regarding these and any other written references. For further information about a specific doctor, you can contact your local medical association. If you call the American Medical Association's offices in Chicago, at 312-464-5000 or in Washington, D.C., at 202-921-4300, they can provide you with the name and address of your local medical association, which can give you information about physicians in your area.

Ethnic Stereotyping and Generalization

Suppose you were raped or robbed by someone from a certain ethnic group. You might generalize your experience and come to fear and hate all persons from that group whether or not they were truly dangerous simply because they are members of that group. In fact, some people from that group may be dangerous and should be avoided. But you won't be able to determine their dangerousness just by knowing their ethnicity. More information will be needed.

Your mistrust of these persons may pose no particular problem until your new supervisor or co-worker turns out to belong to that group or your son or daughter starts dating a member of that group. Then you are trapped—between your trauma-based mistrust and fear and the fear of losing your job, or your relationship with your son or daughter. The following exercise is designed to help you deal double binds like these.

✍ *Exercise: Overgeneralizing*

Refer to your responses in the Assessing Trustworthiness Exercise earlier. Are you overgeneralizing from your trauma experience to the present in any of the relationships you wrote about? For example, do you automatically mistrust people you meet in the present because they have a characteristic similar or identical to the characteristic of someone who betrayed you in the past? In answering this question, consider the extent to which you might have generalized based on concrete, observable characteristics, such as physical appearance, social status, occupation, or sexual or political orientation.

Example A: (Rape Survivor, Homicide Survivor, Assault Survivor)

"Mrs. Z who lied on the witness stand had curly blonde hair. Whenever I see a woman with that kind of hair, I hate her before I even know her name. One of the aerobics teachers at my gym has the same kind of hair that Mrs. Z has. Whenever she teaches a class, I walk out, even if I really need to take the class."

Example B: (Combat Veteran, Police Officer, Rescue Worker, Emergency Room Worker)

"The superior who failed to do his duty and left me stranded had a southern accent. Now, automatically, I don't respect and verbally abuse anyone with a southern accent, and I find ways to discredit anyone with that accent. I won't go on dates with anyone with a southern accent and I refuse to take trips to the southern U.S."

Example C: (Family Abuse Survivor)

"My abuser had a degree in education. I immediately don't trust anyone with a degree in education. I hate them and I think they are fools and I'm always waiting for them to try and cheat me out of something."

For each relationship you listed, how valid is the generalized reason you have for not trusting this person? For example, is it valid to automatically mistrust every short person simply because a short person mishandled your accident claim report? What made this short person harmful to you—his or her size or some other quality?

Just as the hunter needs to learn that it isn't the plant near the swamp, but the crocodile in the swamp, that poses the danger, you need to pinpoint, to the best of your ability, what qualities in people might suggest or signify danger and what qualities are irrelevant with respect to danger. Your search is for the potentially dangerous in the person, not extraneous qualities.

Example A: (Rape Survivor, Homicide Survivor, Assault Survivor)

"Just because someone has blonde curly hair doesn't mean that she is a liar and is out to get me. If Mrs. Z had had brown or red hair, her lies would have had the same impact. It wasn't her hair color that gave her power, it was her being so pretty. The judge was a sucker for pretty women. I now see that what I don't trust about certain women is not their hair color, but if I sense—and have proof—that they use their good looks to get unfair advantage or to hurt others. It was Mrs. Z's willingness to exploit her looks to hurt an innocent person that I hate. That's the crocodile, not her hair color or prettiness.

"My aerobics teacher is pretty, too, but there's no evidence that she's malicious like Mrs. Z. In fact, she's come to me several times at the gym to ask if I needed any help. The fact is this particular woman is not an enemy. She looks like one of my enemies, but she's just an aerobics teacher and she doesn't have the power over me that Mrs. Z did. The pretty blonde in the past nearly destroyed me. This blonde at the gym doesn't have that kind of power. She can't hurt me and, if I let her, she might be able to help me in my work-outs."

Example B: (Combat Veteran, Police Officer, Rescue Worker, Emergency Room Worker)

"It wasn't my superior's southern accent that made him negligent. It was other qualities he had. There are lots of people with southern accents who are responsible and dedicated. When I meet someone, I need to ignore the way they talk and focus on what they are saying and other ways of assessing how ethical and diligent they are."

Example C: (Family Abuse Survivor)

"My abuser didn't abuse me because he had a degree in education. He didn't learn how to be hateful by going to school. When I meet people and want to assess how dangerous they might be, I need to see if they have a history of violence or a substance abuse problem. I need to know whether they become irrationally angry over every little thing or if they make threats. Unless they have an advanced degree in how to commit murder, it doesn't really matter what they studied in college."

Self-Distrust: Projecting
Onto Others

During your traumatic times you may have learned not only to mistrust others, but to mistrust yourself. Indeed one of the most painful aspects of being traumatized is looking back and realizing how you failed to live up to your own standards or ideals. You may have made mistakes, had lapses in functioning, let emotion rule during the trauma and then, in retrospect, wished you had let reason rule; or the opposite, you allowed logic to rule, and then, in retrospect, you wished you had allowed your heart to have been your guide.

If you have been in trauma-focused therapy, you are probably learning about what you did or did not do during the trauma that you consider "unforgivable" and for which you have been punishing yourself, in some way, for quite some time. In your therapy, you should be working on understanding these "unforgivable" feelings, acts, or thoughts in the context of the pressures of the overwhelming demands the traumatic circumstances imposed on your abilities. (If the event did not frighten, overwhelm you, and leave you helpless, then it wasn't a trauma.) This does not mean that "anything goes" and that being in a life-or-death circumstance condones all behavior. However, in assessing your behavior during the trauma, the context of your actions must be taken into account. You also need to be aware of the difference between having a thought, feeling, or impulse and actually *acting* on that thought, feeling, or impulse.

Naturally, if you feel you made a mistake, real or perceived, or exhibited a character flaw, real or perceived, during the trauma, you may be trying very hard not to make that same mistake again and to behave according to the ideals you have set for yourself. To take a very simple example, if you left the front door open and were then robbed, you are probably very careful nowadays about locking your front door. Or, if you were forced to reveal personal information under the pressure of coercion by an abusive family member (or police coercion, or political torture) most likely you are going to be more guarded than most people in giving out personal information in the present.

As a result, you may be highly intolerant of others who exhibit these traits or make the same kind of "mistakes" you made. For you, because of your trauma, these traits or "mistakes" are associated with dire consequences and with great shame and guilt. In nontraumatic circumstances, these same traits and behaviors may or may not result in great danger or shame. In the nontraumatic present, each situation must be evaluated on an individual basis. However, once you've been traumatized, it's hard to divorce a present-day problem behavior or trait from the powerful meaning it had in the past, even when it is in your best interest to do so. Like the hunter with the plant, you can't forget the relationship between the behavior or trait and the sad outcome in the past, even if the present is entirely different.

Kenneth, for example, witnessed a homicide. When he volunteered to testify for the state, he was threatened by the suspect and his friends. Kenneth testified anyway, only to discover that some of the police officers and the homicide suspect were co-conspirators in a drug deal. On the stand, Kenneth felt that *he* was on trial and that he now had two sets of enemies: first, the homicide suspect and his friends and second, certain members of the police department.

Within days after the trial, certain policemen began to harass Kenneth with "surprise inspections" of his business, and his business license was revoked over some minor violation that had been ignored in prior inspections. The paperwork and bureaucratic delays that followed pushed his business into a downward slump from which it never recovered. As Kenneth explains it, "no good deed goes unpunished," and in his view, for which he has substantial grounds, the hassles with his business license were direct retaliation for his testifying. His deepest fear is that the retaliation won't stop with his business. He is afraid that his life and the lives of his family are in danger.

In group therapy, social gatherings, and other settings, Kenneth has trouble sharing on any level and refuses to discuss anything controversial. He feels that if he talks, not only will those who outwardly disagree with him be angry with him (like the homicide suspect and his friends) but that those who say they agree with him (like the corrupt police officers) will become his enemies, too. In essence, because of his trauma, Kenneth has learned to be silent. For Kenneth, talking, speaking up, is dangerous. He's not worried about being unpopular; he's worried about being killed.

Kenneth looks down on anyone who "shows his hand" or talks openly, whether in group therapy or at a family dinner. He chastises his wife and children for confiding to their friends and has a condescending attitude towards co-workers who are friendly and cordial. He calls them "simpletons," "fools," and "dummies" because this is how he views himself for agreeing to do something "stupid" like being a witness in a criminal trial, or having faith in "the system."

Kenneth is in a double bind. He is alienating his family and friends by criticizing them for being sociable, expressing opinions, or sharing their inner feelings. But he feels he is criticizing them only for their own protection, even if they don't appreciate or understand his motives. He entered therapy because he was lonely and wanted to be closer to others. His conflict is that he can't trust people who don't open up to him (because he can't gauge how trustworthy they are), and he can't trust people who do open up (because they are "stupid morons" or "trusting fools" who would say things about him that might endanger him or his family).

Here, Kenneth is placing his feelings about himself that he finds unacceptable onto others. When one places feelings or characteristics that one does not like about oneself onto other people, that process is called *projection*.

The Shadow

The process of projecting parts of ourselves that we do not like onto others becomes even more complicated when the parts of ourselves that we wish to disown are socially taboo. According to psychologist Carl Jung, the human personality has many parts. One part of our personality—the person we present to the world—is called the "persona." The persona has learned socially acceptable traits and knows how to modify certain instincts and desires in order to fit into society and not be punished for breaking societal rules.

Another part of personality, however, is called the shadow. The shadow is the reservoir of many of our desires and feelings that we, or society, feel are unacceptable. Hence the shadow contains our lust, greed, vanity, aggressiveness, pettiness, selfishness, capacity for violence and evil, and all those parts of us that are "bad" and should definitely not be acted upon. Also contained in the shadow are qualities that are not considered "evil" but are socially undesirable, for example, vulnerability and emotionality in men and aggressiveness in women.

Some people are unaware of their shadow. They don't even know it exists. If you ask the average person if he or she has ever lied, cheated, wanted to kill someone, or lusted for someone who was not their mate, most likely that person would say "no." That might not be the actual truth, but to that person, it is the truth because he or she is not aware of his or her shadow. It's too horrible to contemplate. The idea of being murderous or lustful is so unacceptable, the shadow is suppressed out of awareness.

But no matter how much we suppress our shadow, the primitive urges and feelings contained in it continue to emerge. They are very powerful. One way to handle the shadow is to deny it exists, but to satisfy it by watching *other* people act as if motivated by their shadow. That's one reason why movies with lots of sex, killing, and other socially unacceptable behaviors are so popular—people release their shadow urges by watching others act out those urges.

The average person wouldn't dream of robbing a bank, plotting a financial swindle, killing, or raping. But people spend time and money to watch television programs and movies where such things are commonplace. In other words, one way to handle the shadow is to allow it to live vicariously through reading books or watching dramas where people act in ways that we wouldn't dare for fear of being condemned by society.

Trauma survivors have often encountered the shadow; not in movies, but in real life. They have seen people acting out their shadows and may have been in situations where they were forced to act out their shadow, or where their shadow urges were activated. Anyone who has been the victim of sexual assault, war, and other forms of violence has seen people who are acting out shadow urges. Those who have been forced to abuse another person, lie, steal, or cheat, or go against their own moral standards in order to save their own lives or the lives of others were forced to act out parts of their shadow. Even if you were not forced to betray your values as a result of being traumatized, if you've ever felt vengeful or murderous toward those who hurt you, you have met your shadow. Having self-destructive thoughts is also part of the shadow personality, and persons coping with trauma frequently have thoughts of suicide, self-mutilation, and self-abasement.

To go through trauma and not encounter the shadow in oneself or another person is impossible. In fact, it is encountering the shadow in others and oneself that makes trauma so traumatizing. Your trauma has taught you the capacity of others for evil and deceit. You have seen these qualities in others, and, in one way or another, whether you have had to act on them or not, you have seen them in yourself. If you are the survivor of a man-made trauma as opposed to a natural disaster, you are probably acutely aware of the possibility of human evil. However, even those of you who were traumatized by acts of nature may have been exposed to human error and malice.

Projection and the Shadow Self

If you haven't had the opportunity to acknowledge and deal with your shadow self, you may, like the nontraumatized, deal with it by projecting it onto others. In other words, instead of saying that "I am a coward," or "I feel lust," and "Cowardice or lust is a problem for me," you look at someone else and say, "That person is a coward or is lustful and that is the problem. My lust or cowardice isn't a problem because I don't have immoral desires and I am always brave. The problem is that this other person's immoral desires or cowardly tendencies are so strong they may take over." However, the true fear is that your lust or cowardice will come out of the closet and you won't be able to control it.

This process is called "scapegoating" or "projection." On a social scale, the shadow of one group can be projected onto another group with distinct features so that it can be easily identified. Hence, in the past, and even today, some men project what they consider undesirable traits, such as emotionality or vulnerability onto women. For those men, the problem isn't their own emotionality and vulnerability: it's the emotionality and vulnerability of a particular woman in their life, or even of all women.

Many of our racial stereotypes originated in the need to project shadow traits away from ourselves onto a distinct group. Hence white slave owners made much of the unbridled sexuality of their African-American slaves, when in reality it was white slave owners who were taking sexual advantage of their slaves. They projected their own uncontrolled lust onto their victims, calling them "seductive" or "oversexed" or "immoral," when the problem wasn't the sexual desires of the slaves, but the sexual desires of the slave owners.

This tendency to project is very human because it takes a great deal of strength to look into oneself and own one's shadow. The difficulty is compounded if one has been traumatized and the shadow is not just a fleeting thought, but a real action that was observed or a behavior that was enacted. If you've been traumatized, there is a great temptation to project your shadow onto others, to see in others the "evil" or "sins" you feared you might commit or that you were forced to commit under traumatic circumstances.

Joe, a combat veteran, was so frightened during his first firefight that he lost control of his bladder and his bowels. He was taunted by his comrades for being a "chicken," but he didn't need his comrades to ridicule him. He had his own internal censor. Joe's father, also a veteran, had told him that it was a "sin" for a man to be afraid, that "real men" feared nothing.

For the whole time he was in combat, Joe was afraid. But he covered up his fear with a false bravado and tried to prove to his comrades, to himself, and, psychologically, to his father, that he wasn't afraid, by killing randomly.

Today, Joe feels guilty about those random, indiscriminate killings and he is certain that others are out to kill him. He finds it hard to trust that others do not intend to harm him because while he was in combat he lost trust in himself. He, a former altar boy, had thought that as a soldier he would engage only in restrained, disciplined killing. But because of the enormous psychic pressures of combat, he violated his own standards. Because he lost trust in himself he has great difficulty trusting others. Because he hurt innocent people he fears that others will hurt him, even though he is innocent of having done anything to hurt them.

Joe's example may seem extreme. Most of the readers of this book have not taken human life, but many trauma survivors deem themselves to have been more "cowardly" than they wanted to be and have found themselves full of hostile desires as a result of their traumas. It would be the most natural thing in the world for you to project your shadow onto others, but such projection makes it impossible to assess others realistically and to establish safe or enduring attachments.

Another example of projection can be seen in Anna's behavior. Two years ago Anna's sister suffered from deep depression and threatened to commit suicide. Anna got her sister into therapy and tried to cheer her up by taking her out several nights a week. However, one night Anna was supposed to pick her sister up and she was ten minutes late. She found her sister dead.

Anna feels that if she had been on time, she could have prevented the suicide. To this day, she is never late and has an intense dislike for those who are late for appointments. In this, Anna is like many soldiers, rescue workers, and firefighters who value punctuality because they are in situations where if someone is late, someone else may die. In such situations, it is critical for people to show up on time because every second counts.

Anna's punctuality is a major asset on the job and most of her friends appreciate her always being on time. However, she flies into a fury when she's kept waiting. She yells at her children and other family members for being late and she has almost ended relationships with people if they kept her waiting more than once or twice.

"They're horrible!" she'll say.

What she's really saying is that she was horrible for not showing up at the designated time and, in her view, "causing" the suicide. A more rational view of the suicide is that, given the severity of her sister's depression, the suicide might have happened anyway. It might not have happened that day, but it could have happened even if Anna had stayed with her sister twenty-four hours a day. When someone is intent on suicide, sometimes not even psychiatric hospitalization can prevent the act.

On a deeper level, Anna felt "horrible" about more than being late—she felt guilty about her resentment of the burden her sister's depression had imposed on her life. Several times, when she was exhausted from caring for her sister, helping her elderly parents cope with her sister's depression, and managing her own life, she had secretly wished her sister would "just do it and get it over with." When such thoughts had come, Anna had quickly put them out of her mind. To her, those thoughts were absolutely unacceptable.

Anna didn't really want her sister dead. She simply wanted freedom from the long-term burden her sister's illness had placed on her life. Also, Anna was jealous of her sister. As much as she hated to admit it, Anna—like most people—harbored some normal sibling rivalry that had been exacerbated by the fact that her sister, due to the illness, was the center of the family's attention. To make matters worse, her sister had always been her father's favorite and had been considered more attractive and talented than Anna.

"My sister's got the looks, the smarts, a husband, and dad's heart. I'm single, have no boyfriend, and an average IQ. I should have the depression, not her," Anna would sometimes think, and then quickly put those thoughts out of her mind.

For brief moments, Anna's jealousy of her sister would spill over into a kind of hatred. This caused Anna such shame and guilt, that she not only pushed her negative feelings about her sister out of her awareness, she redoubled her efforts to help her sister. But the unacceptable feelings of resentment, jealousy, and hate did not disappear. They became associated with the trauma and the issue of punctuality. Therefore, when people kept Anna waiting, their lateness not only reminded her of the suicide, but became associated with her taboo feelings of sibling rivalry and resentment towards her sister.

Exercise: Projecting Self-Distrust (Your Shadow) Onto Others

In the following exercise, you are going to identify the ways in which you project certain trauma-related self-mistrust onto others.

1. Start by listing three ways you feel you let yourself down during your trauma, or three mistakes you made for which you have regrets, or three aspects of your shadow that the trauma forced you to face.

   Sample:

   a. During the trauma, I failed to stand up for myself.

   b. During the trauma, I was too aggressive or I felt like killing

   _____ .

   c. I should have known that _____ was going to happen and been more prepared.

How did it feel to list the ways you feel you let yourself down? Do you have any uncomfortable sensations in your body? Are you feeling extremely anxious or having destructive thoughts? If you are having any of the reactions listed in the Cautions section in the Introduction, stop reading or working on the writing exercises and follow the suggestions given in the Cautions section. If you are having a strong reaction to questions about how you reacted during the trauma, then it is highly probable that you have more work to do on processing your trauma, especially in the area of understanding why you behaved as you did.

Hopefully, you will seek professional assistance or the assistance of a caring, knowledgeable friend or support group to help you in this area. When you are ready, it is critical that you deal with any unresolved issues about how you acted during the trauma because your unresolved feelings about yourself probably will deeply influence your relationships with others. If you feel you are "evil" or "bad," it will be hard for you to not see others has being "evil" or "bad" also.

2. Refer back to your list in No. 1 above.

   a. How do you react when you see these traits in others?

   b. Does it feel as if the trauma is about to happen again, or is happening now?

   c. How does your body react and what are you thinking when you see these traits or behavior in others?

What were the consequences of such behavior or traits during your trauma? In reality, what are the consequences of other persons making this mistake or exhibiting this flaw today—a major financial burden, a painful emotional state, or just a relatively minor inconvenience? How much of your reaction to these persons' troublesome traits or behaviors is due to your history of trauma and how much is due to the real costs of those traits or behaviors?

Summary

Under traumatic conditions, extreme mistrust of certain persons (especially unknown persons), total trust in others, and quick judgments about whether someone can be trusted are all useful survival tactics. However, these mind-sets are not necessarily life-preserving or life-enhancing in nontraumatic situations. A certain amount of trust is necessary to work with and for others, as well as to have friendships, love relationships, and family ties. Furthermore, total trust or total distrust, or global trust or mistrust, are not useful in situations requiring partial trust.

The trauma survivor needs to respect the lessons about human failings and the capacity of humans to be unjust, uncaring, and evil that were learned all too well during the trauma. Yet it is disadvantageous to treat people in the present, who might be caring and reliable in some important ways, as if they were reincarnations of those people who were associated with mistreatment during your trauma.

One part of healing the ruptures in your relationships that were caused by your trauma is the ability to examine how relationship patterns that evolved during the trauma might be affecting your current relationships. To be as safe as possible in relationships, trauma survivors need to assess the trustworthiness of persons with whom they are involved by using a factually based decision-making process. This process has five steps:

1. gathering information,

2. drawing tentative conclusions,

3. testing the conclusions,

4. revising the conclusions, and

5. then repeating the process, if necessary.

Equally challenging is the task of examining how one has generalized from the characteristics of the people who were dangerous during the trauma to the people in one's life today, and then sorting out what is truly dangerous from what is merely associated with danger. Even harder is the self-examination required to acknowledge how one might be projecting onto others aspects one doesn't trust in oneself or one's shadow.

References

DSM III-R Diagnostic and Statistical Manual of Mental Disorders, Third Edition, Revised. 1987. Washington, D.C. American Psychiatric Association.

Green, Bonnie L. and Jacob Lindy, Mary Grace, Goldine Gleser, et al. 1990. "Buffalo Creek Survivors in the Second Decade: Stability of Stress Symptoms." *American Journal of Orthopsychiatry* 60:1.

Jacob, Lindy, D. 1985. "The Trauma Membrane and Other Clinical Concepts from Psychotherapeutic Work with Survivors of Natural Disasters." *Psychiatric Annals* (March)153–160.

Madakasira, Sudhaker and Kevin O'Brien. 1987. "Acute Post-Traumatic Stress Disorder in Victims of a Natural Disaster." *The Journal of Nervous and Mental Disease* 175:286–292.

4

Relationships and the Physiology of Trauma

How can the wounded heart mend
When it doesn't know
When the memories will come again?

—An old Greek folk song about trauma

In the ancient tale of the Trojan War, the Greeks and the Trojans fought each other for ten bloody years, because Paris, a prince of Troy, kidnapped Helen, the wife of a Greek warrior named Menelaus. After Troy was destroyed, Menelaus and his soldiers returned to Greece and tried to adjust to peacetime living. But their adjustment was disrupted by a visit from Telemachus, the son of the Greek general, Ulysses, who had yet to return from Troy.

Telemachus went to Menelaus' court in search of his missing father, Ulysses. When Menelaus and his men saw Telemachus, war memories flooded their consciousness. Grief and anger consumed them. Nothing, not old wine, cheerful song, good food, or beautiful women, could comfort them. Only Helen had a solution: a magic potion that could stop memories, grief, and anger.

What was Helen's magic potion? An ancient form of Prozac, Trazadone, lithium, or some other antidepressant or anti-anxiety medication, the kinds of drugs given to trauma survivors today to help them sleep, calm down, and shake off depression?

No one knows what was in Helen's magic potion, but everyone knows that once someone has been traumatized, especially if the trauma was severe or repeated, that person is subject to remembering that trauma, at both expected and unexpected times, and not by choice.

Indeed, PTSD has been called a disorder of memory (van der Kolk 1994b) in that chief among its symptoms is the re-experiencing of traumatic memories through nightmares, flashbacks, and intrusive thoughts. These re-experiencing memories are destabilizing because they come unexpectedly and create fear. They also distract the individual from the situation at hand whether it be completing a task or having a conversation.

Over a century ago, Pierre Janet described how traumatized women in a Parisian mental hospital were "tormented by day and by night" by memories of the violence they had experienced (van der Kolk 1994b). Researchers repeatedly have found that it is not simply the traumatic event, but the frequent recall of that event and of the emotions and physical responses associated with it, that causes major problems in everyday life—especially relationships.

This chapter presents some of the basics of our current understanding of the possible physiological reactions to trauma. The 1990s have seen a great expansion in the number of studies on the effects of trauma, including many on the biological effects of prolonged or severe trauma. Some of these studies were done on animals, but many were conducted on human beings, from Holocaust survivors and combat veterans, to survivors of family violence.

Because of space limitations, the results of many of these studies could not be included here. Many of the points made in this chapter will seem like generalities to those who understand that, because of the complexity of human physiology, it is very difficult to study the physical effects of trauma. Nevertheless, certain perhaps sweeping generalities are made because it is necessary to drive home essential concepts about how trauma can affect, sometimes permanently, the way someone reacts to the environment and to other people.

If you do not fully appreciate the physiological effects of trauma, you will tend to misinterpret PTSD or other trauma symptoms as a failure of willpower, or as a lack of willingness to "try harder" or to "forget the past and enjoy life now." You also may tend to view relationship difficulties as signs of personal inadequacies or as a natural predisposition towards being a "loner." Nothing could be further from the truth. The hard truth is that if you have been severely or repeatedly traumatized, your body and your mind will react in self-protective or other ways that are due to the trauma

These physiological reactions and the kinds of memories and feelings that go along with them can be very distressing and can significantly interfere with your personal and work relationships. You may have little choice about whether or not you experience the kinds of biological reactions described in this chapter. You do have some choice, however, over the ways that you *respond* to these physiological reactions and to the memories and emotions that often accompany them. For those readers who find some of the terms used in this chapter a bit daunting, there is a selected list of definitions of some of the more scientific terms at the end of the chapter.

The first step toward understanding how the trauma has affected your ability to have fulfilling relationships is to have a clear understanding of how the trauma affected you physiologically. Once you acquire a basic understanding of some of the major changes in body chemistry that occur as the result of severe or prolonged trauma, you will have a framework with which to understand not only your own inner struggles, but also your relationship problems.

The PTSD Cycle: Hyperarousal and Numbing

The physiological reactions to trauma, and remembering trauma, encompass two seemingly diametrically opposed extremes—*hyperarousal* and *numbing*—or overreacting and underreacting. Although on the surface these two reactions seem like opposites, they are interrelated. Prolonged hyperarousal can lead to numbing and some trauma survivors suffer from both hyperarousal and numbing symptoms within a short period of time.

Hyperarousal symptoms include the following:

- sweating
- rapid heart rate and increased blood pressure
- flashbacks, nightmares, and intrusive thoughts
- the startle response
- sensitivity to noise, sound, pain, or any sudden or intense stimulus
- difficulties controlling emotional responsiveness

Numbing symptoms include the following:
- fatigue and apathy
- sense of emotional emptiness and detachment from others
- inability to focus on and complete a task or social interaction
- numbness to physical pain

Either hyperarousal or numbing symptoms, or both, can occur in response to a trauma or to a reminder of the trauma, or *trigger*.

For example, if Angela sees a flash of light on a windowpane at night, she begins to sweat profusely even if it is the middle of winter and the temperature is freezing. The sudden glow on the window glass reminds her of the flash of light she saw on the gun that killed her sweetheart. Ever since the homicide, she's avoided going out socially for fear that some reminder of the trauma will cause her to sweat, hyperventilate, or emotionally overreact.

Like Angela, Gregory also sweats—whenever he has to ask his supervisor for information or help. It doesn't matter what the temperature is or what he's wearing, asking anybody for anything is a traumatic reminder, or trigger, for Gregory. When he was a child and had to ask his parents for things, he was often ridiculed and beaten. Gregory has lived through three failed marriages, countless broken romances, and is always struggling with his superiors and co-workers on the job.

Angela and Gregory suffer from hyperarousal symptoms. Tony, on the other hand, suffers every summer from a mind and body "shutdown" or numbing reaction. Summers were the times his uncle used to visit and sexually abuse him. In the wintertime Tony is full of life. He plays sports and is active socially. But he spends most of his summers in his room because he feels fatigued and has no interest or energy for anything or anyone.

Lori goes through the same process of "shutting down" and retreating socially during the Christmas holiday. Many years ago, both of her parents committed suicide two days apart over the Christmas holidays. For years she stopped going to church, stopped exercising, stopped making love with her husband, and stopped answering the phone during the Christmas season. Even parenting her children, whom she adored, was a major effort. Until she entered therapy, she never realized that her Christmas "shutdown" was directly linked to the anniversary of her parents' suicides.

Angela, Gregory, Tony, and Lori suffer from the biological effects of severe or prolonged trauma, which affect not only their body temperature, breathing, heart rate, and immune system, but also their ability to feel emotions and their ability and willingness to relate to others. Like many trauma survivors, they tend to judge their reactions as signs of personal failure. They also tend to have trouble connecting their emotional, mental, and physical reactions to the traumatic events that gave rise to these adverse reactions. Their shame at the ways they react causes them to retreat and hide from others and, inwardly, to disparage themselves.

The Mind-Body Connection

Within every human being the mind, body, and emotions are inseparable. The way we feel affects the way we think and the way we think affects the way we feel. The state of our body affects the state of our mind, as well as our emotional state. Endless examples can be provided to illustrate the fact that the mind, body, and emotions are not separate entities, but are intimately related. Nowhere is this more evident than in the case of trauma, where many of the psychological symptoms and relationship problems are not only "in the head," but "in the body," as well.

Like the rest of your body, your central nervous system is vulnerable. Given enough physical or emotional stress, it too can bend or even break. When you lived through your trauma, your central nervous system endured a series of intense shocks. The greater the intensity and the longer the duration of the trauma and the fewer the social supports and comforters you had during that time, the greater the possibility that delicate biochemical balances within your body may have been disrupted.

Despite an increase in research in recent years on the biochemistry of PTSD, there is no single definitive theory as to how trauma affects the body. One theory holds that trauma destabilizes the autonomic nervous system; another that trauma changes body chemistry so that the individual is more prone to anxiety. Still another hypothesis posits that trauma disrupts certain specific biochemical balances, for example, serotonin or catecholamine levels (Murburg 1994, 1996; van der Kolk 1996a, 1996c).

Another theory is that under conditions of danger, the organism coordinates a mental, physical, and emotional effort to respond in a self-preserving manner. After the emergency is over, then the organism returns to the thinking, feeling, and physiological states appropriate to daily (nontraumatic) living. When stress is extreme, however, such as in trauma, or when stress is prolonged, all systems may not return to previous levels of daily functioning. They may remain in a state of emergency. The evidence for this theory is found in studies showing that some survivors continued to live in an altered state of arousal for some twenty years after their traumatic experiences (Giller 1994). Persons with PTSD have been found to excrete more neurohormones of epinephrine or norepinephrine than nontraumatized persons. In fact, persons with PTSD excrete more of those neurohormones than do those suffering from major psychiatric disorders, such as schizophrenia or major depression (van der Kolk 1994a, 1994b, 1996b). Although not all studies of trauma survivors show these results, many do (Murburg 1996).

No single biological explanation is satisfactory in that no one theory can explain the wide range of symptoms exhibited by trauma survivors. But it is an established fact that PTSD for some trauma survivors, especially those subjected to repeated trauma, has both physical and emotional components.

When Dr. Abraham Kardiner, a psychiatrist who treated combat veterans during World War I, described shell shock, he described it as a "physioneurosis" in that the individuals who suffered from war-related PTSD had not only psychic disturbances, but physical ones, as well. These included body tremors, urinary incontinence, heart palpitations, sweating, and increased incidence of heart and other diseases (Kardiner 1941). In fact PTSD was first "discovered" by Charcot, a neurologist in nineteenth-century France, who became intrigued by hospitalized women who exhibited physical complaints and ailments with no known physical basis. Most of these women proved to be victims of child abuse, wife abuse, rape, and other traumas. When they were hypnotized or otherwise encouraged to talk about their trauma and they got in touch with their memories, and their feelings about those memories, many of their physical symptoms disappeared.

The Dangers of Oversimplifying

In recent years, considerable research has been completed on survivors of various traumas, from Holocaust survivors and abused children to rape victims, combat veterans, and car-accident survivors. This research suggests that, in certain cases, profound physiological changes accompany severe or prolonged trauma. The nature of these changes and how they affect relationships is the subject of this chapter. However, it must be emphasized that research on the biology of PTSD is in its infancy and that all statements made in this book regarding the biology of PTSD may well be out of date five years after publication.

The greatest danger in discussing the biology of PTSD is that of oversimplification (Murburg 1994, 1996). The workings of the brain and the way changes in the brain affect emotions, sexuality, physical health, thinking, and memory are still great mysteries and are fraught with controversy. In addition, most of the research on the biology of PTSD and traumatic reactions has been completed only on trauma survivors available for research, namely inpatient psychiatric patients or outpatient mental health patients. Trauma survivors who cannot afford or are not interested in therapy or those who died or became physically ill or psychotic as the result of their traumas have not—for obvious reasons—been included in these studies.

Also, results of the studies have been influenced (and perhaps skewed) by the age and socioeconomic status of the participants, as well as factors like the type and severity of the trauma and the traumatic reactions; the co-existence of traumatic reactions with substance abuse; the presence of clinical depression or other psychiatric disorders; and the physical health and habits of the participants. For example, research results have varied depending on whether the subjects were overweight, smoked, or drank coffee, as well as if they were experiencing current stress in their lives, especially on the job. Research results have also varied depending on the type of technology used, e.g., whether blood samples as opposed to urinary samples were examined, and whether the testing was conducted in a hospital, university, community clinic, or home environment (Murburg 1994, 1996).

Nevertheless, certain general trends have emerged: Mainly that persons who have been severely or chronically traumatized tend either to overreact or underreact to present-day situations, creating anxiety and shame within themselves and chaos in their relationships, including the tendency to withdraw from others. If you have been traumatized, it is critical for you to understand both the immediate and possible long-term biological consequences of the stress you endured. When you "get hyper" and feel as if you just can't sit still another moment or you will explode, or when you "get stupid" and feel dead inside, it may help you to know that these extreme reactions are not signs of moral or emotional deficiency but are continuing reactions to the trauma you lived through.

These extreme reactions, which create so much pain in you and so much havoc in your relationships, are, to a great extent, the result of physiological processes out of your control. They are not acts of will or choice. They are an intrinsic part of survival-based physiological responses, which are largely involuntary. Although there are many ways to moderate the effects of these reactions, if you've been severely or repeatedly traumatized, you may overreact or underreact to situations and relationships for much of your life. However, your first step in managing these reactions, and not allowing them to damage your relationships or cause you to retreat from the world, is to understand what they are and why they are.

Acute Stress Reactions: Fight-Flight-Freeze Reactions—Adrenaline and Noradrenaline

Figure 4.1 illustrates some of the emotional and physiological reactions to trauma. Trauma can give rise to at least four overwhelming emotions: fear, grief, rage, and anxiety. These feelings can be so powerful that to experience them in full force at the time of the trauma would be personally disorganizing and might endanger survival. Therefore, these emotions tend to be suppressed, to some degree.

When emotions are not suppressed during the traumatic event, at least in part, people can become nonfunctional. For example, they may not be able to move or to think clearly due to uncontrolled bouts of weeping or to screaming or hallucinations or any of a number of psychotic breaks from reality. When overwhelmed by emotion during the trauma, some individuals have committed suicide, homicide, or acts of self-mutilation (such as cutting, burning, head banging), which hamper their coping abilities and endanger the safety of others.

The life-threatening nature of trauma also gives rise to physical emergency responses whose function it is to help people survive emergencies like trauma. Included in these responses are the "three F's"— Fight, Flight, and Freeze (see figure 1). Under conditions of danger, the adrenal glands release either adrenaline or noradrenaline. *Adrenaline* enables people to move quickly and powerfully, whether to fight with

Figure 4.1   Traumatic Stressor

Unbearable Affect   **Psysiological Arousal**
                                         (Body's Emergency Response)

Unbearable Affect	Noradrenaline (Freeze)	Adrenaline (Fight-Flight)

1. Overwhelming fear—existential panic at confronting fact of human mortality (death)

Noradrenaline (Freeze)

1. Difficulties moving

Adrenaline (Fight-Flight)

1. Heart rate increases
2. Blood-sugar increases

2. Grief—sadness

2. Slower breathing

3. Muscle tension

3. Rage

3. Biochemical shifts in neurotransmitters

4. Perspiration

4. Heightened anxiety due to powerlessness and danger

5. Blood decreases in arms and legs, blood concentration in head and trunk

6. Dilation of eyes

Possible Effects of Hyperventilation ←————

7. Hyperventilation (rapid, shallow breathing from upper lung vs. normal, gentle breathing from lower lung)

- Irregular heartbeat
- Blurred vision
- Dizziness, lightheadedness
- Muscle pains or spasms
- Shortness of breath
- Chest pain
- Asthma
- Shaking
- Choking sensations
- Lump in throat
- Nausea
- Difficulty swallowing
- Fatigue, weakness
- Heartburn
- Confusion, inability to concentrate
- Numbness or tingling of mouth, hands, feet

8. Biochemical shifts in neurotransmitters

Adapted from *The Body's Emergency Response: Breaking the Panic Cycle for People with Phobias,* by H. R. Wilson, Anxiety Association of America, 1987. Used with permission.

renewed strength or to run (flight) with increased speed. Some rape victims, for example, were so empowered by adrenaline that they were able to fight off attackers three times their strength. In other cases, rape victims have found themselves "frozen"—literally unable to move—or otherwise unable to act on their own behalf because of the release of *noradrenaline*. This numbing reaction is similar to the way some animals play dead when threatened.

Some mugging victims have reported being surprised by how they reacted when they were attacked. One woman says, "I always thought that if I were to be mugged, I'd totally comply with the mugger. I'd hand him my purse, write him a check, do whatever he wanted in the hope that he wouldn't cause me bodily harm. But when I actually was mugged, I fought back. I punched the mugger, pulled his hair, and tried to tear his clothes off of him. He was one foot taller than me and double my weight. It wasn't a matter of logic. Something came over me—a surge of energy—and I just lunged at him like a wild woman. Looking back I can't believe it was me, timid me, who to this day is afraid to swat a fly."

This "timid" woman was struck by a surge of adrenaline that made her feel as physically powerful and daring as a professional boxer. On the other hand, professional boxers and men trained in martial arts have found themselves "frozen" by noradrenaline when they were endangered.

For example, Sam, a former boxer and an ex-Marine, was held up in his home. When he was told to open the safe, much to his amazement, he couldn't remember the combination, even though, until that moment, he had known the numbers by heart.

"My mind froze," Sam says. Then, to Sam's further amazement, when he put his hand in his pocket where his gun was hidden, his hand "froze" too. He couldn't grab the gun. Sam was used to violence and physical aggression, but in this instance, the numbing response flooded his central nervous system, temporarily paralyzing his mind and his limbs.

Similarly, Mike, a combat medic during the Vietnam War, describes how he had been "living on adrenaline" working nonstop on wounded soldiers with an almost superhuman amount of energy for days on end. Then, one day, speeding towards a bleeding soldier, he "froze." He couldn't move, even though he wanted to, and remembers nothing of what happened between the time he first "froze" until he woke up three days later. To this day, he doesn't know what happened during those three days. Not only his body, but his memory had gone numb.

We do not know why some people have the fight or flight response, as opposed to freeze reactions. One theory is that the more severe the trauma, the more likely that a "freeze" reaction will occur, if not initially, then during the traumatic event. This theory holds that at the first sign of danger the body pumps adrenaline, which energizes the organism to respond. However, after a certain threshold of stress is reached (i.e., if the stress is too severe or goes on for too long), the adrenaline flow ceases and a numbing reaction begins.

Perhaps it is analogous to putting your foot on the gas pedal to increase the speed of your car. You press down to go faster, but if you press down too fast or too many times, you flood the engine and everything stops. This is similar to what can happen when adrenaline is pumped too fast or too long: Eventually the energizing adrenaline response ceases and the numbing response takes over.

When experimental laboratory animals are subjected to electric shock or some other form of trauma, at first they secrete massive amounts of adrenaline, epinephrine, and other activating hormones. The animals then run all around their cages trying to find a way out. Or they "fight" the bars of the cage by biting or pushing against them. However, if the electric shock *persists* and the animals see that no matter how much they fight or try to flee, they are still being shocked, the adrenaline surge ceases. The response that takes its place is called the *Stress Induced Analgesia (SIA) response*, which is mediated by the endogenous opioid system (see the section "Opioids: Nature's Stress Absorbers," that follows). The animals become "numb" or "passive." They stop trying to escape and show little interest in food, play, or sex. (These experiments are the basis of Seligman's theory of learned helplessness, described in my book, *I Can't Get Over It: A Handbook for Trauma Survivors* (1996).)

However, not all experimental animals react the same way at the same pace. Some become numb and passive right away, others only after repeated shocks. Are the ones who become numb early on "weaker" for not continuing to fight, or are they "smarter" in that they are able to foresee that putting up a fight is hopeless?

Passing moral judgments on these animals makes as much sense as passing moral judgment on traumatized people, some of whom become numb faster than others for reasons that no one has adequately explained yet. In Western culture, action is more highly valued than inaction, thus trauma survivors who "put up a fight" or try to beat the odds by trying to escape tend to be valued more highly than those who "freeze." However an individual's response may have more to do with the severity and the duration of the traumatic stressor or that person's biologically determined threshold of stress than any character trait. Indeed, the numbing response should be seen as the body's attempt to preserve the organism from unbearable pain and stress, as well as a way to conserve energy for dealing with future stress (Glover 1992). According to Glover, "numbing represents an effort to diminish the psychophysiological experience of stress" (Glover 1992, 644). As van der Kolk explains it, people with PTSD are easily overstimulated.

Because of this tendency to become overstimulated, "they compensate by shutting down" (van der Kolk 1996a, 14). Furthermore, some people have been shown to exhibit both adrenaline and noradrenaline responses within the same traumatic incident, or over a series of traumatic incidents.

As figure 4.1 illustrates, under the influence of increased adrenaline flow, there can be increases in heart rate, blood sugar level, muscle tension, and perspiration. The pupils of the eyes dilate, digestion slows down, and blood coagulates quicker to prevent too much blood being lost. The lungs become more efficient, providing increased oxygen that not only allows more rapid and powerful movements, but also vastly improves the acuteness of all the senses. Sounds, smells, and other sensory data, for example, are perceived more vividly. The brain uses this sensory data to assess the situation, thus maximizing the chances for survival. Furthermore, due to increased oxygen, the brain works more quickly and efficiently to make the best decisions possible.

The emergency alert response of adrenaline strengthens functions essential to survival, such as the abilities to perceive and move, and diminishes nonessential functions, such as digestion and reproduction. Clearly, although digestion and reproduction are important functions, they are not as important as survival itself. Think about it. If you are being chased by a tiger, blood and oxygen are needed in your muscles, so you can run fast, not in your stomach to digest food, or in your genitals for mating or reproduction.

Research on traumatized women has shown that after a certain threshold of stress is reached, reproductive functions such as ovulation can be affected. Hence some abused women cease to menstruate or they have other gynecological problems that are the result of prolonged stress. Bodily resources are directed to essential functions, such as trying to manage the batterer's behavior, protecting children from abuse, and planning how to lessen or get away from the violence, not to the relatively nonessential functions of reproduction.

Even the immune system may shut down temporarily because it's more important to get away from the tiger than to fight microbes and bacteria. This effect of increased adrenaline flow on the immune system explains why persons exposed to prolonged stress (where the emergency response is overextended) are subject to more illnesses and tend to die younger than peers who were not repeatedly traumatized (Perry 1994). Laboratory animals subjected to repeated inescapable shock tend to develop more tumors and other illnesses than control animals (van der Kolk 1996a, 1996b; Murburg 1994).

Increased adrenaline may cause other negative effects, such as hyperventilation, rapid shallow breathing from the upper lung versus normal, gentle breathing from the lower lung. Hyperventilation, in turn, can lead to irregular heart rate and dizziness, shortness of breath, choking sensations, lump in the throat, heartburn, chest pain, blurred vision, muscle pains or spasms, nausea, shaking, and numbness or tingling of the mouth, hands, or feet. It can also generate mental confusion and difficulties with concentration.

Opioids: Nature's Stress Absorbers

Freezing and "numbing" reactions are also caused by the endogenous opioid system, the body's natural tranquilizers and stress-reducing hormones and biochemicals. "Endogenous opioids, which inhibit pain and reduce panic, are secreted after prolonged exposure to severe stress" (van der Kolk 1996a, 227). People subjected to intense and prolonged physical or emotional pain often report that, after a certain point, they "didn't feel pain anymore." For example, it has been found that severely wounded soldiers during World War II did not require as many painkillers as civilians with similar or even lesser wounds (Beecher 1946; Glover 1992).

Similarly, there are numerous documented accounts of refugees, soldiers, and accident victims who have walked great distances with major wounds while reporting only minimal pain. Some abused women and children have reported that, after a certain point, the beatings hurt less and the emotional impact lost much of its intensity. The emotional pain was muted, and so were other more positive emotional states, such as joy and love.

In one case, a woman whose husband beat her and then tried to crush her by piling furniture on top of her, rose from the floor after her husband left and proceeded to cook dinner for her children as if nothing had happened. Only when one of her children noticed the blood and the bone sticking out of her arm did the woman realize she had been badly injured. Yet she felt no physical pain—and no emotion. "I became a robot during that marriage. I fulfilled my duties, but I had no feelings—no anger, no sadness, no joy, no nothing. I just functioned," she says.

In sum, on both the physical and emotional planes, it seems that we are provided a buffer against unbearable or intense pain by means of the SIA, or Stress Induced Analgesia response. According to van der Kolk (1996a, 227), SIA is now believed to be the result of the release of endogenous opioids (Pitman and Orr 1990a, 1990b; van der Kolk and Dicey 1989).

Experimental animals that have been given excess doses of opiates (or the equivalent) become apathetic, lethargic, and drowsy; show less interest in nurturing their young or in sexual activity; show less distress upon separation from a parent; and have been found to not stay in close proximity to one another (Glover 1992). How much can be inferred from animal studies that applies to human behavior is an area of great debate. Yet, like the drugged experimental animals described here, trauma survivors in the numb state show less interest in socializing, mating, and parenting. Even though they may strive to meet their obligations in these areas, doing so requires a great deal of effort and struggle. In my clinical experience and according to available research, individuals who are numb derive much less satisfaction from being with others than persons who are not numb. This often leads family members and friends to view the numb trauma survivor as "cold," "distant," "unemotional" or even "made of ice."

The Biology of Triggers

A *trigger* is anything that reminds you of your trauma and thereby activates stress-related emotions and/or physical symptoms. Triggers can be internal or external. External triggers are located in your environment. Internal triggers arise from within yourself.

External Triggers

External triggers include any current stress or danger, or any sight, smell, sound, touch, or action on the part of others that reminds you of your trauma. The trigger may not remind you of something inherently dangerous, but of something associated with danger in your past. In chapter 3, an example was given of a primitive hunter who learned to associate crocodiles with a certain plant. Even though the plant was not dangerous, he came to fear the plant as much as he feared crocodiles. For him, the plant was a trigger.

For many trauma survivors, crowded places, such as playgrounds, malls, concerts, traffic jams, parades, or even large social gatherings are triggers. The trauma may or may not have happened in such places, but the large number of people, the noise level, and the presence of the uncontrolled movements may remind trauma survivors of the uncontrolled, unpredictable actions of people during the trauma.

Sometimes an inflection or feeling in a person's voice may be a trigger. Mary, for example, responds to anger in other people's voices so fearfully that it is as if she is about to be murdered. In the past, angry others hurt and almost killed her. Therefore, today, when someone expresses hostility, even if it is only a slight annoyance, on some level Mary perceives it as a major threat to her existence. "Logically" Mary knows that the person is simply irritated, not furious, and that she is safe from attack. But on an emotional and physiological level, she is "on guard" waiting for an outburst of violence.

For other trauma survivors, certain words or phrases are triggers. The words may be neutral and harmless, but to the survivor they may be charged with meaning. For example, if Ted were to compliment Anita on her sweater, saying, "That color blue looks good on you," Anita, who is an incest survivor, might react as if she were being sexually assaulted. Ted's intent might not be seductive, but because Anita's abuser always commented on how good Anita looked in blue, she might be "triggered," by his use of the same words.

Internal Triggers

Internal triggers include certain bodily states, such as hunger, sexual arousal, or fatigue, or certain emotional states, such as sadness, happiness, or anxiety that can act as triggers if, for you, one of these states is related to your trauma. For example, working overtime on the job may be a trigger if your trauma included multiple or unrelenting duties that left you physically exhausted. Similarly, grieving for a current loss can trigger memories and thus trigger grieving for traumatic losses. The illness or death of a family member typically can trigger memories of persons who were lost during your trauma.

Triggers can bring forth not only memories of the trauma, but the physiological states of terror and high anxiety (adrenaline) or the physiological states of shutdown and withdrawal (noradrenaline or SIA). People who have been severely or multiply traumatized often live in an "altered state of arousal" and even decades after the event, they may exhibit adrenaline, noradrenaline, or stress-induced analgesic reactions to reminders of the trauma (van der Kolk 1996a, 1996b).

Shutdown

As stated earlier, hyperarousal and numbing are the extreme ends of the emotional spectrum. They may seem like polar opposites, but they are interrelated in that a prolonged state of hyperarousal typically leads to a "shutdown." Emotionally, most people can't tolerate living in a constant state of extreme emotion, whether that emotion be grief, panic, or anger. Physiologically, the body cannot remain in a constant state of hyperarousal without reprieve. The usual response to being in a prolonged state of emotional and physiological flooding (or overload) is a slowing down of all systems—emotional, mental, and physical.

The duration and intensity of the hyperarousal-numbing cycle varies from one individual to the next and varies throughout the life cycle of the individual. For many of the most severely traumatized, for example, for survivors of the Nazi concentration camps, prisoners of war, and genocide survivors life is often a state of being shutdown, punctuated by periods of hyperarousal due to exposure to a trigger. For others, the PTSD hyperarousal-numbing cycle plays only a minor role in their lives, appearing only at anniversaries or other trigger times.

Prolonged Stress

The body's emergency responses were designed to handle emergencies—not daily living. The flow of adrenaline or noradrenaline exists to handle crises of several hours or a few days, not crises that go on for months, years, or a lifetime. The adrenals, like the rest of the body, are not designed to handle prolonged stress. When subjected to repeated trauma or emergencies, the adrenals can be permanently damaged, leading to overfunctioning during subsequent stress, which causes the hyperarousal and numbing phases of PTSD.

Neurotransmitters and Prolonged Stress

In addition to massive secretions of adrenaline or noradrenaline, a variety of neurotransmitters are released when an individual is under severe stress. Neurotransmitters are the chemical substances that enable impulses to be transmitted from one nerve cell to another (Bourne 1990). Among their many functions, neurotransmitters help regulate the intensity of emotions and moods and they are also involved in memory functions.

If you were subjected to repeated or intense trauma or stress, certain of your neurotransmitters may have been depleted. The lack of these "buffer transmitters" can lead to clinical depression and also to mood swings, explosive outbursts, overreactions to subsequent stress, and hyperalertness. Depletion of some neurotransmitters can result in an overdependence on other people, expressed as, "I can't make it without you," or an unrealistically independent or counterdependent stance, expressed as, "I don't need anyone. I can make it on my own." Such depletions can also lead to the development of a self-reinforcing vicious cycle, where in response to the biological changes caused by prolonged stress, the survivor becomes increasingly isolated from others, and the isolation creates still further isolation.

Figures 4.2 and 4.3 illustrate the effects of neurotransmitter depletion and the impact of those effects on relationships in greater detail.

As figure 4.2 illustrates, after you are exposed to a traumatic stressor, your body goes into a state of emergency alert, including the fight-flight-freeze responses. However, if the stress is prolonged or if you are constantly being triggered by your environment, then you run the following risks:

1. Living in a chronic or almost chronic state of hyperarousal: In other words, your baseline heart rate, blood pressure, and anxiety levels are higher than those of nontraumatized persons. It takes less stress to make you anxious, irritable, depressed, or angry than others; once you become distressed, it takes longer for you to calm down.

2. Experiencing a depletion of a variety of neurotransmitters that are essential to your emotional and mental health, your ability to set

Figure 4.2   Repercussions of Prolonged Stress

Arousal of Autonomic Nervous System

- Flashbacks
- Panic attacks
- Visual images and emotions associated with prior trauma
- Abnormal startle response
- Hypersensitivity to noise, temperature, pain, and emotional stimuli

Depletion of a Variety of Neurotransmitters

Serotonin

- Modulates actions of other neurotransmitters
- Responsible for the fine-tuning of emotions
- Buffers emotions—depletion leads to an "all or nothing" response
- Lacking in manic-depressives
- Lacking in lower-level primates with early separation experiences
- Depletion leads to over-reactivity to new stimuli, situations, and people
- Depletion leads to overreactivity to touch, pain
- Depletion leads to hyperexcitability
- Depletion leads to emotional hypersensitivity

Catecholamine

- Modulates aggression—depletion leads to aggressive outbursts
- Hyperactivity to subsequent stress—startle response, nightmares, intrusive recall
- Hostility
- Poor impulse control
- Self-mutilation or aggression towards others

Disregulation of Endogenous Opioid System

- Blunting of emotional and physical pain
- Poor memory
- Lack of motivation
- Emotional deadness
- Symptoms similar to clinical depression
- In extreme form, can lead to loneliness/panic states

Adapted from "Biological Response to Psychic Trauma," by Bessel van der Kolk, in the book, *Posttraumatic Therapy and Victims of Violence*, edited by Frank Ochberg, Brunner/Mazel Publishers, New York, N.Y., 1988, pp. 25–38, and "The Trauma Spectrum," by Bessel van der Kolk, in *Journal of Traumatic Stress*, Vol. 1:3, 1988, pp. 273–290. Used with permission.

goals for yourself and to have relationships, and to see present reality clearly.

3. Experiencing a disregulation of your emergency state response and your SIA or endogenous opioid system.

Initially, the emergency response of increased adrenaline or SIA response functioned to help you get through a crisis. But when these systems are overused due to repeated trauma or repeated exposure to triggers, they don't function as originally intended. Simply put, they "wear out."

Thus, you may find yourself responding to an innocuous situation as if it were a life-and-death emergency, or alternatively, to a genuine threat as if it were nothing extraordinary (see figure 4.2). Your emotional and physiological reactions cannot always be counted on as accurate guides to what is happening in your environment.

Trust and Prolonged Stress

Your awareness that you are overreacting or underreacting, especially if exacerbated by feedback from others telling you that you are overreacting or underreacting, creates even more stress and anxiety, which only intensifies your PTSD and other symptoms, causing even more disregulation of your adrenal and SIA systems.

Once you become aware that your responses do not accurately match reality, you begin to lose trust in yourself, which makes you feel unsafe and vulnerable. As a result, you begin to withdraw. This can create a state of great pain because you find it hard to trust not only others, but yourself. Your alienation from others is compounded by your alienation from yourself. Not only do you feel that others have abandoned and betrayed you, you might also feel as if your "senses" have abandoned and betrayed you (see figure 4.3).

Lest this situation sound hopeless, keep in mind that psychotherapy, medication, and other forms of healing can help stop the vicious cycle illustrated in figure 4.3. Working on relationships can also help. The support of others, especially an intimate partner, can help deflect the damage caused by the hyperarousal-numbing cycle of PTSD. Lack of support from others tends to make it worse.

Consequences of Hyperarousal

Hyperarousal leads to the well-known PTSD symptoms of flashbacks, intrusive thoughts, panic attacks, and hyperalertness, which are accompanied by an increase in heart rate, blood pressure, and other physical changes outlined in figure 4. 1. This heightened state of arousal contributes to problems going to sleep and staying asleep. PTSD sufferers not only have nightmares and panic attacks during the night, but

Figure 4.3
Untreated Traumatic Stress: The Vicious Cycle

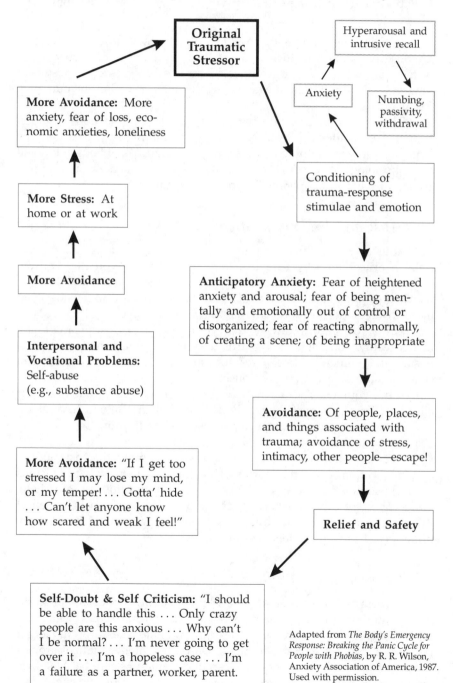

Original Traumatic Stressor

Hyperarousal and intrusive recall

Anxiety

Numbing, passivity, withdrawal

More Avoidance: More anxiety, fear of loss, economic anxieties, loneliness

Conditioning of trauma-response stimulae and emotion

More Stress: At home or at work

More Avoidance

Anticipatory Anxiety: Fear of heightened anxiety and arousal; fear of being mentally and emotionally out of control or disorganized; fear of reacting abnormally, of creating a scene; of being inappropriate

Interpersonal and Vocational Problems: Self-abuse (e.g., substance abuse)

Avoidance: Of people, places, and things associated with trauma; avoidance of stress, intimacy, other people—escape!

More Avoidance: "If I get too stressed I may lose my mind, or my temper!... Gotta' hide ... Can't let anyone know how scared and weak I feel!"

Relief and Safety

Self-Doubt & Self Criticism: "I should be able to handle this ... Only crazy people are this anxious ... Why can't I be normal?... I'm never going to get over it ... I'm a hopeless case ... I'm a failure as a partner, worker, parent.

Adapted from *The Body's Emergency Response: Breaking the Panic Cycle for People with Phobias,* by R. R. Wilson, Anxiety Association of America, 1987. Used with permission.

also equally serious, if less dramatic, forms of sleep disruption, such as midnight awakenings with or without memory of a specific dream and with or without feelings of fear or panic. All in all, trauma survivors with PTSD, depression, or other traumatic reactions suffer from inefficient sleep and/or sleep deprivation, which clouds their ability to think clearly and make sound decisions about anything—from their jobs to their relationships. When a trauma survivor uses drugs, alcohol, or food to get to sleep, the resulting difficulties in focusing on tasks to be completed, or on relationships, are only worsened.

When you are in a state of hyperarousal due to being triggered or to a depletion of your serotonin level or the disregulation of your catecholamine levels, you're on edge and irritable. It's easy for the irritability to turn into strong anger or rage. Hyperarousal is like having too much coffee—but worse, for it involves increased sensitivity to noise, pain, temperature, sudden touch, or any sudden or intense stimulus. Therefore, what to others is just the ring of an alarm clock, is to a trauma survivor, the sound of a siren. What to others is the sound of a book falling, resembles a thunderbolt to the trauma survivor.

It's as if the buffer between you and the environment has worn thin. You feel everything more deeply and intensely than most people. You are like a car that has lost its shock absorbers. Every bump along the road is felt more deeply because your shock absorbers have worn out from overuse. A minor critical remark from a friend feels like major rejection. Your partner forgetting to call as promised feels like adultery, and your tolerance for physical pain may be very low. Hence, when you go to the dentist or have surgery, you may need more anesthesia than others do.

If you, or others, view such hypersensitivity in a negative way, it may become a source of shame and cause you to withdraw. For example, a combat veteran from the Vietnam War who requested time off work to attend group counseling for PTSD, which he explained to his supervisor was a form of shell shock, was later "nicknamed" Shelley by that supervisor. Shelley was not his name. When the veteran's co-workers learned why he was being taunted with that name, they began to tease him every time he left the office, saying things like, "There goes Shelley, shell-shocked Shelley." After enduring two months of such taunts, the veteran quit his job.

Perhaps the most devastating effects of hyperarousal are on the ability to think, reason, and remember. Thousands of years ago survival may have depended on sheer physical strength and endurance—on the ability to flee from and/or fight wild animals, for example. But in today's society, survival depends on mental abilities and the skills necessary to maintain complex social relationships and handle subtle social interactions. Impaired powers of concentration, reasoning, or memory put one at both an economic and social disadvantage.

Many trauma survivors desperately avoid trigger situations or trigger-evoking relationships because they know that once they become sufficiently hyperaroused, they literally "can't think." Research on children, for example, demonstrates that once the fear response has been evoked, learning and other cognitive functioning diminish (James 1994). Research on adults also shows that after a certain level of emotional or physiological arousal is reached, mental abilities, such as organizing, concentrating, calculating, and remembering, are reduced, or even, shut down (van der Kolk 1996a). For example, rats exposed to uncontrollable electric shock not only lose weight and stop grooming themselves, they also can't make correct choices in situations requiring that they pay attention (Murburg 1994).

Indeed, many of the consequences of hyperarousal and numbing are similar. The lists below describe the consequences of hyperarousal and numbing in more detail.

Consequences of Hyperarousal of the Autonomic Nervous System

1. Constant or frequent irritability, which easily leads to outbursts of anger.

2. Sleep problems: Nightmares, difficulty going to sleep or staying asleep, inefficient sleep, waking up in the night (or in the morning) with apprehension and panic with or without conscious memory of a specific nightmare or fear.

3. Increased sensitivity to noise, pain, temperature, sudden touch, or any sudden or intense stimulus.

4. Increased heart rate, blood pressure, or skin conductance, especially in response to triggers like sudden unexpected sounds, smells, sights, or touches, or emotionally charged situations.

5. Agitated movement, tremors at rest, gastric distress, urinary incontinence.

6. Hypervigilance—feeling constantly on guard, threatened, and vulnerable.

7. Lightning bolt responses: Making immediate response to situations: Moving from experiencing an event to reacting to it without being able to think about how to respond or what choices are available.

8. Shame at lack of self-control over irritability, angry outbursts, or immediate response to situations.

9. Increased vulnerability: Can't properly assess situations due to focus on trauma-related aspect of the situation. Attention is focused on sensory or other cues that resemble the trauma or that are new and therefore potentially dangerous.

10. Difficulties concentrating: Feeling of being "scattered."

11. Difficulties focusing on the entire picture: Tendency to focus on as pects of the situation or relationship that are or are perceived as threatening. Perception is biased toward traumatic triggers. Difficulty deciding if a person or situation is safe or dangerous or if an action is rewarding or punishing.

12. Difficulty problem solving: Not free to scan the environment for all the information available. Distracted from attending to the problem at hand by high anxiety level, anger, and other aspects of physiological arousal caused by focus on trauma-related aspects of a situation or relationship.

13. Higher baseline level of arousal: Many trauma survivors have faster heart rates, higher blood pressure, and other features of hyperarousal at "rest" or even when they aren't stressed or triggered.

14. Difficulty calming down: Once aroused by a trigger, epinephrine levels, heart rate, blood pressure, etc. go up. It takes longer for a trauma survivor to calm down than for a nontraumatized person. Simply put, it's easier for a trauma survivor to become distressed and once distressed, it takes longer for him/her to get back to where they were emotionally and physically before the upset began.

15. Feeling "crazy" because often it is not possible to locate or identify the trigger that caused the hyperarousal.

16. Memory problems: You feel as if you are "brain damaged" because you can't remember where or when or what or only part of what is going on now or what happened during the trauma. Difficulty with short-term memory causes shame and a diminished sense of self. (Over time, the hippocampus, which is involved with the storage of memory, shrinks because it can't regulate the Fight-Flight-Freeze reaction of the adrenals, which often fire away as if there is an immediate threat, long after the real danger has passed (van der Kolk 1996a, 231)).

17. Use of substances (alcohol, drugs, food) or compulsive spending, gambling, sexual, or other activity for purposes of soothing and calming.

Consequences of Numbing or Increased Opioid Response

1. Blunting of emotional and physical responsiveness includes not only blunting of emotional and physical pain, but of emotional and physical pleasure. Lack of pleasure. Loss of interest in activities that used to provide joy or satisfaction. Absence of feeling. Feeling "dead" inside.

2. Can't discriminate between pain and pleasure because so little is felt. Easy to be revictimized.

3. Poor memory; clouded thinking.

4. Shame at not being as emotionally responsive as others. Censure from others for not responding emotionally as expected by social conventions or family or community expectations.

5. Increased need for stimulation and stimulants in order to feel alive. Alcohol, drugs, food, gambling, sexual activity, overspending, and dangerous or risk-taking activities are sought out to create energy and excitement to offset the dead feeling within.

6. Sometimes self-mutilation (cutting, burning, or otherwise hurting one's body) is used as a way to feel alive, for to feel pain is to feel something and feeling something is better than feeling nothing.

7. At extreme levels, numbing can lead to feelings of panic and rage.

8. Retreat from life.

9. Increased vulnerability: Emotional and physical reactions cannot guide you.

10. Feelings of detachment and estrangement from others.

11. Can't experience one's own experience. Feeling empty inside.

12. Sexual disinterest and dysfunction.

13. Apathy, lethargy, and mental sluggishness.

Consequences Common to Both Hyperarousal and Numbing

1. Difficulty evaluating situations and people as to whether they are dangerous or not.

2. Difficulty concentrating.

3. Memory problems.

4. Difficulty seeing the whole picture. Distortion of the present.

5. Cannot learn from past mistakes.

6. Not motivated to learn new things or meet new people: Fear that having to do or meet someone new will be disorganizing or cause a shutdown.

7. Emotions are not good guides or signals. The world becomes an unsafe place because one's own emotional and physiological responses can't be trusted.

8. More effort is involved in responding to situations and people. It takes effort to calm oneself down after being hyperaroused and it takes effort to get oneself going after being shut down. When the effort seems too great, the tendency is to retreat from life because handling different situations and relating to people demands a great deal of energy and effort.

9. Impaired reasoning and other mental powers.

10. Depletion of biological and psychological resources necessary to experience a wide range of emotions.

11. Difficulty organizing behavior to achieve a goal or to stay focused on a conversation or social interaction.

12. Involvement in the present is interfered with, which affects learning new social and other skills and which can put old social and other skills into disuse.

13. Shut down of nonessential functions, such as sexuality, immune system, digestion. Rage reactions.

There Is Hope

How do you feel after reading about the biochemistry of PTSD? As if you're involved in a hopeless battle against your own bodily functions? As if you should "give up" because you can't imagine having the energy or strength to fight trigger reactions all of your life?

The bad news is that having intense states of hyperarousal does make life very difficult. Even simple matters, such as standing in line in a store or picking out a movie, can be problematic. Life is harder for you than for someone who hasn't been traumatized because of all the triggers in your environment and within yourself. You may feel sad and angry that you have to work harder than most people just to get through the day and you are entitled to both of these feelings.

The *good* news is that there are many techniques that can help you manage and exert some control over your trigger reactions. Applying these techniques requires a commitment of time and effort, but the results are well worth it. Even though you may be doing the best you can now, there may be even more ways to enhance your efforts or to make them more effective. Although some extra work will be required as you continue to gain control over some of the debilitating effects of hyperarousal or numbing, your self-confidence will increase and you will regain the energy you expend, and more.

Having the trauma and its effects magically disappear is not an option for you. Even in the Greek myth that opens this chapter, Helen's magic potion, which removed memories of anger and grief, worked for only a few hours. Your choices are between taking a good hard look at your triggers and figuring out what you can do about them or allowing your triggers and your biological and emotional reactions to them to dominate your life.

You may try to manage some of your triggers and find that you can't. Some trigger situations are just too powerful and you will need to do your best to avoid those situations at all costs. At least you will have the satisfaction of knowing you tried. The result of your efforts may be valuable information: you may learn that a particular person, place, thing, or situation is so retraumatizing that to love yourself will mean never subjecting yourself to it again, if that is within your power. There should be no shame in this acknowledgment. It reflects the degree of your traumatization—not your moral character or intelligence.

Although there may always be some limits on your life because of your trauma, you may not have an accurate view of your true limits until you do some work on your triggers. The first step is to identify your triggers.

Identifying Your Triggers

In your trauma work with your therapist or support group, you probably were encouraged to acquire as much information about the traumatic event and your secondary wounding experiences as possible. All the details, especially the sensory details, of your traumatic event and its aftermath are potential triggers. The purpose of this exercise is to have you go back over the events you can remember and identify those aspects of your trauma that could be acting as triggers for you in the present.

Note: If you have had difficulties remembering the trauma in your prior trauma work or trauma therapy, you might want to return to therapy, or to a trauma processing book that offers suggestions for mentally reconstructing the trauma (see appendix A). You can then return to this exercise.

✍ *Exercise: Trigger Chart 1*

At this point you will make a trigger chart that will help you first to identify, and later to anticipate, situations in which you might react as if the trauma were recurring.

Go to a fresh sheet of paper in your journal and give it the heading, "Trigger Chart 1." Then draw four columns beneath it. Label the first column "Trigger," the second, "My Reactions, the third, "Traumatic Memory," and the fourth, "How Others Can Help."

In the first column list those instances when you feel the adrenaline rush to fight or flee, or where you shut down and go numb emotionally, physically, or both. Examples of triggers include smells, sights, sounds, people, or objects that remind you of the trauma or of events associated with the trauma. Triggers might also included current stresses, such as the following:

- Interpersonal difficulties at home or at work
- Any kind of work or emotional overload
- Financial or medical problems (including premenstrual syndrome)
- Increased crime or other neighborhood problems
- Witnessing or being involved in a current trauma (a fire, car accident, natural catastrophe, crime, etc.)

In the second column, indicate your reactions to each trigger situation. Your reactions in each situation will not necessarily be the same. Possible responses include the following:

- Anger or rage
- Isolating yourself or overworking
- Self-condemnation
- Increased cravings for food, alcohol, or drugs
- Increased flashbacks
- Self-mutilation
- Numbing
- Self-hatred
- Depression
- Suicidal or homicidal thoughts
- Increased physical pain (headaches, backaches)
- Activation of a chronic medical condition (increased blood sugar if you are diabetic, increased blood pressure if you suffer from hypertension, recurrence of urinary tract infections if you are prone to bladder problems, etc.)

In the third column, try to trace the trigger to the original traumatic event, to a secondary wounding experience, or to an event associated with these experiences. If you cannot remember the original events, do not be overly concerned. The main point of completing this chart is to help you to understand and anticipate when you might be susceptible to triggers. This understanding is the first step toward change and toward control.

In the fourth column, brainstorm about any possible way another human being might help you either before, after, or during an encounter with this trigger. Use your imagination. Don't be restricted in your thinking by what you think others will or will not do for you. Pretend you live in an ideal world where people will go out of their way for you.

Trigger Chart 1

Trigger	My Reactions	Trauma Traumatic	How Others Can Help
Red meat	Nausea; Desire to get away	Mutilated bodies in car crashes	Not eat red meat in front of me and not act as if I'm weird because I can't stand the sight of hamburgers or barbecue
Children playing	Contempt. I want to tell those kids they are stupid for being so happy because soon they will be hurt	Being abused as a child	Listen to my story about how I was hurt; Provide company and support as I learn how to play again
Dead animal in the street; Stories about the abuse of animals in the newspaper	Crying, dissociation, rage	Seeing corpses of children and animals	Understand that I have to stop driving if I see a dead animal in the road; Not make jokes about hurting animals or kids

What could one of those people do that would help, even if it only helped a little bit?

Take a look at the Trigger Chart 1 examples to get an idea of how it works. If you chose to share your chart, or parts of it, with your family members, friends, or an intimate partner, they might be able to add instances as well as suggestions on how they might help. (See the sections that follow on asking for help.)

✍ Exercise: Trigger Chart 2

Your first task in this exercise is to divide your trigger situations from Trigger Chart 1 into four categories:

1. Triggers you feel might be the easiest to endure.

2. Triggers you feel you might be able to handle after a few more months of healing.

3. Triggers you feel you might be able to confront in a few years (maybe).

4. Triggers you plan to avoid for the rest of your life.

Entitle a new page in your journal "Trigger Chart 2" and draw lines to make four columns. Label them, from left to right, "Easiest to Handle," "Possibly Manageable Within a Year," "Possibly Manageable in the Distant Future," and "Impossible to Ever Handle."

Now take your list from Trigger Chart 1 and place each trigger in the appropriate category.

Selecting a Trigger to Work On

When you feel ready to confront a trigger, select one from those you listed in column 1 of Trigger Chart 2—a situation you judge one of the easiest to handle. Beginning with a more difficult trigger, such as one in column 2 or 3, can be a setup for failure because no trigger situation, even one you classified as relatively easy to handle, is truly easy. You have to start somewhere, though, so it is best to start where you have the greatest chance of success.

Trigger Chart 2

Easiest to Handle	Possibly Manageable Within a Year	Possibly Manageable in the Distant Future	Impossible to Ever Handle

Managing Triggers: On Your Own

The task of managing triggers through stress reduction techniques (such as deep breathing and relaxation exercises), therapy, medication, keeping a journal, or structuring your life so as to avoid certain triggers or minimize your contact with difficult situations, is beyond the scope of this book. Suggestions about trigger management are provided in several of the trauma-processing books listed in appendix A.

Quite possibly, your attempts to manage a trigger may not work. This does not mean you are a failure. It may mean that you minimized the severity of the trigger or that you have limits of which you were not aware.

One way to improve your chances of managing a trigger is to enlist the help of other people. The rest of this chapter explores how other people can help you lessen the impact of the physiological effects of triggers.

The Need for Soothing

In Greek, trauma means wounding, and wounded adults, like wounded animals and children, need comfort and care. There is no better way to calm down from a state of hyperarousal, or to be drawn out of a state of numbness, than to be soothed by the caring words, understanding listening, or loving actions and/or touches of another person. Research has verified what may seem like an obvious truth: People who have been traumatized, but are lovingly embraced subsequently by their families or others, are much less likely to develop severe or long-term traumatic reactions than traumatized people who are subsequently rejected or ignored by important others (Shay 1994).

It has been established that the single most important predictor of who develops long-term PTSD or other traumatic reactions is the ability to derive comfort from another human being; not the intensity or duration of the trauma, nor the previous psychiatric history (Johnson 1996). Those trauma survivors who have others around to support them and who are willing and able to receive that help are far more likely to escape long-term or severe PTSD, depression, or other traumatic reactions.

For example, it has been established that when nurses paid attention to the feelings of the sick children in neonatal wards by soothing them when they were crying, the mortality rate went down (James 1994). The moral is that paying attention to feelings can save lives. Having your feelings paid attention to can also save your mental health.

In World War II, when London was being blitzed by the German air force, many children were transported out of the city to the countryside for their safety. Ironically, the children who stayed in London with their parents and endured the bombings, fared better psychologically than the children who were separated from their parents but were physically safer in the countryside (James 1994). A relationship has also been found with losing a parent as a child and the development of certain medical illnesses, immune system deficiencies, and psychiatric problems. However, if the child receives support from another important person, after the death of a parent, these problems tend not to develop (Perry 1994).

According to van der Kolk (1988a), the negative effects of trauma can be mitigated by two factors: (1) the preservation of an attachment system and (2) a strong belief system. If a person can live through horrendous experiences and still emerge with his or her attachment or belief system intact, to some degree, that person is much less likely to develop PTSD (James 1994; Reite and Field 1985; van der Kolk 1996a). For example, the soldier who goes off to war with a strong belief in God or in the value of the military and comes back from war with these same beliefs intact is less likely to develop combat trauma than a soldier who loses his faith in God, as well as his faith in the military, as the result of his war experiences.

Similarly, people who live through their traumas with their attachment systems relatively intact are much less likely to develop PTSD, clinical depression, or other traumatic reactions than those whose attachment system is destroyed or demoralized by the trauma, or those whose partners, friends, or relatives are rejecting or blaming. Most likely some of you who are reading this book are people whose friends, family members, or community were physical injured or emotionally demoralized by your trauma, or people who were (or feel they were) psychologically exiled from their families and community because of their traumas. If the people who loved you before the trauma continued to love and accept you after the trauma and stood by your side like a cheering squad while you healed, you may not have much need for this book.

Supportive relationships have tremendous potential to help you heal. On a biological level, it has been found that positive, and even neutral, social interactions release stress-reducing endorphins that improve your mood and thinking (Glover 1992). Your first task in building a more caring and supportive world for yourself is to generate a support system of a group of people to whom you can turn, when you are triggered into hyperarousal or numbness.

Asking for Help and Needing Others

In Western society, asking for help and needing people tend not to be valued behaviors. To be called "needy" is a put-down and asking others for support is often seen as a sign of childish dependency. Yet children who ask for help are very smart. It is the children who ask for help who become more skilled and independent than those who don't.

Children who don't ask for assistance have major problems growing into adulthood and developing social and vocational skills.

Your purpose in asking for help is not to keep you in a state of dependency forever, but to strengthen you so you can survive the onslaught of periods of hyperarousal and numbing and live your life. As you learn more about your triggers and experience some initial success in dealing with them, most likely your need for support will lessen.

The suffering caused by trauma is humbling, in that such suffering forces you to realize that you need people, even if at first the only person you trust is a therapist or a twelve-step sponsor. Needing people or asking for help isn't a terrible thing to do, neither is it a crime. It is a healthy action to take because, in the long run, if you don't get the help you need to manage your PTSD cycles, you may not develop your capacities to love, work, and play that will allow you to become increasingly independent. You then run the risk of becoming significantly disabled and having to depend on others, or an institution, to take care of you.

Consider, for example, Lisa and Jane, two trauma survivors, who both worked in an office where they were subjected to continued and intense harassment. The stress at work would have been difficult for anyone to handle, but for Lisa and Jane the work harassment triggered memories and symptoms of prior traumas, which plunged them both into clinical depression.

At first, neither sought help, despite the fact that they both spent most of their weekends sleeping, had problems with their families, broke up with their boyfriends, and were making many mistakes on the job, which created even more anxiety. Eventually, Lisa swallowed her pride and went to see a psychiatrist. She also joined a twelve-step program to help her with the overeating that her on-the-job problems had caused. Even more difficult, she told her family about her work problems and her depression.

Initially, her father called her a "weakling" and her brothers acted as if they didn't want to hear her complaints. But, over time, they began to see that Lisa was hurting deeply and they started to call her more often and, in their limited way, gave her their support. Lisa needed to receive more moral and emotional support from her parents and siblings, but if she had never spoken up, she would have never gotten any extra support from her family at all.

Her twelve-step friends were more supportive, and she plugged into that support, sometimes making five or six phone calls a day. It was her twelve-step friends who helped her cope with all the small daily crises at work and within herself. They helped her each day to resist the urge to walk off the job or to harm herself.

In the past, Lisa had been so highly functioning that she had trouble believing her work situation was creating such a severe depression that she was forced to ask for help in so many matters. It hurt her pride to ask for so much help, but she knew that talking to others helped her to complete her job assignments and to cope emotionally, thereby avoiding a poor work performance evaluation. Because it was in her self-interest to do so, she humbled herself and called her friends and increased the frequency of her therapy sessions.

In contrast, Jane refused to share her problems with her family or friends and she would not seek professional help. She was certain she could handle the situation on her own. Over time, she became progressively more depressed and, at times, suicidal. One day, she just quit her job, losing all her retirement funds and other benefits. When her savings ran out, she attempted suicide and had to be hospitalized for months. She then had to go to her family and friends not only for emotional support, but also for financial help.

Had she asked for help earlier, she might not have become so depressed that she quit her job without thinking about the consequences. Furthermore, she would not have needed to ask for the great amount of financial help that was necessary to help her get back on her feet again and to stabilize her emotionally.

Who acted more responsibly, Lisa or Jane? Who was more adult, Lisa who realized she couldn't handle her situation on her own and asked for help before she became even more depressed and unable to make good decisions, or Jane, who was too ashamed to turn to others and who refused to acknowledge the reality of an overwhelming situation? Ironically, Lisa's strength was in her ability to ask for help.

Similarly, for you, it may be far better to ask for a little help right now than to have to ask for massive amounts of help later on down the road. If you can avoid a severe clinical depression, a major "shutdown" in thinking or emotional abilities, or a chronic state of anxious hyperarousal by asking for help, it is in your self-interest to do so. Living in a state of high anxiety does not permit you to do very much except manage your high anxiety levels. It is also far better psychologically (and economically) to turn to a safe human being for soothing than to alcohol, drugs, excess food, or some other addiction, such as compulsive overspending or gambling.

Asking others to support you by listening to you or giving you concrete help during your trigger times is a matter of survival. It is also a means of helping you to grow. As paradoxical as it may sound, depending on certain trusted others to help you get through times of extreme hyperarousal or numbing, or so that you can begin to manage your triggers, most likely will mean that you will need less help in the future. To the Western mind, which values self-sufficiency and believes in the myth of "rugged individualism," it may seem paradoxical that those who ask for help to survive difficult times and to get the strength to grow, do better than those who try to handle overwhelming situations on their own.

We are biologically hard-wired to seek secure attachments. Feeling the protection that comes from a secure bond with at least one person gives us the courage to explore new alternatives and the peace of mind necessary to learn new skills and ultimately become more autonomous, more adventuresome, and more emotionally, socially, and intellectually developed. Research on children has proven this repeatedly (Watenberg 1996; James 1994). Similarly, research on and observations of traumatized adolescents and adults show that those who go to therapy or support groups consistently and those who reach out by sharing their struggles and asking for help, recover faster and in more ways than people who isolate or have no one (or hardly anyone) to turn to for support (Johnson 1996).

Energy Output and Asking for Help

On a biological level, the presence and comfort of other people actually help to lessen the physiological effects of the hyperarousal and/ or numbing cycle. For example, one possible reason for the numbing response (caused by the release of opioids) during prolonged stress is that the body needs to "shut down" to conserve energy. The organism doles out its energy (oxygen, blood, etc.) very cautiously, directing it to those functions essential for survival, such as breathing, and not toward less essential functions, such as feeling, playing, moving around, intellectual or mental activity, or creative or pleasurable pursuits. The organism is so cautious because there is a limited amount of energy available to keep it alive for a long time in very difficult circumstances. Therefore, energy is carefully allotted only to those functions most necessary for survival.

However, once the organism knows that help is available (or on its way) and that the stress doesn't have to be endured alone, there is less need to conserve energy, and, therefore, more energy becomes available for other activities than just keeping the essential organs of the body functioning minimally. Hence, asking for help or knowing that help is on its way makes it less necessary for a traumatized person to shut down, and releases energy in that person. That is why asking for help or soothing is an act of empowerment: because it potentially gives you more energy with which to fight your own battles and pursue your own goals. Asking for help is a weapon to use against the "shutdown response," which can be so disabling. That is also why writing or talking about your trauma, attending support groups, group therapy, or any gathering of people that supports you helps to energize you. It also improves your immune system (Armsworth 1994; Pearlman 1996).

Perhaps an analogy can be made between asking for help and living on a budget. Everything is fine until you have a big unexpected expense (the trauma) and more expenses follow (triggers, retraumatization, secondary wounding experiences). In anticipation of surviving over the long haul, you purchase only the bare necessities—the least expensive food and a minimum of clothing. To save money, you set the thermostat low during the winter, so you are cold, and you have no money for fun, books, movies, etc. However, if you know that a friend is going to loan you some money, or if you plan to get together with some friends who have agreed to help you figure out how to improve your financial situation, you will be able to see beyond your present misery and to feel some hope. With that little bit of hope, you might be willing to worry less about your future and spend a little more on food and heating, which will make you feel better. Because you'll be feeling better, you'll be better able to look for a higher-paying job or to take on a part-time job to improve your life. Also, by eating better and being warmer in the winter, you may be able to concentrate better on finding solutions for your economic problems rather than focusing just on survival.

In an analogous manner, if you know you are going to receive emotional support, the feelings of relief and hope can help motivate you to make any possible improvements in your life. But if you are struggling just to stay alive, you don't have the luxury of thinking deeply about your situation or even of contemplating any changes for the better.

Hyperarousal and Asking for Help

If your problem is not being shut down, but hyperarousal, the presence of supportive others helps to calm the anxiety, which is a part of being hyperaroused. The cause of hyperarousal is fear of annihilation. The reason you are hypervigilant, sweat easily, startle easily, can't sleep, or are extremely reactive to noises, sounds, smells, and other people is because you are still trying to protect yourself from catastrophic danger. During your trauma, when your life or the lives of others were on the line, being hyperaroused kept you alert for danger and helped you find ways to survive. Therefore, now, when you are triggered into a state of hyperarousal, you are, on some level, expecting the original trauma to take place again.

The most difficult part of being triggered into a state of hyperarousal is knowing that even though you feel as though the trauma is happening again, you know it really isn't. For example, when Mary, the formerly battered wife who learned to associate angry words with physical violence, hears her boyfriend speak angrily to a waiter, she begins to breathe hard, sweat profusely, and longs to run out of the restaurant. Her head knows it is very unlikely that her boyfriend will become violent (because he's never been violent and he's not really angry, just annoyed). But her body and emotions react to the tone of his voice as if she were still trapped in a room with her violent ex-husband.

Mary's anxiety is heightened by the fact that she knows she is "overreacting." She feels embarrassed by her response and wants to hide it and "act normal." When someone gets angry at business meetings or at family gatherings, she has the same set of hyperaroused reactions. Her first response to hearing angry words is anxiety. Then, she reacts to her anxiety by becoming more anxious. She worries about what others might think if they knew how distressed she is, or she worries that someone may wonder why she is sweating or breathing hard. She also worries that if she becomes highly anxious she'll be less able to think clearly, speak logically, and act appropriately. Her concerns are legitimate, because high anxiety does impair thinking and speaking abilities.

However, if Mary had a "buddy" (friend, "ally") at her business meetings or family gatherings who could support her in some way, this would help her to ground herself in the present-day reality that the original trauma was not being repeated, and she could calm down faster. Mary would also feel calmer if she knew her buddy would intervene if it became obvious that she was losing control of herself. The knowledge of a "buddy" or "ally" who was there for her would also diminish her anxiety from the very outset, making it less likely that she would experience an anxiety reaction at all, or it would lessen an anxiety reaction if one did occur.

Similarly, if would also be helpful if Mary's boyfriend could learn to say to her something along these lines: "I know it sets you off, when you hear anger in my voice. If I had had your experiences, I'd be upset too if I heard someone talk angrily. But let me assure you, I'm not that mad. I'm just a little irritated at the waiter, that's all. It has nothing to do with you. I'm not going to hurt you, or the waiter, or anyone else. I'm just annoyed that he took so long with our order. Is there anything I can do to help you now?"

Facing a trigger is like going to war. You have a better chance of winning if you don't go alone. In war, the military doesn't send soldiers on solitary missions. There are always at least two soldiers sent out at a time. The presence of at least one comrade helps calm and strengthens both so they can act rationally and achieve their mission. The help a buddy, comrade, or ally gives is not just moral or emotional support. The presence of a supportive other actually causes a decrease in the intensity of potential panic, anxiety, and other hyperarousal symptoms.

Asking for Comfort or Care

Like other people, many trauma survivors have found comfort in music, nature, animals, creative endeavors, and physical activity. These are all excellent sources of courage and soothing. What needs to be added to this list is people. Like a beautiful sunset, a walk in the woods, or petting your cat or dog, people can provide comfort and care, too.

Asking for comfort or care from people sounds good on paper, but it is extremely difficult to do. If you think you are ready to turn to others for soothing and support, it is important to be selective about whom you turn to for help. You must structure your request so that it can be heard properly and you must protect yourself from any additional stresses that might result from the act of asking. For example, it is important that you ask for comfort or care only from those who you feel fairly sure will be open to your request, lest you be rejected and hurt even more than you already have been. It is also important that you be as specific as possible about what you want from the other person.

✍ Exercise: Your Help-Seeking History

The first step in planning how you might reach out to others for comfort and support is to take a good look at what happened in the past when you asked for help, either from family, friends, significant others, or professionals. Start a fresh sheet of paper in your journal and make a list of all the times you asked someone for help, indicating what you asked for and what happened later. Include examples of favorable and unfavorable outcomes.

Then look over your responses and answer the following questions:

1. When you asked for help and got it, what do you think "went right"?

2. Why was your request successful? Was it your attitude, the way you asked, the character of the person you asked, or all of these?

When you examine the incidents that had an unfavorable outcome, ask yourself the following questions:

1. Were you specific or general in your requests? Did someone promise to help you in some way, and then let you down?

2. Did you ever share your pain or vulnerabilities with someone, and then have that person use that information to hurt you?

3. Did you ever ask for help, receive the help you wanted, and then feel so ashamed or guilty afterwards that you decided you would have been better off braving your emotional storm by yourself?

4. With the advantage of hindsight, what could you have done differently that might have improved the likelihood of a favorable outcome?

5. What aspects of the situation were out of your control?

✍ Exercise: Fears About Asking for Help

Start a fresh page in your journal, and based on your answers to the questions above, make a list of your fears about asking others for soothing and care. Take into account the messages about asking for help that you learned from your parents, teachers, peers, and others prior to your trauma, as well as messages you learned about asking for help during the trauma. Use the following sentence as a model:

I am afraid that if I ask for help or soothing, then _____ , _____ , or _____ will happen.

Sample: I'm afraid that if I ask Marty to hold and comfort me because I've been having a lot of nightmares, he'll think I am a weak, pitiful person and feel sorry for me. I don't want pity and I don't want to be seen as weak and helpless.

Sample: I'm afraid that if I ask _____ for _____ now, I won't be able to ask for help in the future. I don't know how many times you can ask people to do something for you or to be there for you without exhausting their patience, or becoming a burden to them.

Sample: I don't want to ask for help now because I'm saving up all my requests for help for a big emergency, like when I feel I'm going to commit suicide or kill someone, or when I know I'm getting so depressed I can barely move. I don't want to use up my "favors" on small things.

Sample: I'm afraid that if I ask _____ for _____ , I'll be obligated to _____ for the rest of my life. This means that if _____ calls me in the middle of the night to get picked up somewhere, I'll have to go no matter how I feel. If someone does something for me, that means I owe that person and I don't have the right to refuse any of their requests.

The sample responses above illustrate some beliefs common to trauma survivors. Stated clearly they are as follows:

- Asking someone for help always imposes a burden on them.

- If someone does something for you, then you owe them whatever they ask for.

- If you ask someone for something one time, you can't ask again.

  These beliefs simply are not true. Let's examine each one individually.

1. How do *you* feel when someone asks *you* for help? It is always a burden or does it sometimes make you feel good to help someone out?

2. If someone does something for you, it doesn't mean you have to put your emotional, physical, or financial well-being at risk for them. You have the right to say "no" to their requests, particularly requests that might cause you harm.

3. The belief that if someone does something for you, then you owe them everything, is a belief that is associated with trauma. During many traumas, people risk their very lives for one another. Perhaps during your trauma someone put his/her life on the line for you

and so now you feel that if someone does something for you, you owe them everything in return, to compensate for the fact that, in the past, someone did everything or almost everything for you.

4. If the person who saved your life or emptied a bank account on your behalf during your trauma should appear and ask you for a favor, it would be understandable for you to feel morally obligated to give that person as much as possible. However, you don't owe others all that you owe this person and, in reality, you could even refuse the person who saved your life.

5. The belief that if you asked once, you can't ask again may be rooted in the feeling that the other person doesn't want to give more than once or doesn't have enough to give you more than once, but feels pressured to consent to your request out of a sense of obligation. You are assuming that the other person cannot say "no" to you, when, in fact, if that other person is an adult, he or she has the right to refuse your additional request. Indeed, someone might refuse your second request but say "yes" to your third or fourth, depending on the circumstances.

6. The idea that you can ask only once is also rooted in pride. You may feel ashamed at having to ask the same person for help two or more times. Yet trauma gives rise to situations where the traumatized individual may need to ask dozens, if not hundreds, of times. If you are using the help to strengthen yourself so that someday you will not need as much help, there is no shame in this. Your need to ask for help more than once is only temporary, it is not forever. If you were planning to spend your life asking for help and never attempt to become more self-sufficient, then there might be cause for shame and you might need to examine your help-seeking behavior.

If a man with no legs is collecting money for a wheelchair so that he can go to work and he needs to ask for financial help more than once, he is using that help to become more independent. If he didn't ask for money to get the wheelchair so he could become employed and had to stay confined to his home, he would be an even greater liability to others.

It is not your responsibility, but that of the person whom you are asking for help, to put limits on what is given. It is your responsibility to strengthen yourself.

Below are two excellent guidelines to follow in deciding what you "owe" someone in nontraumatic circumstances:

1. To fulfill any promises you may have made (such as to return a loan of money in a certain time) and

2. To return a favor in kind or to the same degree as the extent of your original request. For example, if you asked someone to keep you

company during the anniversary of your trauma, you might legitimately feel obligated to keep that person company on a similar occasion, if you were asked. But you aren't obligated to lend that person your car; steal or tell lies for him or her; have that person stay at your home for a month, give that person a large amount of cash; or have sex with him or her.

Since some of the fears and beliefs you have about asking for help may be closely related to your trauma and secondary wounding experiences, it is highly recommended that your work on the following exercise should include input from your therapist, members of your support group, and, if possible, members of your family.

✍ Exercise: Building on Past Successes

In your journal, make a list of what you did on past occasions that you feel helped to make your asking for help successful.

For example, when I ask someone for help, it seems to work better for me if _____ , or _____ .

Sample: When I ask someone for help, it seems to work better for me if I first discuss the idea with a friend or therapist. When I ask someone for help, it seems to work better for me if I tell only a little about my story rather than the whole trauma, or even if I don't mention the story at all.

Generally, people feel more positive about the experience of asking for help or soothing when they acknowledge the possibility that sharing part of their story with someone else may act as a trigger. Then, they can take the possibility of self-triggering into consideration when planning what to share and what parts to keep to themselves, and whether they plan to share at all. Also, people tend to feel more positive about asking for help if they select only those whom they respect and trust and can be counted on to be supportive. (See chapter 13 on sharing your story.)

Caution: The following exercises and recommendations are designed to help you learn how to reach out to others. These recommendations do not apply in situations of abuse or harassment. If you are a survivor of child abuse, spouse abuse, sexual assault, or harassment, none of these exercises or recommendations is designed to help you gain support or comfort from the individuals who have in the past, or are currently, mistreating you. In fact, it is generally recommended not to seek help from someone who has mistreated you.

✍ Exercise: Identifying Supportive Others

Try to create a list of at least five people to whom you think you could turn for help when you feel hyperaroused, or numb, or have to face a situation that could act as a trigger. You may want to refer back to some of the individuals you wrote about in chapter 3 on trust.

1. _____

2. _____

3. _____

4. _____

5. _____

Now, in your journal, list for each person what you would feel comfortable sharing, what you would feel comfortable asking for, and what you fear might happen if you ask for soothing.

Sample: I would feel comfortable telling Sue that this is the anniversary of when I was raped and ask her to have dinner with me. I don't want her to press me for details of the rape. I just want to have her company on that night.

When you ask others for help, it is important that you have a clear idea of:

1. What you want and do not want to share about your trauma, emotional and/or physical state, and

2. What you would like them to do to help you.

You don't have to tell your story if you don't want to, or you may chose to tell only part of it. Alternatively, you could say something simple, and vague, "The twentieth of June is always a hard day for me because something awful happened to me on that day." As repeatedly stated throughout this book, it may well be that talking about what happened during the trauma won't help you at all: it may only serve to retraumatize you. If such is the case, then you need to make that clear to the person you select to help you. For example, you could say, "It would be only natural for you to wonder what happened to me on June twentieth, but talking about it only upsets me more right now. Perhaps I will be able to tell you about it some other time. However, if you will agree to have dinner with me on June twentieth, I would like that very much and it would be helping me out a lot."

It is also best to be as specific as possible about how the other person can help. For example, you can ask someone to drive you somewhere (because you are too hyperaroused or too numb to drive), to do the grocery shopping for you, to take you out, to hold you, or, to listen to your story, if that is your decision. (See chapter 13 on telling your story.)

You might also want to voice your fears about asking for help. For example, you could say, "I'm afraid that if I ask you to be with me (or do something for me), you might throw it in my face later on. If you have any resentments or hesitations about helping me out, I'd rather you would say 'no' now than say 'yes,' out of guilt, or the feeling you can't turn down a friend, than later on to complain about having to help me. It's also important to me that you won't tell my secrets to others, or make fun of me. This has happened to me before and I found it very painful. Can you assure me that, to the best of your ability, it won't happen again? If I didn't respect you—think a lot of you—I wouldn't be asking."

If you aren't exactly sure what you want from the other person, that can be stated also. For example, you could say. "I know I want to have dinner with you, but I might have to leave in the middle if I get too upset. Can you deal with that? On the other hand, I might want company after dinner too. Would you be available then too? Can you deal with me not knowing how I'll feel or what I need until the last minute? Can you be flexible? I might not know until the last minute how I feel. Can you cope with that?"

Sharing Your List of Triggers with Your Partner and Family Members

Your partner and family members, including your children, can be invaluable resources to help you with your triggers. Remember that if you are ashamed of your triggers and trigger reactions or if you do not tell your family that you are distressed for any other reason, they cannot help you.

The first step is for you to share your trigger list with your intimate partner and/or your family. You need to tell them at least what "sets you off"—either into hyperarousal or numbness. It isn't necessary to explain why certain situations or actions trigger you, but at the very minimum you must indicate that you were traumatized or part of an overwhelming (sad, frightening, terrible) event. Communicating such information clearly, however, takes some thought and creativity and the process works best when there is a spirit of cooperation.

However, if your trauma has already resulted in misunderstandings, miscommunications, and estrangement in your family, then the process needs to include the opportunity for your partner or family members to share how your trauma has thus far affected them. Quite possibly your partner or family members hold resentments toward you, have fears about losing you, or feel helpless about helping you in regard to the trauma. If you can discuss these matters openly, without the discussion becoming abusive and the cause of even more misunderstanding, then you may not need the assistance of a neutral helping party. But if you and your partner or family members can't make progress on your own, you may want to seek outside help, at least initially.

Dr. Charles Figley (1988) has proposed a multiphased treatment for families in which one member has been traumatized by events *outside the family*, e.g., rape, war, assault, or homicide. (Clearly, this treatment is not for families in which there is, or was, physical or sexual abuse.) His belief, which has been substantiated by research on war veterans, rape survivors, and suicide and homicide survivors, is that when one person in the family is traumatized by an outside event, the entire family pays the price. Family members must cope with seeing their loved one impaired or disabled by PTSD, clinical depression, or other traumatic reactions. They also live with the fear of losing the survivor, a feeling of helplessness in seeing their loved one in pain or acting destructively, and perhaps with some resentment at the burden the loved one's traumatic reactions impose on family life.

Usually, trauma disrupts the normal course of family living. In addition, trauma makes all the normal family transitions and crises, such as the birth of a child, the rebellion of teenage children, the separation of older children from the family, or a death in the family even harder to manage because such normal family events tend to trigger the traumatized family member.

The first part of Dr. Figley's therapy program involves building a commitment on the part of every family member toward reducing the damaging effects of the trauma. To build this commitment, the suffering the trauma caused *each family member* to experience must be recognized and respected. The traumatized person must share his or her ordeal, or enough of it, so that the other family members can understand the reason for the pain. But this is not enough. The pain, anger, and needs of all of the family members must also be heard. Everyone's psychological agenda is legitimate, not only the trauma survivor's.

According to Figley, there is not just one victim in the family: "the entire family has been victimized" (1988, 133). Therefore, each family member must have the chance to talk about how his or her life was changed by the trauma. The goal is to have all family members be honest about how the trauma affected them, without blaming the trauma survivor, or one another. The ultimate goal is to have all the family members see that the "real enemy" is not others in the family, but the trauma itself.

For example, if John, a Vietnam combat veteran, has trouble staying at his son's birthday parties, especially when his son is given toy guns as presents, the problem is not that John doesn't love his son, but rather that crowds of small children remind him of the orphaned children he saw begging in the streets during his tour of duty. Toy guns are an obvious trigger.

The next stage of Dr. Figley's program consists of reframing the problem so that the positive motivations of family members are brought into the open. For example, if John leaves his son's birthday party, his motivation is to spare his son the embarrassment of seeing his father begin to sweat and possibly go into a flashback. Similarly, when Mary, a formerly abused woman, would fall into a deep depression on the anniversary of her trauma, her adult children tended to avoid her. Mary felt her children were rejecting her and were not willing to help lift her spirits when she needed cheering. In the family therapy sessions, however, the children said that they avoided her because they could not tolerate her pain. Additionally, they said they felt like failures because they felt there was nothing they could do to help her. They felt so guilty and helpless, that in self-protection, they made plans to be with their friends whenever they saw their mother become depressed. Once Mary understood that her children avoided her because of their deep love for her, she was able to reframe her perception of their behavior from signs of "rejection" to signs of "love."

Similarly, when Anthony, a rescue worker, refrained from attending his son's football games, his son felt rejected and hurt. When Anthony explained that seeing young men injured in football games triggered memories of the mutilated bodies he had to deal with in vehicular accidents, his son was able to see that his father wasn't rejecting him, but trying to avoid painful reminders.

The goal is to have the family turn a "tragedy and a terrible burden" into "a challenge" and to call upon the family to see how they can work together to cope with the aftereffects of the trauma, as well as future adversities (Figley 1988, 134).

The third stage of the program is to have each member of the family write a statement describing first how the trauma affected them personally, and then how it affected the family as a whole. (Even young children are encouraged to write, or if they are very young, to say something about how the trauma affected them, and then have an older family member write it for them.) The family then comes together and writes a *combined* statement of what happened to each member individually and to the family as a whole, as a result of the trauma. This combined statement includes each member's perceptions prior to therapy and after therapy. In this healing statement, the family also puts into writing how family members can help each other in the future should a similar traumatic event occur.

Sample Healing Theory Letter

The children of a man who died in an airline crash composed the following healing theory letter:

After our dad died in the crash, our mother would be totally quiet, like a zombie, then she would start screaming at us over nothing. Once she threw the vacuum cleaner at us and tore up our homework. We felt sad that our Dad was dead and we were afraid that we would lose our mother, too, that she would go crazy or even kill herself. She didn't want us around, but she didn't like us to go anywhere, either.

If we went out, we had to call her every hour to tell her where we were and what we were doing. We thought she was punishing us because Dad was dead and that she didn't love us as much as she loved him. Sometimes, we were afraid she was going to put us up for adoption.

Now we know that Mom was acting the way she did because she felt sad and angry about Dad getting killed. Mom was scared too. She had never been on her own and didn't think she could manage everything. She was afraid we were going to get killed too, which is why she didn't want us to see our friends or leave the house. It took her a while to realize that she needed help.

Now she knows why she acts so irrationally at times and she has friends to call when she needs help. Now Mom can help us when we feel sad and angry about our Dad dying. We can plan what we will do on the anniversary of his birthday and his death date instead of picking fights with each other. We appreciate each other more and know that should something bad happen again, we can talk about it and how we feel and we can help each other, instead of having fights. We are glad our mother got help because now we now have our mother back and she can help us if something bad happens to us. She says that if she can survive Dad dying, she can survive anything.

You may want to try some of Dr. Figley's ideas when talking with your family or intimate partner about your triggers. This involves listening to everyone's reactions to the impact of the trauma on the family in a receptive, nonblaming way. If you and your partner or family can discuss these matters without the discussion turning into a name-calling or blaming session, then you will not need the help of a trained professional or neutral trained third party. If, however, your attempt to open communication about the impact of triggers on your family becomes a series of harmful accusations, you need to stop immediately and consider finding professional assistance.

Family Violence and Sexual Assault Survivors: Asking for Soothing from a Family Member or Intimate

If you are a survivor of family violence or sexual aggression within the family, there is a high probability that the person to whom you turned for soothing, protection, and love was also someone who took advantage of your legitimate needs and abused you. Your issues in asking for soothing, especially physical soothing involving touch, may be many, and quite complex. You need to discuss your intentions to approach such an intimate for soothing with a qualified therapist and, ideally, your partner should attend some sessions with you on this issue. The issue is so delicate that it is fairly easy for your partner to become frustrated in trying to support you. Because you were traumatized in so many ways within a relationship, it is easy for your partner, no matter how well-intentioned, to inadvertently retraumatize you.

Definitions of Terms

ACTH: A hormone secreted by the pituitary gland. When the organism is threatened, the pituitary gland secretes increased amounts of ACTH in the blood, which causes the adrenals to respond to the danger. ACTH is a kind of "messenger" from the pituitary gland to the adrenals.

Adrenaline or Epinephrine: Hormone produced by the adrenals. When the adrenals are overtaxed due to excessive use, various illness can result. Low epinephrine levels are associated with depression.

Catecholamines: A group of important neurotransmitters including epinephrine or adrenaline, or noradrenaline, norepinephrine, and dopamine.

Neurotransmitter: Your mind and your body are composed of neurons. Neurotransmitters are chemical substances that enable impulses to be transmitted from one nerve cell to another (Bourne 1990). They have many functions, including helping to regulate the intensity of emotions and moods and to retain memory.

Noradrenaline: Noradrenaline is released by the adrenal glands in response to emergencies. Unlike adrenaline, which provides an energy surge, noradrenaline causes a slowing down of the ability to move, think, and feel. In extreme cases, people feel "frozen" and unable to move. When we say that someone "went into shock" because of a traumatic event or traumatic news, most likely that individual's adrenals pumped him or her with noradrenaline and created a shutdown of the physical, emotional, and mental functions.

Serotonin: This is another neurotransmitter that functions to "fine-tune" and buffer emotions, giving the person time to think and assess a situation and not respond immediately. It is lacking in manic-depressives and in lower level primates with early separation and poor bonding experiences. When serotonin is depleted, an organism may overreact to new stimuli with a great deal of excitement and hyperarousal; overreact to pain and handling; become hypersensitive emotionally and more irritable; and is subject to increased hostility, impulsivity, aggression (including self-directed aggression), more flashbacks, and panic attacks.

Stress-Induced Analgesia (SIA) response: Under life-threatening circumstances, the body may secrete massive amounts of adrenaline or other activating hormones. However, when the life-threatening circumstances are particularly severe or prolonged or are inescapable, the intensity of the stress may cause the body to secrete hormones that create a numbing effect. This is called stress-induced analgesia or SIA. The SIA response is mediated by the body's endogenous (or internal) opioid system. Endogenous opioids are natural substances in our bodies that have effects similar to drugs such as opium and other sedatives. "Nature provides protection against pain by means of SIA" (van der Kolk 1996a, 227). The SIA response helps lessen both pain and panic, thus increasing the individual's chances for survival.

References

Armsworth, Mary. 1994. "Intergenerational Effects of Trauma," Audiotape 94ISTSS, of lecture presented at the 10th Annual Meeting for the International Society for Traumatic Stress. Chicago. November.

Beecher, H. K. 1946. "Pain in Men Wounded in Battle." *Annals of Surgery* 123:93–101.

Bourne, Edmond, J. 1990. *Anxiety and Phobia Workbook*. Oakland, CA: New Harbinger Publications.

Figley, Charles. 1988. "A Five-Phase Treatment of Post-traumatic Stress Disorder in Families." *Journal of Traumatic Stress* 1:127–139.

Giller, Earl. 1994. "Foreword." In *Catecholamine Function in Post-Traumatic Stress Disorder: Emerging Concepts*. M. Murburg, Ed. Washington, D.C.: American Psychiatric Press.

Glover, Hillel. 1992. "Emotional Numbing: A Possible Endorphin-Mediated Phenomenon Associated with Post-Traumatic Stress Disorders and Other Allied Psychopathological States." *Journal of Traumatic Stress Studies* 5:643–676.

James, Beverly, 1994. "Trauma and the Attachment Relationship: Integration of Theory, Assessment, and Treatment, Audiotape 94ISTSS-40 of lecture presented at the 10th Annual Meeting of the International Society for Traumatic Stress Studies. Chicago. November.

Johnson, David. 1996. "Creating Healing Relationships for Couples." Audiotape 96ISTSS-81 of lecture presented at the 12th Annual Meeting of the International Society for Traumatic Stress Studies. San Francisco. November.

Kardiner, Abraham. 1941. The Traumatic Neuroses of War. New York: Hoeber.

Matsakis, Aphrodite. 1996. *I Can't Get Over It: A Handbook for Trauma Survivors*, Second Edition. Oakland, CA: New Harbinger Publications.

Murburg, Michelle, Ed. 1994. *Catecholamine Function in Post-Traumatic Stress Disorder: Emerging Concepts*. Washington, D.C. American Psychiatric Press.

Murburg, Michelle. 1996. "Catecholamines in PTSD: The Up, Down, or Sideways? Debate" Audiotape 96ISTSS-70, lecture presented at the

12th Annual Meeting of the International Society for Traumatic Stress Studies, San Francisco. November.

Murburg, Michelle. Ed. 1994. *Catecholamine Function in Post-Traumatic Stress Disorder: Emerging Concepts.* Washington, D.C.: American Psychiatric Press.

Pearlman, Laura. 1996. "Trauma and the Fulfillment of Human Potential." Audiotape of lecture presented at the 12th Annual Meeting of the International Society for Traumatic Stress Studies, San Francisco. November.

Perry, Bruce. 1996. "Neurobiological Sequelae of Childhood Trauma: PTSD in Children." In *Catecholamine Function in Post-Traumatic Stress Disorder: Emerging Concepts.* Michelle Murburg, Ed. Washington, D.C.: American Psychiatric Press.

Perry, Bruce. 1994. "Psychophysiological Effects of Childhood Trauma: and Their Influence on Development." Audiotape 94 ISTSS-103 of lecture presented at the 10th Annual Meeting of the International Society for Traumatic Stress. Chicago. November.

Pittman, R. and S. P. Orr. 1990a. "The Black Hole of Trauma." 26: 221–223. *Biological Psychiatry* 26:221–223.

Pittman, R. and S. P. Orr. 1990b. "Twenty-Four Hour Urinary Cortisol and Catecholamine Excretion in Combat-Related Post-Traumatic Stress Disorder." *Biological Psychiatry.* 27:245–247.

Reite, Martin and Tiffany Field. 1985. *The Psychobiology of Attachment and Separation.* New York: The Academic Press.

Shay, J. 1994. *Achilles in Vietnam.* New York: Atheneum Press.

van der Kolk, Bessel. 1988a. "The Biological Response to Psychic Trauma." In *Post-Traumatic Therapy and Victims of Violence.* Frank Ochberg, Ed. New York: Brunner/Mazel Publishers.

van der Kolk, Bessel. 1988b. "The Trauma Spectrum." *Journal of Traumatic Stress* 1:273–290.

van der Kolk, Bessel and C. Dicey. 1989. "The Psychobiological Processing of Traumatic Experience: Rorschach Patterns in PTSD. *Journal of Traumatic Stress* 2:259–274.

van der Kolk, Bessel. 1994a. "The Neurobiology of Trauma." Audiotape 94-ISTSS-72 of lecture presented at the 10th Annual Meeting of the International Society for Traumatic Stress Studies. Chicago. November.

van der Kolk, Bessel. 1994b. "The Biological Basis of Traumatic Memory." Audiotape 94-ISTSS-65 of lecture presented at the 10th Annual Meeting of the International Society for Traumatic Stress Studies. Chicago. November.

van der Kolk, Bessel. 1996a "The Body Keeps the Score: Approaches to the Psychobiology of PTSD." In *Traumatic Stress: The Effects of Overwhelming Experience on Mind, Body, and Society.* B. van der Kolk, et al. Eds. New York: Guilford Press.

van der Kolk, Bessel. 1996b. "Brain Imaging Studies in PTSD," Audiotape 95-ISTSS-96, of lecture presented a the 12th Annual Meeting of the International Society for Traumatic Stress Studies. Chicago. November.

van der Kolk, B. A., David Pelcovitz, Susa Roth, Francine Mandel, Alexander Mc Farlane, and Judith Herman. 1996c. "Dissociation, Somatization and Affect Dysregulation: The Complexity of Adaptation to Trauma," *American Journal of Psychiatry* 153:83–93.

Watenberg, Melissa, 1996. "Treating What Time Can't Heal: Three Perspectives on Chronic PTSD."

Audiotape 96-ISTSS-141 of lecture presented at the 12th Annual Meeting of the International Society for Traumatic Stress Studies. San Francisco.

Wilson, R. R., 1987. "The Body's Emergency Response: Breaking the Panic Cycle for People with Phobias." Washington, D.C.: Anxiety Association of America.

5

Limited Psychic Energy: Causes and Coping Techniques

Damn the memories
Damn the sorrows
Must they cloud
My every tomorrow?

I hate this thing called trauma
And to think some think
I'm in it for the drama.

I'm tired of being told
That I'm glad
To be sad.

People don't know how hard I pray
For the pain to go away.

That pain
So deep, so long
How long before it goes away
Only to come back another day?

—Tim, a trauma survivor

Many trauma survivors have said to me, "How can I deal with relationships? I can barely deal with myself." The unhappy truth is that
traumatized people often have less psychic energy available for relationships than other people do, especially if they have never received
appropriate or adequate help. In the words of one of the "fathers" of

PTSD, psychiatrist Abraham Kardiner, who studied combat veterans in World War I, PTSD is basically a problem of "ego constriction."

The ego is the part of the self that interacts with society and manages relationships with the outside world. In Kardiner's view (1941), trauma drains the ego of energy, which causes the ego to constrict, or shrink. This leaves the survivor with the (justifiable) fear that he or she will lack the necessary inner resources to meet the demands of an activity or a relationship. The anxiety that results from expecting to be deficient, incompetent, or unable to cope causes the survivor to avoid social and other involvements. However, avoiding certain people and social activities leads to grieving for the lost pleasures and opportunities inherent in relating to others and pursuing meaningful goals.

Relationships, especially parenting, require an enormous amount of energy, which some trauma survivors lack because of depression or preoccupation with their traumatic experiences. In this regard, some survivors are like some former inmates of the Nazi concentration camps who, due to their focus on their traumatic experiences and subsequent demoralization, have been found to lack the energy to parent (Sigall 1976; Sigall and Rakoff 1971).

If you often feel that it is easier to be alone because you don't have the energy for relationships, your perception may be correct. There are ways, however, to counteract this limited psychic energy. This chapter discusses the possible reasons for a lack of psychic energy for relationships, and, along with each description, there are suggestions for reversing the tendency to isolate and for increasing your social and interpersonal energy levels. Although you may never function as well as you might of had you never been traumatized, there are ways to improve your social functioning and to keep the damages wrought by the trauma at a minimum.

Overview: Causes of Limited Psychic Energy

Some of the reasons for the lack of psychic energy for relationships experienced by many trauma survivors are described below. Some will apply to you. Some will not. Also, if you are in recovery or engaged in a healing process, as your therapy progresses, some of these reasons increasingly will no longer apply to you. As you continue to heal, more of your psychic energy will become available to you for dealing with the present because you'll be spending less of your psychic power trying to suppress the trauma, and the feelings and conflicts associated with it. Also, the more you face the trauma and appreciate the magnitude of the struggles you've been through and the losses you've endured, the less vulnerable you will be to critical or insulting remarks. Even if others don't appreciate you and what you've been through, you will appreciate yourself and what you've been through.

However, until such time that you can safely say that the trauma is almost in the background rather than the forefront of your mind, you may find you have less energy to invest in relating to others for some of the following reasons:

1. Living in two worlds: the world of trauma and your present-day world

2. Unprocessed or unresolved emotions and issues pertaining to the trauma, especially unresolved grief

3. Time and energy spent managing triggers and trigger reactions

4. Medical problems caused by the trauma and medical, financial, and psychological problems caused by histories of addiction

5. Untreated depression

6. Dissociation, depersonalization, and derealization

7. Feelings of low self-worth and lack of assertiveness (see chapter 6)

8. Survivor guilt (see chapter 6)

9. Reenactment and Revictimization (see chapter 12)

10. Relationships with those who died during the trauma (see chapter 10)

Normal Life Stresses: Not included in this chapter are the reasons that almost all people are sometimes emotionally unavailable or disinterested in others. All people tend to withdraw socially when they are ill, when they experience economic stress or problems on the job, when there is an illness or death in the family, or when they are on "overload," not just trauma survivors.

Societal Factors: Societal factors that contribute to social isolation affect all members of society, the traumatized and the nontraumatized alike. In our society it is increasingly difficult for all people, not just trauma survivors, to maintain family ties, friendships, and love relationships because of factors such as the rapid pace of urban life and the growth of solitary entertainments (e.g., television, videos, computer games). Families and communities that wish to spend time together must fight against economic pressures, geographical mobility, transportation difficulties, and the high value put on individual pursuits.

We are an individual-oriented, not a family- or community-oriented society. Making time for family life, friendships, and love relationships requires a concerted effort to coordinate schedules and overcome the demands of other involvements, like work and self-oriented pursuits. Trauma survivors, who have less emotional energy available for relationships, may find it more difficult than others to surmount the societal obstacles that discourage developing and maintaining relationships.

Accurate Labeling

There is nothing more important to a trauma survivor than the truth, for usually, if you've been traumatized, somewhere along the way you've been lied to, or deceived in some fashion. It's also important that you do not, unintentionally, lie to or deceive yourself. Accurately labeling and understanding the reasons for your limited energy are critical to your recovery. You may not be the social person you were prior to the trauma, but if you view your lack of sociability or interest in socializing as due to some characteristic such as being "unpopular," "a loser," "sub-human," "antisocial," or a "goner," then you aren't telling yourself the truth. Your limited psychic energy is far more complex: It's due to the combined effects of many possible factors and cannot be explained away simply by calling yourself a "hopeless case" or a "social misfit." Each contributing factor must be carefully examined to see what can be changed and what cannot be changed, but only accepted.

All too often trauma survivors conclude that they are doomed to be social failures or social outcasts, that they just don't like people or that people don't like them, that they have nothing to give anyone and no one wants to give them anything either. These statements are rarely true. Sometimes, being more assertive in a relationship or limiting certain kinds of interactions can make the relationship enjoyable, as opposed to an exercise in endurance. Also, there are times such as during anniversaries of your trauma, where you will have less energy for relating to others. But this anniversary reaction is not a permanent state of affairs, although while you are in it, it can certainly feel that way. When you are triggered emotionally and physiologically, you are also being triggered mentally into the "all-or-nothing" mind-set of trauma, which believes that the horrible moments of being trapped in a trigger reaction will never end. Yet this is rarely the case. An anniversary reaction generally lifts over time. If it doesn't, then intensive help, perhaps even hospitalization, may be needed.

✍ Exercise: The Terrible Names You Call Yourself

In the spaces below, list the terrible names you call yourself or the terms you apply to yourself when you feel you can't face the prospect of meeting or relating with others, whether family members, friends, co-workers, or intimates. For example, you might be labeling yourself a "social retard," "secret schizo," "failure," "people-hater," "social reject," "ugly," "fat," "stupid-looking," "old," "inadequate," "deformed," "damaged goods," "bad," "crazy," or any number of other pejorative names or adjectives.

1. _____

2. _____

3. _____

4. _____

Now list some of the conclusions you have made about yourself and your social relations. For example, "I don't belong anywhere," or "Nobody will ever like me, " or "I don't fit in with my family," or "I will never have a meaningful relationship with the opposite/same sex."

1. _____

2. _____

3. _____

4. _____

You would probably hate it if others called you by these names or talked to you like this. Yet you may be addressing yourself in this disrespectful manner. If beating up on yourself really motivated you to change, then it might be beneficial. However, self-deprecating statements, like guilt, usually cause people to give up, or become more depressed, or tempt them to drink, do drugs, overeat, undereat, or self-mutilate.

✍ Exercise: Monitoring the Negative Self

Are you aware of how often you call yourself these names and repeat to yourself negative conclusions about your social abilities? In this exercise, you will make a conscious effort to observe yourself putting yourself down. This exercise can be extremely powerful, if you are willing to put the necessary time and energy into doing it correctly.

If you truly want to change the way you talk to yourself, you first must become more conscious of what you tell yourself. For two or three days, on an hourly basis, record in a fresh page of your journal what you tell yourself when you are in a social situation. On an hour-to-hour basis, keep a log of your self-talk and observe how much of it is self-defeating in that it perpetuates a negative self-image that causes you to withdraw or feel alienated from others. As the result of your self-investigation, you may find other names that you call yourself and additional negative conclusions about your life that you may want to add to the names and conclusions you listed above. Add these to your journal entry.

As you read the following sections describing the causes of limited psychic energy, keep in mind how you can change your negative self-blaming self-statements into more accurate statements. For example, instead of telling yourself, "I am doomed to be a social outcast because I cannot attend an upcoming family function," you need to frame a more accurate self-statement, such as the following:

"I have trouble at family functions because some of my family members trigger me. This doesn't mean I am a terrible person, but that terrible things happened to me, which, when I'm reminded of them, cause me so much anger and pain that I can't function for a while. I can try to see the family members who treat me well at another time, apart from those who trigger me, or I can explore with my therapist and/or friends the possibility of trying to manage my reactions to my trigger relatives. That may or may not be possible. But just because I may not be able to handle some of my trigger relatives, does not mean that I can't enjoy relationships with other people or that I lack social skills or that I am socially undesirable."

The purpose of listing the possible causes of limited psychic energy is not to discourage you, but to help you accurately label what is going on within yourself. It should help you to know that if you don't have the "oomph" to stay at a party for three or four hours, that doesn't mean you are "antisocial" or a "social reject" but that your limited energy may be the result of being in the down cycle of a depression. This understanding should give you hope that when the depression lifts, you'll be able to socialize more, and should be the basis of a new way of judging yourself. Instead of beating yourself up for not being able to stay for the whole party, you should be congratulating yourself for getting there and staying as long as you did.

Instead of telling yourself, "I am a miserable failure. I can't even go to a party," you need to say something like, "Wow! I was so triggered last week, my depression got worse. Yet I got out of bed, dressed, and showed up at a party and stayed for two whole hours. That's something to be proud of.

"I wish I could have the kind of party spirit I had before the trauma, but there's nothing I can do about that. It wasn't my fault the trauma happened. I am really strong and brave to go on living, despite what happened, and to keep on trying to make my life a good one. I shouldn't compare myself to others, who seem to be able to laugh and talk for hours on end, and I shouldn't compare myself to who I was before my trauma, because that is setting myself up to feel like a failure. I will judge myself by the determination it took for me to get out and mix with others and I give myself an 'A'."

What would you tell a kid who has lost a leg who is planning to go on a hike with his friends? That he's a slowpoke for not being able to keep up with the others or a hero for going out there with his one leg and doing the best he can? Talk to yourself the way you'd talk to that kid: Don't beat him up for something he can't help and do give him credit for doing what he can.

At the end of this chapter, after you have completed the reading and some of the exercises, we will return to your responses to these questions and see if your perception of yourself has changed.

Living in Two Worlds

Once traumatized, you may find that you now live in two worlds at the same time. In describing the inner life of combat veterans, Rosenheck and Thomson write, "The veteran with PTSD lives in two places and times at once. The fear, anger, grief, and guilt of combat in Vietnam are always close by. His thoughts are periodically wrenched back more than a decade to firefights, atrocities, lost buddies, and to the ensuing experience of being unrecognized, unappreciated, and rejected on his return home. At the same time, he lives in peacetime America. . . . People around him do not think about Vietnam or care to hear his thoughts about the war. He must deal with the here and now as best he can, but, even when he is not thinking explicitly about Vietnam, there remains a sharp sense of betrayal, bitterness, and rage about that experience" (Rosenheck and Thomson 1986, 562).

Many trauma survivors probably can identify with the Vietnam veteran's feeling of living in two worlds at once. There you are going about your business, when something brings your past to mind, and then, all of a sudden, the trauma and all the feelings, especially the fear, anger, and pain, are right there. Yet you are expected to carry on as if you had not had a tragedy in your life, unless you are one of the lucky few who live or work in a supportive environment where you can share your feelings with someone. Most trauma survivors, however, must continue to cope with their daily agendas while being distracted by their trauma memories and reactions. This is a form of "double-duty" which, at the end of the day, can leave them depleted, making it difficult for them to muster the energy to engage socially or relate to others.

Coping Techniques

Nothing can erase or stop memories or feelings of the trauma from intruding into your present-day life. However, the burden can be lifted, somewhat, by sharing with others. Sharing can give you energy.

Are there people in your family or work environment with whom you would feel safe to talk to when the ghosts come for you? Do you carry the phone numbers of people from your twelve-step program or support group with you, so you can call them if there is no one in your family or work environment who is supportive?

If you feel it will make you even more anxious or depressed, or if you don't have the time, you need not go into detail about what you are remembering. You simply need to say, "I'm having a hard time because of a bad memory. I'm calling because I want to connect with someone. I know it (the trauma) is not happening again, but it feels as if it is. I know this feeling will pass, but it's sure hard getting through it. Thanks for caring enough to be there for me."

For example, when Tara's cat became ill, that triggered memories of her marriage to an abusive man. To torment Tara, he would prevent her from taking their children to the pediatrician when they were ill. Typically, he would wait until the children were languishing before he would permit Tara to call the doctor. Tara would have taken a cab to the doctor or asked a friend to drive her to the hospital, but her husband kept strict tabs on her and sometimes would lock her in their home to prevent her from going anywhere. At other times, he would lock the sick child in a room alone, or take the child to a babysitter and leave strict instructions with the sitter that Tara was not to be allowed near the child.

These memories were not new to Tara. She had remembered them before, talked about them with her therapist, and written about them. But when her cat became ill, that brought all those painful memories to the surface once more. She wanted to share them with someone, but was careful not to tell people whom she thought might judge her as "silly" or "crazy" for obsessing about something that happened so long ago. Finally, she decided to talk to a friend, who she thought would be respectful of her anguish, even though he would not totally understand why she was so grieved.

When she told her friend that the cat being sick reminded her of how her husband treated her children when they were ill, the friend laughed and said. "Why are you thinking about that now? The past is the past. You've already talked to me about all that stuff before. Why are you whining about it again?"

This was just the kind of response that Tara had dreaded. She had hoped to hear something more supportive, such as, "I wish those terrible things had never happened to you and your children, but thank goodness you are free from that man." However, despite her friend's harsh response, Tara *did* feel better after talking about her traumatic memory.

"I needed to say it to another human being for my own sake. It would have been better if my friend had been more comforting, but, at this stage in my recovery, it doesn't matter what he thought or said. The point is that I felt I mattered enough to tell someone about it, that I didn't feel ashamed of what had happened in the past or that I was having a flashback about it. For me, as a formerly battered woman whose self-esteem was below zero, to think that I was important enough to tell someone how I felt, even if he didn't understand, is a monumental achievement. I had to tell someone, or do something, to get the memory out of my system and if the person I spoke to wasn't the perfect person with the perfect response, so be it. At least I tried. My goal is to not let my past ruin my present. I've suffered enough. Those memories have power and the only way to reduce their power over me is to get it out, anyway I can, by writing, drawing, singing, and talking, even talking to my cat."

✍ Exercise: Identifying Supportive Others

In your journal, make a list of three people you can call during the mornings, afternoons, and evenings with whom you can share.

- Mornings (list three people)
- Afternoons (list three people)
- Evenings (list three people)

Your phone calls need be neither long nor therapeutic sessions. A simple statement that your past is bothering you again may be enough. Sharing that fact with another person, or writing about it in a journal, helps ground you in the present and will help you to focus better on the task at hand. If all else fails, call your own answering service and tell yourself what is going on, or write yourself a letter and mail it to yourself. E-mail a letter to a fellow survivor, even if all that you write is "SOS. It's happening again and I hate it."

If you don't have a support network like this, you need to develop one. Check with a trained mental health professional, a local hospital, or your local library for a listing of support groups for survivors of various traumas or for persons suffering from depression or various addictions. There may not be support groups available for you, in which case you may need to try to build a network via other associations, such as your place of employment (if it's safe), a church or other group, or neighborhood organizations.

✍ Exercise: What to Do When the Ghosts Come for You and You Are All Alone

If there is no one to talk to, you need a backup plan to express what is you feel inside of you. For example, you could do any of the following:

- Write in your journal
- Meditate
- Go for a walk
- Take a five minute "Time-Out" to talk to yourself
- Listen to music

- Do some exercise
- Make an extra therapy appointment
- Draw a picture of what you are feeling or what happened

Now, make a list of five actions you can take when the "ghosts" come for you and you are all alone.

1. _____

2. _____

3. _____

4. _____

5. _____

It is far healthier for you to spend five to thirty minutes dealing with the trauma's return into your consciousness, than to spend hours in a state of depression, disorganization, or high anxiety.

Unresolved Trauma Issues

There is no such thing as "resolving" your trauma issues and being "done" with your past. For the truly traumatized, there is no "forgetting" and no amount of therapy or mind-control can protect you from traumatic memories, feelings, and conflicts coming back into your life. However, if you have never really attended to the trauma, if your trauma-processing work has been half-hearted or incomplete, then your present-day life is saddled with a major burden: the issues from your traumatic past with which you have not dealt.

If you haven't spent adequate time dealing with the trauma and are trying to suppress or minimize what happened to you, then you are spending your energy fighting yourself. If this is the case, it is no wonder that you are exhausted and have little energy for other people. Most of your energy goes to keeping the trauma in denial or repression and managing your symptoms so they don't get out of control and cause an economic or emotional disaster. Essentially, you are spending your time and strength trying to pretend the trauma never happened, or trying to convince yourself that it wasn't that important and, of course, you can handle it, and the emotions and issues that it raised, all by yourself.

When It's Best to Leave Trauma Issues Alone

Quite possibly, you may not be dealing with your trauma-related issues for good reasons. You may lack the necessary emotional or professional support to do so, or you may be dealing with other survival issues or crises. If there are other immediate crises going on, then survival demands that you deal with those and leave your earlier trauma issues on the back burner until your current crises are under control. For example, if you just lost your job or your partner was just diagnosed with cancer, clearly, this is not the time to probe into the past seeking to resolve prior trauma issues. Even though those issues may affect the way you handle your current crises, the focus of any therapy you receive should be on coping and trying to improve the present, not on delving into the past. Earlier trauma issues will certainly arise, but the therapeutic focus should always be on surviving your present ordeals.

Similarly, if you are emotionally ready to deal with your earlier trauma issues, but there are no supports available to you, it also makes sense not to bring trauma issues to the forefront, lest you become overwhelmed. However, it is imperative that you seek qualified help as soon as possible.

Unresolved Grief

Trauma involves massive losses, some of which may be irreversible. You may have lost some (or all) of your belongings, your identity, your optimism, your sense of safety, you physical and mental health, or someone you loved. Allowing yourself to grieve these losses is an important part of the recovery process. Grieving is exhausting, but fighting the grieving process is even more exhausting.

Although there is no such thing as "resolving once and for all" or "being finished" with grieving, if you have never mourned your losses or did so in an incomplete fashion, you may be grieving in indirect or unconscious ways that detract from your ability to engage in relationships today.

It has been determined that loss is related to medical problems (Reite and Field 1985); that depression can be a defense against grieving; and that underlying many addictions is unresolved grief. Grieving is the hardest emotional task any human being can face. It's no wonder that people will do anything to escape the pain and suffering involved. However, the theory holds that, if you truly grieve a loss on a *conscious level*, it will free up massive amounts of psychic energy that you may have been using to mourn your loss unconsciously; and then you will be free to move on. It is possible to live your present-day life to the fullest degree possible while still honoring and remembering the dead.

Costs of Not Dealing with Trauma Issues

Unresolved trauma issues sap energy. Suppressing trauma-related anger, for example, is like sitting on a volcano: it takes a tremendous amount of energy to hold back the explosions. Suppressing grief is also exhausting, it's like holding back a flood. Suppressing guilt can be like trying to escape from quicksand: you struggle and struggle, but no matter how hard you try to escape, you still feel stuck in a wretched, smelly swamp.

If you were subject to long-term or severe trauma, it may take many years to uncover all of the feelings and inner conflicts that the trauma created in you. There is no "fast fix." But, to counterweight the energy drain spent suppressing the trauma and its emotional toll, you can, if you choose, increase your commitment to dealing with the trauma. For example, some survivors keep a daily journal, talk or write to a supportive other on a more frequent basis, or take their therapy or recovery program even more seriously. Other ways to promote your healing are reading about the subject, seeking or increasing professional help, or becoming involved in healing efforts not directly related to the trauma, e.g., exercise programs, special interest study groups, or community projects.

✍ Exercise: Increasing Your Commitment to Healing

If your schedule and psyche can handle it, what three steps can you take to increase your investment in healing from your traumatic past by dealing with it directly, rather than indirectly, that is, by suppressing feelings and conflicts that may be causing you severe internal energy drain?

Three steps I can take now to commit myself to healing are as follows:

1. _____

2. _____

3. _____

Three steps I can take during the next six months to commit myself to healing are as follows:

1. _____

2. _____

3. _____

If you feel you are being cheated out of your present life because of your trauma, then instead of telling yourself, "It's hopeless. I'm a prisoner of the past," you need to say," It's too soon to tell if it's hopeless or not. I don't have enough information to make that conclusion. I can only come to that conclusion when I've done all I can do to attend to my healing and I haven't done that, yet.

"I'm extremely bound up in the past right now because I haven't had enough help, or the right kind of help, or because, for whatever reasons, I haven't been able to make the time to get the help I need. I can take steps to deal with the trauma, which, in the long run, will free up the energy I now have bound up with the past. I may never have the life I dreamed of before the trauma, but I can have a much better life than I have now—if I take the trauma and its aftereffects seriously and if I love myself enough to make the time to deal with it."

Managing Your Triggers

Managing your triggers is necessary for survival, but it does take time, energy, effort, and, sometimes, money. First, you have to understand your trigger reactions, which takes work, then apply your coping techniques, which also takes work. Using a support system, making calls, going to therapy, writing in your journal, all take effort. The results of your efforts may be extremely beneficial—they will permit you to function in society, in your family, or in a relationship. Nevertheless, they take away from the time and energy you can devote to other endeavors, from personal projects to other relationships.

Having to manage triggers imposes definite limitations on what you can and cannot do. There may be some triggers that you feel you need to avoid entirely, if at all possible. But the limitations extend further than this. You need to allow for the time and energy it takes to manage triggers when making decisions about commitments. Overcommitting and overextending yourself, without leaving adequate time to take care of yourself after your triggers have been activated is a very real danger. The more you were traumatized, the more triggers you need to be concerned about.

This doesn't mean that you should severely limit your life and live in dire fear of being triggered, but rather that you need to respect the fact that, because of your trauma, you will need a lot of time and energy to take care of yourself, if triggered. That means other commitments and obligations may have to be put aside or reduced or shortened, especially during anniversary times or at other predictable times when you know you tend to become highly anxious or depressed.

Coping Techniques

Priority Setting and Time Management Instruction: From business executives, to housewives, to college students, almost anyone who is active in today's world can benefit from learning about priority setting and time management. Courses and books on these subjects abound in our society and they are relevant for all people, especially trauma survivors. Part of taking care of yourself is being selective about what you do, and setting priorities. When you start feeling overwhelmed because of a trigger, you need to be able to look at your day, or week, and know what absolutely must be dealt with and what can be put on the shelf for a while.

Theoretically, you probably could figure out your priorities in the middle of a panic attack or a dip into depression, but it's better if you figure them out in advance. This prepares you for the eventuality of a trigger being activated and makes it less threatening.

Trauma survivors need to plan their lives carefully to avoid undue stress. This may mean excluding certain activities or relationships entirely but, alternatively, it may only mean doing less in each area or in each relationship. You need to set limits on what you can and cannot do, because you need to save some time and energy for managing your triggers. It may not be a pleasant fact of life, but it is a reality that you may not be able to do as much as easily as those who have not been traumatized. In the past, you carried a big load (the trauma). It stole energy and psychic resources from you and wore you out, so, now, if you can't carry as large a load as others do, it doesn't mean you are inadequate. It means you might be emotionally, physically, and mentally exhausted from having had to manage an overwhelmingly heavy ordeal in your past.

✍ Exercise: Writing Your Own Script

Almost everyone has a fantasy image of being a superperson— the "ideal" man or woman—with a constant smile and loving heart, who is all things to all people at all times with no wear and tear on the self. Sometimes, trauma survivors try to be superpersons to compensate for having trauma-related symptoms or to atone for trauma-related guilt. They try to be superpersons by overdoing or overgiving in their relationships and all their roles. However, trying to be a superperson can be costly. It is important that you write your own script for each of your roles and relationships, tailored to your talents, and your limitations.

Brainstorm a list of adjectives describing the cultural ideal or stereotype of this super or "perfect" person. Perhaps you see such a person as always being tidy, punctual, cheerful, helpful, and caught up on all his/her paperwork. Next, brainstorm a list of personal costs and costs to others that are the price of this ideal image. For instance, you may think of the ideal person as always saying "yes" to someone in need, especially to a fellow trauma survivor or someone in your support group. This could cost time and money that might be spent on yourself, or meeting family obligations, or keeping commitments to nontherapy friends.

For example, a mother might write the following script:

My children expect me to be all-giving all the time and perhaps that is my supermother image of myself. But it isn't realistic or healthy for me or the children. In order to be a giving mother, I need to be able to give to myself. I'll spend half of my free time on myself and the other half on the children. If there are six free hours on a weekend day after the chores are done, I'll do whatever *I* want to do for three hours and be available to the kids for the next three. Or I'll spend Saturday with the kids and Sunday on myself.

If one of the kids has a special need, I'll need to change my fifty-fifty plan and give more time to the child in need. If I have a special need, such as managing a trigger reaction or getting through an anniversary time, I may not be able to give what I want to give to the kids. During those times I cannot commit to any activities that will involve stress or even more triggers because I will already be stressed and triggered by my own internal responses to the anniversary or the trigger at hand.

Now, on a fresh page in your journal, write your own personal script, not a superperson script, for one of your roles, taking into account some of your triggers and anniversary times. (This exercise can be completed for additional roles also.)

✍ *Exercise: Junk Versus Joy*

The "Junk Versus Joy" exercise is another version of "Writing Your Own Script."

Think about what is truly important about being a parent, friend, co-worker, partner, neighbor, sister or brother, daughter, or son. What activities are really necessary for each role? You may have the qualities of honesty and consistency, or of being a good listener, or never forgetting birthdays or other important dates. Maybe you play an instrument or tell entertaining stories or good jokes. Maybe you cook great meals or know how to fix appliances. Perhaps you can baby-sit or provide nursing help. These are all qualities that you can bring to relationships. Which of your qualities do you really want to share with your family? Your co-workers? Your neighbors?

For example, what does it mean to be a Mom? Is there a difference between being loving and baking cupcakes? Do the cupcakes ever get in the way of the loving?

The point of this exercise is to separate the junk from the joy of the roles in order have more of the joy and less of the junk. On a separate sheet of paper, draw a line dividing the paper in half. Label one side "joy" and the other "junk." Underneath the label, list the junk versus the joy from your various roles as parent, spouse partner, friend, neighbor, co-worker, or any other roles that matter to you.

Nontraditional Solutions to Common Relationship Conflicts

The more you can write your own script or focus on the joy versus the junk in your roles and relationships, the less energy you will spend on the nonessential or draining aspects of those relationships and the more energy you will have for the aspects that nourish and reward you. One sure way to drain yourself of psychic energy is to be involved in those aspects of relationships that set off a trigger for you or are inherently boring or distasteful to you. In order to write your own script and create more joy in your relationships, you will have to contemplate nontraditional creative alternatives.

If you've been traumatized, you have not had a traditional life and you probably never will have a traditional life. Your relationships are not going to be like those of the people you see in the media or of certain cultural ideals. But your life, and relationships, can be satisfying and meaningful if you can figure out how to meet the emotional needs of significant others, while not overstressing yourself or knowingly putting yourself in situations that set off your triggers.

To accomplish that goal, the two key words here are *compromise* and *creativity*. If you restrict yourself to traditional solutions and if you don't enlist the help of others to solve relationship issues, your chances of resolving those issues will be small.

For example, suppose your child asks you to volunteer to be a room parent at school and you are feeling overextended, not just by the demands of being a worker and a parent, but by the demands of recovering from your trauma. Or, perhaps, there is something about being a room parent that is distasteful to you, or triggers you.

You want to be a good parent, but you also need to keep your limits in mind. You may cause yourself damage by agreeing to be room mother (or father) and becoming overextended and, later on, becoming resentful. Yet you may feel you would hurt yourself and your child by refusing to participate in your child's school because you do not want your trauma to rob you of contributing to a good relationship with your child.

Your choices are not all-or-nothing. With a little creativity, you can come up with a way to participate in your child's school and still not overextend yourself. For example, you could agree to be a room parent every other month, instead of every month, or you could find another parent who could share the responsibility. This may not be an established pattern at the school, but why not start a new pattern? Probably other parents, who are also very busy, would appreciate the opportunity to share room parenting, without having to shoulder the complete responsibility all the time.

Alternatively, you could say "no" to being a room parent, but agree to participate in a special project or event for the class. The key action you need to take is to ask your child what matters to him or her.

For example, you could say, "I love you very much and want to be a part of your school. But I won't be able to be a room parent this year. Maybe next year I will be able to manage it, but not this year. Yet I very much want to do something to be a part of your school life. If you could have your wish come true, how would you like me to help out at your school? What could I do for your school that would make you happy and feel as if you had a parent who really cared, because I *do* really care."

Don't be surprised if even a very young child has good ideas about how you could participate and some of these ideas might be more manageable for you than being a room parent. It may be that it isn't that important to the child that you be a room parent, but it is important that you be involved in some way. It may be that it doesn't matter to the child at all.

One common problem some trauma survivors have is becoming anxious when confined, or when they *feel* confined. For some survivors, attending sports events, concerts, or other large gatherings of people is extremely stressful. Yet their child may be involved in sports or school performances. Some children want their parents to come to PTA meetings, or other such gatherings.

Lisa, an incest survivor, who had spent many hours of her life trapped in small, confining rooms with her abuser, abhorred feeling "stuck" in closed spaces. When she attended her daughter's dance concerts, which sometimes lasted four or five hours, she'd sweat and break out in hives and it would take her two to three days to recover from being triggered by the confinement.

Lisa felt trapped. She didn't want to let her daughter down. On the other hand, she didn't want to subject herself to being triggered in such an extreme way. Once, while attending a dance concert, she had had a panic attack and had been forced to leave early.

Her daughter was in tears. "Mommy, you left before my best dance."

"But Mommy stayed for most of the concert. Then Mommy got sick and had to go home," Lisa tried to explain.

"But Mommy, you missed the best part. All the other moms stayed for the whole thing. Why couldn't you?"

Lisa felt as if she was being asked to make an impossible choice, between her sanity and her daughter's well-being. Eventually, she had a talk with her daughter and tried to effect a compromise. She said, "I love you very much and am so proud of how well you dance. But it's hard for me to be in any one room for a long time. I can stay for two hours, but I can't stay too much longer. Which two hours would you like me to come?"

"Mommy, I want you there the whole time to see all my dances. Why can't you stay like all the other mommies?"

"Let's see. How can I see all your dances? How about I come for the first part of the concert on Friday night and then I come to the last part on Saturday night? Or, I could come to one of your practices and see the dances. What do you think? And, then, what about if the next day or the weekend after, we have a party for you and your friends to celebrate the wonderful dance performances?"

Lisa's daughter wanted her mother to be "like all the other moms." But Lisa could not be like the other moms, because she had a different history and that history imposed limits on what she could and could not comfortably do. That was the hard reality of the situation. Her daughter had to accept that Lisa was not and could not be a storybook mom, but she would also know that her mother deeply cared for her.

When Lisa divided her obligatory attendance at the dance performance into two parts, and then showered her daughter with extra love by throwing a small party for all the performers, she more than satisfied her daughter's needs. Lisa felt like a responsible and caring mom and her daughter felt that she had a mother who really cared about her.

Lisa could have beaten herself up by telling herself, "I am a failure as a parent because I can't do what other parents can do because of my depression, or PTSD, or other traumatic symptoms." Instead, she told herself, "I need to take care of myself and I need to take care of my responsibilities toward my child. If I think hard enough and even ask others for advice if I have to, I can probably come up with a way to satisfy my need not to become exhausted or triggered, as well as my need to take care of my daughter. I must stop wasting my time beating myself up over things I can't help and try to solve the problem at hand."

If you cannot do what is usually expected, think about what you can contribute that may be equally meaningful, if not necessarily traditional. For example, suppose you are triggered by certain family gatherings and cannot attend as expected. You can send a special gift or make something special for the occasion, a painting, a poem, a flower arrangement, or something uniquely you, and creative. Or perhaps you can contribute in some other manner than a way that triggers you. Not all family members will understand, and you may still be criticized by some, but if you do what you can, that's all you can do, and doing what you can, even if it isn't what is expected or customary in your family, is better than doing nothing.

For example, Bob, a combat vet, saw exchanging holiday presents as a superficial commercial tradition that contradicted the true spirit of Christmas. He saw so much poverty overseas, that when he came home he felt that buying presents for relatives, who already had so much, was a waste of money. For him, buying what he considered to be unnecessary gifts felt like a violation of his values and a betrayal of what his trauma had taught him, which was, an appreciation for human suffering. He thought that all the money he normally would spend on holiday gifts should go to those in need. Yet, exchanging gifts was part of his family's tradition.

What was Bob to do? Be true to himself and alienate his family? Or do what his family expected and betray himself?

After considerable thought, Bob decided to give the amount of money that he would have spent on presents to a local charity in the name of all his relatives He also decided to spend part of Christmas and Thanksgiving at a homeless shelter preparing food for the homeless. In addition, he offered each of his adult relatives two or three nights (or days) of baby-sitting and a day of his time to do house repairs, or chores, whatever they needed done, such as weeding, or washing cars. For the children, he offered to teach them certain games or take them on day trips to museums or parks.

Although some family members did not appreciate Bob's nontraditional gifts, others were delighted and praised him for his humanitarian concerns and his creative gift-giving ideas. The most positive result of Bob's actions was that he didn't alienate himself from his family over the issue of how to celebrate Christmas. Instead of totally rejecting the holidays, which was his first impulse, he modified the holiday traditions to match his values. In his view, he chose the "joy" and left out the "junk."

Initially, Bob's "breaking the rules" about Christmas gift giving caused some concern in the family. But eventually they got used to it. Over time, Bob's gifts of doing gardening and household chores became a tradition in itself. Relatives began talking about how they put off certain chores until the holidays because they were counting on Bob's "fabulous" offer of help. Three years after the start of this new Christmas tradition, Bob's brother, who had made fun of his new ideas about celebrating Christmas, admitted that he had ridiculed Bob because he was jealous of Bob's social consciousness and courage in challenging family traditions.

Much to Bob's surprise, this brother pointed him out to his children as a role model. "See your Uncle Bob. He has the true Christmas spirit. He gives his money to the needy and feeds the homeless on holidays instead of stuffing his face and getting fat like your Daddy," the brother told his children. Then he asked Bob to take his nieces and nephews with him the next time he volunteered at the homeless shelter. He wanted his children to learn to be as socially conscious as Bob.

While you try to find creative untraditional solutions to being a part of a relationship and still respect the limitations imposed on you by your triggers, keep in mind that nothing is forever. What is true now about your limitations regarding certain triggers, as well as what others might want or expect from you, can change over time. For example, five years from now Lisa may have fewer problems with the sense of confinement as a trigger than she does now. She needs to view the problem as a current problem, not a forever problem; she needs to tell her daughter that this year Mommy can't stay for a four-hour concert, but maybe next year she will. Similarly, in the future, Bob may still want to volunteer at shelters to celebrate the holidays, but he also might want to spend the day with his family and do his volunteer work at other times of the year.

How you will be in terms of managing your triggers and what you can and cannot do in the future is unknown. Most likely, the further along you are in the healing process and the better able you are at managing your triggers, the easier it will be for you to relate to others and to fulfill social obligations. Also, over time, as you become more skilled at managing triggers, the process of trigger management will become less taxing, which will leave you more time and energy for meeting your own goals, and for relationships.

To the best of your ability, try to adopt a realistic, neutral attitude towards managing your triggers, no matter how that impinges on your relationships. Think of taking care of your triggers as taking care of physical battle wounds.

For example, Saul has a war-related leg injury that requires two hours of his time a day. If he doesn't do certain exercises and stretches as prescribed, his ability to walk suffers greatly. This means that when he comes home from work, he must take two hours to care for his leg before he can help his children with their homework, be with his wife, go out with friends, or participate in other activities. If he wants to do something that starts right after work, he has to leave work early so he will have the time to take care of his leg.

Saul's family is supportive because war injuries tend to be honored. However, other injuries that are also trauma-related, are not as honored, and tend to be mislabeled and misunderstood. For example, Lisa's high anxiety about being confined is a problem that most people don't understand. Yet her high anxiety is just as much of a "battle scar" of her years of being abused as Saul's wounded leg.

Medical Problems Caused by the Trauma

Trauma often leads to medical problems that need attention. If you have no trauma-related medical problems, then most likely you will have more time and energy for relationships than someone who is struggling with a severe or chronic medical condition.

The interrelationship of the immune system and the brain is well documented (McDaniel et al. 1994). Even under nontraumatic circumstances, the loss of loved ones has been found to suppress the immune system, making the bereaved more susceptible to many illnesses, such as viral infections. Also, stressful life events have been found to correlate with a wide variety of heart problems (McDaniel et al. 1994; *Science News* 1997; Schnurr 1996).

Trauma can give rise to clinical depression or worsen a pre-existing one, and it has been found that some parts of the immune system are affected by depression. Of course, not all people with depression have a lowered immune system, but many do. A 1997 summary of the research on the effects of depression on cancer and heart disease suggests that individuals suffering from depression have a greater risk of developing various kinds of cancer. This is most likely because "depression weakens the immune system's ability to control the spread of cancerous cells" (*Science News* 1997, 15). Although some studies contradict this finding, other studies suggest that depressed people suffer from higher cancer rates because they tend to smoke more to improve their mood. It is their smoking, rather than their weakened immune system, that "accounts for the link between depression and lung cancer" (*Science News* 1997, 15).

The research on the relationship between depression and heart disease is clearer: individuals with major depression are much likelier to suffer from heart attacks (*Science News* 1997; Jiang et al. 1996; McDaniel 1994). There are also several animal studies that indicate when animals are artificially stimulated adrenally, that is, "triggered" by inescapable shock, they tend to become ill at higher rates than other animals. The implication is that when events set off hyperarousal symptoms for trauma survivors who experienced many adrenaline surges during their trauma and afterwards, they may also be subject to contracting more illnesses (McDaniel et al. 1944).

In studying female crime victims, Koss (1991) found that victims, as opposed to nonvictims, reported more health problems. Similarly, Golding (1994), who studied women who had been sexually assaulted, found that the assaulted women were more likely to experience a wide range of medical problems, unrelated to the assault, than women who had never been assaulted. Vietnam veterans have been found to suffer from poorer health than other veterans of that era who did not see combat (Kulka et al. 1990). In a 1996 review of the literature on PTSD and health, Dr. Schnurr of the National Center for PTSD at Dartmouth Medical School concludes that "the literature on trauma and health consistently shows that exposure to trauma is related to poor health outcomes" (Schnurr 1996, 3).

Coping Suggestions

Have you sought medical care for your problem? Are you following medical suggestions related to your problem? Are you doing all you can to help yourself heal from the injury or to manage the medical problem? If you can answer "yes" to all these questions, then you are doing all you can do. If, instead, you have delayed seeking medical help or are not following medical instructions, then you need to ask yourself why not and talk to a professional counselor about why you are harming yourself by not taking the appropriate actions to take care of yourself.

If medical care is not available to you for financial reasons, then you need to call your local social services and see what forms of pubic medical assistance are available to you.

Effects of Substance Abuse and Eating Disorders

If, in the past, you abused controlled substances or suffered from an eating disorder as a way of coping with your trauma, your physical health may have been affected. The longer and the more severely you abused your body with alcohol, drugs, overeating, undereating, or binging and vomiting, the greater the likelihood that today you are coping with the physical consequences of your former addiction. The fact that you have to commit time, energy, and money to take care of any physical or medical problems that resulted from your prior addiction detracts from the time, energy, and money you have for relationships. However, if you do not take care of these problems, your health will suffer, which ultimately will cause an even greater drain on your emotional and physical resources.

Dealing with the medical consequences of a long-term addiction is one of the bitterest pills many trauma survivors have to swallow. Often these consequences are the source of much shame. "It's my fault my teeth are falling out," says a former bulimic whose gums were eroded by the acid left in her mouth after purging. "If I wasn't such an idiot, I wouldn't have hepatitis," says a former alcoholic. "If I didn't share needles, I wouldn't be stuck with Hepatitis C," says a former drug addict.

If you blame yourself for the medical or physical consequences of an addiction acquired in response to your trauma, then you are only sapping your strength further. You probably need to do more work on understanding how your addiction began. As self-destructive as the addiction may have been, it may also have been the only means of survival you had available to you at the time of the trauma or afterwards. This is not an "excuse" for such harmful behavior, but rather a recognition that the addiction didn't give birth to itself: something started it, and often that something was a trauma and lack of support afterwards.

Coping Techniques

For further work on learning to accept your addictive past and its present-day scars, you may want to consult one of the trauma-processing books listed in appendix A or to seek professional help. If you suffer from clinical depression, are subject to depressive episodes during anniversary times of your trauma, or have strong persistent feelings of guilt related to your trauma, these also contribute to your lack of energy. (The subject of guilt is treated more extensively in chapter 6.)

1. Obtain a psychiatric evaluation of your depression and consider the psychiatrist's recommendations. Since psychiatrists often differ in their approach, you may want to obtain a second opinion and then decide which recommendations to follow.

2. Follow the suggestions for coping with depression that are available in any of a number of self-help books on depression, such as *The Depression Workbook* by Mary Ellen Copeland (1992), *Feeling Good: The New Mood Therapy* by David. D. Burns (1980); *First Aid for Depression* by Louis Presnall (1988); *Here Comes the Sun* by Gail Rosellini and Mark Warden (1988); *Waking Up Alive: The Descent, The Suicide Attempt, and the Return,* by Richard Heckler (1994). (See the References section at the end of this chapter for complete references.)

The suggestions in these books include examining negative thinking patterns, an exercise program, a healthy diet, an emotional support network, and structured activities.

Dissociation, Derealization, and Depersonalization

Dissociation, derealization, and depersonalization are forms of emotional and physical numbing common among trauma survivors. Episodes of dissociation, derealization, and depersonalization vary in intensity and duration. Sometimes they last a few minutes, sometimes a few hours, sometimes for years.

There are many kinds of dissociation, but basically dissociation refers to a split between one's mind and body, a disconnection between experience and emotion, like drawing a "blank" emotionally during an emotionally arousing experience. "It's like a glass wall around me," or "It's like I'm outside my body observing myself," or "It's like I know I should be feeling something but I don't feel anything" or "I have no idea what I'm feeling," are some of the ways that trauma survivors describe dissociation.

Derealization and depersonalization involve feeling dead, mechanical, and disconnected from your emotions, body, and mind. Depersonalization refers to periods of time where you feel you aren't a person or that others aren't people. You feel more like a robot than a thinking, feeling, living person. During periods of derealization, you don't feel as if you, or what is going on around you, is real. There's an altered sense of time and a feeling of detachment, as if you were watching a movie about these moving objects called people. Nothing feels real, not even yourself. "I feel as if I'm in a dream," or "I feel like I'm in a play, and I don't even know if the play is real or not," some survivors have said about this state.

During states of dissociation, derealization, or depersonalization, as with other forms of numbing, the experiences of pain and fear are lessened. For example, suppose someone cut a large hole in your leg. In a state of dissociation, derealization, or depersonalization, you would see your blood flowing and not feel much fear, or pain. Your attitude towards your wounded leg would be detached and analytical, rather than emotional. Instead of becoming anxious and scared, which would be appropriate to the situation and which would propel you to seek medical care, you would calmly observe your blood flowing and feel little physical pain or concern about your well-being.

During these states, there is little motivation to take care of yourself, or others, except in a mechanical way. These states, only briefly described here, make it difficult to be emotionally and mentally present. Your body may be present, but emotionally you feel dead, and mentally you are confused, disoriented, and have trouble remembering. Your thought processes are slowed down and it's hard to concentrate or to make plans. These are the times when you might forget what you are doing or what you planned to do or when you may say things to others that, later on, you won't be able to remember.

These states are dreadful because you can lose so much control over yourself. In extreme states of dissociation, for example, survivors can be driving and forget where they are going or not remember what they did for hours at a time. "It was 9 p.m. when I came home, then for six hours I don't know what I did. Before I knew it, it was 3 a.m. I couldn't tell you what I did, where I went, if I had dinner, watched TV, or took a bath," states Sarah. Sarah had dissociated for six hours. Because she is subject to dissociative spells, Sarah doesn't make promises to others. She's afraid she won't be able to keep them. She is afraid of making any kind of commitment to do anything, because she may dissociate and not be able to follow through.

When you are in a state of dissociation, depersonalization, or derealization, relating to others is very hard. It takes so much work to overcome the inertia, confusion, apathy, and self-focus of these states and concentrate on what another person is saying or doing, that the decision to withdraw makes perfect sense. Yet many survivors forge on and, in the midst of depersonalization or derealization episodes, continue trying to relate to co-workers, friends, partners, children, and others. Usually, they are driven by a sense of obligation toward these others or by a determination not to let their symptoms interfere with their lives. However, when they heroically try to fight their natural tendency to isolate and just "give in" to these numbing states, they may find that their abilities to think, respond, or even talk, have been impaired. Then, although they try even harder, they find themselves becoming more and more tired. These states are energy-draining, no matter how determined one might be to not let them "win."

Coping Suggestions

Professional Help: It is beyond the scope of this book to discuss treatment for dissociation, derealization, or depersonalization except to emphasize that professional assistance aimed at examining trauma-related issues, which are the root causes of these states, is mandatory.

Using a Support Network: It also helps to be aware of these episodes—to document them in some way and to be able to talk about them while you are in them. If you have friends or family members who live with you or nearby who could be supportive, you could share what you are feeling with them. If you don't, then you need to develop a telephone support group of people you can call when you are feeling distressed.

These individuals need to be screened carefully, in that you want to minimize the probability of calling when you are feeling hurt or disoriented, only to be hurt further by a nonsupportive response. You need to know enough about these individuals to feel sure they would be understanding if you call at a difficult time. Have they talked with you about PTSD, depression, dissociation, or trauma in ways that indicate they feel compassion for those who suffer from these disorders? Are they in therapy or recovery programs themselves?

It is important to have an understanding with the members of your telephone support group about your calls. Are they willing to accept calls from you? Are there restrictions on when they will not accept calls from you? If they are unable to take your call, for whatever reason, how can this be handled so as not to cause you further stress? What if you call them and *they* are experiencing a depression or otherwise need help? Are you willing to help them? Can you spell out these issues well in advance of ever calling to avoid misunderstandings and hurt feelings in the future?

You need at least five (ideally ten) people on your telephone support list, which you can carry with you at all times. You need people you can call at various times of the day or night on that list. Perhaps there are people who work at night, or are usually up very late at night, who would be willing to accept calls from you.

When you call, you don't have to describe the specifics of your trauma or any other intimate details of your life. All you need to do is share how your are feeling at the moment and whatever conflicts you are feeling inside. For example, you could call someone in your telephone support network and say:

"Today I feel like a piece of wood. I'm going through the motions of living, but I have no feeling. I hate this! How long is this going to last? How do I know what I'm supposed to do next when I'm like this? Should I cancel my plans for this evening and stay home alone, numb, where no one can see me and I can take it easy, or I should I push myself to go out and be with people. If I stay home, it'll be okay, up to a certain point. Then I'll get lonely. But if I go out, I might feel more miserable because I can't mix like others and I might get so tired from trying and pretending that I won't be able to drive home."

Your support friend might help you figure out how to handle whatever situation lies before you. The following exercise is intended to help you deal with relationships when you are in one of these states.

✍️ Exercise: Partial Involvement

If you are going through a period of frequent dissociation, derealization, or depersonalization episodes, what should you do about being with others? At such a time, your natural tendency is to withdraw, which is perfectly understandable given your limited resources for relating to others and your fears that you may not be able to talk or act or feel the way you think you should. That is, why go to dinner with someone when you feel so empty within? You have nothing to say and are afraid you couldn't even pretend to be interested in what the other person has to say.

Many trauma survivors have entire storerooms of excuses for withdrawing from social engagements or getting away from their families when they are going through one of these states. Choosing not to be with others can be a self-protecting alternative. However, if you can avoid thinking of the social situation ahead of you in "all-or-nothing" terms, you might be able to be with others. You have more than just the two choices of (1) avoid others or (2) be with others and do everything you think is expected of you.

When faced with attending a social situation or answering an invitation, you need to examine it carefully to figure out if there is a way you can restructure it so that it might be manageable for you. One way is to limit the time or the demands made upon you. The truth is you do have a limitation; for whatever reason, you're dissociating or struggling with feelings of unreality. But that doesn't necessarily mean you have to hide in your room (or the basement) until these states lift. When you try to decide whether to interact with another person or stay by yourself, consider the following factors:

1. Limiting Time
   Would it help to limit the time of the social interaction? For example, if you are invited to a party from 9 p.m. to 2 a.m., could you go for two hours and not feel as if you had to stay for the entire event? If you are invited to a three-hour play at a theater which is an hour away, can you suggest a two-hour movie at a theater near your home instead? If someone wants to have lunch and then go to a museum with you, can you tell that person you can have lunch, or go to the museum, but you can't do both?

If you're low on psychic energy, but still want to be with other people, and you know you can't handle a lengthy situation, try to estimate the amount of time you could handle and make arrangements to socialize just for that amount of time.

2. Structuring Activities to Meet Your Needs
   Some social activities are much more demanding than others, especially when you are feeling numb. For example, it's easier to go to a movie or watch a video with someone than to have a deep conversation, a political argument, or make love. When you're feeling numb, try to find ways to structure activities so that they are low-key and relatively nondemanding. This may not always be possible, but if there's some way to participate without feeling overly stressed, it could be worth a try.

   If you would like company, but don't want to feel you have to "perform" or "give" a lot, spectator sports and entertainments or activities where the focus isn't on the relationship, but on something external, are often easier to manage when you're feeling numb.

3. Having an Exit
   No matter what it is you plan to do, have an exit plan. If you are following some of the suggestions in this book and trying to get out of the prison of isolation, no matter how well you pre-think the situation to avoid being triggered or overwhelmed, you never know how you might react or what unplanned event might occur. You are experimenting—finding out what you can handle and what is just not worth the effort. In the process of experimenting socially, you may make a few miscalculations. You might find yourself in a situation that you need to remove yourself from as quickly as possible and to do that, you need a plan.

   If there is one "rule" trauma survivors should remember before they do anything, it's to have a way out. The essence of trauma is being trapped, being held captive in an intolerable situation. If you are socializing and you start to feel an extreme state of dissociation or derealization begin, and you think you can't leave the situation or you don't have a plan for doing so, then you will feel you are in a state of entrapment reminiscent of your trauma, which will only heighten your symptoms.

   If you are out socially and you find that you need to be alone, be ready to excuse yourself in a manner that is respectful of the others, as well as yourself. You don't need to expose your vulnerabilities to others and take the chance that you might be misunderstood. For example, you don't need to say, "I have PTSD because I was traumatized and I'm going through mood swings and depersonalization reactions because it's the anniversary of such and such." Most people won't know what you are talking about and they will ask questions and you will end up having to talk about your trauma and your traumatic reactions, which will only make you feel more anxious or exhausted. When you are already feeling out of control and need to be surrounded by quiet and in an environment where you are in control, that is not the time to tell your story.

Instead, you can simply say, "I'm sorry. I'm not feeling well and need to leave. This is unexpected. I had hoped to stay longer, but I can't. Thank you for having me."

This type of statement is not an "excuse" or a lie. Every word is true. You are not feeling well. You didn't plan it and you wish you could stay longer.

You can even set the stage to make it easier on yourself. For instance, if you plan to go to a party, meeting, or any sort of gathering, don't promise to stay for the entire event, for then if you have to leave, you will feel you have broken your promise in addition to your other difficulties. When you accept the invitation, or before you go to the event, you can (if you want to) tell the host or hostess that you're planning to come, but you don't know how long you can stay. (This is the truth, isn't it?) Or you could tell your friend in advance that you may need to leave early. You don't have to tell a lie or give elaborate excuses or explain why you may need to leave early, all you need to say is the truth: you may need to leave early.

If you set the stage for leaving early, when you make your exit (if you need to), your departure is expected and thus less abrupt. If you are going somewhere with someone, discuss the possibility that you may need to leave at an earlier time *before* the event, not *at* the event. If you are riding with others and you think you may need to leave before they do, arrange for alternative transportation home in advance, so you know you can leave if you want to. This is called taking care of yourself.

Low Self-Worth and Lack of Assertiveness

Trauma engenders low self-esteem and lack of assertiveness in many people, especially in women. Even if you had self-esteem issues and were not assertive before your trauma, the trauma probably lowered your self-esteem even further and made you less assertive than ever. Traumatized women have particular problems with being assertive because of their cultural conditioning to put the needs of others first and to be submissive and obedient. To be assertive means to express opinions, to ask for one's needs to be met, and to stand up for one's rights. Women who were physically, sexually, or emotionally abused, especially if this abuse took place when they were children, learned that it was dangerous to speak up, about anything, much less their needs.

Like women, soldiers are expected to be obedient. Self-assertion is not a military value. Hence, many combat veterans lack assertiveness skills, as do survivors of refugee and concentration camps and survivors of all kinds of family violence.

In relationships, we seek to meet our needs for companionship, validation, protection, and connection and to meet those needs in others. If your low self-esteem and your lack of assertiveness interfere with your ability to ask for your needs to be met, speak freely, or stand up for your rights, then it is no wonder that relating to others may seem unappealing, and that interacting with others leaves you feeling drained, rather than fulfilled.

Coping Suggestions

Low self-esteem needs to be dealt with in a therapeutic context where the full meaning of the effects of the trauma on all the aspects of your life is carefully examined. Assertiveness skills can be learned from self-help books or from courses offered by the community or by mental health associations. But only when you feel you deserve to be assertive will you actually use those skills.

Guilt

Trauma is the breeding ground for all kinds of guilt—survivor guilt, moral guilt, competency guilt, and other kinds of guilt. Feeling that you deserve the esteem, affection, and care of another is difficult when you are burdened with guilt. Separating from and setting limits on others, as well as standing up for one's rights in a relationship are also complicated by the feelings of guilt and shame that are the legacy of the trauma. In every way, guilt is psychically exhausting and can make relationships seem as if they are more trouble than they are worth. (See chapter 6 for an extended discussion of guilt.)

Reenactment and Revictimization

When a trauma has not been adequately processed and the feelings and belief systems associated with the trauma have not been brought into conscious awareness, trauma survivors are subject to reenacting their traumas in their relationships and being revictimized by others. Needless to say, both reenactment and revictimization make life even more difficult and contribute to an overall lack of psychic energy. (See chapter 12 for a more complete discussion of these subjects.)

Relationships with Those Who Died During the Trauma

If you lost someone (or more than one) during your trauma, even though that person is dead, your relationship with him/her is still a part of you. Even if you have truly grieved the loss, you still have a relationship. He or she may no longer be alive, but if the person who died really mattered to you, to some extent you still have a relationship.

However, if you haven't fully grieved the loss of that person or you feel guilt or other troubling feelings about him or her, then he/she may actually be an active part of your current emotional life, even though dead. Those feelings may be affecting your relationships with people who are alive today. Your relationship with the dead may even be a source of comfort, validation, and strength for you. Nevertheless, it may drain energy away from your current relationships and prevent you from asking for comfort, validation, and having your needs met from the people who are currently part of your life.

For some trauma survivors, an ongoing active relationship with someone who died during the trauma competes with the need to form relationships in the present. There is a difference between having some small part of your psychic energy bound forever to those whom you lost during your trauma, and having the largest part of your psyche preoccupied with thinking about, talking to, or living for those who are gone. Your relationship with your dead may be a major deterrent to your ability to become involved with others in your present-day life.

✍ Exercise: Accurate Labeling

Go back to the first exercises in this chapter and reread your journal pages where you listed the terrible names you call yourself and the negative conclusions you came to about your social skills and social desirability. Then, after reading this chapter about the various causes of low psychic energy, on a fresh sheet of paper, re-evaluate the way you described yourself and the vision you have for yourself in the future.

Sample:

I no longer believe that I am _____ (include the names you used from The Terrible Names You Call Yourself exercise) or forever doomed to _____ (include negative conclusions you drew about your life in the Monitoring the Negative Self exercise, the second exercise in this chapter).

After reading this chapter, I believe that the following factors contribute to my social withdrawal: _____,
_____, _____.

To the best of my ability, I plan to take the following three steps to boost my psychic energy level:

1. _____

2. _____

3. _____

References

Burns, David. 1980. *Feeling Good: The New Mood Therapy.* New York: Signet Books.

Copeland, Mary Ellen. 1992. *The Depression Workbook*. Oakland, CA: New Harbinger Publications.

Golding, J. M. 1994. "Sexual Assault History and Physical Health in Randomly Selected Los Angeles Women. *Health Psychology* 13: 14–138.

Heckler, Richard. 1994. *Waking Up Alive: The Descent, the Suicide Attempt, and the Return*. New York: Grosset Putnam Books.

Jiang, Wei, B. Michael, D. Krantz, R. Waugh, E. Coleman, M. Hanson, D. Frid, S. McNutly, J. Morris, C. O'Conner, and J. Blumenthal. 1996. "Mental Stress-Induced Myocardial Ischemia and Cardiac Events." *Journal of the American Medical Association* 275:21 1651–1656.

Kardiner, A. 1941. *The Traumatic Neuroses of War*. New York: Hoeber.

Koss, M. P., P. Koss, and W. Woodruff. 1991. "Deleterious Effects of Criminal Victimization on Women's Health and Medical Utilization." Archives of Internal Medicine 151:342–347.

Kulka, R., W. Schlenger, J. Fairbank, B. Jordan, C. Marmar, and D. Weiss. 1990. *Trauma and the Vietnam War Generation: Report of findings from the National Vietnam Veterans Readjustment Study*. New York: Brunner-Mazel.

McDaniel, Stephen, M. Moran, J. Levenson, and A. Stoudiemire. 1994. "Psychological Factors Affecting Medical Conditions." In *The American Psychiatric Press Textbook of Psychiatry*, Second Edition. Eds. R. Hales, S. Yadofsky and J. Talbott. Washington, D. C. : The American Psychiatric Press.

Presnall, Louis. 1988. *First Aid for Depression*. Center City, MN: Hazeldon Educational Materials.

Reite, Martin and Tiffany Field, Eds. 1985. *The Psychobiology of Attachment and Separation*. New York: The Academic Press, Inc., Harcourt Brace Jovanovich, Publishers.

Rosellini, Gail and M. Warden. 1988. *Here Comes the Sun*. Center City, MN; Hazeldon Educational Materials.

Rosenheck, Robert and Jane Thomson. 1986. "Detoxification of Vietnam War Trauma: A Combined Individual Approach." *Family Process* 559–570.

Schnurr, Paula. 1996. "Trauma, PTSD and Physical Health." *PTSD Research Quarterly* 7(3):1–7.

Science News. 1997. "Depression Puffs Up Lung Cancer and May Lie Heavy on the Heart." 151.

Sigall, John J. 1976. "Effects of Paternal Exposure to Prolonged Stress on the Mental Health of the Spouse and Children," *Canadian Psychiatric Association Journal* vol. 21 169–172.

Sigall, John J. and Vivian Rakoff. 1971. "Concentration Camp Survival: A Pilot Study of Effects on the Second Generation. "*Canadian Psychiatric Association Journal* vol. 16 393–397.

6

Guilt

Trauma-related guilt can powerfully stunt both personal growth and relationships. Although guilt is no longer considered a symptom of post-traumatic stress disorder, it is very common among trauma survivors. For example, in a survey of formerly battered women and combat veterans Kubany (1996) found that very few of these trauma survivors were guilt-free. One-half of the formerly battered women reported moderate or greater guilt in relation to being abused and one in four reported considerable guilt about being beaten. Less than four percent of the battered women he interviewed felt no guilt at all. Among the combat veterans, two out of three reported moderate to great guilt in relation to their war experiences. The percentages were even higher among combat veterans who were seeking professional help.

What Is Guilt?

Although there are many definitions of guilt, in this chapter, the definition used is Kubany's. He defines *guilt* as a negative feeling state that is triggered by the belief that one should have thought, felt, or acted differently (1996). Trauma is a fertile breeding ground for the many types of guilt that are described below.

Survivor Guilt

Survivor guilt is a form of self-blame. Do you feel guilty because you made it out alive and others did not? Perhaps you feel guilty because you were less injured than others? It is not uncommon for trauma survivors to feel this way.

Survivor guilt is not just compassion for those who suffered more than you did. It is also a way of saying, "If I had suffered more, they would have suffered less." Such thinking is not logical, but it makes emotional sense. It can be a defense against the pain you felt at seeing others hurt. Survivor guilt hearkens back to atavistic notions about sacrificing to the gods to assure a desired outcome. The idea is that by punishing yourself, you can undo the damage or, at least, keep bad things from happening again. But, of course, the world doesn't really work that way.

Survivor guilt also involves gratitude. But it is difficult to accept being grateful that it was someone else who suffered. "It sounds heartless," survivors will say, "but if someone had to die, I'm glad it was someone else, not me." However hard this feeling is to face, it is nothing more than an expression of the natural and vital instinct for self-preservation.

Competency Guilt

Competency guilt involves feeling guilty for not having acted as efficiently or as wisely as you think you should have acted. In truth, you may not have been functioning at your best or meeting your personal performance standards during your trauma. However, you need to consider the bigger picture—the fact that you were operating under traumatic conditions.

As Kubany (1996) points out, different decision-making rules apply during trauma than during everyday life. In the first place, trauma is usually both unexpected and chaotic. Even though your senses may have been on hyperalert, there is usually so much going on during a trauma, and at such a rapid pace, that no one person can accurately observe all that is taking place. A whole team of people would be needed to obtain a more complete view of the situation and come up afterwards with a list of viable options and an effective plan of action.

If, for instance, you were held up by an armed bandit, you most likely found yourself focused on his gun, not his face or clothing. You may or may not have seen that there was another gunman with him, or that there was a police officer one block away. Such information could have influenced what you decided to do or not do. But all the information necessary for the best possible decision wasn't available to you, because under traumatic conditions there is a tendency to pay attention only to the most life-threatening aspect of the situation. In the mugging situation, for example, your attention would probably have been focused on the gun—not on any other aspects of the situation— because that gun had the power to destroy you.

In the second place, during a trauma, time is precious. You do not have the luxury of brainstorming alternatives and carefully examining all of the options available before you make a decision. If you are running away from a rapist or a mugger, or have only a few seconds to escape from a fire or flood, you can't think of all your options and carefully select the best one. You have to act right away, or risk death or injury, to yourself or others. You also have to act under the following constraints:

1. Without having the time to ask those who may know more about what to do.

2. At a time when your mind may not be functioning at its best, because of the terror and stress.

3. At a time when strong emotions, such as fear and panic, take over and you have no choice but to endure them and try to make a good decision in spite of how you feel.

Hindsight Bias

Kubany (1994, 1996) defines hindsight bias as the tendency to think you were smarter than you actually were during the trauma, or to think that you knew things while you were living through the trauma that you understood only after the trauma had ended. For example, trauma survivors tend to evaluate what they did or didn't do based on the information they *currently* have about the outcome of the trauma or on options they thought of long after the trauma was over, rather than on the information they actually had and options they thought of during the time of the trauma itself.

For example, a man in an war-ravaged city that was almost depleted of food, water, and medical care decided to send his family to a rural hiding place. He loaded his family on a truck bound for a small village and thought they were safe, only to find out later that the truck had been ambushed and all the passengers killed. He blames himself for not anticipating that the truck could have been ambushed, and for not considering that had he thought the truck might be captured, he would have kept his family with him.

His intention was to save his family, not to send them to their deaths. But his hindsight bias has resulted in a deep and abiding sense of guilt.

Other Causes of Trauma-Related Guilt

There are many possible causes of guilt. Guilt can result from religious beliefs, personal moral convictions, or even "brainwashing" by a more powerful person or group. There is also guilt by association, when a person feels guilty for acts he/she did not commit or even see as desirable, but for which that person feels guilty because of being associated with a person or group that committed those acts. For example, some German citizens feel guilt by association for the Holocaust, even though they were not even born until twenty years after World War II. Similarly, some veterans feel guilt for atrocities committed by their comrades, even though they themselves refrained from the abuse of military violence.

Catch-22 Situations

Trauma is full of lose-lose situations, where all the choices available are unacceptable or involve a violation of personal ethics. Usually, no matter what choice you make, you must betray yourself, or an important value. The battered wife who leaves her husband may feel guilty for depriving her children of a father and a comfortable standard of living. But if she chooses to stay, she may feel guilty for exposing her children to violence and to a chaotic lifestyle. The combat veteran who shot a grenade-laden toddler may feel guilty about having killed a child. But if he hadn't killed the child and the grenades had gone off and killed his squad, then he would feel guilty about not having prevented the deaths of his comrades.

The mother of a teenage boy who committed suicide may feel guilty about not having supervised her son's every move. If only she had kept tighter control over him, she could have caught him before he took that overdose of pills. On the other hand, if she had kept watch over her son every minute, she would have felt guilty about not permitting him the freedom to enjoy the activities and friendships that gave her son some pleasure. Also, she would have been told by others that she was adding to his depression by being "overcontrolling" and not allowing him enough autonomy.

Kubany calls this type of guilt "Catch-22" guilt because no matter what choice is made, there is an undesirable outcome (1994, 1996). In these situations, the least bad choice is the best choice, but trauma survivors rarely view matters in this way. They tend to evaluate their choice against a wished-for, magical, or unrealistic ideal choice that was not available at the time of the trauma (Kubany 1996). Until they can examine their behavior, feelings, and thoughts in a rational light, their suffering from guilt may be enormous. Indeed, this type of guilt is often at the root of substance abuse problems, eating disorders, and suicidal depressions.

Difficulty Making Amends

In everyday life, when people do something they feel guilty about, they sometimes try to make themselves feel less guilty by making amends for what they believe they did wrong. But with trauma, there might not be a way to make amends, because some of the losses are irreversible. If you steal five dollars from your mother's purse, you can give her back the five dollars. But if you drive the car that slams into a truck and your mother, who is riding with you, loses her life, there is no way you can make amends to her.

Trauma involves irreversible losses. Amends cannot be made if the trauma involves death, dismemberment, physical or mental disability, or other forms of permanent damage. All too often there is no way to make up for the damage you think you caused. Therefore, you are stuck carrying your guilt with no way to lighten the load. Under such circumstances, it is easy to carry that unresolved guilt into your present-day relationships—your relationship with yourself and with others.

Guilt Over Helplessness and Powerlessness

Some trauma survivors feel guilty about having been helpless and powerless during the trauma; but being helpless and powerless in the face of great danger is the defining characteristic of trauma. Because people prefer to believe that they are able to control their lives, it is easier to blame themselves for negative events than to acknowledge that life is sometimes unfair and that innocent people often are victimized for no reason at all.

Guilt Over the Fight-Flight-Freeze
Response or Other Reactions to Trauma

Some trauma survivors feel guilty about having intense fight-flight-freeze reactions. or other strong emotional or physical reactions. (See chapter 4 on the physiology of trauma.) Yet all of these reactions are involuntary. The combat medic whose hands trembled as the result of extreme combat trauma didn't choose to develop those tremors. The rescue worker who became overwhelmed with fear didn't choose to be afraid. The rape victim who "froze" and couldn't defend herself didn't choose to "freeze." On the other hand, the rape victim who did fight back didn't choose to become enraged by an adrenaline surge, attack her attacker, and then be beaten for it.

Sexual abuse survivors may feel guilt if they become sexually aroused during the abuse. Yet sexual arousal as a result of sexual stimulation is not an act of will or choice, but an involuntary, biologically programmed, hard-wired, physical response. Nevertheless, guilt over involuntary reactions such as these can last a lifetime.

Examining Guilt

Examining your trauma-related guilt is an important part of your trauma-processing therapy. In your individual or group therapy or recovery program, it is critical for you to examine the different ways you feel guilty about how you acted (or didn't act), how you felt (or didn't feel), or what you thought (or didn't think) during the trauma. If you have survived more than one traumatic incident, then the guilt involved in each incident may need to be examined.

Healing involves a realistic appraisal of what your options were during the trauma. It isn't fair to judge what you did, felt, or thought by some fantasy or ideal that was not available to you. For example, if you feel someone in your family committed suicide partly because your family did not have the funds to provide good mental health care, then judging what you did or did not do for the deceased according to an ideal situation, where you had unlimited funds or unlimited time off from work to take care of that person, is neither a fair nor logical standard.

Not all guilt is bad and there may be aspects of your trauma about which you feel, for personal reasons, that you should feel guilty. It is more likely, however, that there are many parts of your trauma about which you deserve to feel less guilt, or no guilt at all.

This major issue, dealing with your guilt, belongs to the realm of your individualized trauma-processing work and will not be covered in this book. Some of the books listed in appendix A provide guidance on examining guilt in the light of the realities of trauma. The chapter called "Honoring What You Did to Survive," in *The Courage to Heal* by Laura Davis and Ellen Bass, and numerous exercises in *The Courage to Heal Workbook* by Laura Davis and in *I Can't Get Over It* by Aphrodite Matsakis deal directly with trauma-related guilt. The exercises in this chapter focus on how guilt affects your relationships.

The Issue of Shame

For trauma survivors, the issue of shame is closely related to the issue of guilt. *Shame* can be defined as feeling unacceptable, not good enough, and, quite possibly, of never being good enough. Shame is the deeply felt fear expressed in the following sentences: "If they really knew me, they would despise and reject me. It's the fear of being rejected by others" (Valerio 1997). Like the issue of guilt, the issue of shame belongs to the realm of individual trauma-processing work and will not be covered in this book. Some of the books listed in appendix A address this issue.

How Trauma-Related Guilt Affects Relationships

Your trauma-related guilt could be so strong that you not only feel that no one could ever love or care for you, but that you don't deserve love either. There may be people in your life who care for you a great deal, or who are beginning to show signs of caring for you and who could possibly come to care about you even more (if you let them). Yet you might find yourself seeking ways to reject these people or keep them at arm's length.

There are many ways to cancel someone's affection for you, whether that affection is familial, platonic, or romantic. You may be doing things that alienate others without conscious intent—perhaps because of trauma-related guilt.

Alienating Others

You may find yourself doing things that alienate others and be surprised at your own behavior. For example, you may not return phone calls, or you may show up late or not show up at all for a planned date, or you may disregard a previously agreed-upon agenda. You may even find yourself paying no attention to the known needs of the other person. If you are burdened with trauma-related guilt, the roots of such behavior are very likely much deeper and more complex than simple self-centeredness, sheer insensitivity, or outright cruelty. Those roots lie in your need to create emotional distance and in your ambivalent feelings about being close to anyone.

You may want to be close, but be afraid to trust or not be sure how much to trust the other person. Or, when you begin to get close, your trauma-related guilt surfaces and tells you that you don't deserve to be close or that it's dangerous to be close because you might reveal aspects of yourself about which you feel great shame or guilt.

Your reasons for pushing others away may have very painful origins. Nevertheless, not showing up as planned, not returning calls, not adhering to previously agreed-upon plans, and not being considerate of the other person's needs send a powerful message. These behaviors communicate that you don't care much about the other peoples' time, feelings, or your relationships with them. Obviously, insulting or physically attacking other people or their property communicates the same message.

Another way trauma survivors create distance for themselves is to start a quarrel over trivial or meaningless matters. Instead of saying, "I need space or quiet time," you may hurl an insult or say or do something that you know will trigger a negative response. Although unpleasantries result, you will have achieved the goal of emotional distance.

How much easier it would be to simply say, "Look, I need a little time to myself right now. I'm not rejecting you, neither am I angry with you. I simply don't have the energy to relate to you right now." But if, deep down, you feel guilty or ashamed of something related to your trauma, then you may feel you don't deserve to have your needs for personal space and quiet respected.

It's all too easy to start a quarrel and blame the disagreement on something the other person did, then realize later on that you started the conflict. You will then probably feel guilty about your behavior and realize that you were taking out your frustrations with yourself on the other person. What you may not realize, however, is that your guilt about hurting or distancing someone who wants to be close to you is a way of *punishing* yourself for whatever trauma-related guilt you still carry deep within your heart. In essence, you feel guilty about some aspect of your trauma, and to punish yourself you become involved in situations that create more guilt, present-day guilt, for which you can punish yourself again. It's a vicious cycle.

Present-Day Guilt as a Punishment for Trauma-Related Guilt

Here, present-day guilt is used as a punishment for trauma-related guilt, and it is a powerful punishment, indeed, for few feelings are as horrible as guilt. For many trauma survivors, feelings of guilt and shame quickly become transformed into either depression, or rage. If the rage is acted upon, for example, if you yell at or verbally or physically abuse someone, destroy property, or hurt animals, then you create even more guilt in yourself, which leads to more anger, which leads to more guilt, and thus a self-perpetuating cycle is established. Your partner, child, or friend is also a part of this cycle, in that after an unpleasant encounter, that person is less likely to be considerate of your feelings or to show you affection, or he/she might even retaliate in certain ways, any of which may provoke greater anger from you.

The uncaring or hostile reactions of others may make you mad; but, fundamentally, you may feel that you deserve the rejections or hostile treatment you receive from others. Not only did you "cause" these people to be angry with you because of the way you treated them, but on a level that you may not even be aware of, you may believe that you *deserve* rejection and anger, as a punishment for something that happened during your trauma.

The Death Taint

Trauma-related guilt not only can make you feel as if you don't deserve the support and love of others, it can also make you feel that you should not get close to other people for their own good. Some survivors of war or other traumas involving death feel as if they carry a "death taint." If you were in a trauma where many people died and, to some extent you feel guilty about some aspects of those deaths, you may fear that if you become close to someone, that person will be affected by your "death taint" and will also die. The thinking goes, "If I love you and get close to you, then you may die. So, if I truly love you, I will stay away to save you."

Some trauma survivors sincerely fear that, as punishment for their incompetence or some other aspect of the trauma about which they feel guilty, their loved ones or people they are close to will be injured or die. For example, when Joe's wife developed cancer, he was certain that the cause of his wife's illness was the fact that he had killed women during his participation in the Vietnam War. After his wife died, he never remarried, or even dated, because he was sure that any woman he loved would be punished for his sins. He even withdrew from his children for fear that being near them might cause them to come to harm.

Pointing out to Joe that many soldiers killed female civilians or female combatants during their tours of duty, and that few of these soldiers' wives died, did not convince Joe that he was not responsible for his wife's death. Joe could have benefited from more counseling but he quit therapy abruptly, saying that he didn't even deserve to receive help.

If someone in your family becomes ill, dies, has a major mishap, or even a minor disappointment, you may feel that you are the cause of it because of your trauma-related guilt. Despite all evidence to the contrary, you may feel convinced that you are responsible for your niece being raped, your son flunking math, your partner developing a chronic illness, or your cousin's house being destroyed in a flood. People who feel guilty expect to be punished and there is no bigger punishment than for something awful to befall someone you love, especially to one of your children.

You may conclude, therefore, that it's best not to get close to others, for when they are hurt (because of you), you don't want to feel the pain of feeling responsible. You fear that if you feel the depth of that pain, you may want to commit suicide, hurt someone or destroy property as a form of revenge, or lose your mind. Such fears are realistic because, in fact, sometimes the precipitating event that causes some trauma survivors to plunge into a deep depression, have a psychotic breakdown, or come close to suicide or homicide is the misfortune or death of a loved one. Too often, the trauma survivors feel they are responsible for the tragedies due to their trauma-related guilt and feelings of carrying a "death taint."

The alternative possibility is that when someone close to you gets hurt, you may be surprised to find that you feel no emotion at all; that you feel "shutdown" and not sympathetic. Then, you may feel subhuman because you don't feel any concern about a loved one's misfortune. Such a response only convinces you that what your trauma taught you was right: You are "damaged goods," an inferior kind of person who is fated to suffer and to cause suffering. This kind of thinking can launch you into a deep depression, or a rage reaction, either of which will render you emotionally unavailable to those persons who are hurting and counting on you for assistance during the current crisis.

Your inability to respond as you would like to during the immediate crisis may remind you of your trauma when you were similarly unable to respond as you would have liked, and where you felt helpless and powerless to save either yourself or others. Even though the current situation may not be a hopeless one, and even though there may be many ways that you could be helpful, your past guilt can paralyze you into a form of inertia and fear that is both humiliating, and infuriating. Once again, you aren't acting, feeling, or thinking in an adequate way. The present can feel just like a replay of the past and, once again, you find yourself living in hell.

If you are fortunate, the people around you are understanding. But if they don't understand your trauma-related reactions and become critical or angry with you for not helping or not even displaying emotion, you are made to feel guiltier. This added guilt can cause you to "tune out" even further emotionally, or to leave the situation (which causes more anger and hurt in the others), or to explode. Or, you may be tempted to return to alcohol, drugs, or a food or gambling addiction. This scenario illustrates the wreckage that can be caused by unexamined trauma-related guilt.

Building an emotional wall around yourself is another consequence of trauma-related guilt. You fear becoming close to others because if you become truly comfortable and relaxed around another person, one day you may talk about aspects of the trauma about which you feel guilt and shame. Then that person may reject or leave you. You don't trust that you can have a close relationship and not, inadvertently, mention something about the trauma that will frighten or disgust the other person. As a result, you wall out other people, or are very guarded about how close you let anyone come to you.

Lack of Assertiveness

Another reason you may distance yourself from others is that your trauma-related guilt prevents you from being assertive or for standing up for your rights in a relationship. If you have trouble expressing your opinions or desires, or stopping others when they hurt or take advantage of you, it's no wonder that you would rather stay to yourself.

Although lack of assertiveness can have many origins, trauma-related guilt can also play a role. On some level, you may feel you deserve pain and suffering and that you don't deserve to have choices in a relationship because of the guilt you carry over the trauma. As a result of such guilt, some survivors allow themselves to be financially exploited by a wide range of persons, from employers and friends, to family members, intimates, or members of their therapy or support groups. Some trauma survivors have even been taken advantage of by their physicians or therapists.

Anthony, a police officer, feels considerable guilt about the death of one of his fellow police officers and about having shot and wounded people in the line of duty. As a result, when others don't repay the money he has lent them, he says nothing. Joanne, the mother of a teenager who committed suicide is the same way. She lets people borrow her belongings and money and says nothing when these items aren't returned. She also permits her living children to verbally abuse her and her employer to sexually harass her. On some level, she feels she doesn't deserve respect, because, in her distorted, guilt-ridden view, the reason her son killed himself was because she was a failure as a mother. Similarly, Allen stayed in an emotionally and sexually dead marriage for ten years, because, in his own words, "I feel so guilty about what happened during the trauma."

Although traumatic experiences cause some people to seek revenge by exploiting or harming others, many of the people I work with are so burdened with guilt that they stay enmeshed in unrewarding, or even punishing, relationships. Often they are unable to protect themselves from financial and other forms of exploitation or mistreatments; or they sabotage positive, nurturing relationships, due their to trauma-related guilt.

For example, it is not uncommon for trauma-survivors with intense trauma-related guilt to abdicate many of their financial and custody rights during divorce proceedings. They feel they don't deserve justice; they are more concerned about causing harm to others than being harmed themselves. If they feel there is a possibility that they might injure their ex-spouse or the children, this evokes guilt about harm they believe they caused or could have prevented during the trauma. Whether they actually caused or could have prevented that harm during the trauma is, to them, irrelevant. What is relevant is that they believe they could have—and that belief results in guilt. This guilt continues to play a major role in their in their present-day decisions.

Overgiving and Separation Difficulties

Two other ways trauma-related guilt manifest in a relationship are (1) overgiving, which can reflect a generous spirit, but also be an attempt to atone for trauma-related guilt, and (2) difficulties with separations.

Overgiving

What is overgiving? Everyone's standard of what constitutes an appropriate amount of time, love, money, or service to give to another human being, or group, is a highly individual matter. However, *overgiving* can be defined as giving to the point where there are serious negative financial, emotional, physical, or other consequences that result from the giving. For example, if a survivor gives away so much money that his/her own family suffers or that he/she does not have enough money to provide for his/her own medical care, that is "overgiving." Alternatively, if survivors spend so much time helping others that they neglect themselves or others to whom they have made commitments, this situation can also be called "overgiving."

It is not uncommon for rape survivors (male or female) to overgive in intimate relationships from a sense of guilt. Similarly, formerly battered women often overgive to their children because of the profound guilt they feel for having exposed their children to violence. Generous giving in a relationship is good. It is healthy. But when the emotional or physical price tag for the generosity includes harm to oneself or others, or puts one at physical, mental, or financial risk, then it is highly likely that trauma-related guilt is playing a role.

For example, Joanne, who left a violent marriage, found herself unable to say "no" to her children's requests for money or for her time. "I can't refuse them," she would explain to her therapist. "Not after all they have been through." She took an additional part-time job to be able to give her children more money. The job left her with less time to assist them with their school projects and even less time for herself. As a result, she became irritable in the evenings and even began to slap the children, which only compounded her guilt. "I'm hitting them, which I swore I would never do," she'd say.

In therapy, she realized that by taking on a part-time job and saying "yes" to most of her children's' requests, she was defeating her purpose of providing her children with a stable, nurturing, *nonviolent* environment. Her intentions in saying "yes" to them and earning extra money for their sake were good, but they were also fraught with guilt— guilt over having married the man she had and over the psychological damage the children had suffered from living in a violent home. In therapy, Joanne realized that she needed to deal with her trauma-related guilt before she could learn less self-defeating ways of being a good mother.

Separations

Separations and other forms of "good-bye" are difficult for most people, but they can become torturous for trauma survivors if the separation triggers survivor guilt. During the trauma, leaving others may have meant leaving them to their deaths or leaving them in the hands of those who you knew would harm them.

For example, Lily, an incest survivor, ran away from home when she was fourteen, leaving behind two younger sisters. To this day, Lily feels guilty about leaving home because while she was there she tried to protect her sisters from incestuous attacks. Even while Lily was at home, her sisters were being abused. Yet Lily still feels that it was her departure that was responsible for her sisters being abused.

This trauma-related guilt is so strong in Lily that she has trouble breaking away from acquaintances (both men and women) who, for one reason or another, she doesn't want to spend time with. She also had great difficulty saying "good-bye" to her original church family. She had found another church which she felt better met her spiritual needs, but she felt that by leaving she put the people in her original church in jeopardy. An objective examination of the situation revealed that the only "harm" Lily caused by changing churches was the loss of revenue to the first church and the loss of her time and work contributions to some committees. But no one became ill, or died, or was abused because she left, which is what Lily unconsciously had thought would happen.

For Lily, every separation hearkens back to the separation from her sisters. Almost every time Lily has to say "good-bye," even to her pets when she leaves for work, she feels the pain of the past and has to examine her decision to leave carefully to be certain she is not causing harm.

For many trauma survivors, saying "good-bye" even to casual acquaintances or attachments is not an easy matter. It can be so agonizing that they choose to stay in unrewarding relationships rather than go through the guilt of initiating a separation. Guilt is frequently a part of most separations, but for trauma survivors separation guilt may be very intense because it contains guilt feelings belonging to the trauma. The decision to terminate, or lessen the degree of involvement in a relationship, is even more conflictual and problematic if the relationship is a significant one, such as with a sexual partner.

Trauma-related guilt can also affect involve employment decisions and relationships.

For example, Peter, a nurse, had the opportunity to leave his nursing position and become a medical administrator. The decision involved many factors, but he couldn't be totally rational about making the decision because of a trauma he had suffered as a teenager. He had just received his driver's license and, to celebrate, had taken his mother and grandmother out for a ride. His car ran out of gas, and he left his mother and grandmother in the car while he walked to a near-by gas station. During his absence, his mother and grandmother were beaten, robbed, and raped. He felt responsible for these heinous crimes because he believed it was his fault that his car had run out of gas, even though the gas gauge had broken the day before. For Peter, leaving a nursing job where he took care of adults and the elderly was emotionally tantamount to leaving his mother and grandmother vulnerable to attack. He had to do extensive work in therapy to work through his guilt feelings about the attacks on his relatives before he could accurately assess whether or not he wanted to make a career change.

In another instance of separation guilt, Marianne, the ex-wife of a violent alcoholic, did everything in her power to protect her son from her husband's physical abuse. But she did not always succeed. As a result, she was plagued with guilt. After she left her husband, she began working as a bank teller. Over time, because of her intelligence and diligence, she was offered one training after the next and soon she was offered a job as a high ranking bank official. Marianne was thrilled, but she went into a panic when she found out the position involved travel.

How could she leave her son? If she left town, her former husband might seek out her son and hurt him, as he had in the past when she was still married. But this was fifteen years later. Her son was now twenty-five years old and perfectly capable of defending himself against his father. In fact, her ex-husband had recently had a heart attack and back surgery and he hadn't attacked anyone in more than ten years. But Marianne's fear of his violence, as well as her trauma-related guilt over the abuse of her son, is just as alive in the present as it was in the past, when she lived with her abuser. To an outside observer, Marianne's fears about her son's well-being may seem "irrational." But underneath Marianne's fear there is an enormous amount of guilt about the times she failed to protect her son from harm.

Marianne had to work hard in therapy to distinguish her son's present needs from his past needs for protection. In the process, she had to confront her guilt not only for not being able to protect her son in the past, but many other guilts, for example, for marrying a man who later proved to be abusive, for having had children with him, and for not leaving him sooner.

Overprotectiveness and Perfectionism

As Peter and Marianne's dilemmas illustrate, overprotectiveness in relationships is one of the possible consequences of trauma-related guilt. Perfectionism is another. (Perfectionism is dealt with in greater detail in chapter 7.) Peter and Marianne are not unique. When dealing with current relationships and decisions, many trauma survivors encounter long-buried or insufficiently resolved trauma-related guilt issues. For many survivors, trauma-related guilt affects all of their relationships in many ways. The following exercises are designed to help you achieve a clearer understanding of how trauma-related guilt may play a role in your relationships today.

✍ Exercise: Relationships and Guilt

In chapter 1, you wrote about three sets of relationships: those you had prior to the trauma, those you had during the trauma, and those you have had since the trauma. You were asked to pick three relationships within each of these time frames and write about some of the positive and negative aspects of those relationships.

In this exercise, you will go back to your journal entries for those relationships and reread what you wrote for evidence of behavior that might have been motivated by guilt. As you review your journal writing, consider the following questions and on a fresh sheet of paper write down any thoughts you might have.

1. Looking at the relationships you had *prior to* the trauma, how did feelings of guilt and low-self-esteem affect them? What kinds of guilt, if any, did you experience in these relationships? How did your guilt help each relationship? How did it not help?

2. Looking at the relationships you had during the trauma, did any of them involve guilt feelings? Describe your guilt feelings as fully as you can. How did feeling guilty help matters during your trauma? How did it not help?

3. Was part of your guilt similar to the kind of guilt you felt in relationships prior to your trauma? In other words, did the trauma reinforce or make stronger certain kinds of guilt feelings you had prior the trauma or was all of your guilt in the relationship you are considering entirely due to the trauma? Did the trauma increase tendencies toward feeling guilty that you had in the past, create new kinds of guilt, or both?

Now, look at your journal entries about three of your *current* relationships and consider the following questions for each relationship:

1. How do the guilt feelings you had prior to the trauma affect these relationships? How do the guilt feelings you acquired as the result of the trauma affect them? How does your guilt help each relationship? How does your guilt not help each relationship?

2. Suppose you had never been traumatized and never acquired trauma-related guilt, how do you think the three current relationships you are writing about would be different? If you had a magic wand and could wipe away the trauma and the guilt feelings it generated in you, how would things be different in your relationships in general?

3. How did it feel to write about the role of guilt in your relationships? Are you feeling angry, sad, afraid? Did you learn that you might need to do some more trauma-processing work about your guilt feelings? If so, avail yourself of the help you need. Don't let your trauma-related guilt keep you from helping yourself and improving your relationships.

✍ Exercise: Guilt and Separation

Now, take a fresh sheet of paper in your journal and answer the following questions as completely as you can.

1. In your traumatic experiences, were you forced, or for other reasons, did you leave others behind? What happened to those people? Were any of them hurt or killed after you left? During your traumatic experiences, were others injured, killed, or otherwise harmed because you were not at a certain place at a certain time?

2. Do you feel guilt about leaving or not being with others during certain times of the trauma? Have you examined your guilt feelings in the light of the real options that were available to you at the time and the pressures of the traumatic situation? If not, why not?

3. Do your feelings of guilt about leaving or separating from certain people during the trauma affect your ability to limit or end relationships with other people, with organizations, with therapists or support groups, or with intimates today? If so, how?

4. Compare what happened to those you left behind during the trauma with what you think may happen if you leave people or groups today. For example, if, after you left during the trauma some people died, do you now feel that if you leave certain relationships, that person or persons will die? If the person doesn't die, how might he/she be harmed? What evidence do you have that the harm you anticipate happening will actually occur? To what extent might the person actually be harmed and to what extent are you projecting what happened in the past onto the future?

✍ Exercise: Role and Responsibility Guilt

If you had a position of responsibility during the trauma, it is possible that you developed some trauma-related guilt as the result of being responsible for the welfare of others. Kubany (1996) stresses that parents, teachers, squad leaders, airline pilots, head nurses, and all those who have obligations toward others tend to feel responsible for any negative outcomes experienced by those they are responsible for because *they confuse their assigned responsibilities with being accountable for the trauma.*

Hence, if a fire chief sends out staff to fight a fire and three firefighters die as a result, there is a high probability that this chief will feel a keener sense of guilt than other employees who don't have such a responsible role. Chiefs are responsible for taking care of their staffs—training them, making sure they have the right equipment, and enabling them to do their job as safely and effectively as possible. But chiefs are not responsible for causing huge uncontrollable fires or unforeseen events. Yet they and others in responsible positions still tend to feel accountable for such events because of their designated responsibilities.

"I'll always be the squad leader," says Jim. "I left Vietnam twenty years ago, but in my bones I still feel responsible for my men. I always felt responsible for my squad while I was their leader. When one of them got hurt or killed, I felt it was my fault, even if they got themselves killed driving drunk while they were out on R and R (Rest and Recreation). I figured I should have taught them better about acting crazy.

"Even after I got wounded and was flown back to the U.S., whenever I found out that one of the guys had died or got wounded on the field, I felt guilty. I should have been there to instruct and protect them. I should have never left them, even though I had no choice because I was wounded so bad I couldn't do my job.

"When it comes to my survivor guilt, logic makes no difference. A squad leader is responsible for his men. That's it. No exceptions. Even now, when some of them call me about their nightmares and flashbacks I feel like I have to be there for them, even though listening to them talk about their PTSD triggers my PTSD and I end up having night sweats, anxiety attacks, flashbacks, and nightmares, too. Sometimes, I just want to hang up the phone and never see or talk to those guys again, because listening to them brings back all the guilt—and all the pain. But I can't cut myself off from them, no matter how much talking to them damages me. In my heart, they are still my men. I'm their squad leader and I'm responsible for them—till the day I die."

Now, answer the following questions in your journal if they apply to you.

1. If you held a position of responsibility during your trauma, do you feel any guilt about what happened to the people you were responsible for during the trauma?

2. Are you currently in a position of responsibility? For example, are you a parent, grandparent, supervisor, manager, or director?

3. How do guilt feelings left over from your trauma affect your current responsible role? Do you find yourself being overprotective, perfectionist, overly controlling, or fearful of making a mistake? If you are, what are the benefits of having these qualities? What are the drawbacks?

4. If you had never been traumatized, how do you think you would act, think, or feel in your current role? For example, if you are the parent of a sexually abused child or a child who committed suicide, how would you parent your other children, relate to your partner or intimate friend, or relate to your family members and other friends, if you didn't feel guilt about your child having been sexually abused or having committed suicide?

5. To what extent do you fear a "disaster" similar to the trauma happening within the realm of your responsible role today? For instance, if one of your children was abused or committed suicide, how much do you fear that one of your other children, or one of your nieces or nephews or grandchildren, will suffer a similar fate? What is the probability that the disaster might repeat itself? What do you see as your role in preventing such a disaster?

Suppose you had never been traumatized yourself, but were nevertheless aware of the possibility of negative events happening, such as child abuse or teen suicide. In your role as a responsible person, what actions might you take to help prevent these negative events? How does this set of actions compare with what you are actually doing today or think you should be doing?

References

Davis, Laura. 1990. *The Courage to Heal Workbook*. New York: Harper and Row.

Davis, Laura and Ellen Bass. 1988. *The Courage to Heal*. New York: Harper and Row.

Kubany, Edward 1994. "A Cognitive Model of Guilt Typology in Combat-Related PTSD." *Journal of Traumatic Stress* 7 (1) 3–19.

Kubany, Edward. 1996. "Cognitive Therapy for Trauma-Related Guilt" Audiotapes 96-ISTSS-25 and 26 of lecture presented at the 12th Annual Conference of the International Society for Traumatic Stress Studies. San Francisco. November.

Matsakis, Aphrodite. 1996. *I Can't Get Over It*. Second Edition. Oakland, CA: New Harbinger Publications.

Valerio, Peter. 1997. "On Shame." Unpublished paper. Baltimore, MD: Department of Veterans' Affairs, Readjustment Counseling Center.

7

Mind-Sets

Trauma-Related Mind-Sets

Just as trauma can change your biochemistry, it can change the way you think. After you have undergone a trauma, your assumption that the world is a safe and loving place is destroyed. You feel vulnerable in ways and to a degree that you never felt vulnerable before. When new people or events come into your life, you tend to automatically view them as threats, or potential threats, instead of opportunities, or potential opportunities, for good, or for pleasure.

Because you were helpless during the trauma, you fear being helpless again, and justifiably so. To protect yourself against that fear, you may approach new situations and people with mind-sets or ways of thinking that the trauma taught you.

In this chapter, three common trauma-related mind-sets are described: all-or-nothing, now-or-never thinking; perfectionism or intolerance of mistakes; and denial of personal difficulties. These mind-sets are not inherently "bad," "dysfunctional," "sinful," or "psychologically incorrect." In fact, they probably helped you to survive the trauma. These mind-sets may still be extremely useful in some areas of your life today. In other areas, however, they may distort your perceptions and reactions and not serve you well. In still other areas, your challenge will be to modify or adapt these mind-sets to meet your personal goals and improve your relationships.

As you become aware of your mind-sets, you will become able to catch yourself thinking in these predictable ways. You can then stop yourself and consider whether thinking in these ways is best for the situation or relationship at hand. Just as during your trauma your first priority was to do what was best for you or for a valued relationship, now and forever, your first tendency may be to think in ways the trauma taught you to think. In some circumstances, it may make sense to think along those lines; in other circumstances, however, that may not be to your advantage.

You may never be able to stop trauma-related ways of thinking from coming into your mind almost automatically, but if you can become aware of *how* your are thinking, then that thinking need not determine your behavior. The hard part is catching yourself in a trauma-related mind-set. Once you do that, the next challenge will be to see if other points of view might be beneficial. This is no small feat, but if you can do it, then you will have choices as to how you respond.

How you view a relationship determines how you will act and react in that relationship. Your way of viewing a relationship no longer need be based on the fear that the trauma is happening again, unless, of course, it is happening again, either in whole or in part.

Mind-Set 1: All-or-Nothing and Now-or-Never Thinking

Absolutist, or all-or-nothing thinking, is characteristic of individuals who have been traumatized. Because so much is at stake during a traumatic incident, issues tend to become black or white. Either you let the violent family member attack your child or risk your safety trying to protect that child. Either you take a risk and fight the mugger or surrender and hope that he shows you mercy. In war, either you kill the enemy or he kills you.

There is no such thing as fighting a child abuser or a mugger "in moderation" or killing the enemy "just a little bit." In a trauma, "moderate" and "medium" responses are not effective and are often not possible. You have to take a stand. If moderation in action and thought was possible, then, by definition, you were probably not in a traumatic situation.

During a trauma, people are either friends, or enemies—there are no in-betweens. (Chapter 3 discusses this topic of trust in more detail.) When this thinking is carried into everyday situations, you might approach others, from intimates to salespersons to professionals with an all-or-nothing attitude. For example, you might find yourself thinking, "Either this caseworker is going to take care of all my needs, with no intrusive questioning or mounds of paperwork, or he is just another crook who is out to get me."

When you are plagued with this kind of black-and-white thinking, the caseworker cannot be viewed as just an ordinary human being who is afraid he might lose his job or the opportunity for a promotion if he doesn't make you complete all the paperwork. In your love life, you may think, "Either he loves me enough to marry me (or have sex with me, or let me live with him) or he doesn't care about me at all and is using me." This is black-and-white thinking. The truth may be somewhere in-between. For example, he may care for you, but not enough to marry you. Or he may be confused about how he feels. Perhaps his current state of lukewarm affection is only temporary and in the future he may grow to love you, even enough to want to marry you.

But if you practice all-or-nothing thinking, then you probably practice now-or-never thinking too, because during a trauma, there is no past or future, only the horrible present.

During trauma, all that matters is the moment at hand. It doesn't matter if your father was kind to you when you were six or that he will bail you out of jail when you are sixteen. All that matters is that he is assaulting you right now. It doesn't matter if an ambulance driver has always responded to emergency calls promptly in the past and will be given a prize for being the best ambulance driver of the year. All that matters is that he shows up for you when you are hurt. If you are being raped, it doesn't matter that the rapist used to be your friend or that, in the future, he will spend his life serving the poor. All that matters is what he is doing to you, right now.

When applied to yourself, all-or-nothing and now-or-never thinking leads to you judging yourself in the same black-and-white terms. You see yourself as a total failure or a total success. You make few allowances for partial successes or partial failures and your eyes are focused solely on the present, not on the past or the future. You don't take into consideration what you did in the past or what you might do in the future. All that matters is what you are doing or feeling right now.

You put your feelings into extreme categories and assess them according to extreme standards. For example, if you aren't willing to risk your life for someone, you conclude you don't love that person. This leaves out the possibility of varying degrees of affection and commitment. If you are depressed during the anniversary of your trauma, you assume you will feel this depressed every single day of your life. This leaves out the possibility that you might not always feel this miserable. Similarly, life is either all bad and hopeless or a bowl of cherries with endless possibilities.

If you were traumatized during childhood or adolescence, you may be especially prone to such all-or-nothing and now-or-never thinking, especially if you suffer from depression. Absolutist or all-or-nothing thinking is characteristic of individuals who suffer from depression. Given that an estimated fifty percent of those who suffer from PTSD also suffer from clinical depression, it is not surprising that many survivors tend to view themselves, others, and life situations in simple all-or-nothing terms.

✍ *Exercise: All-or-Nothing Thinking*

Chapter 3 provides exercises that address the tendency some survivors have to trust some people almost entirely and some people not at all, and to help you learn that different levels of trust are appropriate for different people. The following exercise is designed to help you examine some of the other ways that you might be viewing your relationships with others in absolutist ways.

The questions that follow are particularly difficult to answer because during the traumatic event, you probably were more focused on how you felt and what you needed to do to survive, or to help others, than on your mind-set. There is also a tendency to "forget" what you were told or not told before or during the trauma, because, unless the words were directions to cause harm, what people said might have seemed as important as what people were doing (or not doing). Yet it may be that the directions, suggestions, or views from that time have taught you how to think in traumatic terms.

Similarly, after the trauma, when you reflected on the traumatic events, you may have been concerned about what you did or didn't do during the trauma, that you discounted the importance of the instructions, suggestions, or life-perspectives you heard from others involved in your trauma. Those others might have included authority figures, but they could also have been fellow survivors or just bystanders to the trauma.

Before you begin writing, you may want to take a few minutes of quiet time and ask yourself the following questions:

- Who was there during the trauma, or immediately before or after the trauma?

- Were there fellow survivors, authority figures, rescuers, or bystanders?

- What did they say? Did anyone give instructions or orders or threats?

- Did anyone make all-or-nothing comments?

- Did your thinking change because of what others said, or did not say, right before, during, or immediately following the trauma? How did your thinking change?

Now, take a fresh sheet of paper in your journal and answer the following questions:

Note: If you can write more than six or seven sentences, do so; be sure to stop if you sense that you are becoming overwhelmed. Refer back to the Cautions section in the Introduction for a listing of specific signs of becoming overwhelmed.

1. During the trauma, were you taught all-or-nothing ways of viewing people? Were you given all-or-nothing labels by people who had power over you? Were you subject to some form of subtle or overt brainwashing that used all-or-nothing terms to describe others or yourself?

   For example, if you are a rape or incest survivor, were you told by the rapist that there were two kinds of people: sexy and unsexy, and that you were one of the "sexy" ones who "liked it"? Is it now hard for you to view yourself, or others, as not being either sexy or unsexy, but as a mix of both? Has the brainwashing you were subjected to by the rapist made it difficult for you to see yourself and others as having fluctuations in attractiveness or sexual desire?

If you are a soldier, police officer, or rescue worker were you told (directly or indirectly) that anyone who flinches on the job is a "coward"? As a result of this teaching, do you view yourself as a coward whenever you have a few moments of fear? Do you also consider those who hesitate or feel anxiety before taking a major risk, or doing something dangerous, as cowardly?

If you are a victim of political torture or oppression, were you told by your captors that there were only two kinds of people: loyal and disloyal, patriots and traitors? Do you now categorize people according to these two labels? If someone agrees with you, does that mean that person deserves to be praised? If that person disagrees with you, do you feel that person needs to be punished, as you were, or even killed, as you almost were? What happens when you meet someone who agrees with some, but not all, of your political views?

If you were a victim of child abuse, were you told that only "sissies" or "weaklings" cried or complained about being beaten or otherwise abused? Do you now categorize people as "strong" or "weak" depending on how they act when they are under stress or hurting? What happens to your all-or-nothing categories if you find out that the same person who is stoic under one kind of stress, exhibits signs of strain under another kind of stress?

2. In what ways and to what extent do you judge yourself by the kinds of absolutist standards taught to you during your trauma? Did the all-or-nothing or now-or-never thinking you learned from your abusers, captors, or instructors during your trauma somehow become a part of your value system?

   If you still believe in some of the all-or-nothing or now-or-never thinking that you were exposed to during the trauma, how do you feel about this? Proud? Ashamed? Frightened? Confused?

   Even if you do not like the standards that were imposed upon you during the trauma, are they still a part of you? Do you still find yourself evaluating yourself as if you were back in the trauma?

   Do not be ashamed if this is the case. Even if the people who once had power over you during the trauma are now dead, or behind bars, their voices may still be echoing in your head. Why would they not be? After all, these people had ultimate power over you. How could you possibly forget what they told you? Their words might be branded in your mind as if placed there by a hot branding iron.

   Your struggle will be to decide whether you want to continue to act or react according to their precepts or standards or whether you want to respond to life and people in different ways. It is quite possible that you want to keep some of their "all-or-nothing" thinking. But you may want to disregard some of it, or change yourself to suit your life's purposes today.

3. In what ways and to what extent do you judge members of your family, your friends, your co-workers, members of your therapy group, or members of the helping professions by these standards?

4. Take a close look at the relationships you wrote about in chapter 1: the three that occurred during the trauma and the three that are going on in the present. Do you view these people, or aspects of these relationships, in all-or-nothing or now-or-never terms?

5. For each relationship, explain how it helps to use all-or-nothing or now-or-never standards to evaluate this person and to deal with this relationship. Explain how these ways of thinking might not help.

6. Are you having trouble answering these questions? Are you confused? If so, is it true that during the trauma you received conflicting all-or-nothing messages?

   Think back to the trauma and search your memories to see if you received mixed messages about all-or-nothing standards for personal behavior. What were those mixed messages? For example, if you were a soldier, firefighter, rescue worker, or police officer, were you told that those who were killed in the line of duty were "fools," but also told that they were "heroes"?

   If you were abused as a child, were you told that "good children obey their parents," but also told that you lacked "spunk" or "ambition" and therefore "deserved a beating"?

   If you are an incest survivor, were you told that you were "everything" by the person who abused you and that the family's welfare depended on you. But then, at other times, were you told that you were "worthless" and that if you didn't behave as expected, you would be cast out of the family, and, furthermore, that the family would be better off without you?

   If you were a battered spouse, were you told that you were a "saint" or an "angel" for enduring the abuse for the sake of the family but also the "devil" who started it all? Were you praised for sacrificing yourself for the family, but then criticized for having a masochistic, self-defeating personality?

7. Do you find yourself judging others in your life by conflicting all-or-nothing standards? If so, what are the consequences of such judgments on those relationships? In answering this last question, pay special attention to the three current relationships you wrote about in chapter 1.

Mind-Set 2: Intolerance of Mistakes and Perfectionism

During certain traumatic events (combat, fires, floods, and family violence) and in certain occupations that involve injury and death (nursing, rescue work, firefighting, police work), mistakes are intolerable. Even the tiniest error can result in death or injury to others or to oneself. If you have been in such a work situation, it is very likely that you have seen how the mistakes of others caused needless deaths, injuries, and other losses. As a result, you may have developed a mind-set of "no mistakes" allowed.

This same mind-set can develop during secondary wounding experiences in which you feel that if you make even the slightest mistake you will be denied help or be mistreated by authorities or others. Or perhaps you have attributed the denial, discounting, or other secondary wounding experiences you have had to "mistakes" you made in how you presented yourself or how you handled your interactions with others. Alternatively, you may still be livid over the "mistakes" made by those who were supposed to help you, but who kept you waiting inordinate amounts of time or otherwise failed to fulfill their prescribed role of providing you the assistance and care you needed after your trauma.

Usually, both abused children and abused spouses try to avoid "mistakes" at all costs, because making a mistake, even a small one, can be an excuse for a beating or some other form of torture. People trapped in domestic violence situations often develop the mind-set that if they are "perfect," they can stop the abuse and win the abuser's much desired love, affection, and protection. The abuse, however, is always more a function of the abuser's internal state than the victim's behavior.

Exercise: When Others Make Errors Similar to Your Trauma-Related Mistakes

In chapter 3 you were asked to list mistakes you made during the trauma. Add to this list mistakes that others made during the trauma that proved costly to those involved. In your journal, write about what happened when these mistakes were made during the trauma. Try to distinguish between mistakes that led to death and injury and those that led to relatively inconsequential results.

Think of two or three instances when someone (a child, spouse, co-worker, friend, or stranger) made a mistake that was identical or similar to a mistake you or someone else made during your trauma. Consider the following questions for each case:

- For which of these mistakes were the consequences life threatening or costly in other ways?

- Did your response to the person making the mistake make matters better and help avert a disaster or a serious negative consequence?

- Did your response make matters worse in any way? How did your attitude or behavior affect the relationship?

- For which of these mistakes were the consequences relatively inconsequential or unimportant?

- How did the way you responded help matters?

- Did the way you responded to the mistake make matters worse in any way? If so, how?

Suppose you had never been traumatized and had never seen these kinds of mistakes made in a traumatic situation, how do you think you might react to someone making such mistakes? How would this reaction compare to the way you tend to react in reality? For example, suppose during your trauma you saw someone who wasn't wearing a seat belt die in a car accident. Not wearing a seat belt is viewed as a serious mistake by you now. Many people would probably agree with you. When you are driving with someone who isn't wearing a seat belt, what is your attitude and behavior? Suppose you had never witnessed that car accident, what would be your attitude and behavior toward the person not wearing the seat belt?

Now that you have carefully examined how you react when others make mistakes, do some more writing about how you would like to respond in the future when someone makes a mistake that is associated with a traumatic memory for you. What attitudes and behaviors do you think would be most constructive for the relationship, as well as for reaching the goal of averting a catastrophe or misfortune? For example, what do you think might be the best way to get someone you are driving with to wear a seat belt?

✍ Exercise: Perfectionism—Pros and Cons

Perfectionism creates problems for many people, including those who have never been traumatized. Perfectionist standards impose a heavy weight on you as a trauma survivor, and they can affect your relationships in the following ways:

1. You may impose the same perfectionist standards you place on yourself onto others, thus making them feel incompetent or inadequate or angering or alienating them by your high standards.

2. Your need to be perfect may stand in the way of developing relationships. For example, you may be spending so much time trying to meet your perfectionist standards that you don't have time for other people.

3. You may have such high standards for how you behave in a relationship that the minute you don't live up to your own perfectionist

ideals, you conclude you are a failure and withdraw from the relationship (either permanently or temporarily).

4. When someone else fails to meet one of your high standards, you reject that person entirely.

Perfectionism has sometimes been labeled a "disease" or a "character defect," but for many trauma survivors it hearkens back to the trauma, where being perfect, or trying to be perfect, in some areas of life was an absolute necessity. For example, in the military, keeping one's living area spotless and keeping one's weapons immaculately clean is a requirement based on the need for soldiers to be constantly ready. In case of a surprise attack, there is no time to scramble through one's untidy messes or to clean a gun. Everything has to be ready to go!

Soldiers learn to equate neatness with their dedication to the military and to the country, with self-preservation, and with the preservation of one's unit. Often soldiers are punished severely for any form of untidiness or unreadiness. But what happens to soldiers when they become parents of messy children?

"I go ballistic," says John, a former military officer. "My wife wants to know why I'm acting like it's the end of the world because the kids don't clean up their room. To me, a messy room *is* the end of the world . . . at least that's how it was when I was in the service."

John finds his family's messiness intolerable. They, in turn, find his meticulous neatness equally intolerable. John can't feel safe in the midst of clutter, and his family can't relax if they feel they have to constantly pick up after themselves to keep John from yelling at them.

Who is right and who is wrong? It doesn't matter. What matters is that John and his family were able to talk about the situation. The family promised to try to be a little neater, but they made it clear they could never be as neat as John would like them to be. John, on the other hand, promised to stop yelling and name-calling when the house is messy. It was also decided that John would have one room in the house just for his own use that he could keep as perfectly neat as he needed it to be. He would be able to retreat to this room when the family's clutter might trigger him with traumatic memories.

John's wife and children were well-intentioned but, being human, they soon returned to their not-so-neat ways. John still had his private "neat room," but sometimes the rest of the house looks like a battlefield—strewn with broken toys, dolls, clothes, and papers. John has been tempted to start yelling again but, so far, he's been able to talk himself out of it.

"Look," he tells himself, "in the army, being neat was mandatory and essential for survival. Here at home, the messiness annoys me to no end, but it isn't life threatening. No one is going to die or get wounded because this house is a mess. If I want to have a good relationship with my wife and children, I have to stop the yelling and the name-calling.

"I can't believe I call them the same names my drill instructor called me—'lazy,' 'stupid,' and 'good for nothing.' I wasn't lazy, stupid, or good-for-nothing and neither are my wife and children.

"And what good did it do for that drill instructor to keep putting us men down all the time? No good at all. We did what he told us to, because we were scared of him, but behind his back we made fun of him for yelling over little things. When he yelled about important things, like not checking the safety equipment, we respected him. But when he called us names because we got a drop of water on the floor, we thought he was a jerk.

"Is that what my wife and kids think of me? That I'm a jerk because I get upset that the newspapers aren't folded right or that there are a few sweaters laying around? Why don't I save my yelling and screaming for the big things, like safety checks and let the little things go?

"It's going to be hard, because when I scream at the mess in the house, I'm really screaming at my memories—the dolls on the floor remind me of the dead kids, the clothes on the floor, remind me of discarded uniforms; the broken toys look like the wreckage of war. These memories hurt.

"Screaming at the family relieves the hurt for me, for a while, but it only creates more pain. My sons will think I don't love them. I could give them an inferiority complex, like my drill instructor gave me. Is that what I want to do?

"If I can fight in a war, I can fight the temptation to blast away at my family. I want to feel powerful in the family, but yelling at everyone only takes away my power. And, when I just can't stand it any more, I can go into my neat room and calm myself down."

The solution John and his family arrived at was not perfect, either for John or for his family, and it may not be suitable for you. It is presented simply as an example wherein all concerned tried to compromise and where the trauma survivor, John, was able to reevaluate his perfectionist standards in light of present-day realities, not the realities of the past.

Ideally, John's family would have totally respected his need for order, but the trauma survivor who has a family that instantly and consistently accommodates his or her needs in all ways is the exception. In most instances, it is the trauma survivor who has to change his or her very high standards for the sake of the family.

Joellen was a perfectionist about keeping the kitchen clean. However, with four teenagers in the house, this was nearly impossible. Yet for Joellen, keeping the kitchen clean was an imperative. When she was a child, her mother would get so upset when the kitchen was messy that she would beat Joellen's younger brother. From the age of seven on, Joellen had taken it upon herself to keep the kitchen clean, in order to keep her brother from being beaten.

Joellen understood that her perfectionist standards had important and meaningful origins. But she couldn't help but be triggered whenever the sink was full of dirty dishes. All the coping techniques and therapy sessions in the world could not erase the memories of the anguish she had felt as a little girl when her mother would hurt her little brother. Yet Joellen came to realize that she was only alienating her children by nagging them all the time and creating tension in her home by doing the dishes herself and resenting every minute of it.

"Look, Mom's being the martyr again," her children would say when they would see her cleaning up their messes in the kitchen.

Finally Joellen told her children, "I get very upset about a messy kitchen because I have terrible memories about it. My head knows that nothing catastrophic will happen if you don't pick up after yourselves, but emotionally I react very intensely. I don't want to nag you and I don't want be your maid. I don't want to ruin our times together because of this problem, but I can't help getting very upset. Frankly, I don't know what to do about it. Do you kids have any suggestions?"

Like John's children, Joellen's children promised to try harder to keep the kitchen tidy. They were well-intentioned, but they were children and they sometimes forgot their promises. Keeping the kitchen clean was Joellen's priority—not theirs.

Joellen had to evaluate her options realistically. Did she really want her children to be as she had been when she was young—terrorized by an adult's anger? Then it struck her. She was acting just like her mother, although for very different reasons. When her mother saw a messy kitchen, she'd start complaining and berating her children and then beat one of them. When Joellen saw a messy kitchen, she'd get livid and act just like her mother, except for the hitting part.

"Oh no," Joellen groaned. "I'm re-creating the past. I hoped that my kids would help stop this scene, but they won't cooperate. So I guess it's up to me.

"The last thing in the world I want to do is leave my children with the same memories my mother left me: that of a woman yelling about a dirty kitchen. The dirty dishes aren't important, what is important is what went on because of those dishes.

"Joellen," she told herself, "you can respect the past and all the pain in that torturous past and, at the same time, you can try to make your present and future better by not dominating all of your interactions with your children by talking and yelling about these dishes. Learn to be the mother to them that your mother couldn't be to you."

At the suggestion of her youngest daughter, Joellen invested in paper plates. "It hurts the trees to make paper plates," the daughter said. "But it's better that trees hurt than you hurt, Mommy."

Shoulds

The following list of "shoulds" (McKay and Fanning, 1987) imposes burdens on many people. Do you subscribe to any of the following?

- I should be the epitome of generosity and unselfishness.
- I should be the perfect lover, friend, parent, teacher, student, spouse, and so on.
- I should be able to find a quick solution to every problem.
- I should never feel hurt. I should always feel happy and serene.
- I should be completely competent.
- I should know, understand, and foresee everything.
- I should never feel certain emotions such as anger or jealousy.
- I should be totally self-reliant.
- I should never be afraid.
- I should have achievements that bring me status, wealth, and power.
- I should always be busy; to relax is to waste my time and my life.
- I should not take time just for my own pleasure.

✍ Exercise: Perfectionism

In your journal, consider those areas of life for which you might hold perfectionist standards, such as those listed above. Why were these standards a necessity during your trauma or during the secondary wounding events that followed? When or how are such perfectionist standards useful today? How do they benefit your ability to relate to others? How do they detract from your relationships? Which of these standards do you want to keep and which do you want to modify, or disregard entirely?

Are there any relationships, for example, with your co-workers, family members, neighbors, or children where you find yourself judging them by perfectionist standards, such as those listed above? How does applying those standards help these relationships? How does it hurt them? Which of those standards do you want to keep in these relationships? Which do you want to modify, change, or disregard? Can you ask others to help you makes these changes?

Mind-Set 3: Denial of Personal Difficulties

Certain occupations, for instance, medicine, police work, combat duty, and rescue work emphasize the necessity for solid thinking, quick action, and endurance, both physical and psychological. There is little room for expression of emotions or for personal weaknesses. Hence, from firefighters to combat soldiers, those who are involved in life-and-death situations tend to keep their personal difficulties to themselves. The legitimate fear of such workers is that if they are emotionally open, they may be viewed as cowards, weaklings, incompetents, or otherwise unfit for the work they do.

Victims of crime, childhood physical and sexual abuse, battering, and natural catastrophes may also deny personal problems for fear of being seen as weak or defective because of their experiences. To avoid this stigma, some trauma survivors assume a macho or stoic facade.

It makes absolute sense for you not to share your personal difficulties with individuals who are apt to denigrate you or who have already done so. However, in intimate relationships, and during the healing process, denial of personal pain, conflicts, and other psychological or physical symptoms is counterproductive and can lead to addictive behavior, psychosomatic problems, or worse. You owe it to the wounded part of yourself to find at least a few people whom you can trust sufficiently to share your emotions with openly, both friends and professionals.

Decisions about who to talk to and how much to tell are complex. It is important that you take care of yourself first, by being selective about those with whom you share your thoughts and feelings. Chapter 13 provides guidelines and exercises for sharing your story and the personal problems you experienced as a result of being traumatized. Always keep in mind that if you take the risk of sharing with someone, and he or she is not receptive or supportive, you can bring the conversation to a close as quickly and search elsewhere for solace.

References

McKay, Matthew and Patrick Fanning. 1987. *Self-Esteem: A Proven Program of Cognitive Techniques for Assessing, Improving, and Maintaining Your Self-Esteem.* Oakland, CA: New Harbinger Publications.

8

When Your Loved Ones Set Off Your Triggers

One of the most complex and wrenching dilemmas you might find your-self in occurs when someone you love sets off your triggers. What could be worse than being put into a state of anxious hyperarousal or lifeless numbing by a child, parent, spouse, or other person whom you deeply cherish? Of course, this chapter does not concern relationships with family members or others who have hurt you physically, emotionally, sexually, or financially. The suggestions in this chapter pertain only to loved ones who have not traumatized you, but who nonetheless activate your triggers.

It is normal to have conflicting feelings about people, even about people you love. Sometimes you have conflicting feelings about *yourself*, don't you? But when the conflicting feelings are too intense, you can become totally confused and hopeless about ever being able to feel emotionally secure in a relationship.

Perhaps your inner dialogue goes something like this:

"If I can't feel safe around my mother/father/sister/brother/partner/child/ favorite aunt/uncle/niece/nephew/ or best friend, then who can I feel safe around?

"I know I love this person. I'd do almost anything for him/her. Yet he/she triggers me so intensely that I'm better off not being around him/her and trying to avoid him/her as much as possible. But how can I do that? They're my family (best friend/wife/husband/brother). What should I do—divorce my own mother (father/sibling/child/spouse/aunt/uncle)? Then what will I have? Just me? That would get very lonely.

"I can't stand that person sometimes, yet I know he/she loves me and is one of the few people who was there for me and who will be there for me in the future. To be sure, he/she wasn't there for me one-hundred percent in the past, but so what? Who was?

"At least he/she was there thirty percent (or forty percent or sixty percent), which is more than most people were. And because he/she is my spouse (family/best friend), I know that if I'm really desperate, that he/she will at least try to help.

"But he/she always sets off my triggers. What oh what am I going to do?"

Within all of us, there is always some tension between the need to be autonomous and independent and the need to rely on others. As much as our society worships the idea of self-sufficiency, it is a myth. There is no sane person alive who isn't dependent on someone in some way. Those who feel they are one-hundred percent self-sufficient, or who act as if they are, are usually out of touch with reality and end up dependent on family members or an institution for their care.

It is normal to need others and the logical place most people turn to for meeting some of their emotional and financial security needs is their family, either their family of origin or the family they have created through marriage or cohabitation. Hence, when loved ones in your family set off your triggers, the dilemma is one of major proportions. You can probably find ways to avoid or minimize contact with some of your neighbors, co-workers, and casual friends, but it's much harder to stay away from parents, partners, close friends, or children. Avoiding family members or any of your close circle of friends usually leads to guilt or to negative responses from other family members or good friends.

For example, if you are a formerly abused child, you can choose not to be around people who are violent or exploitative, but what happens during the holidays, or at other times, when most people visit members of their original families?

Going home may be a trigger for you. Obviously, if your abuser is around, he or she will set off your triggers. But the concern here is your relationship with family members or friends who didn't directly hurt you, but who are associated with the abuse because they were a part of your life when the abuse occurred. You may want to be with them, yet they activate your triggers. If you don't go home, unless you have created a new home for yourself, you won't have a home to go to, and for many people that will elicit painful feelings of abandonment. The difficult question is, which is more intolerable: being triggered by your loved ones or distancing yourself from those loved ones; in essence, having loved ones in name only, or feeling alone and abandoned in the world?

Neither of these alternatives is satisfying. However, choosing between the pain of being triggered or the pain of disconnecting from people you love (or feel committed to) may not be your only option. Before you make such an all-or-nothing, now-or-never decision, consider taking certain steps. These steps may help to reduce the impact of the way your loved ones set off your triggers and help you find ways to control your interactions with them so that you can better manage your reactions. If some of these people are capable of and interested in helping you, they may be able to accommodate some of your needs and help make it less stressful for you to be with them.

✍ *Exercise: Specifying Exact Triggers*

"My _____ triggers me." Stay with that thought. When you say that a certain person triggers you, what image or sensation comes to your mind? What exactly is that person doing, saying, looking like, wearing, or smelling like that brings forth such a negative reaction from you?

It's probably not the case that *everything* this individual does or says triggers you, only certain very specific actions, statements, or attributes. You could also be responding to your perception of what the other person expects of you at the moment, for example, to be happy when you feel sad, to be calm when you feel anxious, to lead the way when you feel confused, or to "be over it" (the trauma) when you aren't over it, yet.

Your first task in this exercise is to try to specify exactly what it is about the other that sets off your triggers. This may require some thinking and some "research" or self-observation. You may not be fully aware of how and why this person causes your triggers to go off until you take the time to pay attention to what that person does, says, or "is." Your second task will be to draw the connection between what triggers you about that person and your trauma, if such a connection exists. As with previous exercises, this one will require you to do some writing in your journal.

1. Identify three people whom you love who trigger you. These may include some of the individuals you wrote about in chapter 1 or they can be different people.

2. For each person, try to identify what they do, say, or symbolize that sets off your triggers. Be as specific as possible in describing how each person triggers you.

3. For each trigger, what traumatic event is brought to mind?

4. How is this person related to the traumatic event? To what extent is this person responsible for the traumatic event?

5. What is the difference between the way this person looks or behaves and what happened during your trauma? Write about how you might be confusing aspects of this person with people or events related to the trauma.

6. Are you placing any feelings that belong to the traumatic event onto this person? Describe this in as much detail as possible.

7. List the ways in which each of the three people you are writing about *do not* trigger you.

8. Make a "plus" and "minus" list for each person. On the "plus" side indicate the qualities you like and the positive feelings you have for that individual. On the "minus" side, indicate the qualities you dislike and the negative feelings you have. Now, answer this question: Which of the "negative" qualities you listed might seem less negative if they were not associated with the trauma? In other words, if you had never been traumatized, would your "plus"and "minus" lists be different?

Examining the Elements of a Trigger

Joanne, a formerly abused woman, found that her daughter set off her triggers. "My daughter puts me into a rage. I know seven-year olds can be annoying, but I overreact to her and want to wallop her—over nothing. I don't know what comes over me. I love my girl, but sometimes I feel that, if I could, I'd erase her from my life," Joanne told her therapist.

Therapist: What about her triggers you?

Joanne: I don't know.

Therapist: Think about it. Does she trigger you all the time, or just sometimes?

Joanne: I hate the way she eats.

Therapist: What do you hate about the way she eats?

Joanne: The way she picks up her fork and spoon and the way she chews her food.

Therapist: Tell me more.

Joanne: I bet you think I'm crazy, hating my kid because of the way she eats. Funny, I don't get mad at her for misbehaving, but the way she eats reminds me of . . .

Therapist: Of what?

Joanne: I don't believe it . . . of my ex-husband. He holds his fork and spoon the same way she does.

Therapist: So when you see your daughter eating, you have memories of your ex-husband?

Joanne: I used to hate the way he ate.

Therapist: Why?

Joanne: Because he used to think he had better manners than me and if I didn't eat properly, he'd punish me.

Therapist: Let's go back to your daughter now. Her eating habits trigger memories of abuse, right? What else about her reminds you of him?

Joanne: Well, at times she looks like him. After all, he is her father. Sometimes she smirks the way he does and she has some of his mannerisms, too. I think she acts like him to torment me.

Therapist: You think she acts like him on purpose?

Joanne: Well, no, but it feels that way. Yet probably she acts like him because she's learned to imitate him, the way she imitates me.

Therapist: Are you saying she is not copying him to torment you and that even though she acts the way he does sometimes, her purpose isn't the same as his? His purpose was to torment you, but your daughter is just imitating a parent, which is what kids do. Is that how you see it?

Joanne continued to identify the ways her daughter triggered her. She made associations between her daughter's specific behaviors and specific traumatic memories. Then the therapist asked Joanne to think about how her daughter's behavior, intentions, thoughts, and feelings were different from those of her ex-husband who had created the trauma.

This process helped Joanne to distinguish her past from her present more clearly and reduced the degree to which she was susceptible to being triggered when her daughter acted like her ex-husband. As the result of following the steps outlined in the exercise above, Joanne was able to look at her daughter when her daughter's behaviors were about to activate her triggers, and say to herself:

"My daughter is triggering me because she eats just the way my ex-husband used to eat. He used to eat that way before he hurt me. She's not eating that way to hurt me, but because that's the way he taught her to eat. It's not her fault if she's copying her father's eating habits. My anger should be directed at him, not her. I'm not a terrible mother for being triggered by my daughter. I really love my daughter. I wish she didn't remind me of my ex-husband and I wish I never ever had to think about him or my past again. But that's not the way it is. The best I can do is try not to ruin my relationship with my daughter by overreacting to her and making her the target of the anger I still feel toward her father. He's ruined enough of my life already."

But Joanne's hostility towards her daughter went deeper than her daughter simply reminding her of the abuser. It had to do with the daughter's role in Joanne's traumatic marriage. Joanne told her therapist:

"This was the child who was supposed to make my ex-husband happy and stop him from hurting me. This was the child who was supposed to give me fulfillment. Instead, having a child became just another reason to stay married for as long as I did. If I had not had this child, I'd have left him long before I did. But having a child tied me down and made me feel even guiltier about wanting to leave."

Therapist: So who are you really angry at?

Joanne: Me. I'm mad at myself for believing the myth that a having a baby can solve marriage problems and for not seeing sooner that staying in that marriage was a lost cause.

Therapist: So you aren't angry at your daughter, but at yourself?

Joanne: It's not her fault she was born. She didn't start the abuse.

Therapist: Are you sure you aren't angry at your daughter for any other reason?

Joanne: I'm mad at her for the usual things mothers get mad about . . . but this trauma stuff has nothing to do with her. She's innocent. It's not her fault I was brainwashed into thinking that having a man was the be-all and end-all of a woman's life.

By drawing a sharp and clear distinction between her feelings about her past and her feelings about her daughter, Joanne was able to reduce the degree to which her daughter set off her triggers. You can do the same, the more you clarify the differences between the people and forces that played a role in your trauma and the loved one who is triggering you in the present.

Clarifying Expectations

Unstated expectations are a major problem in many human relationships. Many unnecessary interpersonal conflicts result from people not being sufficiently clear about what they expect of one another. From parents and teachers who order children to "do as I say," without specifying what it is they want their children to do, to lovers who fear expressing their true desires because they think their partner "expects" different words or behaviors, the issue of expectations is a major source of misunderstanding.

Consider checking out whether your perception of others' expectations is accurate. For example, you may think that your loved one expects you to do such and such, or to be a particular way. If you feel that you cannot meet those expectations, any resulting sense of inadequacy or guilt on your part may bring to the fore, or trigger, feelings of inadequacy and guilt related to your trauma. It may be the case, however, that other people don't hold the expectations of you that you think they do, or that their expectations of you may be quite different from what you think they are.

Martin, for example, was triggered by his girlfriend because he felt she expected him to be amorous every time they were together. After discussing the matter, he found out that his girlfriend didn't always want to make love. Although she didn't want a sexless relationship, having to make love every time was an expectation that Martin— not his girlfriend—was imposing on the relationship. Martin was able to trace this expectation back to some traumatic origins and, as a result, he felt less threatened when he was with his girlfriend.

Even with children it is possible to discuss expectations and clarify what it is the other expects, and what you will or will not do in the relationship.

Structure and Control

If someone you love sets off your triggers, and writing and thinking about the sources of your triggers does not sufficiently reduce the degree to which you are being triggered, you may need to treat your relationship with that person as you would any other trigger. You will need to find ways to structure and control your interaction with that person so as to minimize the degree of hyperarousal, or numbing, that is triggered. This may mean limiting the time spent with that person or structuring the time so as to cause minimum damage to your inner peace. You will need to use some of the same coping methods you would use on any other trigger.

The first step, however, is to give yourself permission to structure and control your relationship with that person so as to minimize the degree to which you are triggered. This isn't always easy, because by trying to arrange the relationship so that you can manage it, you may have to change some of the family's "rules" about how family members get together or you may have to fly in the face of family traditions or social custom. For example, you might decide that you could tolerate a holiday dinner with some of the members of your family if it wasn't held at your parents' home because that home holds bad memories for you. When you suggest having the family dinner at a restaurant, you may meet resistance from family members who, unlike you, have fond memories of the parental home, or who do not wish to get together in an unfamiliar, commercial setting.

It isn't always possible to arrange relationships to accommodate your needs, but you can try. As you think about the close relationships that trigger you, keep in mind the following question: Are there any ways to change or modify part of the relationship? For example, can the time, the place, and/or the nature of the activities be changed to make it more tolerable for you? Can you present some of these ideas to the other person involved in a nonblaming manner as a way of enhancing or improving the relationship?

For example, if your child (partner, sibling, close friend) wants you to do things with him/her that trigger you, can you put a time limit on these activities or suggest other activities? If being with a certain loved one is tolerable for only one or two hours, can you try to arrange for your interactions to be of this length?

Your need to structure and control these interactions may change over time. Do not fall victim to all-or-nothing, now-or-never thinking. Just because this year you need to limit your interactions with a loved one, doesn't meant that such will be the case forever. Over time, you may change and feel more comfortable around this person or situation, especially if the other person shows some willingness to respect your needs.

For example, some trauma survivors find it difficult to be away from home for long periods of time because their home is their "safe place" where they can control their environment and feel protected from intrusion.

Tim, for example, liked to spend most of his free time at home, yet he also wanted to date. However, dating meant leaving home, taking dates out, or visiting in their homes. When Tim first met women, he didn't tell them about the anxiety he inevitably would feel after three or four hours away from his home. He simply arranged his dates so that they wouldn't last more than three or four hours at a time.

When he became intimately involved with Laura, however, he wanted to spend more than just a few hours with her. Yet being away from home for more than three or four hours, even when he was with Laura, continued to be extremely anxiety-provoking. To make matters worse, Laura liked to go on long bike rides and weekend trips.

Tim greatly feared Laura would leave him if she discovered that he could not participate easily in the kinds of activities most people view as "normal." Yet he could no longer continue to make excuses about why he couldn't do things with her that involved long periods of time away from his home. It took all of his courage, but Tim finally revealed his limitations to Laura. "My central nervous system can't take too much noise, too many people, or too many hours away from home," he stated.

Laura responded lovingly. She was willing to keep their outings short and even suggested making a stay at his home into a "vacation" by renting special movies, buying special foods, and using the money that would be saved on new clothes for both of them.

Whenever they would go out, Laura wouldn't wait for Tim to announce that it was time to go home because he was beginning to feel anxious. To spare him the ordeal of having to announce his increasing anxiety, Laura would take the initiative and ask him if he wanted to go home. She knew that he felt guilty about cutting short their times away from home. By taking the initiative, she spared Tim the embarrassment he always felt about leaving early.

Over time, as Tim and Laura grew closer, Tim began to feel increasingly secure in the world. In Laura he had a "buddy" who was there for him, should he become anxious. The fact that help and comfort were so readily at hand helped to reduce Tim's anxiety level and he began to feel safer when he was not at home. He became able to stay out longer and longer. Within two years of dating Laura, Tim was able to take a seven-day vacation without suffering any major anxiety attacks. The fact that Laura respected his limitation and treated it in a matter-of-fact manner, rather than as a sign that Tim was defective, helped him to expand past his former limits and to participate in more activities outside his home than at any time since his trauma.

✍ *Exercise: Structure and Control*

In this exercise you are asked about ways in which you can structure and control certain relationships so that you will feel more comfortable. The goal is not to be totally free of anxiety or stress, for that goal may be unattainable. Rather, the goal is to have the anxiety or stress become manageable, not overwhelming.

You may want to write in your journal about the current relationships you listed in chapter 1, or you may want to consider other relationships that are important to you. Select three relationships you want to work on and list the names of the individuals involved below or use a separate sheet in your journal for each person.

1. _____

2. _____

3. _____

For each of the individuals you entered above, list at least one way in which that person reminds you of your trauma or behaves in a manner that sets off memories of the trauma. If there is more than one way that this person brings to the fore some of your emotional or physical stress symptoms, you may make your list longer.

1. _____ causes me distress when he/she _____ .
   When he/she acts in these ways, I am reminded of _____
   which occurred during the trauma and I tend to react by _____
   _____ .

2. _____ causes me distress when he/she _____ .
   When he/she acts in these ways, I am reminded of _____

which occurred during the trauma and I tend to react by _____
_____ .

3. _____ causes me distress when he/she _____ .
When he/she acts in these ways, I am reminded of _____
which occurred during the trauma and I tend to react by _____
_____ .

The last part of this exercise consists of trying to think of at least two ways that you can structure or control your relationship with each person named above so that you feel safer and less afraid of becoming hyperaroused, depressed, or dissociated. In your journal, or in the space provided below, list two ways you might arrange certain aspects of the relationship so as to feel more comfortable and less afraid of having to experience a stress-related emotional or physical symptom.

1. When _____ does or says _____ ,
   I can _____ or I can _____ .

2. When _____ does or says _____ ,
   I can _____ or I can _____ .

3. When _____ does or says _____ ,
   I can _____ or I can _____ .

For example, suppose you selected your relationship with your brother, Joe, to work on for improvement. Either in your journal or in the space provided above, you would first write about how Joe's words or deeds bring memories of your trauma to the fore. Then you would take a few minutes to think about how you could arrange your times with Joe so as to minimize the power of those memories.

Sample:

When Joe makes certain jokes or comments, I am reminded of the trauma. I react by becoming very angry and wanting to yell at him, or by shutting down and feeling like a mummy. In the future, when Joe makes these kinds of comments, I can tell him that I need to excuse myself for a minute. I don't have to tell him why I need to excuse myself if I don't want to. All I have to say is, "Sorry to interrupt, but I need to excuse myself for a minute. I'll be back as soon as I can," then, I'll go to the bathroom or the hall and practice some deep breathing techniques and decide what to do.

Another step I can take is to tell Joe how I feel when I hear his jokes. I don't have to criticize him, but I can say, "I feel sad when I hear you talk about _____ ."

Sample:

Or, suppose you select your relationship with your child Annie to work on. When Annie, who is five years old, knocks on the door to your room and unexpectedly wants to come in and "talk," it may remind you of how an abusive family member would come into your room unexpectedly, supposedly to "talk," but in reality to criticize, hit, and/or molest you. You might write something like the following:

My daughter is not abusive and she has every right to expect me to be available to her for conversation. But I can't tolerate feeling "stuck" in the room with her, even though she's my child and I know I am not really "trapped" in a room with an abuser, as I was in the past.

To feel more comfortable, I could limit the time I spend with Annie. But I don't want to do that. I want to be a good parent to her, which means not cutting short the time she needs to spend with me. Another possibility would be to leave the door open when we talk, and I could sit near the open door, so that I won't feel trapped. If Annie objects to the door being open because she wants to talk confidentially, I can ask her to whisper in my ear or I can suggest that we go to her room or to a larger room in the house. I feel less trapped in rooms that are not my bedroom, because it was in my bedroom that I was always abused.

Family Life Cycle Triggers

Families go through certain changes over time. New members are added through birth or marriage and old members die, change, or move away. There are certain normal transitions in family life such as a child leaving home or marrying, or an older adult becoming dependent. In some cases, these normal transitions in the family may trigger trauma-related memories for a survivor.

If, in any way, the change brings about a loss, the loss may trigger memories of losses associated with the trauma. For example, a child leaving home for college can take on additional emotional meaning for a survivor and, to those who haven't been traumatized, the survivor's reaction may seem "abnormal" or "extreme." As Douglas Scaturo and Peter Hayman (1990, 67) write, "for the combat veteran who has frequently observed the loss of significant friendships often instantaneously, randomly, and brutally on the battlefield, the normative transitional events of family life may take on exaggerated emotional proportions by the standards of those who have never been traumatized." Thus the event of children leaving home is experienced not only as a step towards the child's independence and maturation, but also as agony and betrayal. A child's leaving, however appropriate or innocent, brings to the surface the veteran's "feelings of total abandonment, isolation, and helplessness previously experienced during combat."

The same uncomfortable feelings might be experienced by survivors of vehicular accidents, family violence, suicide, stranger crime, or a natural catastrophe if the trauma involved the loss of a loved one or a separation. If you fall into this category, then you might find yourself being triggered by a loved one simply because he/she is making a transition in the normal family life cycle. At the very time that you want to get the most out of your relationship with a certain loved one, you may become furious with him or her for "leaving you" (even though he or she isn't really leaving you, but following the path of the ordinary life cycle of leaving home, taking a partner, growing older) and you may be struck with a host of trauma-related feelings. Your reaction can make it difficult for you to relate to that person at the time when you want to function best in your relationship with him or her.

At these times, it is important to know what is going on inside yourself: that you are reacting on two levels—the normal family life-cycle level and the trauma-related level. All families go through upheavals of some sort when there is a transition, but you may also have trauma-related reactions with which to contend, which make these transitions more complex and more painful.

🖎 Exercise: Family Life Cycle Triggers

The purpose of the following questions is to help you make the connections between events occurring in your family today because of the normal transitions of families and events that are related to your trauma. Read each of the following questions carefully and respond to each question by writing your answers in your journal.

1. Is there a change going on in your family right now? Has there been an addition or subtraction due to birth, marriage, illness, death, or the relocation of a family member? Are you going through a transition in relation to your family, i.e., are you leaving home, getting married, divorcing, about to become a parent or grandparent?

2. How does the transition your family is undergoing right now remind you of your trauma? What trauma-related memories and feelings must you deal with in addition to the feelings the transition is bringing up for you? How would you react to this transition if you had never been traumatized?

3. Do you feel that additional support at this time, either through a support group, trusted friend, or therapist, might help you?

4. How is your reaction to this transition affecting other family members?

5. Although you may not be able to change your feelings, is there something you want to say or do that you haven't said or done yet with respect to what is going on in the family that you feel would be beneficial to you and/or other family members? What prevents you from acting?

For example, if your son is leaving for college, does this bring back memories of young men you saw die in a trauma? These memories may have kept you from recognizing your son's achievements the way you would like. Is there some way you want to honor your son? Don't let the terrible past keep you from doing what you would like to do in the present.

Age-Related Trigger Reactions

You might find yourself being triggered by someone in your family because they have reached an age that you associate with a trauma. For example, if you were raped at age seven, when your child reaches seven, you might find yourself having a type of anniversary reaction related to your child's age. You might feel especially protective of, or repelled by, your child, or have a variety of feelings more related to what you experienced when you were seven than to your seven-year old's behaviors. If you were sent to war at age nineteen, when your son or daughter turns nineteen, you might have trigger reactions to your child's age. Or if someone who abused you was fifteen when the abuse began, you might be triggered when someone in the family turns fifteen.

These kinds of age-related anniversary reactions in family members have been documented among all kinds of people. For example, several researchers have found a remarkable correlation between the age at which people develop certain psychiatric or physical problems and the age of the death of a family member, especially if the loss was a traumatic one. Hilgard (1953, 1969) found that parents develop symptoms when one of their children reaches the age at which the parent experienced a traumatic episode or significant loss in childhood.

She and other researchers documented many instances where adults developed physical illness, psychosis, and clinical depression when their children reached the age the adults had been when they lost a parent or sibling. Some adults develop such problems when they reach the age of a parent who died during their childhood. For example, in one study it was found that if someone's parent died in childhood and that person later married and had children, if that person was later hospitalized for mental illness, it was likely "beyond chance expectancy" to occur "when the oldest child of that person was within one year of the age the person was when the parent died" (Hilgard 1969, 198).

✍ Exercise: Age-Related Trigger Reactions

Take a fresh sheet of paper and answer these questions in your journal.

1. What ages are the loved ones who set off your triggers?

2. Given what you know about your past, is there any special significance associated with any of these ages? Was there a loss or a traumatic

incident associated with any of these ages? How old were the people who died in your trauma? How old were you when you were traumatized?

3. To what extent are your trigger reactions to this particular loved one fueled by the significance of his or her age?

4. How might awareness of the trauma-related aspects of this individual's age help you to manage the relationship better? Now that you have an additional awareness about why you are being triggered, is this a relationship you want to keep or not keep? If you decide to keep this relationship, how can it be changed to make it more rewarding?

References

Hilgard, Josephine R. 1953. "Anniversary Reactions in Parents Precipitated by Children." *Psychiatry* vol. XVI:73–80.

Hilgard, Josephine R. 1969. "Depressive and Psychotic States as Anniversary Reactions to Sibling Death in Childhood." *International Psychiatry Clinics* vol. VI:197–211.

Scaturo, Douglas and Peter Hayman. 1990. "The Impact of Combat Trauma Across the Family Life Cycle: Clinical Considerations." *Journal of Traumatic Stress Studies* vol. 5:2 (April) 273–288.

9

Positive Contributions of Trauma to Relationships

Out of pain
Great sorrow flows
And then the sorrow
Gave birth to love.

—Tanya, incest survivor

Positive Aftereffects of Trauma

According to an ancient Greek myth, Haphaestus, son of Zeus and Hera, had post-traumatic stress disorder. His trauma was being born to warring parents who beat him, called him names, and wished that he had never been born. In one version of the myth, Haphaestus was beaten by his mother, Hera, because he was born with a deformed leg and disgraced her status as the Queen of the gods by being a cripple. In another version of the myth, Haphaestus was beaten and almost drowned by his father, Zeus, for trying to protect his mother, when Zeus attempted to assault her physically. In this version, Haphaestus acquired his deformed leg by being thrown off Mount Olympus by his angry father.

Of all the gods on Mount Olympus, Haphaestus was the only one who was physically disabled and who suffered from depressions. Whenever Haphaestus would become enraged, he'd dash off to a small island and hide until his rage passed and he could be "civilized" again. Once on the island, he would descend into a cave where he hid from everyone—mother, father, friends, foe, and even beautiful goddesses—until he could work off his anger and emerge ready to cope with the world again. But this was no ordinary island, for this island was really the top of a volcano. There is great emotional symbolism in the fact that Haphaestus's cave was part of a volcano in that depression can be viewed as repressed anger—or as the result of keeping anger "underground."

Haphaestus's cave was unique in that it was also a studio and artist's workshop. Haphaestus (called Vulcan in Latin) was a master craftsman. When he was hiding from others in his cave, he made beautiful pottery and jewelry. He also made exquisite swords, bejeweled and sturdy chariots, and many other practical tools and weapons. He took all the energy involved in the anger and pain of being abused, unloved, and deformed and used that energy to create beautiful works of art and magnificent tools. Haphaestus was wounded by life, but his wounds were the source of his creativity and his determination to make beautiful things.

According to the myth, Zeus once threw Haphaestus into the ocean in the hope that he would drown. Haphaestus would have died if he had not been saved by two sea nymphs. They saved his life not only physically but also emotionally, by providing soothing and comfort. They also saved his life psychologically in another way: they taught him how to work and how to create. From the nymphs, he learned the fundamentals of metalwork and the value of being productive and creative. Ironically, Haphaestus's curse—his black moods, his "outcast" status among the gods, his crippled leg, his hypersensitivity to criticism and ridicule, his being the only god on Mount Olympus who knew what it was like to hurt, physically and emotionally—was the source of his creative gift and beautiful products, which were sought after by all the gods.

Haphaestus might have been the social "leper" of Mount Olympus; he couldn't compete with the other male gods in terms of looks or wealth, but he was highly valued for his creative work. Using his talents, rather than his looks, he was able to succeed in obtaining what every other god on Mount Olympus and man on Earth wanted but could not get: the goddess of love and beauty, the goddess Aphrodite, as his wife. Just as several positive results came out of Haphaestus's various traumas, something positive came out of yours. You just might not recognize it. It is so easy for trauma survivors to focus only on the negative—on the opportunities they missed, on the emotional and physical limitations they must constantly contend with, on the time and energy they must spend managing their triggers—that it is easy to overlook some of the positive traits that can result from being traumatized.

In this chapter some of the positive personality characteristics that can come from being traumatized are discussed, and you will be asked to identify how you grew and developed as a result of your trauma. This work is not an attempt to sugarcoat your experience and make it seem as if "everything is fine." If you've been traumatized, everything isn't fine, but that does not mean that you may not have acquired certain strengths and insights as the result of your experience.

The Appreciation of Life

Having come close to death, or seen death, you may now appreciate life in a way that someone who is still in denial about death cannot do. Because you have suffered, you can have empathy for those who are suffering in this world, and there are plenty of those. Their traumas might not have been like your trauma, but you know what it's like to be humbled by pain and, if you've learned anything from your trauma, you know not to mock those who suffer and not to feel that you are superior to them. If you've been touched by pain, your heart may now be open to the many people in this world who have been unjustly treated or who suffer misfortunes of various kinds.

Although your trauma may have isolated you or cut you off from those who are only concerned with appearances or materialistic values, it can bind you to the multitudes of human beings on this planet who struggle to keep their sanity and who go through their days with hearts full of grief and loss. You now have a bond with trauma survivors throughout the world. Just one look at the daily newspaper will show you that there are thousands of people in the world with whom you have something in common.

Perhaps this perspective can help to ease the pain you felt if you were stigmatized or excluded by members of your family or social circle after you were traumatized. You may have felt like an outcast then. But if you are an outcast, there are millions like you. Just open your eyes and look around. Human misery is everywhere and you, because of your trauma, can understand the father who lost his children in a fire, the woman who was beaten by her husband, the young man who was disfigured in a car accident, and the teenager who was mugged and raped.

Finding Meaning in Suffering

This new empathy for human suffering can open up the world of relationships in a new way for you. Although some people may slam their doors in your face because they look down on someone who has been through what you've been through, there are probably many others who would welcome an understanding heart and a sympathetic conversation. Should you decide to reach out, there are countless opportunities for you to help alleviate human suffering. Indeed, many trauma survivors find great meaning and comfort in volunteer work or in helping those who were similarly traumatized or who suffered great losses.

Victor Frankl, a psychiatrist who survived the Nazi concentration camps, has written much about finding meaning in suffering (1959). If suffering is part of life, he says, it must have a purpose, one of which is that it binds us to the rest of humanity. In his philosophy of healing from trauma, he stresses the need for finding meaning and purpose in life, often by helping others who are hurting or by making a positive contribution to society, similar to the beautiful metalwork of Haphaestus.

When Haphaestus was in his cave, he was overflowing with psychic energy—anger, hurt, the desire for revenge, and the desire to feel powerful. He smoldered and seethed and while he smoldered, he created. Having been powerless to stop the other gods from making fun of his leg and powerless to stop his parents from fighting and hurting him, he wanted—needed—a way to feel powerful. So he created. Other trauma survivors have used that kind of Haphaestian creative energy to create and organize political and social movements.

Support Groups

Mothers Against Drunk Driving (MADD) was founded by a mother whose child was killed by a drunk driver. Rape crisis and battered women's crisis centers were originally started by women who had been raped or abused. The "founding mothers" of these groups were like Haphaestus—full of anger and pain. Often these women had experienced rejection from their husbands, families, and communities because in many places victims of rape or battering are still judged as having "deserved" or "provoked" the rape or the beating.

These women had been wounded, but they banded together and started crisis centers and hot lines for other women in need. Some of them worked long hours for little or no wages. But it didn't matter—they had the energy, Haphaestian trauma-generated energy. It has been said, "No one works harder than survivors." The saying is a true one, especially if the survivors are working to help other survivors or others in need.

This kind of creative energy has also been demonstrated by survivors of airline crashes, who have organized and formed powerful lobbies to influence legislation pertaining to airline safety and the treatment of survivors of airline disasters. The Stroke Club is another example of survivor energy at work in the world. It was founded by a handful of people who had been disabled by strokes. Initially, they joined together to give each other emotional support. Later, they expanded to arrange for services, such as the assistance of occupation or physical therapists. What began as a conversation between two or three people in a hospital room has mushroomed into dozens of Stroke Clubs throughout the U.S.

If there is no support group for survivors of your type of trauma, perhaps you can start one. Or perhaps you can do something else to give meaning and purpose to your painful experience. According to another myth, Ares (Mars), the god of war, had two horses. Their names were Fear and Panic and Ares never went anywhere without them, and without him, they went wild. Without Ares to direct them, the horses' movements were erratic, directionless, and had no purpose. But when Ares firmly gripped their reins and directed their powerful energy, there was no goal that could not be won. There are two messages in this myth: the first is that fear and panic are inseparable from trauma. (Even the god of war was always accompanied by fear and panic.) The second message is that when the power inherent in fear and panic (adrenaline reactions and intense emotions associated with trauma) are harnessed and directed toward specific goals, much can be accomplished.

History offers many examples of men and women who were traumatized but subsequently used their trauma-related energies and perspectives to create empires, works of art, and major humanitarian efforts and institutions. Peter the Great of Russia had PTSD. His high adrenaline levels caused him nightmares and seizures; they were also the basis of his efforts to rebuild and modernize what was then Czarist Russia. Beethoven was a trauma survivor. His symphonies did not arise from a man who had a well-balanced, middle-class life, but from one who, like Haphaestus, had known parental rejection and abuse. Haphaestus went to a cave to create beautiful objects: Beethoven went to his room and created beautiful music.

Some survivors have been able to create literature from their sufferings. For example, in her recent autobiography (1997), Linda Cutting describes the relationship between her successful career as a concert pianist and her history of childhood sexual abuse. One critic's response was that Cutting created a "powerful piece from the dark melodies and painful dissonances of her lost childhood" (Zuckerman 1997, 5).

Institutional Support

Because of secondary wounding experiences, trauma survivors become well-acquainted with political and social realities. If you've been traumatized and have had to seek help from the government, the courts, insurance companies, and various other institutions, you probably learned quickly about the inadequacies of these institutions as assistance-providers. You probably also learned that the way certain organizations operate often doesn't match the way they are supposed to operate. You are no longer socially or politically naive. This may be painful, but it is a valuable asset when trying to function in today's world. Your insights might also be helpful to others.

Survivor Skills

Your trauma taught you humility; it also taught you about the power of emotions. You can no longer pretend that feelings are not important or that it's "easy" to acquire emotional stability. You know how powerful and disruptive feelings can be. If you've ever been suicidal, homicidal, or severely depressed, you know that feelings have the potential to kill. Just as you've learned to respect the power of social and legal institutions, you've learned to respect the power of emotions. This helps prepare you for life, including future relationships, because you will never be naive enough to believe that you can "handle anything" and, hopefully, you have learned not to disregard your feelings, or the feelings of others.

Because you've experienced so many feelings, some of them extremely uncomfortable, you have acquired an endurance to a wide range of human emotion. Unlike others who have yet to be tested emotionally by trauma or hard times, you have demonstrated that you can tolerate a wide range of feelings. This is no mean feat. It is a source of strength.

Like it or not, you have survivor skills. You have borne what for many people is unbearable. Like Haphaestus with his broken leg and depressive episodes, you may have physical and emotional scars. But you are still here, and given the high suicide and hospitalization rates for certain kinds of trauma survivors, still being here, i.e., alive, is a major accomplishment. This accomplishment takes on even more significance if you are clean, sober, and free of addiction. This is why you can call yourself a survivor—because you survived. You did not die or lose your mind. Yes, you have times where you don't feel emotionally stable or when your mind doesn't function well. But you aren't dead and you aren't permanently locked up in a back ward of a state hospital. You are alive, and still trying to lead a rich, full life.

This is an asset you may fail to appreciate and others, too, may fail to appreciate, unless they are struck by tragedy. Hopefully, those you know and love will not meet with undue hardships in life, but if and when they do, they have the perfect person to turn to for advice, encouragement, and example—you. If your brother's house burns down, if your neighbor is in a car wreck that leaves him paralyzed, if your co-worker's mother commits suicide, if your nephew comes home from war, or if your cousin is raped, you will know something about what that feels like. You, who may have been scorned or rejected by some of these people, may be sought after because of the wisdom, insight, and perseverance you had to have to live through what you have lived through. Just like Haphaestus, who was ridiculed at parties where all the other Olympian gods were beautiful, healthy, and knew nothing of physical or emotional pain, you, who once felt like "Frankenstein," may be sought after the way the gods flocked to Haphaestus because they wanted the beautiful objects he created.

After the large number of earthquakes, fires, and floods our country experienced in recent decades, Vietnam veterans' groups volunteered to help in rescue efforts and counseling survivors. Many of these men and women had been rejected by their communities because of their psychological scars. But then they were turned to as sources of information and pillars of strength on how to handle trauma. You may experience this same turn of events. Someday, you may be valued because of your hard-won survivor skills and your ability to endure.

Another quality that trauma can foster is loyalty. People who have been traumatized sometimes develop an intense loyalty to fellow survivors as well as to those who helped them in their time of need. Just as you will never forget your trauma and never forget those who were callous or hurtful, you will never forget those who were kind to you. Your loyalty to those people can be intense and long-lasting. Because of your trauma, you may have a capacity for loyalty to a person, a job, or to a religious, social, or political effort, that is simply enormous. Others will value you for your ability to be loyal and you should learn to value that aspect of yourself.

✎ Exercise: Identifying Strengths

It is easy to lose sight of your strengths. The tendency among survivors is to look at how the trauma disabled them and how scarred they are or how the trauma made it difficult for them to achieve certain goals. The purpose of this exercise is to counter that tendency and help you identify what you did and what strengths you displayed *despite* the negative events that happened to you and despite your PTSD, depression, or other disabling mental health problems. In your journal write complete answers to the following questions.

1. What strengths did you display during the trauma or afterwards that helped you to survive and to function?

2. Despite the trauma and the reactions you had to it, what strengths have you displayed and what have you achieved since the trauma ended? Do you have increased appreciation for life, empathy for human suffering, humility, knowledge of emotional realities, knowledge of political and social realities, an ability to tolerate a wide range of feelings, or an ability to be loyal? Despite the trauma, have you been able to maintain some relationships, take care of your physical needs, keep a job, or develop an artistic talent? What else have you achieved despite the trauma and its impact?

3. In which of your current relationships are the trauma-related strengths you just identified useful?

✎ Exercise: Identifying Hidden Strengths

Sometimes survivors have difficulty recognizing their strengths because they've given negative labels to those strengths. As Torem (1994) points out, sometimes survivors call themselves "stupid or silly," when, in fact, they were simply "naive" or "innocent." Those who call themselves "rebellious" may, in fact, be creative. Those who had to lie or pretend during their trauma may call themselves "phony." In fact, they were simply being smart survivors. If you call yourself "confused" or "mixed up," is it not that you simply have the courage to face ambivalence and the wisdom to see the many sides of a situation?

Relabeling these traits may sound like just a mind game, but it isn't. Relabeling these traits in terms of their function or usefulness during the trauma is being accurate and honest. Mislabeling them in an unnecessarily derogatory way, or glamorizing them, would constitute a mind game. Giving negative labels to traits that were helpful during the trauma is unnecessary criticism and makes you feel like "damaged goods." Now, go to your journal and on a fresh sheet of paper write complete answers to the following two questions:

1. What negative labels do you give yourself? Are these negative labels disguised forms of positive qualities?

2. What negative labels do others apply to you? What positive qualities might lie underneath these negative labels? For example, a rape survivor who was working hard at a rape awareness seminar was called "hyper" and a "workaholic" by some of her friends. "I'm not 'hyper,' I'm high energy and I'm not a 'workaholic,' I'm a dedicated committed worker," she told them, thus reframing negative labels into positive ones, which were also more accurate.

The Mental Illness Label and Pop Psychology

All too often trauma survivors are stigmatized and, in a sense, revictimized by mental illness labels. Your first encounter with a mental illness label may have been at a doctor's office or at a mental health clinic. Some psychiatric diagnoses sound better than others. For example, most people would prefer to be diagnosed as having an "adult adjustment disorder," "an acute stress reaction," or "post-traumatic stress disorder," than as having a "borderline personality," "an anti-social personality," or a "character disorder." Certain psychiatric diagnoses have extremely stigmatizing connotations and imply that you, the sufferer, are deficient in important respects, as well as being a hopeless case. Indeed, in the mental health field, it is not unusual for persons with diagnoses of borderline personality, character disorder, or antisocial personality to be viewed as less desirable clients and difficult to treat.

Even if you think the labels you have been given are accurate and fair, to be given any mental illness label can feel extremely degrading and dehumanizing. The problem with a psychiatric label in our day and age is that, in a sense, the mental health field has almost replaced the clergy in terms of deciding who is "good" and who is "bad." People use psychological concepts to evaluate themselves and one another in the manner that, centuries ago, religious concepts were used as standards for "good" and "evil."

To those whose knowledge of psychology is limited to talk shows and pop psychology, a mental health label is an all-or-nothing concept. To those who are unaware of the complexity of illnesses such as depression, post-traumatic stress disorder, or addiction, once you have been labeled, that label explains everything about you and defines your entire personality, not only as it is now, but as it was the past and as it will be in the future. There is no room for change in the future, nor can it be conceived that there are parts of you that may not have been affected by the trauma or its aftereffects.

For example, if you have PTSD, then all your thoughts and behavior are seen as reflecting your PTSD, from the way you hold hands to the kind of movies you like. But if you were diabetic, everything you do or think would not be seen as reflecting your diabetes. People often refer to someone, for example, as a "manic-depressive." But do people refer to someone with cancer as cancerous? Of course not.

Cancer is accepted as a true illness. But manic-depressive illness and other illnesses, such as depression, panic disorder, paranoia, post-traumatic stress disorder, and other psychiatric disorders are often not accepted as true illness in that it is commonly believed that if a person "tried harder" or "really wanted to get better," the illness would go away.

Of course, such is not the case. Having PTSD, depression, panic disorder, or any of the various mental health problems associated with trauma is not your choice. It is not your dream come true. More accurately, it is your nightmare come true, yet people who don't suffer from the kinds of problems you do often have trouble recognizing that no matter how hard you try to overcome what happened to you, certain scars and patterns remain. You don't like it either. In fact, you can't stand it, which is why you are in therapy, or reading this book, or going to twelve-step programs, or other support groups.

Talk shows and other media presentations that show survivors "getting well" after one or two therapy sessions or after they meet the love of their life do a major disservice to survivors who must struggle, often for years, to cope with the aftereffects of their trauma. This is a microwave society: we like instant food and instant fixes. But recovery doesn't work that way. It takes time and effort to get better. It also takes the support of others and the recognition that even though you might have a mental illness label and that label reflects real symptoms, your mental illness is not all you are. It doesn't define your entire being. Not everything you think, do, or feel is the result of your trauma.

You were a person before the trauma and some of those parts of you have not changed. You have a first name and a last name and those names are not PTSD, panic disorder, depression, or borderline personality disorder. These labels may be a part of you, but they are not all of you. These labels are designed to identify only those parts of you that were hurt by the trauma—not your strengths. Mental illness labels tend to define you in terms of what you cannot do or cannot do well. Their purpose is not to provide a complete personality description, even though that is how they are sometimes used by helping professionals, survivors, and their loved ones. Do not allow those labels to define you and, most importantly, do not define yourself by such labels.

✍ Exercise: Disarming the Mental Illness Labels

Take a fresh sheet of paper in your journal and answer the following questions as completely as you can.

1. What mental health diagnoses have you been given?

2. Have you looked up these diagnoses, read about them, or asked your doctor or therapist what they mean?

3. Does the diagnosis fit? Is there a possibility that you might have been misdiagnosed?

4. If you have received an inaccurate label, do you want to discuss this with the mental health or medical person who gave you this label?

5. What parts of yourself were relatively untouched by the trauma? Have those parts been viewed by others or yourself through the lenses of a mental health diagnosis? How accurate are these views?

Remember that you know more about your inner life and past experiences than anyone else in the world.

The Wish for a Magic Rescuer

When you were being traumatized, you probably prayed for a magic rescuer. You wanted one during the trauma and you probably could use one now as you try to manage your traumatic stress reactions and the difficulties they impose on your life and your relationships. The problem is that there is no such thing as a magic rescuer, neither is there emotional security, no matter how great the need you may feel for both.

Your need for someone to love you, understand you, and be there for you is even greater than the need most people have for such a person because once you have been traumatized, your internal sense of safety has been violated. You aren't as self-confident as you were before the trauma and now it's even harder for you to trust in yourself, because you don't know when, or to what degree, you might be triggered and how you might react once triggered. If you are suffering from PTSD or depression, it's hard for you to predict what mood you will be in or how well you will be able to think. You simply can't take yourself for granted, the way you might have been able to before the trauma.

At the same time that you may be feeling insecure within yourself, you may also be unsure about where and how you fit in the world. The trauma changed so many things—the way you feel, the way you think, your sociopolitical awareness, and your basic values system. However, with so many aspects of your personality changing, you may be undergoing an identity change, as well as a traumatic reaction. At such times it is understandable that you would wish for another person who could provide you with both a sense of safety within yourself and a sense of connection with the outside world. You may even be thinking that once you find this person, you'll be able to be yourself again and belong somewhere again.

Other people, especially a cherished intimate, can provide you with a certain amount of comfort, some sense of belonging and a certain degree of emotional security in the face of your inner turmoil. But no one person, whether it be a therapist or a lover, can "fix" you or erase your past, provide you with self-love, or with a sense of self-acceptance of who you are and what the trauma did to you. Neither can a single relationship be a substitute for the many relationships necessary to make a life rich and meaningful.

If you are lucky, you have a special person in your life and there may be a great deal of mutual love between the two of you. But even that person cannot be parent, sibling, spiritual advisor, therapist, "buddy," and lover, at all times. Neither can that one person compensate for anyone you lost during the trauma. Although you may certainly feel you "belong" to that person, you still will need other people to feel connected to, and a role in society that you believe to be meaningful in order to feel that your life is purposeful.

"If someone would love me, I could love myself" is a common feeling. Perhaps you hope that another person, will "rescue" you, not only from your self-doubts, but from your pain, confusion, grief, and any other aftereffects of the trauma.

However, neither sex nor the love and strength of another person can deliver you from dealing with your past or with your present problems at home or work. You cannot place the responsibility for your life on another person. While the love and support of others can make all the difference in the world and, indeed, the purpose of this book is to help you expand your loving connections, there is no "magic rescuer" who will meet all your needs or save you from yourself. Erich Fromm (1941), one of the first therapists to describe the human struggle against social and personal pressures to conform, called the wish for a magic rescuer the attempt to "escape from freedom." If you look to someone else to take charge of your life, it will be restricted by narrow borders and you may never develop a healthy self-reliance.

No one out there can meet your many needs or take away all your pain, and if you put this expectation on another person and it isn't met, then you may interpret this as further evidence that people are no good and life is not worth living. The truth is that healthy living requires a balance between self-reliance and reliance on others. Either extreme isn't realistic and is doomed to failure. If you expect to get everything you want in life from another person, you won't be forced to extend yourself and struggle for what you want, intellectually or emotionally. Your dependence on that person wouldn't eliminate your feelings of helplessness, anxiety, or insecurity: it would only perpetuate them. You would live in a state of fear that the other person might abandon you. If you were dependent on a magic rescuer, you might find yourself spending much of your energy figuring out how to please that person so as not to lose him or her. Or, rather than take responsibility for your own life, you might spend your energy manipulating your rescuer so he or she would continue to guide, protect, and strengthen you.

If you do have someone whom you see as your magic rescuer, as much as you desire and need that person, you may find yourself resentful of your dependency on him or her. You may find yourself rebelling against or having hostile feelings towards that person. Since you might think it is dangerous to be angry with someone you need so much, you might hide or repress your feelings. This would create still another internal conflict for you, adding to your stress.

✍ Exercise: The Wish for a Magic Rescuer

In your journal write complete answers to the following questions:

1. If you could have a magic rescuer, what would that person do for you? Can you think of at least three things that person would do for you?

2. Can you do any of these things for yourself or can the three (or more) needs you identified in the previous question be met by three different persons rather than by the same person?

3. Is there someone in your life, or has there ever been someone in your life, whom you viewed as a "magic rescuer"? Do any of the people you wrote about in chapter 1 in the Relationship Inventory, fall into the category of "magic rescuer"? What was that person able to give to you? What were that person's limitations?

4. What happens when someone whom you turn to as a "magic rescuer" disappoints you? What feelings and problems are you left with because the "magic rescuer" wasn't there to help? Is there a way to manage these problems better, or must some of these feelings and problems simply be endured?

5. If you met yourself and tried to be your own magic rescuer, what could you do for yourself? What stops you from doing these things for yourself?

6. Give some thought to a somewhat philosophical question: What can one human being actually do for another human being? What are the limits of human love and affection? Are you expecting others to do for you what you could not possibly do for yourself, if you were in their position?

7. If you give up the hope for a magic rescuer, what kinds of feelings of loss, anger, and betrayal are you left with?

References

Cutting, Linda. 1997. *Memory Slips*. New York: Harper Collins.

Frankl, Victor. 1959. *Man's Search for Meaning*. New York: Simon and Schuster.

Fromm, Erich. 1941. *Escape From Freedom*. New York: Rinehart & Co., Inc.

Torem, Morshin. 1994. "Trauma Work: Now, Later or Never." Audiotape 94-ISTSS-95 of lecture presented at the 10th Annual Meeting of the International Society for Traumatic Stress. Chicago. November.

Zuckerman, Eugenia. 1997. "Overture to a Recovery." *Washington Post*. Bookworld. February 3.

10

You and Your Traumatized Self

Coming to Terms with Your Traumatized Self

"Lots of times when I cry, it's not me crying, but her," says Nancy. "I'm a full-grown woman who functions well and is responsible and mature, except sometimes with food. But inside me there's a crippled little girl. She's ugly and battered, with a bloody nose, black eyes, a busted lip, and aches and pains all over from where she was kicked. But she's me, and until I realized that she was me, as much me as my grown-up self, I had no peace and could not stay clean and sober and free from overeating.

"I used to hate her because she brought so much pain into my life. But I've made friends with her and every morning when I wake up, I look in the mirror and tell her that I love her and I will protect her and take care of her. I won't let her get too tired, or take her to places that frighten her or set off any of her triggers. She has a protector now—me—and I'll never abandon her the way I was abandoned."

For many years Nancy denied the crippled girl deep within her. Nobody had loved this little girl, so why should she? Having been abused was something the Nancy of today wanted to forget. It was nothing to be proud of. Let bygones be bygones. The Nancy of the past was useless and she stood in the way of everything a good life had to offer now.

Nancy wanted to bury the little girl, but she would not stay buried. When the little girl became suicidal, the grown-up Nancy would suffer from depressions that didn't allow her to function very well. When the little girl would become angry, the grown-up Nancy would want to stop the anger with cakes and pies and alcohol, as she had in the past. When the little Nancy would become sad and lonely, she'd try to comfort herself the way she had in the past—by stealing, lying, overspending, and overeating.

Sometimes Nancy felt as if she had a split personality. Although Nancy didn't suffer from Multiple Personality Disorder (MPD), there were times the traumatized little Nancy took over, which left the grown-up Nancy feeling as helpless and hopeless as she had as a child. Until Nancy made friends with her traumatized self and came to respect the crippled girl inside of her, even the little girl's need to drink and overeat and tell lies, Nancy had trouble making headway in her twelve-step programs of recovery from alcohol abuse and compulsive overeating.

The challenge facing every trauma survivor is to confront his or her traumatized self and make some kind of healthy alliance with that part. Too often, trauma survivors punish their traumatized selves, or deny that they are even there. Because there is no relationship between the present self and the traumatized self, it is easy for the traumatized self to erupt, at times, to get out of control and take over the trauma survivor's life. Of course this creates problems because the traumatized self is still living in the reality of the trauma, not the reality of the present.

Coming to terms with your traumatized self is the work of trauma-processing. If you feel you've already done a lot of personal trauma work, the following exercises may seem redundant and unnecessary to you. You may want to look them over, however, and complete them anyway, to solidify the gains you have made in your individual or group trauma work.

If you are right in the middle of your trauma-processingwork, the following exercises may be helpful to you. However, you may need to work with a mental health professional in completing these written assignments or, at the very minimum, reread the Cautions section in the Introduction and monitor yourself for the reactions described there. As stated in the Cautions section, this book may not be suitable for persons suffering from MPD. If you suffer from MPD, you should use this book only under the guidance and careful monitoring of a qualified mental health professional.

The Importance of Knowing Your Traumatized Self

It is frequently said that you can't have good relationships with others unless you first have a good relationship with yourself. This is a simplistic platitude in that it implies that having a good relationship with yourself is an easy matter, which it is not. It can take a lifetime to come to terms with parts of yourself. This platitude is also misleading in that it suggests that you have to "fix yourself" first, before attempting to enter into and sustain relationships. People in recovery programs or therapy often are told by well-intentioned, but misguided, counselors, sponsors, or friends, that they need to "focus on yourself" and avoid relationships until a certain level of self-acceptance and self-understanding is reached. Yet it is only through relationships with others that we encounter ourselves. That is, strong positive or negative reactions to others tell us about our inner needs and struggles.

Nevertheless, there is considerable merit in looking inward and examining different parts of ourselves. Most human beings are very complex and full of contradictions which, in some cases, no amount of therapy can totally erase. We all have parts of us that war within. For example, many people experience a tug of war between the need for security and the need for adventure; the desire to be generous and the fear about giving; the desire for intimacy and the fear of closeness. It is no sign of psychological inferiority to struggle internally and be "mixed up" about certain issues: it is part of the human condition. It is a rare person who is always sure of his or her views or feelings and there should be no shame attached holding contradictory feelings. Yet in our society, people who are ambivalent are sometimes pejoratively labeled as "wishy-washy" or "weak," and the people who are admired tend to be those who are unequivocally certain about what they want and "go for it" by pursuing their goals without internal doubts or fear of external obstacles.

When you've been traumatized, this task of understanding the divergent contradictory parts of yourself and focusing your energies toward certain goals is even more complex, for deep within you there lives a very powerful person—your traumatized self. You may be safe now and, like Nancy, you may want to disown the part of you that was traumatized, but that part is still there and your inborn drive for self-preservation is not going to permit the knowledge and experiences of that traumatized person simply to disappear. The woman who was battered, the girl who was raped, the warrior who killed, the parent whose child was killed, will always be a part of the traumatized self. While you may wish, with all your heart, for that part of you not to be there anymore, that cannot be.

All too often trauma survivors despise their traumatized selves because during the trauma they were helpless, victimized, confused, or engaged in acts for which they now feel great shame and guilt. It is easy to put down or punish your traumatized self, but fighting him or her, ridiculing and shaming him or her uses up psychic energy, leaving less energy for engaging in relationships or pursuing other goals.

If you really want to reduce the impact of your traumatized self, you need to know that part of yourself and, ultimately, to make friends with him or her, no matter how much you don't like that person or wish he or she were different. You need to build a working relationship with your traumatized self that will empower you to have fulfilling relationships with others.

Building a Healthy Relationship with Your Traumatized Self

The way to build a relationship with your traumatized self is the same way you'd build a relationship with any other person—you talk to that person, try to see his or her point of view, and try to understand why he or she feels or acts the way they do and figure out what they need.

One way to do this is to write a letter to your traumatized self and have that self write a letter back. You may need to write many letters or find other ways to converse with the traumatized yourself. If you are seeing a therapist, Gestalt techniques such as talking to parts of yourself in therapy, might be very helpful.

✍ Exercise: Writing a Letter to Your Traumatized Self

Part 1: Writing a Letter to Your Traumatized Self

Imagine yourself during part of the trauma. How old were you? What did you look like? What were your hobbies? Who were your friends? Where were you living? What did you think about? With a picture of your traumatized self in your mind, write a letter to that person. For example, Nancy's first letter to her traumatized self went as follows:

Dear You,
I can't write a letter to "Dear Me." You aren't me. You're this horrible creature I lived in for a few years. You're disgusting. I can't stand you. I wish you had never been born. You were so stupid, believing everything that man told you. How dumb can you get? It's your fault you were used. You let it happen out of your own ignorance. You aren't part of me. I'm a grown woman now, successful in every way. I wish you'd just go away and die. I hate thinking about you and I hate the stupid exercises these therapists make me do.

Part 2: The Traumatized Self Replies

After you write the letter to your traumatized self, have that self respond and write a letter back, and continue the interaction. For example, Nancy's abused self wrote back:

Dear Nancy:
Thank you for talking to me. Hardly anyone ever talks to me. You're right, I was bad and I probably deserved the treatment I got. But I didn't like it. No matter what anyone says, I didn't like it. I tried to fight back, but I couldn't. I didn't know what to do. I still don't know what to do. I'm only seven years' old. I don't know how to talk like a big person.

I wish you had been there when all those awful things happened to me. I needed a big person to take my hand and tell me I didn't have to stay in that bedroom and there was a way out. But nobody helped me. I guess I deserve to be miserable. I'm just a bad person.

Part 3: Dialoguing

To get the most out of this exercise, you need to maintain a dialogue between yourself and your traumatized self. You can write to each other back and forth as much as you can. (Reread the Cautions section in the Introduction and monitor your reactions as you do this exercise. Professional help may be needed if this dialoguing becomes overwhelming.) For example, Nancy wrote back to her traumatized self:

You don't make any sense. You weren't bad. He was. If I could go back in time, I'd have helped you. You didn't deserve it. No little kid deserves what happened to you. He's the bad one, not you.

The abused self wrote back: Really? Can you help me now? Can you be there for me when I'm scared? Can I really have a Mommy or a friend to help me when I'm scared?

Nancy: Yes, and I promise to stop calling you stupid and telling you how bad you were. I promise to help take care of you and not hate you for being so little, helpless, and trusting.

When writing these letters, Nancy came to realize that she hated the part of herself that trusted, which was a significant obstacle to her ability to develop relationships. She also hated her beauty, because she felt her beauty had been the cause of the abuse. This made it difficult for her to interact with men. She came to realize that she had spent considerable emotional energy despising and punishing her sexually abused self and that this energy would be better spent trying to protect and understand that part of herself.

Despite her difficulties, Nancy had married and had children. She was a model mother, who lavished her children with love and attention. She did not express her rejection of her abused self by rejecting her own children, but rather by rejecting other people's children. For example, when she would see parents playing with young children at picnics or family events, she would become enraged. She'd complain about the noise the children made and would fantasize that those children would be hurt in accidents, so they would suffer the way she had.

She had zero tolerance for her small nephews and nieces and had trouble going to baby showers or birthday parties for the young children of her friends. Sometimes, she purposely tried to ruin the fun the children were having nearby and several times, much to her shame, she stole or destroyed some of their dolls and toys. She wanted to punish them because they had what she had never had: a happy childhood with parents who played with, protected, and cherished them. Nancy was not only a victim of sexual abuse, but also of gross neglect. She had never known what it was like to be loved.

Her hostility toward other people's small children created problems in many of her relationships, but this hostility was only the reflection of the hostility she felt toward the traumatized child she had been. Until she began talking to her traumatized self, she hid all the pictures she had of herself as a child. But after completing the exercise of writing a letter to her traumatized self (and doing other trauma work), she put a childhood picture of herself on her dresser.

Whenever she had a decision to make, she'd look at that picture and say, "If I do this (such and such), will it be fair to you? Will you be scared?" Then she would decide whether she could, in fact, protect the little girl inside her and be safe.

Note that if you cannot complete the exercise, that is, if you can't write or talk to your traumatized self, then do some writing about why you can't. Discussing this issue with a qualified therapist is highly recommended.

Writing a Letter to Your Disfigurements and Disabilities

Are there parts of yourself, the way you think, feel, or look that you don't like? Are any of these parts associated with your trauma? Do you have physical or emotional scars, personal limitations, and particular disabilities that were the result of your trauma?

Can you write a letter to those parts of yourself and have those parts answer? Can you keep up this process of writing and responding, until you reach some kind of inner peace and recognition of the strengths and insights you acquired as the result of the trauma? As a rule, writing about your scars and disabilities will lead you to an awareness of your strengths.

If there is a part of your body, a personality trait, or some physical or mental limitation that represents the damage done by the trauma, then you might write to that part. For example, you might write to the part of you that has trouble remembering, the part of you that becomes aggressive waiting in lines or in traffic jams, the part of you that can no longer be creative, the sad part of you.

You might want to write to your medical problems that were caused by long years of substance abuse or other addictions. For example, you could write a letter to your bad back, your liver problems, or to any part of you that you feel is scarred and deformed and keeps you from feeling normal and relating freely to others.

Substance Abuse

For those of you who turned to substances to medicate yourself from the feelings associated with the trauma, there may be physical and medical scars associated with your addiction, rather than the trauma itself. But if the trauma was the cause of the addiction, or made an ongoing addiction worse, then these addiction-related problems can be considered trauma-related. For example, it has been found that a high percentage of children from dysfunctional homes, where there is child abuse, sexual abuse, wife battering, or emotional neglect develop addictions (Bingham and Resnick 1990; Herman 1992; Kunzman 1990; van der Kolk 1996). Eating disorders, from anorexia nervosa and bulimia to compulsive overeating, are common among female survivors of childhood abuse. Abused women may turn to alcohol or drugs for comfort, and persons who develop disabilities as the result of vehicular accidents, work-related accidents, war, or crime often medicate their anguish with alcohol, drugs, or food. Indeed, there is a marked correlation between physical disability and alcoholism and/or obesity (Dailey 1979; Hendrickson 1992).

Abuse of Food

Although being overweight may not seem like much of a disability compared to the loss of a limb or the loss of certain mental functions, there is marked discrimination against obese men and women in school systems and in the world of work, as well as in the military. Slimness pays off in terms of dollars, position, and promotions, and overweight persons are often seen as "lazy," "stupid," "careless," and not as competent as those of normal weight. For women, the curse of obesity extends into the social world where, in general, overweight women are not seen as attractive or as desirable as slim women.

Obesity is also a disability in that it contributes to the development of many medical problems, from diabetes and heart disease, to back problems and arthritis, all of which compound the original disability for which food is used as a relief. For example, Rebecca was in a car accident that left her flat on her back for six months. During that time, she put on some weight due to her immobility, but her weight gain was moderate. Upon returning to work, however, she was not able to function as well as she had in the past, partly due to the ongoing pain she had as the result of the accident, as well as to memory problems that arose when she was triggered. To quell her anxiety over her diminished performance, she turned to food again. But overeating only made her mind more sluggish, thus decreasing her ability to concentrate. Her subsequent weight gain increased the pressure on her legs and back, which had been injured during the accident, which led to more physical pain, which further detracted from her ability to concentrate on the job.

Then she would turn to food to cope with her guilt and shame about not being able to do her job. Thus a vicious cycle was established which ended only when she joined a twelve-step program for overeating (Overeaters Anonymous).

Overeating is a problem for male survivors as well as for women, especially those men who are committed to staying clean and sober. It is not uncommon for individuals who have achieved recovery from alcohol or drugs (which they had turned to because of a prior trauma) to turn to food if they are traumatized again. If alcohol and drugs are out-of-bounds for them and their twelve-step program doesn't permit sexual promiscuity or gambling, what's left? Only food.

Food is legal and, compared to other addictions, is relatively inexpensive. Few people consider overeating a mortal sin or major problem, as alcohol or drug addictions are thought to be. Hence, it is very easy for anyone to begin to use food to stop nightmares, manage anger and anxiety, and cope with relationships after being retraumatized, perhaps for the second or third time.

Therefore, when you write a letter to your scar or disability, keep your mind open to a wide range of possible scars or disabilities. You may have a disfigurement such as obesity that you don't see as directly trauma-related, even though the trauma may have created or contributed to the development of the problem.

Marsha, for example, wrote a letter to her thighs, which showed signs of food abuse. As a young girl, Marsha had used compulsive overeating and bulimia to cope with her numerous traumas. When she finally entered a recovery program for eating disorders, she was able to stabilize her weight and achieve a normal-looking body. But her thighs, which had been stretched and shrunk numerous times, not only were still heavy but also retained hanging folds of skin; "elephant skin" she called it.

Her "elephant skin" swung and swayed whenever she moved and was, indeed, unattractive. In desperation, Marsha consulted a plastic surgeon. She was told that her "elephant skin" was not fat, but loose skin. No corrective surgery could remove it. Exercise wouldn't fix it either. She was told she could build muscle by weight lifting, but the folds of skin would always be there, a permanent reminder of her hellish past.

Marsha never wore shorts or went swimming and she made love only with the lights off. She said no to many invitations for pool parties, hikes, picnics, and barbecues because of her shame about her thighs. Her sexuality was greatly inhibited by her fear that her partner would see her thighs and reject her. She had a storehouse of excuses for not showing up at certain events, and for making love in the dark. Making these excuses was emotionally exhausting and made Marsha feel like an "oddball" or like an obese, deformed monster destined to a life of loneliness.

Finally, her therapist instructed her to write a letter to her thighs. She wrote the following letter:

Hi thighs. You are ugly, but I need to learn to love you. Yes, you are big and parts of you hang loose and flap when I walk. But that's because you were treated so badly. Eating was your way of coping with all those years of physical and sexual abuse.

But you survived. Didn't you? You came out of hell with a head on your shoulders and love in your heart. So many were against you, but you prevailed. Your large somewhat misshapen body is not a sign of failure, but a testimony to your strength. Don't be ashamed, be proud of yourself. Besides, your lower body is just part of you, not all of you and, thank goodness, you can find ways to keep the ugly parts hidden. Just think if you were scarred on the face, like some people are.

After Marsha wrote this letter, she was overcome with tears. Finally, she felt good about the most despised parts of her flesh. She was certain that she would never hate herself again, for as long as she lived, and that the good feeling she had about herself would last forever. But it didn't. In situation after situation, she was passed over for girls with better bodies and great legs.

"Lookism" is real. In our society physical attractiveness counts a lot. It may not be fair, but that's how it is. Marsha realized that, to some extent, she would be disadvantaged forever because of a physical part of her being that she couldn't correct. All of her positive self-talk would not change the reality that in our society people with "normal" bodies and cover girl looks are privy to advantages that people with physical deformities do not have. Indeed, PTSD and other traumatic reactions have been found to be more prevalent, and more intense, among persons whose injuries show or disfigure them.

One night Marsha went to bed sobbing about the fact that she would never be able to go to the beach like other people, or wear shorts, and at the general unfairness of it all. She had a dream that reflected the dialoguing exercise where she conversed with her disfigurements. She wrote the following entry in her journal:

Last night I dreamt I was having lunch with a skinny-minny cover girl. I realize now that I carry this cover girl critic with me everywhere I go. She torments me, but in this dream I put her in her place—out of my life.

This was the dream: The cover girl was dressed all in pink, with perfectly matching lipstick and nail polish and a pink flowered belt around her tiny waist. She seemed like a little girl rather than an adult woman except when she started shaking her adorable curls at me and we had the following conversation:

Cover Girl: You know what everyone says about you? That you are a scatterbrain because you don't wear a girdle even though your hips and thighs waddle.

Marsha: But I have broken capillaries around my upper thighs from the abuse.

Cover Girl: And you don't blow dry or mousse your hair either.

Marsha: I don't have time. I have children and a job.

Cover Girl: You're due for a manicure too. Everybody knows that long painted nails take away attention from chubby arms, and legs, like yours.

Marsha: Ma'am. Do you have to work for a living?

Cover Girl: Why I'd be ashamed to walk out of the house if I looked like you.

Marsha: Ms. Cover Girl, do you know how to spell the word "work"?

Cover Girl: You need to do one-hundred sit-ups every morning and night, aerobics four times a week, and lift weights to even get to the half-way normal range. Then you'll need a tummy tuck and liposuction too.

Marsha: I told you, I'm raising children on my own and I have to work. I exercise for health, but even if I exercised more, it wouldn't do that much good. The damage to my body is too great.

Cover Girl: (Giggling) I hear your house isn't dusted either.

Marsha: (Roaring) I don't have time!

Cover Girl: Your arms, hon. They shake when you shout that loud. Weight lifting might fix the flabby parts, but it would take you at least a year.

Marsha: Look lady, I survived an abusive childhood and an abusive marriage. I've overcome a devastating eating disorder and a long-time alcohol addiction. I lost one-hundred pounds twice—and since the last time I lost it, I've kept it off for ten years. I'm a walking miracle. Isn't that enough?

Cover Girl: Hon, your elbows—they are a disgrace. I can recommend the best little pumice stone. It takes away all the gray uglies. Use it at least twice a day. Your breasts, too dear. Don't you need a little help there? There are these great new bras, only fifty dollars. Everyone will think it's you. And for fifty dollars more, you can get a control body corset that will do wonders for that tummy of yours and those wobbly thighs. I might get one today too because I've gained one pound and I am totally frantic about it.

Marsha: (In a firm and commanding tone) Go. Just go. Go and don't ever come back!

Cover Girl: (Amazed) You want me to leave? We've been together for so many years. You need me, don't you? You like to feel bad. That's why you were abused, isn't it? Because you like pain. You'll never get rid of me. Here's a good starvation diet.

Marsha: No thanks.

Cover Girl: You just want to stay fat forever.

Marsha: There are some things people can't help and that they just have to live with. For me, my body is one of them. I'm fine the way I am. Now please leave.

Cover Girl: You aren't fine and you know it.

Marsha: I'm just fine and, as a matter of fact, the madder I get at you, the finer I feel.

Cover Girl: You aren't being very nice to me.

Marsha: And you, my dear cover girl, have *never* been very nice to me. Now get out of my life and out of my heart and out of my mind and never come near me again.

The cover girl wiped her little pink lips with her little pink napkin and walked away. And, with that I woke up happy, joyous, and free and ever so glad just to be me.

Marsha has been in therapy for more than fifteen years. Only in her tenth year of counseling did she achieve sufficient self-love to admit to herself that she cared about her physical appearance. Prior to that time, she did not feel worth enough to care about how she looked. Also, she had not been emotionally strong enough to bear the sorrow she felt when she thought about the abuse and neglect she had suffered in her childhood.

In her dream, Marsha confronted one of her inner critics and made progress in understanding the harsh voice within that was always condemning her because she didn't look a certain way. But this dream, as important as it was, was not a "magic cure."

Marsha's low self-esteem returned. However, it was not as strong as it had been; furthermore, those feelings were not the only feelings that she experienced. Whenever the critical voice in her head began to berate her for not looking like a cover girl, another part of her being began to list her strengths and to congratulate her for having endured and survived so much emotional and physical pain.

As her feelings of low self-esteem shrank and her acknowledgment of her accomplishments grew, Marsha began to have a more balanced view of herself. Although it was true that she never was and never could be a beauty queen, she could take pride in many other aspects of her being. Nevertheless, there were still times when she still wished she had a magic wand and could relive her life so she would grow up unscarred by abuse and addiction.

At such times she had to do more writing, more talking to her therapist, and more sharing in her twelve-step program and with other friends. Sometimes, Marsha resented the fact that despite all of her efforts, the critical voice within did not totally disappear. As time went on, she took the risk of telling some of her friends about how ugly and unworthy she felt and some friends took similar risks and told her about their own deep pain about similar issues.

Marsha bonded with those friends in a very special way, and, at times, even felt grateful for her physical defects. "If I didn't know what it felt like to be called a 'rhino skin lady,' I would never have been able to talk to and help my friend Maxine. I probably would never even have met her. Now we are like sisters," Marsha told her therapist.

"I wanted to be pretty so that people would love and accept me. But these friends love and accept me the way I am. They don't care what I look like. And when I feel emotionally close to others and am able to help them and accept their help, I feel so cared about and so useful, I don't give a thought to my looks.

"To me, to be able to live without that inner voice tormenting me is true freedom. And the more I talk about my feelings without being ashamed of them, with people who understand, of course, those times of freedom grow longer and take up more and more of my life. The part of me that is jealous and insecure is still there, but it is much smaller than it used to be."

✍ *Exercise: Writing a Letter to Your Traumatized Self*

Now, in your journal, write a letter to your traumatized self. You may write to the whole person you were during your trauma or you may choose a specific part of yourself. For example, a quality you displayed during the trauma (such as kindness, fear, selfishness, generosity, seductiveness), or to a part of your body that you associate with the trauma. As you write, try to focus on those aspects of your traumatized self that have caused you emotional pain, anger, or confusion, or the parts of your behavior or appearance that other people have commented upon, or that make you feel as if you are "different," "not normal," or "not attractive."

Take as many pages as you need. If you have several body parts you are concerned about or if you have been traumatized many times, start with one incident. Later, you can write about other incidents.

Before you begin to write, read the following directions carefully.

1. **Visualizing:** Create a picture in your mind of who you were during the traumatic incident. What did you look like? What were your in-

terests? Who were your friends? What did you do during the trauma that you wish you hadn't done?

2. **The Letter:** Hold the picture of your traumatized self in your mind. Now, write a letter to that person.

3. **The Reply:** After you write the letter to your traumatized self, have that self respond and write back to you to continue the interchange.

4. **Dialoguing:** To get the most out of this exercise, you need to maintain a dialogue between your self and your traumatized self. Write to each other, back and forth, as much as you can. (Reread the Cautions section in the Introduction and monitor your reactions as you complete this exercise. Stop if you begin to feel overwhelmed. You may need some professional help.)

You and Your Dead

In the previous section, you did some work on clearing up a major obstacle to your ability to develop relationships in the present—tensions between your traumatized self and your self-definition. In this section, you will do some work on understanding another obstacle to developing relationships in the present—your relationships with those who died or were lost during your trauma.

The emotional ties that may form between people during a trauma are intense, long-lasting, and irreplaceable. The bonding that takes place among those who are engaged in a common struggle for survival can equal, and sometimes surpass, the bonding that develops in a family, one of whose purposes is the protection and support of its individual members for purposes of survival. Many combat veterans consider their war buddies closer to them than their actual brothers. Many rescue workers, policemen, and firefighters consider their co-workers closer to them than their siblings. Parents who lose a child to suicide, homicide, or in a vehicular accident often become closer as a couple, if the loss doesn't drive them apart.

During trauma, the people involved become a family and if they are already family, they may become an even more tightly knit family. A car-accident survivor explains:

"My entire family was in the car when we were hit by an eighteen-wheeler. As I saw the truck plow into the car, I felt my life was over. I prayed not for myself, but that my kids would make it through. My wife and I had only minor injuries, but my son was in the hospital for a year and my daughter needed four surgeries. Both of the kids were invalids for a long time.

"After the accident, sometimes my wife and I would just look at each other and start to cry. We'd just cry and cry. We were stressed out, caring for the kids in the hospital and at home. Medical insurance didn't cover everything and money was tight. We were emotionally wrung out and financially almost bankrupt, but we were never closer.

"That was years ago. Everyone's well now, but sometimes I miss those times, how close we were, how much we appreciated each other, how we cooperated for the sake of the common good. When we argue now, about small things, I think back to the time of the accident, when we were all willing to put aside our individual preferences and made helping each other our number one priority. We all rose above our selfish selves and came together to save money and find ways to make things work. We didn't argue about little things then. In *A Tale of Two Cities*, Charles Dickens wrote, 'It was the best of times, it was the worst of times.' That's how I feel about the time after the accident. It was terrible because we didn't know if the kids were going to make it, but it was wonderful because we were really a close-knit family."

Trauma can create the kind of closeness between people that extends beyond the grave. If you lost someone during the trauma, that person is lost to you physically, but you still have a relationship with that person. You think about them, you may even talk to them, and your memories of them may influence your thoughts, actions, and feelings. There is nothing psychologically unhealthy about this. Throughout the ages people have maintained contact with dead relatives and loved ones. Not forgetting the dead is part of being human and a truly loving person.

There are instances, however, where major unresolved issues between yourself and those who died carry over into your present-day relationships. For example, you may be disappointed that the intensity of some of your current relationships doesn't match the intensity of the relationships you had with those you were with during the trauma, especially if the natural intensity of those trauma relationships was heightened by the death of the other person. You may not have had the opportunity to grieve the loss of the person or persons who died in the trauma for a variety of reasons. Perhaps you had too many other matters to attend to or you lacked the support necessary to truly grieve. It may be that unresolved grieving is affecting your present-day relationships, especially if you are fraught with survivor guilt.

If you still suffer from survivor guilt, you may feel you should not go on with life. You may secretly be giving up a part of your life as a tribute to your dead friend or loved one. For example, you may have given up an activity that gave you joy as a way to honor the deceased or you may feel you aren't entitled to have children, an intimate love relationship, or good friends because it would be disrespectful to those who died.

"Every time I have sex, I think of the guys who didn't make it home. Some of them were virgins. Whenever I look at my kids, I think of the guys who died and never had the chance to have a family. This makes me pull away from my wife and family, it feels like I don't deserve to have them," explains a combat veteran.

"My husband and son died in the car crash," explains a widow. "Even though it was years ago, I feel I must not go out socially, or ever remarry, or have any more children. I know that being a recluse and staying home won't bring them back from the dead. I also know that my husband and son would want me to go on with my life, but I feel that doing so would dishonor their memory and I just won't do it. My grief is the only thing I have left. It's my only relationship with them. I can't give it up. I was in that car crash. I should have died too."

🖎 Exercise: The Dead and the Living

In your journal, answer the following questions as completely as possible. Use a separate sheet of paper for each person you write about.

1. Make a list of persons you lost during or because of the trauma. In chapter 1, you wrote about three relationships that you developed during the trauma. Are these persons all still alive?

2. How does the memory of these people affect your life today?

3. How do your feelings about the dead impact on your relationships today? Take a look at the three present-day relationships you wrote about in chapter 1. Does your grief or survivor guilt affect these three relationships in any way?

4. Do you find yourself denying or holding back in certain relationships because of your memory of the dead?

5. Do you ever have mental conversations with the dead? Do you feel closer to the dead than to living? When you are having conflicts with people in your present-day life, do you seek out the dead to converse with? Do you feel that those who died understood you better and appreciated you more than those around you today? Are there times you feel the dead are sitting next to you or walking with you? Do you take them with you sometimes?

Don't be afraid to answer "yes" to any of the questions above. If you have an active relationship with those who died during your trauma, don't think that you are being "crazy." It is quite common for trauma survivors to maintain ongoing and significant relationship with those who died during the trauma. To help you understand this better, you may want to do some writing about your relationships with each person you identified. Sometimes writing that person a letter is very helpful.

This writing assignment has two parts: first, writing about the death of the loved one (or about the life of that loved one) and second, how the loss of that loved one affects your life today, with a special emphasis on how that person's death affects your present-day relationships. For example, if your trauma involved the death of a sibling, you may want to write about that sibling's death, or write a letter to that sibling. But you must also do some thinking and writing about how that sibling's death affects your relationships today, within your family, your circle of friends, and other relationships. To what extent does that person's death influence your choice of friends or sexual relationships, or the degree to which you can become close to another person?

For example, Eileen grew up in a home where her brother died as the result of the most common form of child abuse; child neglect. Although her brother was never beaten, his asthma and other medical problems were not attended to by his alcoholic parents and he died at age five. Eileen, who was ten at the time of her brother's death, is now fifty-seven. But in therapy she discovered that her brother's death had profoundly shaped her psyche and all her relationships all of her life.

In the course of her therapy she wrote him the following letter:

Dearest Brother, Seeing you laying on the floor, breathing hard, so frightened and so weak is the worst memory of my childhood. I felt so guilty that I couldn't save you, but I couldn't. Mom and Dad wouldn't listen to me. I told them you needed help, but they wouldn't pay any attention to me. I even called for the ambulance to come, but when it came, Mom and Dad told the rescue workers to go home. I should have told the rescue people that Mom and Dad were wrong: that there was a little boy in the other room who couldn't breathe.

But I was scared of Mom and Dad. They told me I was driving them crazy by worrying about you all the time and that they didn't have money to pay for doctors to take care of you. They said it was your fault you were so sick all the time, that you were a "weakling" child who should never have been born. They told me to get the inhalers for you and that they would work, as they usually did. But they didn't work as usual and you died.

Then Mom and Dad blamed me for your dying. They said I didn't do the inhalers right. But the doctors who came later said you were having such a terrible asthma attack that the inhalers weren't enough, that you needed to be in a hospital, that even if I had helped you with the inhalers perfectly, you would have died anyway. I know I'm not to blame, but I still feel guilty and my memories make me sick.

And how does your death affect me today? I think it's the reason I go into a panic anytime one of my children is sick, even with something minor, and if someone at work is ill, I break out in a cold sweat and can't concentrate. I feel as if I have to do something to help them, even if it isn't my job. Like my boss has allergies and minor asthma attacks. He's a grown man, with a loving wife, but when he gets sick, I get mentally ill and I start feeling responsible, even though I'm not. Then, because I feel so sorry for him, I let him take advantage of me professionally. Also, I feel I can't say "no" to people who are sick because I don't want to add any extra stress to their lives by refusing their requests, no matter how costly those requests might be to me.

If I had to summarize it, I'd say that because of your death, I feel guilty and responsible when others are sick; I feel scared of the worst when someone's ill, no matter how ill they really are; and if I feel someone has a medical problem, I have trouble being assertive with that person or remembering my personal limits and needs. I feel I have to give all I have to them, to save them, as I didn't get to save you. I should have given my all for you—I should have risked Mom and Dad's anger and maybe you'd be alive today.

Eileen's unresolved grief about her brother's death permeated all of her relationships. Her operating mode was that it was her obligation to save any sick people she knew by giving them her all. Yet sometimes the way she "gave her all" had nothing to do with helping the sick person get better. For example, if her boss asked her to work overtime without pay, how could that help him with his medical problems? Yet in her mind, there was a connection between "giving her all" and saving a life. Eileen needed to examine the logical relationship between "giving her all" and a positive gain, for anyone. For example, when she worked overtime, was she helping her boss with his medical problems or supporting his workaholism, which contributed to his poor physical health? If she became ill because of overextending herself at work and became increasingly resentful, who would that help?

What was Eileen hoping to accomplish by overgiving in certain relationships, over and over again? She wrote:

"On some level, I've been trying to atone for not standing up for my brother and hoping that if I overdo for my boss, or any other person, I not only will save them, I will bring my brother back. But my brother is gone. I can sacrifice myself all I want, for whomever I want, and he's not coming back. I have to accept the pain of that loss. I've grieved that loss many times, but giving up the fantasy that by overgiving now I can remedy the past, fills me with sorrow again, on a deeper level. But it also frees me to be more self-protective and assertive in my relationships and to have relationships where I can receive, as well as give."

Andrew, a combat veteran, wrote the following letter to a little girl who died in Vietnam:

Dear Little Girl: I don't even know your name, but I will never forget your eyes. We picked you up after your village had been bombed. I held you and your dying mother in my arms on the chopper that was taking you and all the other wounded villagers to a base hospital. Your mother died on the plane, and then you clung to me as if I was the last person in the world.

When it was time to get off the helicopter, you wouldn't let go of my hand and when I pushed you away, you fell to the ground and wept like the baby that you were. I wanted to take you with me, but I would not have been permitted to do that. I thought about hiding you among my things, to comfort you just a little longer, but eventually you would have been found and taken away. Then what would have happened to you? It was better that you went with the wounded. I thought that perhaps some of your relatives were among them and that they would take care of you.

At the airbase where you and the other civilians were unloaded, a truck was waiting to transport you to a hospital. You didn't want to be separated from me and it took a soldier to take you from me and force you on the truck. You even managed to jump off of the truck and ran towards me, but I motioned you to go back. I turned my back on you as the soldiers forced you aboard.

Once the truck was on its way, I turned back to look at it, hoping to see your face. Then, in a flash, the truck exploded into flames. It had been blown up by the Viet Cong.

If only I had kept you for that little while, you'd have been saved. But then, after you would have been taken away from me, you might have been killed anyway, or forced into prostitution, or you might have survived it all and developed PTSD, like me. Maybe it's best you died. Or maybe not.

Dear Little Girl, You have a special place in my heart and there must be a special place in heaven for little children like you and all the other unhappy victims of stupid wars.

During his tour of duty, Andrew saw children dying not only of war wounds, but also of malnutrition and disease. Some had even been purposely mutilated by adults so that they would be "good beggars." Of all of Andrew's wartime memories, those of the dead and dying children he saw have tormented him the most, making it difficult for him to relate to all children, especially his own.

Not just combat veterans, but many individuals who are exposed to the sufferings of children, such as police officers, emergency room workers, firefighters, and social workers, have accounts similar to Andrew's account of the Vietnamese girl. All too often their traumatic experiences affect their relationships with other children, especially their own.

For example, in completing the first part of this exercise, Joshua, an emergency room worker, wrote a letter to a poorly nourished toddler who had been beaten to death by her parents. The toddler was just one of dozens of dead or badly injured children Joshua had seen in the course of his work. In the second part of the exercise, Joshua worked on understanding how those dead and injured children were affecting his present-day relationships. He realized that he felt an intense anger directed at well-nourished, protected children, including his own. Whenever he would see that his children were happy, he would scold them for being so and remind them that there were children in their own city who were starving to death or were being killed or maimed by their relatives.

Joshua would become so angry when he preached about how spoiled and materialistic his children were, that they would dissolve in tears. Joshua's anger at his children was fueled by his anger over the circumstances of the toddler's death and his powerlessness to help her and all the other innocent children whom he saw die in the emergency room at the hospital.

Joshua didn't enter therapy until his children were adults. Not until he was almost fifty years old did he realize that he had made his children afraid to be happy in front of him and that he had taught them to feel guilty about being alive. The survivor guilt had been passed on to them. As so often happens, his trauma was passed on to the second generation of survivors.

In a therapy session with Joshua and his twenty-seven-year-old son, the son wept, explaining to his father that he had felt as powerless to help his father as his father had felt to help the abused children he had tried to save. Joshua's son told him the following:

"You were so angry all the time, and it seemed like you hated us because we had what those poor kids didn't have. I felt as if I had to finish what you couldn't finish—so I decided to go into law, so I could push for tougher laws against child abusers to save kids. I figured if I could save kids, it would help you feel less guilty and angry.

"My sister and I felt like we were never enough, like the abused kids were more important to you than we were, that the only way you would love us the way you loved those kids was to get sick or hurt or be killed ourselves.

"My sister and I were scared to be around you, Dad, because if we were sad, you'd get all upset and if we were happy, you'd get all upset too. It seemed that no matter how we were, we could never be right. So, sometimes, we tried to stay away from you, but then you'd be furious and insist that we stay home so you could watch us and be sure we were safe. So we were stuck, and sad, and scared, just like you were in the emergency room when it was too late to save a kid's life."

Joshua was grieved and shocked to learn that he had had such a negative effect on his children and he is determined not to repeat the pattern with his grandchildren.

Replacement Children

Some children are "replacement children" in that they are conceived or perceived as substitutes for a child or person who was lost during the trauma. If a child is lost to suicide, homicide, or in an accident or natural catastrophe, another child may be conceived to replace the lost child, or an existing child may be expected to take the place of the child that was lost. A child may be named after a dead buddy or friend or relative who died during the trauma and then the child may have an important symbolic identity.

That child may be highly valued and, in some cases, may become the survivor's only real reason for living. As the child grows, he or she will feel the burden of meeting the parental expectations to replace the person who died. At times, the child may feel wanted more because of his or her "replacement value" than for himself or herself.

✍ Exercise: Replacement Children

In your journal take a fresh sheet of paper and answer the following questions as completely as possible.

1. Are any of your children "replacement children?" If so, do some writing about the importance of that child in your life. What might happen, for example, if you lost the replacement child? How are you going to handle the child's growth and eventual separation from the family? What kinds of support do you need to help you bear not only your original loss, but the slow loss of the replacement child to the natural life cycle? Can you find the meaning you now find in the replacement child in other relationships or activities?

2. How might you feel if you were a replacement child? Perhaps you were a replacement child yourself. Is your replacement child in any way a replacement for yourself as you might have liked your life to be?

Healing Your Traumatized Self

Therapy or healing involves many different processes. One of the major processes is that of learning how to know and claim *all* of yourself: the parts that you (and perhaps others) admire and the parts that you (and perhaps others) wish did not exist. Knowing and claiming all the parts of yourself does not mean that you have to act on or express any of those parts, except those that you choose.

For example, in therapy you may discover that you feel certain jealousies. Yet such an awareness does not mean that you must or will

act on those jealousies. In fact, knowing that you are jealous in a particular area will probably give you more control over the jealousy than
if you were unaware of its existence.

Similarly, healing from trauma involves recognizing parts of yourself that you find either undesirable or taboo. It means knowing, and
owning, your traumatized self. Regardless of whether you esteem or
despise aspects of your traumatized self, you need to know as much
as possible about him/her because he/she exists and exerts some power
over your emotions and ways of thinking, and consequently, over your
actions and decisions.

In this chapter, you were asked to participate in endeavors that
required considerable courage: that of getting to know your traumatized
self and forming an alliance or friendship with the part of you that was
traumatized. Part of your traumatized identity includes those who died
as the result of the trauma and you were asked to undergo the painful
process of recognizing how their deaths impacted upon your life.

Although much of the process of accepting your traumatized self
and the role of the memories of those who died may be painful, the
intended result of your efforts is to achieve some measure of joy and
serenity and a definite increase in energy. The joy results from the fact
that you will no longer have to spend emotional energy suppressing or
fighting those aspects of your traumatized self that you previously rejected or mercilessly tortured with shame or ridicule. Increased peace
of mind will follow the slow demise of the civil war that was raging
within you. You will have more time and more psychic energy to pursue
other goals, including the goal of developing your relationships. And,
if you are aware of your relationships with the dead, you will be able
to allow your ties with those who are gone to strengthen, not weaken
or distort, your ties to those who are still with you.

References

Bingham, Denise and Patricia Resnick. 1990. "Victimization in a Chemi-
cally Dependent Population." Paper presented at the International
Society for Traumatic Stress Studies Annual Conference. New Or-
leans, LA.

Dailey, Ann Louise. 1979. "Physically Handicapped Women." *The Counseling Psychologist* 8(1) 41–42.

Hendrickson, Jacqueline. 1992. "Disability and Addiction." Presentation,
Veterans Center 0213, Department of Veterans Affairs, Silver Spring,
MD.

Herman, Judith. 1992. *Trauma and Recovery: The Aftermath of Violence—
From Domestic Abuse to Political Terror.* New York: Basic Books.

Kunzman, Kristin. 1990. *Adult Recovery from Child Sexual Abuse*. Center City, MN: Hazelden Educational Materials.

van der Kolk, Bessel. 1996. "The Complexity of Adaptation to Trauma." In *Traumatic Stress: The Effects of Overwhelming Experience on Mind, Body, and Society*. B. van der Kolk, A. McFarlane, and L. Weisaeth, Eds. New York: Guilford Press.

11

Protectiveness, Entitlement, and Jealousy

Protectiveness

A sense of protectiveness and a sense of urgency are two characteristics that describe the way that some trauma survivors relate to
others. Although some trauma survivors tend to withdraw from others
and even to distance themselves from partners, children, family members, and friends, there is also a tendency to be extremely protective
toward those whom the trauma survivor considers to be in his or her
inner circle.

"If you're one of mine, I'm bound and sworn to take care of you.
I'm responsible for you and must do everything in my power to protect
you from harm," is the underlying feeling that propels trauma survivors
to triple-check seatbelts, double-bolt doors, and engage in lengthy in-
vestigations of anyone coming near a loved one, whether that person
be a friend, co-worker, doctor, auto mechanic, or therapist.

If you lost someone during your trauma or you saw people get
hurt or die, you don't ever want to see such a scene again. Because
of the horror of what you've been through you are motivated to do
everything possible to make the world safe, not only for you, but for
those you care about, those whom you consider your "charges" or responsibility.

"Once a squad leader, always a squad leader. Once a medic, always
a medic. Once the mother of a child who committed suicide, always a
mother on guard against it happening again to someone else," describes
the feeling. This feeling is deep and it is unchangeable. No amount of
talking about the "past is the past" or about "detachment" or "letting
go" or any kind of pop psychology or "logical thinking" can make a

dent in your indelible memory of the trauma or the sense of danger and responsibility you feel toward others that was born during your traumatic episode.

Overprotectiveness

Perhaps your loved ones call you "overprotective," but whether you are being protective or overprotective is a matter of judgment. The truth is there is danger in the world. Some of your "overprotectiveness" may not be overprotective at all, but a healthy caution about potential danger. You learned something during your trauma—you acquired valuable information about all the ways things can go wrong: about human error, human frailty, human corruptibility, and about the breakdown of machinery, bureaucracies, and other man-made objects and systems designed to function well to help protect people, but which often do not function as intended. An exercise later in this chapter will help you decide if you are indeed being "overprotective" or just being careful and prudent.

You and your loved ones are just as vulnerable to traffic accidents, criminal victimization, medical or bureaucratic malpractice, natural catastrophes, or technological disasters as anyone else. But unlike most nontraumatized people, you as a trauma survivor, expect the worst and are determined to be prepared for it. "Never again" is the motto of many trauma survivors, who have vowed deep in their hearts never again to be unprepared or vulnerable to human or man-made disaster.

You may, therefore, be supercautious about everything, from the seatbelt to the fanbelt in your car, to the kind of restaurant you will patronize. A part of you trusts nothing and no one, so you check out people, places, and objects for possible danger, or deceit. When purchasing an appliance, you read the directions and warranty several times and ask the salesperson extensive questions. If your child or partner has to visit a physician, you check out the physician's credentials by going to the library, questioning the physician, or talking to others.

You don't want any more mistakes. You saw enough "mistakes" during the trauma and the cost of those mistakes. And you don't have to rush to make decisions as you did during the trauma, so you can investigate and deliberate whatever is necessary to assure safety. "If something goes wrong this time, it's not going to be my fault for not making the effort to be sure things were safe. I'm going to do everything in my power to be sure that me and mine are as safe as possible in this unpredictable world," is probably how you think.

You may have a persistent fear that something terrible is going to happen to your loved ones. When they are out of your sight or hearing range, you may experience tremendous anxiety about their safety. If you are in the same vicinity, you'd be near enough to know if something was amiss and you could do something to help. But if they are out of the range of your help, you're powerless to be of immediate assistance. Therefore you may not want your loved ones to be far from you. You may insist that they call you when they arrive at a destination or just before they are to come home.

Your loved ones may feel you are being overcontrolling and intrusive, but your goals are to protect them and to reduce the horrible anxiety you feel about their safety. You may *also* be trying to control them, but that is a different issue. Even if you do have tendencies toward being controlling, when you are a trauma survivor your need to know where others are and to be sure of their safety is based on your concern for their welfare—and your concern is an urgent one.

You and your loved ones need to work out a plan that respects their need for autonomy and mobility, as well as your need to be protective and assured of their safety. For example, the wife of a trauma survivor stated the issue this way:

"I don't want to feel that I have to constantly check in with my husband. He wants me to call him when I get to work, before I go to lunch, when I get back from lunch, and before I leave to come home. If I'm even ten minutes late, he's a nervous wreck. He starts thinking I was in a car accident or abducted or killed. When I walk in the door, I'll find him sweating and pacing the floors or lifting weights to manage his anxiety.

"I know he acts this way because he cares about me, but his insistence on me telling him what I'm doing all the time, takes all the spontaneity out of life. I can't decide to go shopping or see a friend after work, without having to tell my husband and get his okay. Then I have to tell him exactly how long I'm going to be, so he won't get anxious. Well, I don't always know to the exact minute how long I'm going to be, but he has to know or he says he'll lose his mind with worry.

"He sometimes drives me crazy with his overprotectiveness, but I know why he is this way, and I am his wife and an adult and I can put up with it. But our kids can't stand it and won't tolerate it and the arguments over his overprotectiveness are splitting this family apart," she said.

Protectiveness and Adolescent Children

A trauma survivor's protectiveness and concerns about safety can create conflict with adolescent children who are rebelling against adult authority and needing to free themselves from childhood restrictions. Adolescence is a stage of life where children test boundaries and like to take risks. These are normal behaviors that most parents find unsettling, but trauma-survivor parents especially find such behaviors extremely anxiety-provoking and a cause for anger. At such times, the trauma survivor's anxiety level may be raised to almost an intolerable level, which may lead to eruptions of verbal or physical aggression. Such eruptions, although understandable, only create further alienation and tension between all concerned.

No child likes to feel burdened by a parent's anxiety, but adolescents especially want to be free of having to "report to" or give an accounting to their parents. At the same time, if adolescents are aware that a parent becomes highly anxious about safety issues, they may fear that the parent will have an anxiety or panic attack or lapse into a deep depression if they try to assert their independence. The tension between not wanting to aggravate a parent who is seen as wounded and vulnerable, and wanting to prove their grown-up identities can create internal conflict for adolescents, which only adds to their normal conflicts about needing to be attached to their parents for purposes of security, and needing to rebel against their parents to prove their independent identity. One teenager put it this way:

"If I don't call my mom when I decide to stay after school for a while, I'm afraid she's going to have a heart attack or do something awful. Once when I forgot to call, I came home and found that she had ripped the curtains off the windows. Another time she stayed in bed for four days, saying that my not calling triggered memories of her trauma and caused her to relapse into a terrible depression. She even had to go on pills again.

"I don't want to hurt my mom, but I can't always be so careful about calling. I feel I can't just have fun and just do things on the spur of the moment like the other kids do, because of my mom. All the other kids think I'm acting like a child because I 'have to call Mommy.' They don't know about my mom and what she's been through. I know she had a rough time and that I mean a lot to her. If anything happened to me, I'm afraid she might commit suicide or something. I know she worries a lot because of all that hell she went through, but I have to live, too.

"Does my life have to be messed up because someone messed up her life? Now I worry about her, the way she worries about me. The worrying is being passed down from one generation to the next. I want to be able to relax and have fun like the other kids, and not worry about my mother 'freaking out' because I changed plans or I'm not home when I said I was going to be home."

This young man wants his mother to "hang loose," but "hanging loose" is an impossible mode for some trauma survivors. "Hanging loose" and trusting that things are going to be all right is the last thing a trauma survivor can do if he or she thinks a loved one might be in danger. "I don't want my son to feel like prisoner of my anxiety," the mother explains, "But I can't help myself. I know I'm overprotective and I know that sometimes being overprotective creates distance and tension between me and my son, the very thing I don't want to happen, but I can't change."

This mother, like other trauma survivors, may not be able to change completely, but there are ways that her need to be protective, which some people may call "overprotective," can be modified and integrated into a family system or relationship. The following exercises are designed to help you with this issue of protectiveness.

✍ Exercise: Evaluating Your Protective Behavior

1. Open a new page in your journal and then make a list of the things you do that you, or your family members or friends, consider "over-protective." Try to think of at least five things you do on a consistent basis that are seen as "overreacting" or "overdoing" by others, but which you feel are necessary precautionary measures.

2. Each of the behaviors on your list must be evaluated independently of the others. (There is a tendency in families to overgeneralize from one behavior to all behaviors. If one of the things you do is really "overprotective" then *all* your cautions about safety might be dismissed as "overprotective," when in fact, some of those cautions might be extremely helpful and prudent.) In this exercise, you are going to examine each of the protective behaviors in the light of the current reality of danger.

For each behavior, e.g., triple-checking seatbelts in the car, write about the usefulness of your behavior. How does it help promote safety and well-being? How does it not help? If others see your behavior as "extreme," why do they think this? Are they unrealistically minimizing the possibility of danger because they are not as aware of danger as you are, or are they accurate in their assessment that you are overestimating the degree of danger? Is it possible to obtain an objective assessment of danger from a neutral third party? How does the danger you feel exists in the present situation compare with the danger present during your trauma?

There is always the chance that something terrible will happen, but what is the probability of something terrible happening if you don't engage in the protective behavior? For example, if you were in a fire in a crowded building, you may not want to go to restaurants or movie theaters for fear that there will be another fire and you will be trapped in the crowd, as you were during your trauma. In addition, you may not want your family members to go to restaurants or movie theaters for fear that the trauma will repeat itself.

Anything is possible. A fire could happen anywhere, at anytime. However, you might want to determine the probability of a fire in a restaurant or movie theater by looking up the statistics on the number of fires that took place in restaurants or movie theaters in your area in recent years. Then, you will have a clearer picture of the probability of danger. If two percent of movie theaters had a fire in the past ten years, then, when you or your loved ones go to the movies, you will know that the odds are roughly two out of one-hundred that a fire will occur. This doesn't mean your loved ones are totally safe, but at least you will know that the odds are relatively small that something terrible will happen. In addition, if you find that a particular restaurant had five fires in the past six years, it would be reasonable to want to avoid that restaurant and to have your loved ones avoid it, too. For each of the fears you listed that generate your protective behavior, it is important to acquire as much objective evidence as possible. Objective evidence may be sparse, or hard to come by, but all you can do is get as much information as possible.

- In the first part of this exercise, you began to distinguish between those protective behaviors that are based on the probability of real danger and those that have more to do with your past trauma. Can you discuss with family members and friends the differences between these types of protective behaviors? Can you explain your need for caution in some areas as being based on the true probability of danger? Can you also explain how some of your fears are more related to past, rather than present, danger? Can you work out a plan whereby your trauma-related fears are acknowledged and respected, along with the needs of others to act freely without being hampered by your fears?

- How can you manage your anxiety and other reactions if your loved ones are not willing to compromise or go along with the steps that you feel are necessary for them to be safe?

Such a discussion may not be as easy. You may need a neutral third party to mediate the issue. In a family or any other situation where there is true caring, the needs of all concerned must be met. Just because one of your fears is more rooted in the past than the present, does not mean your fear is "silly" and that it should be disregarded or ridiculed by others. On the other hand, others cannot organize their lives around your fears without building up resentments. Just as your loved ones may have to make some concessions to your fears, you have to make some concessions to their needs.

Anger and Adolescents

Studies of the children of Holocaust survivors and combat veterans have shown that some of these children are exquisitely sensitive to the needs of their traumatized parents. Some of these children put their own lives "on hold" and suppressed the normal anger children often feel toward parents so as not to hurt or upset a parent whom they saw as vulnerable or emotionally unstable. In extreme forms, some of these children became parental caretakers, taking the responsibility for healing their traumatized parent through their love. Ultimately, some of these children ended up feeling as helpless and powerless to heal their parent as their parent felt during the trauma.

Suppressed anger in children can lead to the same array of problems it does in adults: low self-esteem, clinical depression, or "acting out" behaviors such as drug or alcohol addiction or sexual promiscuity. Such children do not express their anger because they do not want the guilt associated with hurting an obviously already hurt parent. Yet the frustration these children feel can rise to intense levels. It can be internalized in the form of psychological symptoms or externalized in the form of aggression toward others or animals and, sometimes, toward a parent. Sometimes, the nontraumatized parent is the target for anger meant for the traumatized parent because the child assumes that the nontraumatized parent is "stronger" and can "take it," and that the traumatized parent might lose control or develop more symptoms if faced with the child's anger or rebellion.

If you are a parent, it is important that your child be able to speak freely to you about his or her anger and/or frustration with your need to protect him or her. The child needs to be able to talk to you without being afraid that you will lash out in rage or "fall apart" psychologically. Each of the security measures you have for your family must be discussed, individually, on its own merits. You need to hear your child's side of the story, just as the child needs to hear your concerns. Hopefully, you will be able to compromise on some of these issues. However, on some issues, compromises may be difficult to effect; in which case the price to be paid is either your high anxiety level at not being able to protect your family member as you would like, or the child's resentment for having to adhere to your protective measures.

It is important to view each problem in its complexity and not engage in "black-and-white" thinking. The choices are not that your child must totally obey you or that he or she must totally disregard your demands. If you can break the problem down into all its parts, you may be able to reach a compromise on some parts of the problem, although not all.

For example, Joan, a victim of stranger rape as well as family violence, felt extremely protective of her fifteen-year-old daughter, Betty. She did not want to restrict Betty socially, but she couldn't tolerate it when Betty would tell her she was going "out," without specifying what time she would return or where she would be going. Joan insisted that Betty had to be home by midnight on weekends—no matter what the circumstances might be.

In a family meeting, Joan's daughter explained that since she was dependent on others for transportation, she couldn't always guarantee that she would be home by midnight and that if she insisted that the friends who gave her rides promise to bring her home by that hour, many would be unwilling to take her to parties and social gatherings, since they were permitted to stay out later. Betty also explained that sometimes she and her friends went to one party, and then moved on to another, and that she did not want to be burdened with having to call her mother every time the party shifted from one location to another.

Joan thought that she could not tolerate not knowing where her daughter was or what time she would be coming home. She imagined her daughter at parties with out-of-control adolescents and at the mercy of drinking or drug-abusing teenagers. Joan wanted a black-and-white strict rule to cover all of her daughter's social behavior. A rule such as "home by midnight" would have allowed Joan to breathe easy, but such a rule was impossible to effect.

Joan and Betty tried to consider each social situation separately. Sometimes Joan would agree to pick Betty up at midnight or to provide her with cab money, so that she could leave potentially dangerous situations. Betty promised Joan that she wouldn't get into cars with drivers who had been drinking or taking drugs and promised to call her once per night. Joan would have liked Betty to call her every hour on the hour, but that was unacceptable to the young woman.

Betty compromised by agreeing to call at least once a night and to negotiate with her mother on a situation-by-situation basis. Some weekend nights she would come home by midnight, as her mother wished. At other times, she might stay out later. The important fact is that both mother and daughter were able to communicate and to respect each other's position. Joan was able to accept Betty's needs to socialize in a relaxed manner and Betty was able to accept her mother's need to be assured of her daughter's safety.

Their mutual acceptance of each other's position made it possible for them to work out arrangements for even the most complicated evenings. If, however, either Joan or Betty had become rigid in their position and condemned the other for her position, a struggle would have taken place where no one would have "won." Betty might have given in to her mother's demands with resentment (and found ways to express that resentment), or Joan might have agreed to her daughter's wishes, and then punished her daughter in other ways.

If you cannot work out a compromise with your family members or loved ones, it is highly recommended that you seek a neutral third party with whom to discuss matters. Especially when dealing with children and adolescents, the time and money spent ironing out these conflicts is a wise investment. When such conflicts are left to fester, the result can be addiction, teenage run-aways, and psychological disorders that are much more expensive and difficult to treat.

What Will You Do If Bad Things Happen to One You Love?

How will you manage your anxiety and other unpleasant feelings if your loved ones do not adhere to an agreed-upon plan or ignore your need to feel that they are safe in other ways? The best laid plan devised by the best therapist with the most willing family members, partners, or friends is not foolproof. Human beings make mistakes. Human beings forget. However well-intentioned, your loved ones may not keep their part of the agreement and you will, predictably, suffer from intense feelings of apprehension, anger, and fear. You need to have a plan for what to do when the plans you make go awry.

For example, what memories can you expect to have if a loved one decides to go walking in an area you consider dangerous, drive a car you believe to be unsafe, or socialize with someone you suspect is sadistic? How can you state your concerns in a way that will be heard, and not dismissed, by the other? Can you present objective reasons for your concerns about safety and avoid name-calling, yelling, and other behavior that distracts from your main point—that you are afraid they will be harmed? If a loved one disregards your advice, what are you going to do?

Can you give yourself credit for at least trying to be helpful, even if your intervention is not appreciated or respected?

If some harm does befall the individual in question, how might you respond? Are you going to blame yourself even though your concerns were not heeded? If the other person chose to ignore your warnings, what were your options at the time? What would have happened if you had used physical force or some other means of coercion to force them pay attention to your warnings? What problems would using such means have created?

If someone you love is harmed or hurt, your first impulse might be to blame either yourself or the person who was hurt for not following your advice. It is important to compare your self-blame with the reality of what happened to your loved one. In what ways are you responsible? In what ways are you not? Unless you actually hurt the individual yourself, how did you influence the unfortunate event? In our society, there is such an emphasis on individualism, that we often forget how much other people can matter to us. Aside from our own instinctive desire for survival, there is also a desire to assure the safety of those whom we love, especially our children.

In an ancient Greek myth, Thetis, a sea goddess, wanted to be sure that nothing harmful would befall her newborn baby boy, Achilles. As a goddess, Thetis was immortal, but her baby was half-mortal because he was the child of her union with a human. Because of his mortal parentage he could not live forever. So, to protect the baby from harm she held him by his heel and dipped him into the magic waters of the river Styx.

All the parts of the baby's body that were touched by the magic waters became invulnerable—save for the one part his mother had held him by—his heel. When Achilles became a warrior, many arrows and swords assaulted his arms, legs, and torso, but he was never wounded. His mother's magical protection kept him invincible. Ultimately, though, an arrow did pierce the one small spot on his body that the magic river had not touched, and he died of that wound.

The myth of Thetis symbolizes the universal human desire to provide loved ones with invisible shields of protection. However, unlike Thetis, we are mortal and so are our children and other loved ones, no matter how godlike they may seem to us. Just as Thetis had to grieve the loss of her son, when bad things happen to those we love, there is no other option but to grieve.

Grief and Action

If your child is molested or badly beaten by a bully, or if a relative is hurt in a traffic accident, assaulted, or murdered, there are two appropriate responses: grief and action. If the loved one is now dead, how can you help yourself through your grieving and, if you can, help the others who loved this person cope with their grief? If your loved one is injured but alive, what can you do to help?

Having been traumatized yourself, you know what not to do and what not to say. You know better than to blame the victim or to judge in any way the person who is hurting when what that person needs most is caring, emotional support, and whatever concrete assistance you may be able to provide. You might be tempted to say, "I told you so," but if that person is truly injured, you don't need to tell him/her that. That person already knows, beyond a doubt, that your warnings and concern were justified. There is a high probability that he/she is silently thinking, "Why didn't I listen to . . . ?"

In sum, if something traumatic happens to someone you love, ask what you can do to help and show compassion for the suffering. Do for that person what you wish others had done for you when you were traumatized and in need of human assurance and help. If your loved one dies as a result of the traumatic event, all you can do is grieve. There is nothing more you can do, except to take whatever precautions are possible to avert a repeat of the traumatic event.

Superiority, Entitlement, and Jealousy

Coming to terms with contradictory feelings within ourselves is one of the hardest parts of being human. Life would be so much simpler if we felt only one way about ourselves and others, instead of feeling one way one time, and a different way the next time, and sometimes feeling two contradictory ways at the same time.

Not all trauma survivors feel both inferior and superior to others at the same time, neither do they feel they deserve nothing and are entitled to almost everything at the same time. But some trauma survivors do feel such contradictory feelings, and for them the tension between these kinds of extreme feelings creates its own confusion and pain.

This section will not apply to all readers, but it does apply to you if you answer "yes" to the following questions:

- Have you ever felt so worthless, ashamed, and guilty because of your trauma and the scars it left that you feel you deserve very little out of life?

- On the other hand, do you sometimes feel that precisely because you suffered so much as the result of your trauma, you are now superior to others and entitled to the best that life has to offer?

- Do you sometimes think, "I've paid my dues. Now the world owes me!"?

- Does a part of you feel ashamed of your scars (whether they be psychological, physical, or both) while another part of you wears them as a badge of honor?

- Do you feel that the hardships you've had set you *above* those who have never known true suffering or defeat?

If you experience these kinds of contradictory feelings, feelings of inferiority alternating with feelings of superiority and feelings of worthlessness alternating with feelings of entitlement, you may discover that when relating to others you are simultaneously both jealous and contemptuous.

For example, you may be jealous of others because they don't have to deal with nightmares, flashbacks, intrusive thoughts, or triggers and life seems to have dealt them a better hand, whereas you have been cheated of aspects of your physical and mental health, and perhaps, years of your life. On the other hand, you may be contemptuous of the nontraumatized because they don't know what "real life" is all about. Unlike you, they haven't been tested and they still naively believe that the world is just and fair and that people are basically good at heart. You know better. You know about cruelty and injustice, or bad luck and in that knowledge you might feel superior to those who assume that life is one positive experience after another, interrupted only by the ordinary, normal stresses of life, such as flat tires or lost baggage at airline terminals.

You may feel that, because of all you have been through, the rest of your life should not be stressful and that you are entitled to an easier time of it than others. At the very least, you may feel that no more traumas should ever happen to you again because, after all, you've had your share. Furthermore, allowances should be made for you at work, in relationships, or elsewhere that take into account your limitations and triggers.

It would be wonderful if the world was organized that way—but it isn't. Having been traumatized once does not inoculate you or keep you safe from future trauma. There is no "quota" in misfortune. Furthermore, in most circumstances, whether on the job or with the family, you are probably held to the same standards and expectations as anyone else. Your employer is not going to make an exception and allow you to come in an hour late on those days that you suffer from depression, neither will your work be permitted to fall below par because you are experiencing intrusive thoughts or problems concentrating. You are judged just like anyone else, even though, because of your trauma, you aren't like everyone else and during your trauma anniversary and other difficult times, it's harder for you to do what is expected than it is for others.

This might not seem fair and perhaps it isn't. But it is reality, a reality that can feed your jealousy and resentment toward those who do not seem to have to struggle as hard as you do to get through the hour, the day, or the week. You may find yourself resenting not only co-workers and neighbors, but members of your own family, even your own children, if these people don't have to suffer with extra burdens as you do. Such resentments and jealousies toward loved ones can create rifts in your relationships with them, especially if your jealousy turns to anger or if you hide your jealousy and then feel guilty about it.

Some survivors, in their resentment at not feeling as whole as they did prior to their traumas, verbally attack and criticize family members and friends whom they see as being "superior" or more capable than they are. The survivor might think, "I wish I could be normal like you. I know you have your up's and down's, but you don't know what it's like to be out-of-control or feel vulnerable all the time. I'd give anything to sleep through the night (or have no more nightmares or intrusive thoughts) and for you, it's the most natural thing in the world to go through a day without a psychological symptom of any kind. For me, it would be a miracle." But, instead of voicing such thoughts, the survivor might say, "You really don't know how to _____ very well. It's getting impossible around here with you constantly making this mistake," or "I thought I was stupid until I met you," or other such derogatory comments.

✍ Exercise: Being Honest About Feeling Superior

Go back to the beginning of your journal and look over the trauma-related and post-traumatic relationships you wrote about in chapter 1.

Do you feel superior to any of those people? It is not illegal or immoral to feel superior to others and, if you feel this way, it is important to acknowledge it and to understand the reasons for your feeling. Now, start a new page and answer the following questions:

1. (a) If you feel superior to others, why do you feel this way? (b) Does a part of you also feel inferior to any of these people? Why?

2. How do your feelings of superiority (and/or inferiority) express themselves in each relationship you wrote about in the previous question? How appropriate do you think it is to feel superior (and/or inferior) to each of these persons?

3. Do you feel entitled to special favors or services from others because you have been traumatized and have suffered? What are the special favors or exceptions you feel you deserve? Have you directly asked for these special arrangements in any of your relationships? Have you asked for them, or expected them, indirectly? Have you not asked for these certain arrangements either directly or indirectly, and then become angry when were not been provided?

4. Which of the above special favors or services that you feel you deserve do you realistically think can be provided for you? For example, are there special services that are legally mandated for people like you? If your community organizations or others do not offer you such services, are there any you can provide for yourself?

5. Can these services be worked for politically or socially by organizing with other survivors? Have you considered taking such action?

🖎 Exercise: Being Honest About Being Jealous

People are often reluctant to admit to feelings of jealousy because such an admission reveals a lack in one's self. Yet jealousy is a normal human emotion and, if you have the courage to look at your jealousy, who you are jealous of and why, you can learn much from the process and possibly activate dormant parts of yourself that have not had the chance to develop.

There are two types of jealousy:

- The first is a kind of pathological possessiveness of another person that seeks to control that person and keep that person all to oneself. In this type of jealousy, you aren't jealous of the qualities of the person, you are afraid of losing that person's affection or commitment to you. You seek to ensure that person's allegiance through various means of control, and you possessively guard that person from being influenced by others. Almost anyone, or any force outside of your relationship is seen as a potential threat to the relationship, for example, the other person's family, vocational interests, friends, intellectual interests, or, indeed, any interest other than you is viewed as threatening.

In this type of jealousy, you perceive others as better than you in some manner, and fear that the person you care about is going to abandon you for someone who is superior to you, i.e., in some way more attractive, talented, smarter, or desirable than you are. Not only do you view certain others as being better than you in one or more ways, but the gap between what you are and what they are seems so enormous that you feel there is no way you can compete and there is no question but that you will be the loser in any contest.

For example, suppose you are in a romantic relationship and constantly fear that your beloved will leave you for someone else. Your fear may be irrational in that your beloved has expressed a commitment toward you and, thus far, has given you no evidence of having lost interest in you or of being disloyal. Yet you find yourself filled with jealousy at the mere approach of an attractive stranger. This type of jealousy has more to do with your personal insecurity than with the behavior of your partner

- The second type of jealousy is jealousy of another person's traits or achievements, which you admire and wish you had. You may see a dancer in a movie, for example, and be jealous of the dancer's grace and skill. You may hear someone give a speech and envy the smoothness and effectiveness of the presentation. You may read an essay written by a friend and be envious of your friend's achievement.

These kinds of jealousies can point you to undeveloped potentials within yourself. Your jealousy of the dancer, for example, might lead you to take dance lessons; of the speech giver, to take a speech-writing class; of the writer, to pursue your own writing talents. If you are jealous of someone else's neat appearance, well-kept home, well-balanced financial accounts, or ability to speak a foreign language, these are all goals toward which you could choose to work. Here, your jealousy could be the spur that would activate you to develop new parts of yourself. Perhaps all you need is the permission to do so.

In some other cases, you may feel jealous over qualities or abilities you do not have and cannot ever aspire to obtain. For example, you may feel jealous of the youthfulness of your children or friends, especially if they are the age you were when your trauma happened. When you envision their unblighted future, it is natural for you to wish that such good fortune had been your fate, and to wish that you could be young again and able to relive your life without trauma. Jealousy in such a situation is natural; it reflects your sense of loss.

There are no written exercises or positive affirmations that can fix this kind of jealousy or turn back time and give you what was lost. The only positive action that can be taken is to not permit your jealousy to interfere with the positive aspects of your relationship with the person you are jealous of and to carefully examine your present options and continue to do what you can for yourself.

Exercise: Channeling Your Jealous Energies Productively

Re-examine the three relationships you wrote about in chapter 1: relationships prior to, during, and after the trauma. Then, answer the following questions in your journal. Use a fresh sheet of paper for each person.

1. Were you jealous of any of these people? Did you want to control them so that you could be assured of their affection for you? What did you fear would happen if you lost that person?

2. Were you the object of someone else's jealousy? What do you think this person was afraid of if he/she lost you? If you have left this person, what happened following your departure?

3. If you are currently behaving in a jealous manner toward someone, how does your behavior affect the relationship? Is your behavior useful in controlling the other and assuring you that this person won't leave you, or does your behavior have another effect? What is that effect?

4. Examine the relationships you wrote about in chapter 1 again. Were any of these relationships affected by jealousy arising from your insecurity? How did your jealousy affect the relationship? Are you currently feeling insecure and jealous within an important relationship? What is the source of your insecurity? How does your jealousy affect you and the relationship?

5. Are you, or have you been, jealous of what someone else is doing or how someone else behaves? Would you like to be more like that person? In what ways is possible for you to become what you are jealous of? In what ways it not possible? In what ways is your jealousy a mirror of the losses you sustained as a result of the trauma?

6. What stops you from becoming the kind of person of whom you are jealous? For example, if you are jealous of people who are physically fit, what stops you from emulating them and becoming more fit? Even if you take steps to become more like the person you envy, what might be the limits of such action? What can you realistically hope to achieve?

12

Revictimization and Reenactment

Revictimization

It is a sad truth that people who have been victimized in their families or by people they trust run a high risk of being victimized again by others. For example, some studies show that those who were physically or sexually abused as children run a higher than average risk of being raped or criminally assaulted as adults than do those who were not abused as children. Incest survivors have been found to experience higher rates of battering and rape as adults and higher rates of prostitution, suicidality, and substance abuse than those with no history of incest. Similarly, women who have been raped once are more likely to be raped again, and women who were abused as children are more likely to be revictimized as adults (Finkelhor and Brown 1985; Gelinas 1983; James and Meyerding 1977; van der Kolk 1989).

This tendency toward revictimization does not occur because abuse survivors "like" being abused or getting hurt. But if those who were abused as children did not receive adequate or appropriate help, they often remain demoralized and suffer from low self-esteem. Thus they become easy prey for manipulative, exploitive persons. Additionally, those with histories of abuse may not have developed the ability to sense danger and to get away from it.

Dissociation

If you dissociated as a child as a way of coping with abuse, you may, therefore, still tend to dissociate when you sense danger. As an adult, you are likely to be less able to identify and cope with dangerous or potentially dangerous situations or people. If you "tune-out" when you start to feel afraid or exploited, then your coping mechanism of dissociation may interfere with or obstruct your ability to accurately assess a present-day situation and take steps to protect yourself. Dissociation may have been an effective way of coping with childhood abuse, but it will not serve you well in the present.

If the stress-induced analgesia response (dissociation) (see chapter 4) is activated when you are under severe stress, you cannot accurately perceive current situations and you will tend to minimize your feelings, including any emotional or physical pain. You could be hurting and not really feel it. In extreme states of dissociation, you could even be bleeding or severely injured and feel very little physical pain. Or you might be experiencing emotional abuse or economic exploitation and feel little or no reactions. The dissociation protects you from the pain, but it also prevents you from understanding that a particular situation or relationship is not good for you and, in fact, may be harming you.

Similarly, if you have total or partial amnesia about the abuse in your past, you can't use your abuse history as a basis of information for assessing the safety of current situations because you can't remember the abuse well enough to analyze it, understand it, and therefore recognize current abuse situations.

Recognizing Anger

Another theory about revictimization is that people who have histories of being abused have trouble recognizing their own anger because, in the past, they downplayed their perception of threat in order to minimize the intensity of their emotions so that they could handle the situation. Therefore, in the present, they may downplay their sense of the danger involved in a situation, which can minimize their sense of urgency to leave or change a potentially dangerous situation.

Self-Harm and Aggression Toward Others

Self-mutilation, including cutting, burning, and head-banging, are all forms of revictimization, as are substance abuse and eating disorders. Harming the self is a way of repeating the pattern of victimization experienced at the hands of others. Harming others or other living beings is also a form of revictimization. The issues of self-harm and harming others are, however, beyond the scope of this book. If you practice self-mutilation or other self-abuse or if you hurt others or animals, you need to seek professional assistance immediately.

Revictimization in Relationships

This section on revictimization focuses on the ways in which you might be revictimized in your current relationships. As a child or young person, you may have been victimized more than once because others took advantage of your age, relative helplessness, and your dependency on adults. As a child, you were not responsible for the chaos, violence, or abuse inflicted on you. But as an adult, you can learn to protect yourself from being revictimized in relationships. Obviously, if you are being assaulted by someone with a weapon or are outnumbered or overpowered in some way, then you may have no choice but to be victimized again. However, in relationships in which you have choices, you don't have to be physically or sexually abused, emotionally or financially exploited, or otherwise used.

The first step toward self-protection is to know what abuse is and is not. If you were abused as a child and were told by your abuser that you were being hit or raped as a sign of "love" or affection, you still may have a lot of confusion about what is caring behavior and what is abuse. For starters, you will need to review definitions of abuse so that you will recognize it when you see it.

Physical abuse includes any form of physical coercion, from confinement and slapping of the wrists, to punches with fists or stomping with feet. Being tied up, confined, or subjected to extreme temperatures, starvation, dehydration, or deprived of needed medical care are also forms of physical abuse. Threats of bodily harm are also considered abuse.

Sexual abuse includes any form of sexual coercion; it is not limited to penetration. Being stimulated when you don't want to be stimulated, being forced to watch or participate in pornographic movies, being penetrated by objects, or being forced to engage in any kind of unwanted sexual activity are all forms of sexual abuse.

Emotional abuse includes taunting, ridiculing, name-calling, and yelling. Economic exploitation includes not only being robbed, but not having control over your earnings, and not being paid a fair wage in a timely manner.

✍ Exercise: Recognizing Revictimization

In your journal write complete answers to the following questions:

1. In your adult years, have you ever been subject to revictimization? How were you victimized?

2. *Are you still being revictimized? If so, seek help immediately. Written exercises are not what you need. You need guidance and support to find ways to end your revictimization.*

3. What are the warning signs of abuse that you have trouble recognizing because of your own history of being abused and dissociating?

Elizabeth was sexually abused by her mother from the age of five to seventeen. The fact that she slept with her mother was always portrayed by her mother as "loving and "helping." As a child, Elizabeth was accustomed not only to sexual contact with her mother, but to helping her mother with all her parental responsibilities and social relationships. Elizabeth learned to equate family duty with sexual love and complying with everything that a lover requested.

When Elizabeth married, she immediately assumed that she should help her husband with his many goals, including his work goals. She also assumed that she had to have sex with him whenever he wanted. These were the definitions of "love" and "family duty" she had learned in her family of origin. Her husband exploited her by having her do some of his work, keeping some of her earnings, and disregarding her sexual preferences. But, for Elizabeth, such behavior was a "normal" part of family life. She had vague feelings of discontent, but she didn't feel they were legitimate because she had no standard of a healthy relationship against which to judge her marriage.

Only when her husband began to harm her physically did she realize she was in an abusive, exploitive relationship. But there were many other forms of exploitation going on in the marriage prior to the first physical attack. Elizabeth did not know enough to call them "abuse" because she was accustomed to such treatment and because, like many abuse survivors, she tended to dissociate and minimize her feelings.

In her current life, Elizabeth is "on guard" against potentially exploitive men by staying aware of her personal warning signs. She knows that in the past, when she was being used, she tended to dissociate, not have strong feelings, lose her sex drive, and be driven by "duty." Now she knows that if she is working for or dating someone and she starts thinking about "duty" more than her own needs and begins to find herself "spacing out" or "tuning out" a great deal, that some aspect of the relationship is probably exploitive.

What are your personal "warning signs" that something may be amiss in one of your relationships?

✍ Exercise: Protecting Yourself: Being Your Own Guardian Angel

1. How can you help yourself be on guard for potentially dangerous or exploitive people? For example, are you willing to discuss problems you are having in a relationship with friends or a neutral third party? Are you willing to introduce the person in question to family members, neighbors, or others who have your interests at heart? Are you willing to compare notes on your relationship with others and look at the relationship in an objective manner?

2. Assume that somehow you find yourself in an exploitive relationship. Do you have a plan for rescuing yourself or for getting out of the

relationship? What would prevent you from ending an exploitive relationship?

Now, find a quiet place and think about why you are in this exploitive relationship. Perhaps some people have told you that you are a masochist who likes pain and suffering. In most cases, this is not true. This popular theory, that people stay in relationships that are hurtful to them because they are masochists, is usually a myth. People stay in relationships for solid, compelling reasons; for example, because the relationship meets certain important needs or provides some kind of protection from further harm.

You might be in an exploitive relationship because the other person threatened to physically harm you, others, or a pet; or that person threatened to harm you economically by damaging your career; or threatened to damage you psychologically and socially by smearing your name, or by revealing some of your secrets to family members or others.

You might stay in an exploitive relationship for financial reasons. If you were not in this relationship, perhaps you would be faced with poverty, or lose your health insurance for yourself and your children. Your beliefs and values may also play a role, in that you adhere to a religious tenet that requires you to persevere even in an exploitive relationship.

Regardless of what you decide to do, whether to stay or go, it is important for you to be aware of the reasons for your choice and to examine them carefully to determine how realistic those reasons are. For example, if you are staying for financial reasons, are there other sources of help available to you that might make it possible for you to leave? If you are staying for fear that this person will harm you or someone you love if you leave, how realistic is this fear, and what protection, if any, would be available to you and to others who have been threatened? If your job or career has been threatened, are there ways to protect your employment?

If you are staying because you fear being alone, are you willing to explore this issue with a therapist or trusted friend? If you are disabled and you need the exploitive person's assistance to manage daily life, are there any other people or resources to help you besides this person?

3. Now, in your journal, make a list of the ways that staying in an exploitive relationship helps you and compare it to a list of the ways that the relationship endangers or harms you. You can also make a list of your fears—about staying in the relationship and about leaving it. Include in your list of fears not only those fears that you believe are "logical," such as losing financial help, but also those you think other people might find "irrational," such as the exploitive person is very sexually attractive to you and you fear that you will never meet anyone again who will seem so desirable to you.

Reenactment

Harming yourself or finding yourself in situations or relationships where you are harmed or misused are both forms of revictimization and of reenactment, or a reliving of your trauma. The incest survivor who engages in prostitution or in sexual activity when she is in a dissociated state and the formerly battered wife who permits her employer to harass her without protest are not only being revictimized, they are also reenacting part of their traumas.

There are basically two kinds of traumatic reenactment:

- The first is a repetition of the behavior or actions associated with the trauma, such as the incest survivor who has sex when she is in a dissociated state or the combat veteran who chooses a career in police work, rescue operations, or other kinds of high-action, high-risk occupations.

- The second type of reenactment is a symbolic re-creation of the original traumatic event. For example, a mother who lost two of her pre-school children in a car accident transformed her two cats into "substitute children." She comes home at lunch to "check on the cats," the way she used to check on her children. She leaves social engagements early to "be with the cats" because the "cats miss her," just as she used to restrict her social activities for her young children. When she doesn't keep up this kind of contact with her pets, she experiences extreme anxiety, confusion, and pain. Without her "symbolic children," she plummets into a deep depression which can take days to overcome. Her relationship with her cats is a symbolic reenactment of her trauma, which helps her keep her traumatic memories and emotions in check.

One theory holds that traumatic reenactments are attempts at mastery: that by trying to "redo" or "relive" the trauma, the individual hopes that the negative outcome of the original trauma can be changed and that, if he/she does things "right," a positive outcome can be effected. For example, the mother who lost her children can be viewed as trying to be the very best mother possible, in the hope that her attentiveness will protect her children from harm. Unconsciously she may hope that if she is an excellent mother to her cats, her children will be returned to her. Through her actions, she's trying to reverse the negative outcome of her trauma. When she stops engaging in the reenactment, she will realize that taking care of the cats, or any other living thing, is not going to undo the harsh reality of the loss of her children.

Similarly, the combat veteran engaged in dangerous police work may be "undoing" some of his combat trauma. For example, by risking his life as a police officer, he may be trying to compensate for those times during combat when he felt he didn't act courageously enough. Or he may be trying to complete some other unfinished trauma-related business.

Another theory about traumatic reenactment is that reenactments are familiar ways to deal with an unsafe world. A trauma survivor may feel "stuck" in repeating certain reenactments, but there is a comforting familiarity in repeating certain reenactments and it certainly may feel safer than facing an unknown world or unknown group of persons.

✍ Exercise: Recognizing Reenactments

Recognizing reenactment can be extremely difficult. If you are reenacting an aspect of your trauma, usually you are not doing so consciously. It is hard, therefore, to look at your behavior and identify a reenactment. Also, recognizing reenactment requires you to be aware of your trauma. If you have not done much trauma work, still suffer from amnesia, or only partly recall the details of your traumatic experiences, it is, understandably, difficult, if not impossible, for you to recognize reenactment. An indirect approach, rather than a direct one, is often most helpful when trying to uncover reenactments.

In your journal, answer the following questions. Use a separate sheet of paper for each activity.

1. Are there any activities or behaviors you engage in which, when you don't have the time or opportunity to do them, leave you feeling extremely restless, angry, or unhappy? Is your emotional reaction out of proportion to the absence of the activity? For example, if you can't do a certain thing or go to a certain place at a certain time, do you find yourself in a state of turmoil that may be somewhat extreme, given the circumstances?

For example, Betty went to shopping malls almost every Saturday afternoon, whether she needed to purchase anything or not. If she didn't go to a mall and look around, she would break out in a sweat or fall asleep from depression. When the weather did not permit her to go shopping, she'd become highly anxious or almost robotlike: i.e., she would become either hyperaroused or shutdown. And if someone suggested an alternative activity or interfered with her trip to the mall on Saturday, she would withdraw from the relationship.

The severity of Betty's reaction when she was not able to go shopping on Saturdays and the fact that going to the mall was more important than being with any of the people in her current life were major clues that Betty's behavior was tied to a significant traumatic event. On the surface, shopping at a mall seemed unrelated to any trauma in Betty's life, but upon closer examination, Betty found the connection.

When she was small, her parents quarreled a great deal. There was frequent violence and Betty was afraid not only that a parent would be hurt, but that she and her younger siblings would be injured also. Betty functioned as a protector to her younger siblings and kept them from crying when her parents cursed and hit each other by giving them small pieces of candy. She got the candy on weekly Saturday shopping trips with her mother.

When she was a child, Saturday was a special day for Betty. Her father was always on his best behavior that day because his parents visited the family on Saturdays. While her father was busy with his parents, Betty's mother would take Betty shopping and buy her small treats and gifts. At these times, Betty's mother would assure Betty that the fighting was going to end and that someday their family would be happy. While Betty was shopping with her mother, her siblings were home with her father and his parents. She knew that her siblings were safe because her father always acted like a model parent when his parents were visiting.

Betty came to associate shopping trips at the mall with the rare occasions when she received nurturing from her mother, as well as with the purchase of protection (candy for the younger siblings) for the impending fights between her parents.

When the adult Betty stopped going on her shopping trips, she reexperienced the feelings she had felt as a child during her parent's ongoing abuse of each other. At times, she became so afraid that she went numb. At other times, she became hyperalert and highly anxious. Eventually, she realized that her Saturday shopping trips were forms of reenactment in that she was soothing herself by repeating the one family event in her childhood that had provided her with some nurturing and hope. She had to learn to deal with her feelings about her childhood before she could to to the mall on Saturdays as a matter of choice, rather than as a psychological necessity.

2. Do you feel you need to do certain activities or see certain people at specific times of the day or days of the week or seasons of the year? Is there a relationship between the timing of your trauma and these activities, or the specific times that you want or need to see certain people?

3. Have others commented to you about certain behaviors of yours, wondering why you need to do such and such? Is there any possibility that they are noting some kind of reenactment on your part?

4. If you've been able to identify a reenactment, can you draw a clear parallel between your behavior and your trauma?

5. What function does the reenactment serve for you? How does it help you to reenact your trauma in this way? How does it not help you?

6. How does your reenactment affect your partner, children, or other family members? How does your reenactment affect your work and extracurricular activities? More specifically, look at the three post-trauma relationships you wrote about in chapter 1. Do your reenactments affect any of these relationships?

7. Are any of your current relationships reenactment or repeats of past relationships? Are any of your current relationships substitutes for or similar to relationships you had during your trauma?

8. What happens when you don't engage in reenactment behavior? What are the uncomfortable thoughts and feelings you must endure? Can you discuss these with anyone?

References

Finkelhor, D. and A. Brown. 1985. "The Traumatic Impact of Child Sexual Abuse." *American Journal of Orthopsychiatry* 55:530–541.

Gelinas, D. M. 1983. "The Persistent Negative Effects of Incest." *Psychiatry* 46:312–332.

James, J. and J. Meyerding. 1977. "Early Sexual Experiences as a Factor in Prostitution." *Archives Of Sexual Behavior* 7:31–42.

van der Kolk, Bessel. 1989. "The Compulsion to Repeat the Trauma: Reenactment, Revictimization, and Masochism." *Psychiatric Clinics of North America* 12:2 389–411.

13

Telling Your Story

Telling the story of your trauma won't make the trauma happen again. Telling your story won't undo the trauma or make it go away either. People who hear your story, no matter how compassionate and understanding they might be, do not have any magical powers. They cannot make the pain, or the scars, totally disappear. But telling your story can help *lessen* the pain and shrink the scars and, by telling just one person about your trauma, you can begin to feel reconnected to the human race again.

Telling the story of your trauma is much like therapy. There is healing in the telling.

Being able to tell the story of your trauma, or even parts of it, means you have some sense of the sequence of the events during the trauma and some sense of your own actions and motivations. Having this kind of understanding means you have achieved a major milestone in the recovery process. But that doesn't mean you need to tell all of your story to everyone, that you have to share your traumatic experiences with whomever asks, or that your need to share today will be constant over time. Your need to share, or not share, may be different next year, the year after that, or ten years from now.

As always, unless you are being held hostage, you have choices. This chapter examines some of the issues and choices that arise when you share your story. These issues include which parts of your story to share and with whom, when not to share or to stop sharing, and telling your children about your trauma.

The Need to Tell

Many survivors have a deep legitimate need to tell the story of what happened to them, especially family abuse and sexual assault survivors who were silenced in the past. Telling your story validates you because when you tell another person your story, you are telling the world, "This awful thing happened to me. It truly happened and it has affected me ever since."

Telling helps lift the veil of denial, mystery, and silence that so often shrouds trauma. Family abuse, rape, and political-torture survivors in particular usually had to bear their pain in silence because their abusers warned them "not to tell—or else." Telling breaks the power of the perpetrator's injunction to stay silent at all costs. Even combat veterans, concentration camp survivors, police officers, rescue workers, and survivors of other kinds of traumas don't readily talk about their experiences. Often they fear that telling will alienate or emotionally disturb others, or that others will judge them harshly for their actions during the trauma or see them as deficient human beings because they happened to be caught in a trauma. As chapter 2 explained in detail, some of these fears are grounded in reality. Many people do condemn and reject trauma survivors, for the variety of reasons discussed in that chapter.

Yet telling the story to someone, sometime, is an imperative. You survived to tell the story and you may need to tell the story to survive. Telling your story helps you to organize the chaos of the trauma and to know yourself. You may need to tell your story many times in order to remember the details and to make sense of what happened, as well as to understand how the different people and events in your trauma relate to one another.

Initially, telling your story may set off a trigger or retraumatize you. Nevertheless, in the long run, telling your story can help desensitize, you to the trauma. The more times you can tell the tale, the more you will be able to integrate all the pieces of the trauma with each other, and the more you will be able to put the trauma into perspective. With each new insight you will gain in understanding what happened and why; you will also regain a bit of the control you lost during the trauma and slowly, very slowly, the trauma will lose some of the power it holds over you.

If you were traumatized, you were in a great drama. However, unless you were very fortunate, you probably had no place to talk about it. You, as a trauma survivor, need a place to speak the truth of what happened to you. Telling your story—under the right conditions—helps to detoxify any shame and guilt you may feel and, as such, empowers you. Telling your story helps give you a sense of who you are and where you are going and helps you to construct meaning not only from your symptoms, but for your life. By telling what happened in the past, you can begin to think about a future (Armsworth 1994).

When It's Safe to Share and When It's Not

It is important not to engage in black-and-white thinking in regard to telling your story. For example, there is a common misconception that "getting it all out" or "sharing all your secrets" will cure you. Sometimes media portrayals of trauma recovery show individuals experiencing a major emotional catharsis when they tell all the details of their trauma to a doctor or loved one with great emotion. When they finish talking, they are immediately "cured" of the trauma. This is a myth. No truly traumatized person has ever been "cured" in a single session, no matter how emotional the session was. Such portrayals of the healing process do not do justice to the long hard work involved in understanding and processing severe trauma. It takes years, not hours, to undo the damage wrought by trauma.

Therefore, contrary to the message given by media presentations and pop psychologists, there is no rule that to get better you have to "get it all out" or "tell all." In fact, talking a lot about your trauma when you are still being overwhelmed by the feelings associated with it, or when you are still abusing substances, could cause you to regress and develop even more psychological distress symptoms than you already have. Under no conditions should anyone, even a therapist, push you to tell all of your story before you are ready to do so. Reread the Cautions section in the Introduction which will guide you in knowing when to stop, not only when reading this book, but when talking about your trauma.

Who to Tell Your Story To

Telling your story to a nonsupportive person could be extremely damaging to you. It is important that your first self-disclosure be with a supportive person or a trained therapist. In general, it is not wise to tell your story to someone you just met or whom you don't know very well, even though you may have a strong impulse to do so. You may want the other person to get to know you quickly and feel that he or she cannot possibly know you unless they know about your trauma. Or you may want to get the sharing of the trauma "over with," so that you can be sure whether other people have accepted you or not. If they are accepting, you can proceed with the relationship. If they are not, you may want to end the relationship immediately and you would rather find out sooner than later whether a person is someone to whom you can relate.

However, there is a middle ground between telling a new person right away and waiting for a long time to share your story. Your trauma isn't all of you. It doesn't define every aspect of your personality or dominate every thought, act, or feeling, even though at times you feel it has defined and shaped who you are.

Before telling other people about your past, let them get to know the other parts of you first. If they are familiar with you to some degree before you begin to talk about your trauma, they will have some basis for relating to you and a context in which to understand your trauma. Telling the horrific details of your trauma cold to someone does not set the stage for a warm reception. Other people may not know you well enough to respond in a helpful manner. Also, you do not know them well enough to interpret what their responses mean. For example, some people may not show their emotions in their facial expressions, yet they may be reacting very deeply to what you are saying. If you do not know this about the person, you may perceive that person as "cold" and unresponsive to your pain.

How to Tell Your Story

During your trauma you had no or little control. You couldn't stop anything. But when telling your story, you can change the subject whenever you feel the need. Just because you may feel like telling your story, doesn't mean you have to act on that feeling. You can stop yourself from acting on the impulse to share if you intuitively sense that the time isn't right.

When to Stop Telling

Also, once you start sharing it, you can stop telling your story whenever you want, at any place. Just because you begin with the intention to tell the whole tale, does not mean you have to complete it, especially if you find that you are being triggered by the telling or that the listener is not responding as you had hoped. Stop telling your story, even if you must do so in an abrupt manner, under the following conditions. Suggestions are also given below on how to stop. These are just suggestions. You may have your own way of backing off.

- Stop if you find yourself being triggered by your story into a state of hyperarousal, dissociation, or any of the conditions listed in the Cautions section of the Introduction. In such a situation, you could simply say, "I want to share with you, but I find myself becoming too distraught, so I must stop. The fact that I stopped telling my story to you has nothing to do with you. It's because I'm becoming overwhelmed. Thanks for listening as much as you did. Maybe I can finish my story another time."

   If you say this, your listener may accept it or may push you to continue sharing, at which point you will need to stand firm in your resolution to take care of yourself. In the worst case, you'll receive a teasing, discounting, or critical comeback such as, "Why do you have to be so hysterical all the time?" or "Come on, now. Isn't it time you got over this thing by getting it out and letting it go?" or "You are overly sensitive. It's hard to be around you because you are always overreacting and I never know what to say. I can't feel free around you because you are always so emotional. You're always having one kind of attack or another. It's impossible to have a logical conversation with you."

The message here is that something is wrong with you and that you are a social failure. This kind of message hurts. If you want to, you can tell that person that he/she is being hurtful, but such an admission may lead to that person becoming defensive or attacking you further. He or she may think they are being helpful by telling you not to be so sensitive and to "get over it," and may feel frustrated because they want to be supportive and don't know how. When you tell the listener that he or she has hurt rather than helped you, if the listener's original intention was to be helpful, he/she may feel like a failure and then respond with his/her own negative feelings, or even lash out at you to say that you are the problem.

There is no real way to "fix" this kind of interaction and make it positive. Indeed, it is this kind of interaction that most trauma survivors dread and that causes many trauma survivors to withdraw from others or stay silent about their traumatic histories. If you find yourself in this kind of awkward situation, the most you can do is not make it worse by attacking the other person or by compromising your own dignity and self-respect. You can make a statement such as the following: "This conversation hasn't turned out the way I wanted. I feel bad and I sense you are feeling bad. Frankly, I don't know what I can do or say to make things better right now. Maybe it's best to stop the conversation or change the subject rather than take the risk of causing more misunderstandings. It's hard for me to talk when I'm upset and I am upset. But that doesn't mean I'm rejecting you. I need a time-out now. How about you?"

Although it's important to ask how the other person is feeling, if you need to stop the interaction, do so. Listen to what the other has to say, acknowledge what has been said and then, if you need to, end the interaction. You can then think about whether you want to share your story with this person again, and under what conditions.

- Consider stopping if your listener seems to be losing interest, as indicated by yawning, darting eyes, irrelevant comments, or changing the subject. In this type of situation you could simply say, "I need to stop talking about this right now," without any long excuse or explanation. You can then excuse yourself, if necessary, saying something like "I need to go right now," once again, without any explanation, or change the subject.

If you choose to, you can point out that the other person doesn't seem to want to listen, and deal with the response to your observation. Or you can avoid a confrontation and simply excuse yourself or change the subject. You may have to deal with this issue later, however, if the other person asks you why you stopped talking about your trauma, or you may decide you want to confront that person with the fact that he or she didn't seem interested in listening to something important to you.

- Stop if your listener appears overwhelmed, looks horrified or disbelieving, or begins to hyperventilate or show any of the warning signs listed in the Cautions section. Once again, you don't have to explain why you are stopping. You can just announce, "I need to change the subject right now. Let's talk about something else." Note that if the other person displays some of the warning signs listed in the Cautions section, it may be that hearing about your trauma has triggered a repressed traumatic memory or a repressed strong emotion and that person may need the kind of assistance also discussed in the Cautions section.

- Stop if your listener begins to make disbelieving or derogatory comments such as, "That couldn't happen," "You're exaggerating," or "It's your fault. You should have known such and such," or "That could never happen to me," or "You really enjoy talking about all that gore, don't you?" Again, you can excuse yourself or state that you need to change the subject. Or you can say, "I don't find your response supportive, so let's drop the subject."

- Stop if you discover that your listener has a sadistic side, or you have reason to suspect that he or she may ridicule you for what you might share, or use it against you. You can indicate to the other person that he or she is not being supportive or you can avoid a confrontation and simply excuse yourself or change the subject.

- Seriously consider *not* telling your story to someone in a position of authority over you, for example, a supervisor at work. Such a person could be placed in a difficult position by knowing this personal information about you. (This suggestion does not apply to circumstances involving lawsuits, in which case you must follow the advice of an attorney in regard to what information to disclose and what to keep confidential.)

- Stop if your listener responds to one of your statements in a way that indicates you have been misunderstood.

- Stop if you realize that you don't know the listener that well or that the listener has a vested interest or emotional involvement with individuals or institutions that violated you. For example, part of your trauma may have included negative experiences with the military, the criminal justice system, or some other organization or particular person. As you share, you may realize that the listener is emotionally involved with the individual who hurt you or that the listener strongly believes in the organization that you consider has damaged you. For the listener to believe you, might mean shattering his or her strong attachment to the individual or organization in question.

The listener is then caught in a bind—the same bind you were caught in when you first learned that a cherished person or respected institution was capable of causing, or allowing, harm to be done to you. Remember how you felt when your faith in someone, or some institution, was shattered? Remember how your experience threatened your previous beliefs, and your sense of identity?

That is how your listener might feel, if he or she is truly listening and has an investment in believing in the goodness of the person or institution that was part of your trauma. If a listener in this position does not respond in a sympathetic manner, it doesn't mean that you are wrong or bad or that you shouldn't have opened up to that person. It doesn't necessarily mean that the other person doesn't care about you or is an inhumane monster either. It can mean simply that the information you are giving by telling your story is too psychologically threatening or too emotionally overwhelming for that person to handle. When you sense this is the case, it is probably time to stop sharing your story. To continue might cause you to feel more misunderstood and uncared for, and might cause more fear and anxiety in your listener, who, because of such anxiety and fear, might withdraw from you or verbally attack you.

Deciding whether to tell your story, or to stop telling your story once you have started, can be a complex dilemma. When you share your story, you need support. However, your listener may be overwhelmed or may not be able to handle your suffering. When you sense your listener is anxious or rejecting, you need to protect yourself by ending the conversation.

Generally, it is best to share only with those who are trained in trauma work or people whom you know care about you and have proven that they understand and respect human sorrow and fear and who do not mock those in emotional pain. One approach is to share a little bit and observe how the other person reacts before you share more. (Clients "test" therapists this way, sharing bits and pieces of the trauma that they consider safe to see how the therapist reacts. If the therapist seems to be able to handle and respond appropriately to "lesser" or "safer" parts of the trauma, then clients feel comfortable talking about the more emotionally problematic or more horrifying aspects of the trauma.) You can even ask your listener how he or she is feeling or reacting, or whether he or she is willing to listen to more, or wants you to stop.

Remember, no one can walk in your shoes. No matter how understanding someone is, no one can ever appreciate everything that happened to you during your trauma and because of it—not even the most qualified, caring, or highly-paid therapist.

Caution: This chapter is *not* a guide to confronting someone who has harmed you or to telling your story to members of your immediate or extended family when your trauma was childhood abuse or sexual violation within your family.

Telling Your Story—Fears Related to the Past

In the past, part of your trauma may have been the fact that you could not talk about it. You might have been warned not to tell or known that if you told, you would be punished, or hurt. In many traumatic situations, secrecy about the events and silence about reactions to those events is expected, if not mandatory. To have talked in the past, may have put you at risk emotionally, financially, physically, or sexually.

In the present, it is important that telling your story does not put you at risk, which is why it is generally advisable not to share your story with supervisors or persons in positions of authority over you, unless you have good reason to trust these persons. You also need to have good reason to believe that these authority figures will maintain the confidentiality of your story and stand behind you, if for some reason, they have to choose between being loyal to you or complying with a directive from a superior to demote you or remove you from your position. Although there are laws protecting those with disabilities (and PTSD is considered a legal disability), there is no reason to let others use your trauma-related pain in an inaccurate or demeaning way or as a means of humiliating or disqualifying you.

It is also important, however, not to let your fears about what might happen determine your decision about telling your story. Remember, you don't have to tell all of your story. You can share in a general way or share only those aspects you feel are suitable to the situation and safe for you to disclose at work. For example, if you are a combat veteran or a police officer, you do not have to reveal every gory detail of every death you have ever seen. You can simply say, "For several years I served as a _____ and I saw many deaths." If you are an abuse survivor, you don't have to describe specifics about how you were physically and psychologically humiliated. For instance, you don't have to say that you were forced to perform obscene dances for your abuser. All you need say is something general that communicates your point. For example, you could say, "I know the hell of having someone use force and threats to control me."

✍ Exercise: Fears About Telling

The following exercise is designed to help you understand the consequences of telling your story in the past, versus the consequences of telling your story in the present.

In your journal, answer the following questions as completely as possible. If you have had more than one trauma, use a separate sheet of paper to discuss each trauma that you choose to write about. You may write about as many traumas as you choose. Do not, however, write about more than one trauma at one sitting. At a later point, you can write about the additional traumas. Keep in mind the necessity of protecting yourself from becoming overwhelmed with traumatic memories and feelings and the importance of learning about yourself in a slow, but thorough, manner.

1. During your trauma, were you explicitly told "not to tell" what was happening or "not to talk" about how you felt? Who told you not to tell or to talk? What would have been the punishment for telling or talking?

2. Were you ever punished or hurt in the past for telling or talking about your trauma? If so, what happened?

3. In the present, what is the likelihood that the past will repeat itself and that you will be punished or made to suffer in ways similar to the ways you would have been punished or hurt during the original trauma, if you told your story (or part of it)?

✍ Exercise: Deciding What to Share

Your story has many parts and many levels. Telling your story doesn't mean sharing every aspect of it with everyone. You can decide in advance what parts of your story you feel comfortable about sharing and what parts you want to keep to yourself. There may be some parts you feel comfortable sharing with one person, but not with another.

In your journal, answer the following questions as completely as possible.

1. Are there parts of your story you don't want to share with anyone? What are those parts?

2. Are there parts of your story you would share only with a therapist or a best friend or partner, but no one else?

3. Have you shared your story in the past? Looking back on the times you shared your story, what do you wish you had done differently?

Are there parts of your story you wish you had talked about? Are there parts you wish you had kept to yourself? With what types of people did you feel comfortable sharing? What kinds of responses were discouraging or deflating? What did you learn from these past experiences about what to share and with whom to share?

4. Consider three people in your life today with whom you would like to share your story, or more of your story. You might want to consider the three persons you wrote about in chapter 1 or you might want to consider others. For each person, list what you think you would be willing to share and what you are not willing to share. For each relationship, write about how you hope the other person will respond and write about what you hope will be the outcome of your sharing. For example, are you hoping the other person will understand some of your difficulties? Are you hoping the other person will love and appreciate you more? Are you hoping the other person will come to see that some of the current tensions in your relationship are due to your trauma?

5. What are your goals in sharing? Are you looking for emotional support, financial assistance, changes in the relationship, revenge, validation, or an apology? Is there something specific you want the other person to do for you or do you want some change to take place in the way the other person views you?

6. Can you tell the other person your goals in sharing? For example, can you say, "I want to tell you what happened to me because I want us to be closer," or "Because I want you to understand why it's so hard for me to visit your mother (or go to violent movies)" or "Because I feel so unhappy about what happened I need to share my unhappiness with another human being and I think that you would be understanding and supportive"?

7. Preparing for the worst. For each relationship, write about how you might feel if the person you are sharing with is rejecting instead of accepting. What other risks might you be taking by sharing your story in each situation?

8. Weighing the pros and cons of sharing in each situation, what do you think is best for you to do in terms of sharing? In other words, what is your plan for sharing with each person?

✍ *Exercise: Deciding How to Share*

Your story is important and your sharing should be thought of and treated as an important occasion. It is essential not to leave the sharing of your story to chance. You must take as much control as is possible over the circumstances under which you will disclose such a significant part of your life. By answering the following questions as carefully as possible, you can structure the situation so that you and your story are given the dignity that your story deserves.

Before you begin to write in your journal, take a few minutes to think about where and when you would like to tell your story. For example, would you like to talk outdoors? Can you be specific about where you would like to be, for example, in the woods, at a beach, in your backyard? If you would rather talk indoors, do you want to share your story in your own home or elsewhere?

You might want to arrange for a quiet place where you will not be distracted or interrupted. In addition, you might want to tell the other person in advance that you have something important to share and that you would like them to be able to give you the necessary time and attention. For instance, if you are sharing your story with family members and you go to their home at a time when two of their children are ill and their basement is flooded with rainwater, you cannot legitimately expect those family members to attend to you.

You need to set up a time when they can focus on you and what you have to say. It is permissible to ask others to make the kind of arrangements necessary so that they can be emotionally available to you. You are sharing emotionally sensitive material and you need to set the stage so that the others have the ability to listen carefully without being distracted by other pressing needs.

1. Now, in your journal, write at least six or seven sentences in response to the following question: How can you set the time and the place and other aspects of the situation for telling your story so that you increase your chance of being truly heard?

2. An alternative way to tell your story is to describe the specific events only in the most general terms and focus your account on what your feelings were during the trauma. You can talk about the sadness, the terror, the sense of helplessness, the shame, and the anger. You can also briefly mention the events, but focus instead on the symptoms you have had to cope with since the trauma, i.e., numbing.

   For example, instead of sharing the specifics of what happened when you were mugged, raped, or in a firefight, you might want to say you were in a "violent event" or in a "terrible accident," and talk more about what it felt like. Some survivors, for example, choose to say, "I was mugged. I don't want to talk about the details, but I want you to know that during the mugging, my entire life flashed before me and I had regrets about such-and-such and I realized such-and-such. Although I thought I was going to die, I promised myself that if I lived, I would _____.
   Even though the mugging happened four years ago, I still feel _____ and _____.
   I'm still triggered by _____ and _____."
   You might want to state your feelings about the person you are

talking to or how they can help you or what they mean to you. For example, "Because of what I went through, I appreciate such and such about you," or "I have such and such a goal for our relationship."

3. Now, do some writing about how you can tell your story in terms of *feelings*, rather than the details of the events. Add to this writing your thoughts about how you can tell your story in terms of the kinds of struggles you have in your daily life today. For example, Andrew, a combat veteran, often had nightmares where he relived certain battles. He'd sweat so much the sheets would be drenched and he would wake up screaming. Although his girlfriend wanted to hear details about his dreams and the battles, Andrew didn't want to talk about his war experiences. Talking about the war triggered him. What he could share with his girlfriend was his feelings: "I wake up afraid" or "In the dreams I'm attacked, and angry," or "I'm afraid you are going to leave me because of my nightmares."

4. In your journal, write down what you could say to the person who is listening to you about the importance of your relationship to you and about how he/she can be (or already has been) supportive of you.

Checking In with the Other Person

An important part of sharing is being aware of the other person, not only in terms of that person's potential to reject or hurt you, but also in terms of that person's needs. Your story, or the feelings you are sharing, may be upsetting or even overwhelming to that person. He or she may become numb or hyperaroused in response to hearing about your trauma similar to the ways you become numb and hyperaroused when triggered. You need to be prepared for such reactions because they are quite normal. You cannot expect someone to listen to a traumatic story and not have some kind of reaction. If there is no reaction at all, you might interpret that as disinterest or disregard; but it may be numbing or the individual's need to distance from your pain. On the other hand, it could be that the person seeks to distance himself/herself from your pain, so as not to personally feel the pain.

At different points in your sharing, you may want to ask the other person if they are able to hear more or to ask how they are feeling. If you are in a therapy session, you shouldn't have to concern yourself with how the therapist feels. But if you are with a partner, friend, relative, or someone who isn't a trained mental health professional, you must understand that person has feelings too and deserves choices, especially if that person is a child.

It may be that the person can't listen to all of your story, even if you are willing to tell it, because your story stimulates painful or angry feelings. That person may be vicariously traumatized by your trauma. This does not mean that person doesn't care about you or doesn't respect your sharing. It simply means that person is human and subject to the same kinds of traumatic reactions as you are and were.

The Pros and Cons of Disclosing Your Trauma to Children

At the 1994 convention of the International Society for Traumatic Stress Studies, a panel of trauma experts discussed the effects of parental trauma on children. Most of the discussion centered around the children of Holocaust survivors and children of incest survivors. However, many parallels can be drawn between these children and the children of rape and criminal assault survivors, children of combat veterans, and children of war survivors, such as civilians caught in war situations, refugees, and political-torture survivors (Albeck, Armsworth, Auerhaln, et al. 1994).

The panel emphasized that the relationship between parental trauma and the child's emotional and mental development is highly complex because of the following factors:

- Traumatized parents are not all the same and each individual reacts to his or her trauma in his own way.

- Parental trauma, whether it is disclosed or not, is not the only factor affecting a child.

- Parents vary in the ways and degree to which they disclose aspects of their traumatic pasts.

- Parents vary in their motives for such disclosure.

For example, in a recent study (Armsworth 1994), women survivors of incest were questioned about whether they had disclosed the fact of their sexual abuse to their children. The women who had told their children that someone in the family had committed incest on them when they were children varied in their motives. The motives included the following:

- "I didn't want to keep it a secret anymore."

- My children had witnessed confrontations and arguments between me and others in my family and I didn't want the kids to keep guessing about what was going on."

- "I didn't want my children to feel responsible for the way adults in the family, including myself, were acting or feeling."

- "I wanted support and understanding from my kids."

- "I told my children because they guessed the truth and I needed to validate their observations."

Mothers who had decided not to tell their children gave the following reasons for not disclosing:

- "It was bad enough I went through it. Why should my kids even know about it?"
- "I wish my past was not my own, so I don't tell anyone about it, not even my kids."
- "I want my children to have good relationships with everyone in the family, even those who abused me."
- "I don't want to pass on the shame and the fear."
- "I am too ashamed to self-disclose."

In this study (Armsworth 1944), children reacted in a variety of ways. Although some children showed empathy toward their mothers, most children did not respond in an understanding manner. Some children were indifferent. Others said they already knew about the incest, or were angry at the abuser, or at the mother for taking away the trust they had in the abuser. Some children felt ashamed, as if they had been contaminated by the abuse the mother had suffered, and some children became depressed because they experienced a conflict of loyalty between their mother and their mother's abuser. Some children wept and expressed fear that they would be abused, or revealed their own abuse. Some children were so horrified that they asked their mother to never talk about it again.

Reasons for sharing with children vary, as do children's reactions. Your work is to be clear about your motives for revealing your trauma to your children and to be prepared for the fact that you cannot predict how your child will react to your disclosure, no matter how well you think you know your child.

Also, be aware that the effects of trauma do not go just from parent to child, but also from child to parent. Kathi Nader, for example, points out that trauma does not move just up and down, from the older generation to the younger, but back and forth, from the younger to the older and vice versa (Albeck, Armsworth, Auerhaln, et al. 1994).

Nader gives an example of a World War II veteran who lost his hair after his son was sent to Vietnam. After his son returned, the father's hair grew back. This is an instance of how a child entering the type of situation that was traumatic for the parent can greatly affect the parent.

In my experience, many Vietnam veterans did not seek help for their combat stress until their sons or daughters were sent overseas (or were in danger of being sent) to serve in the Persian Gulf conflict. Some of these veterans had experienced PTSD symptoms during and after their tour of duty in Vietnam. But their symptoms did not distress them enough to seek help until one of their children was endangered.

Similarly, some family abuse survivors, particularly incest survivors, sought help only after one of their children had been assaulted or in a vehicular accident. Some of the abuse survivors had experienced PTSD symptoms but they had all been able to maintain their jobs and relationships until one of their children was traumatized.

Sex and Aggression in Children

The panel also pointed out that a child's growth can activate a survivor's memories and feelings about the trauma. Children's aggressive feelings, especially when directed toward the trauma survivor or other family members, and a child's emerging sexuality can also activate strong feelings in trauma survivors. The trauma survivor may try to hide his or her reactions from the children, but children cannot help but observe their parent's increased distress or other symptoms.

As a result, children may come to feel that their normal growth processes, feelings of aggression, or evolving sexuality are threatening or troublesome for their parent. Children then may feel guilty, as if they were wounding an already hurt parent. At the same time, children may *resent* feeling guilty, as well as becoming angry for not being allowed to grow up and "be normal" like other children.

The panel concluded that in homes where a parent is a trauma survivor, the effect of the parent's trauma on the children is complex, for the child is not a blank slate upon which the parent's trauma is written. Children have their own issues and conflicts, which interact with their knowledge of, or fantasies about, their parent's traumatic history.

In homes where the survivor is obviously suffering, but there is no talk about the trauma or why the parent (or sibling or other relative) is so sad, angry, or confused, the child is exposed to the survivor's pain and depression with little understanding as to why the survivor is so tormented. In these cases, children come up with their own explanations. On the simplest level they may feel that they are at fault and think: "If only I were a more lovable, more obedient, or more [something] child, my [relative] would not be so unhappy." Or they may fantasize. For example, if the survivor has a physical disability or scar from the trauma, the children may surmise that the survivor is very ill and perhaps dying. But they don't know if their thoughts are true and they may become quite confused.

If children are told nothing about a parent's trauma, yet know their parent was in a trauma, they may fantasize about it and mix their fantasy with whatever partial knowledge they do have. For example, if they know their mother was abused, their knowledge about child or wife abuse may have been obtained from the media or from other non-familial sources who may have inadvertently dropped small bits of information.

For example, a child may have heard from the media or friends that child abuse survivors sometimes grow up to abuse animals or their own children. Even though their parent may have never harmed a living thing, the child may wonder whether the parent did hurt children or animals. If the parent is a combat veteran, the child may have learned in school or from the media that soldiers sometimes kill women and children. Even though the parent may not have hurt civilians and never discussed having to kill while in the military, the child may fantasize and wonder whether the parent did kill or hurt children while serving in the military.

If, at the same time, children are struggling with jealous feelings toward a younger sibling, step-siblings, or other new members of the family, the fantasies about a parent's imagined aggressive behavior can fuse with their own fantasies about hurting the young rival. As a result, the guilt a child might feel about wishing harm to a newborn sibling, niece, nephew, or grandchild may be intensified by any guilt the child might be carrying regarding the parent's fantasized acts of cruelty to animals or other children.

Guilt and Aggression in Children

The affected child may be quite young or an adolescent. For example, Susan, age eighteen, is the youngest of three children born to a combat veteran. As the youngest and only daughter, she was adored by her parents, aunts, and uncles. However, when Susan's oldest brother married and had a baby girl, the new baby became the center of the family's attention and replaced Susan as the family's "little darling."

Susan felt she was too old to be jealous, yet she resented her young niece. When Susan baby-sat for her niece, she was distressed to find herself fantasizing slitting the child's throat, as she had imagined her father had done to enemy infants. Imprinted in her mind were photographs of dead civilians who were killed in wartime, which she had seen in a magazine at her school library.

"Your father fought in a war, didn't he?" a schoolmate had taunted her.

As a soldier, Susan's father had not killed any children. But Susan did not know that. All she knew was that her father did not talk about his war experiences and refused to answer any questions about what had done or not done. He refrained from discussing his military career with his children to protect them from being traumatized, but the lack of discussion left many unanswered questions in Susan's mind about what her father had done. Due to her classmate's and others' assumption that most soldiers committed atrocities, Susan began to feel guilt over what her father might have done as a combat soldier. This guilt, combined with her own guilt over her own murderous wishes toward her baby niece, became an enormous burden. But she could not tell anyone her thoughts about her father or her niece. She was certain she would be judged an evil person if she talked about her jealousy about her niece and as a disloyal daughter if she expressed concerns about her father's combat role.

The normal aggression a child feels for a parent also may play a role in the child's reaction to a parent's trauma.

John, age seven, was feeling the normal kind of rivalry that Freud postulated exists between a father and a son of this age, when his father was injured in an auto accident. His father was hospitalized for several months, but no one told John how severe his father's injuries were in an effort to spare the child. John was allowed to speak to his father on the phone, but not to visit him in the hospital for his father had had severe facial injuries that required multiple plastic surgeries.

John overheard his mother weeping and he was aware of increasing financial pressures at home because the insurance company was late making payments to the doctors and his father had used up all his sick leave at work and was on leave without pay. When John turned eight, his mother could not afford to throw a big birthday party for him, as had been the family's custom. She was concerned that John would feel slighted and angry; but John was relieved—for deep down, he felt that he had contributed to his father's accident.

Although John had not seen his injured father, he had seen many pictures of vehicular accident victims on television and in the movies. In addition, John played games of "shoot'em up" and "kill 'em" with his friends. At times during these games, John had fantasized about harming his father, because he was angry at some of the restrictions his father had placed on his activities and also because he held some unconscious anger at this father due to the Oedipal rivalry typical of his age.

In John's mind, his visions of traffic accident victims, of people he had shot dead or injured while playing games, and of his hurt-hospitalized father merged. "Logically," he knew he had had nothing to do with the accident, but on some level he felt that if he had been a "better boy" or a "more lovable son," his father might have stayed home with him on the day of the accident, instead of driving to where he had been going when the accident occurred.

When it was time for his father to return home, John pretended to be glad, but he was filled with dread. He was certain that his father knew of his aggressive feelings toward him, that his father blamed him for the accident, and that his father would retaliate. John's psyche was torn between his love and his fear for his father. This normal Oedipal conflict was exacerbated by the car accident, leading to periods of depression that alternated with aggressive outbursts.

John would sit on the living room couch in an almost inert state of depression for hours; then he would erupt into destructive behavior, such as smashing furniture and toys. In these ways, he expressed his guilt, confusion, and anger. He was angry that his father had been hurt, he was angry that his father was not available to help him with his sports and school activities, he was angry at his mother for being less emotionally available to him since the car accident, and he was angry at himself for having conflicting feelings about his father.

After his father came home, he was bedridden for quite some time and not available to give John the attention and affirmation he craved. Also, John's mother had less time for him due to having to nurse her husband and take on a part-time job to help meet the bills. John believed that he was being punished by both parents for his confused and angry feelings and withdrew even further. He did not know how to say that he was angry that his father had been in an accident and that he was angry because the accident had caused so many changes in the family.

In John's home, as in many homes, his parents only knew how to stifle anger or to let it explode indiscriminately. Hence John had no role model for other ways of expressing anger. He did not know how to express anger in a open, direct manner or how to identify the frustrated need and disappointment that had given rise to the anger. Even if someone in his family had had the ability to help him express his emotions, the family was under so much economic and psychological stress, that neither parent had the time or energy to help him learn how to identify emotions, how to express them accurately, or how to find constructive ways of coping.

When anger cannot be freely or safely expressed at home, children act out their frustrations in school. Counselors who have worked with children of parents who have PTSD or other traumatic reactions report that school is the area where children are most likely to vent the anger they cannot reveal at home. When children are young, their anger is usually expressed in terms of minor acts of disobedience toward the teachers or minor infractions of school rules. As children grow older, their behavior becomes more rebellious and, in some cases, more dangerous to others or themselves. Teenagers who become promiscuous, engage in petty crime, or abuse alcohol or drugs, and run away from home may be acting out their anger, as well as their other feelings toward their families.

Conflicts About Sexuality in Children

Another problem for children of trauma survivors, especially adolescents, concerns their parent's sexual behavior during traumas such as rape, incest, combat and other wartime experiences, such as refugee and political-torture experiences. If children know the parent was sexually abused as a child, as a civilian in wartime, or as a prisoner in a refugee or political concentration camp, they may wonder what happened to their parent. They may wonder whether their parent is like the highly sexualized portrayals of sexual abuse survivors in the media. If the children are subjected to society's common misperceptions about incest and sexual assault, they may wonder if their parent "enjoyed" or "provoked" the sexual assault. Just having to think of a parent in sexual terms can be distressing to a child, especially if there is no one the child can talk to about his or her feelings or thoughts.

Talk shows and movies about sexual assault and highly distorted media portrayals of persons with multiple-personality disorder or histories of sexual abuse may make the child's fantasies about what happened to their parent much worse than what actually occurred. Due to media portrayals of sexual assault, the child may expect their traumatized parent to have "flashbacks" or "a nervous breakdown" or to develop another personality at some unexpected time. Children may fear that their own sexuality, or some other aspect of themselves, may trigger an extreme reaction in the parent. Hence children's fear of and ambivalence toward their sexuality fuses with fear about the parent's mental and emotional stability and fear about what happened to the parent when that parent was traumatized.

Children of combat veterans may wonder whether their father had sexual relationships with enemy women during their wartime experience. When children see the TV stories about the rape and mistreatment of women and girls in present-day wars and political uprisings, they cannot help but wonder whether their father was involved in such behavior himself. They may also wonder whether their father frequented prostitutes in other countries or coerced girls or women into sexual acts with him.

These questions take on special importance if the veteran was already married to their mother while in the service. If children think that their father had sexual relations with other women than their mother while he was in the military, they may feel he betrayed and belittled their mother by his behavior, in addition to any feelings they might have regarding their father as a sexual being.

If such questions are raised when the child is entering adolescence or struggling with his or her own sexual issues, the child's sexual identity and values may be affected. On the other hand, open communication between parent and children on the issue of the father's relations with other women during his military career is extremely difficult. Not only is sex a largely taboo topic in many families, but the subject may hold traumatic memories for the father.

In addition, a veteran may feel, quite justifiably, that his wife and children cannot handle the truth about his sexual behavior in the military. If a veteran told his wife or children that he raped women or had sex with preadolescent prostitutes during wartime, he might destroy his marriage, as well as his children's faith in him. Also, he may have trouble remembering or accepting such behavior himself, and therefore be unable to talk about it at all, even with his therapist, much less with his family members.

Similarly, family abuse survivors who were forced to harm other family members or animals may, justifiably, feel that their spouse and children would be harmed by learning that the survivors were not only victims, but also perpetrators, and the survivors fear rejection for that reason. The survivors may still be trying to reconcile the facts of having been both victim and victimizer in therapy and be in no position to make their former torturous position an open topic of conversation.

On the other hand, in the case of both the veteran and the family abuse survivor, the child's fantasies about the parent's behavior might be much worse than the parent's actual actions. For example, children might wonder whether their veteran dads had fathered and abandoned other children overseas. Such questions might be sparked by the publicity given to the abandoned children of American soldiers in Vietnam and elsewhere. Children may feel great anger and bewilderment with their fathers if they suspect they have half-brothers or sisters in a far away country. They may reason that if their father abandoned his overseas children, he might also abandon them. Then, again, they might feel relieved that they do not have to contend with step-siblings. In those cases where a veteran and his wife have adopted a child from the country where the father served, the veteran's natural child may wonder if the adopted child is a substitute for a child left overseas.

Parents with histories of abuse may find themselves in situations similar to a combat veteran father. Media portrayals of female incest and sexual abuse survivors who became prostitutes or sexually promiscuous and who subsequently had abortions or neglected their children may cause the children of sex abuse survivors to wonder whether their mothers had other children whom they aborted, put up for adoption, neglected, or abused. Media portrayals of male sexual abuse survivors who became abusers themselves, or career criminals, alcoholics, or drug addicts, may also cause children to wonder whether their survivor parent ever played any of those roles. When a parent tries to shield the child from the ugly facts of his or her own abuse as a child, the child may wonder about what really happened not only during the abuse, but *because* of the abuse.

Parental Double Binds

Research on the effects on children of exposure to a father's combat trauma or a parent's abuse or other trauma history is extremely limited. It appears to me that in this situation caring parents are put in a true double bind. If a parent tells the children nothing about his/her traumatic experiences, then the child is left to imagine what happened or did not happen. The child's fantasies, along with whatever information or misinformation about the trauma presented by the media or obtained from family members, can dominate the child's perception of the parent's experiences.

On the other hand, to talk about the trauma may overwhelm the child. Ideally, the information should be presented to the child in an age-appropriate manner and the child's reactions to the information should be discussed with the child also in an age-appropriate manner. In general, sharing traumatic stories with a child without also providing support for coping with that information has the potential of complicating the child's healthy development. In other words, partial knowledge or incompletely processed knowledge has the potential for creating as much emotional conflict and pain for the child as not knowing at all.

Parents may wonder what is the right thing to do, but there is no single answer. Some children may be relieved to hear the truth because the truth is more benign than their fantasies. On the other hand, when told the truth, some children may feel outraged and angry. The knowledge given to them about the trauma may help to foster negative self-esteem and the children may come to feel as scarred, unlovable, tainted or "abnormal" as their traumatized parent.

The problem with trauma is that it just doesn't go away. Whether the parent talks about it or not, whether traumatic material is shared with the children or not, trauma makes its impact. The crucial factor is how the trauma is discussed in the family and the support available to those who were traumatized or who live with someone who was. It is also crucial, yet very difficult, for traumatized parents and their families to be able to identify whether it is the trauma or its aftermath that is upsetting their lives or if some other stress is causing the upset. When parents can draw a connection between a family problem and the trauma, they may be spared the self-defeating assessment that the family problem is a sign of someone's personal or moral failure, unlovableness, or incompetence.

On the other hand, there are very real dangers associated with telling a child too much about one's trauma or turning to that child for emotional comfort or other forms of support.

Secondary Traumatization

One type of dysfunctional family is called the *enmeshed* family. This is where the personalities of some of the family members are fused together and individuals are not allowed to become their own person. Such enmeshment can occur when one or more of the children becomes traumatized by a parent's traumatic experiences. This process, called "secondary traumatization," has been found among children of the sur-vivors of the Nazi Holocaust, children of World War II and Vietnam War veterans, and children of adult survivors of child abuse (Epstein 1979; Rosenheck and Nathan 1985; Rosenheck 1986; Sigal 1976; Silver-man 1989).

In secondary traumatization, the child, in some manner, relives the parent's traumatic experiences or becomes obsessed with the trauma-related issues that concern the parent. The child may even manifest symptoms similar to the parent who was traumatized. The child may have nightmares about the parent's trauma or worry a great deal about death or injury. In some cases, children as young as three or four have learned to imitate their parent in certain hyperalert symptoms. Whether the children actually experience fear or are simply imitating their parent is not known.

In families of World War II veterans where there was secondary traumatization, Rosenheck and Nathan (1985) found that "for some of the veteran's offspring, their father was, by far, the most important per-son in their lives. It is as if they were constantly together, constantly embroiled in a shared emotional cauldron. For these children, life seems to have been a series of anticipation of, and reactions to, their father's moods, impulses, and obsessions" (Rosenheck and Nathan 1985, 538–539).

Rosenheck and Nathan (1985) also cite the case of Alan, the ten-year-old son of a Vietnam veteran who, although he did not have night-mares, had great difficulty sleeping because he worried about "being killed or kidnapped. His main fear was that he, like his father, or both, would be shot 'like in the war.' In many of his [Alan's] fantasies, it was as if he were living in one of his father's flashbacks rather than in his own reality" (page 538).

In a study of counseling centers serving combat veterans, about 65 percent of the counselors polled observed symptoms similar to the veteran's in his children. This does not mean that 65 percent of children of Vietnam veterans evidence symptoms similar to their fathers' symp-toms, but rather that 65 percent of the counselors said that they had witnessed this phenomenon in some children of veterans (Matsakis 1996).

I have observed several children evidencing secondary traumati-zation. Like the ten-year old described above, Ben was obsessed with power and violence. He constantly played war games, read war comics, and wanted only war toys for Christmas. It was impossible to have a conversation with Ben without his mentioning Vietnam and his father's various heroic feats. Despite his superior IQ, he had trouble concentrat-ing in school and was in frequent fights. His participation in sports was intense and, he admitted, a way to prove to his father that he was as strong and brave as any Vietnam veteran. Ben also attacked his sisters and neighbors with plastic swords, hurling anti-Vietnamese epithets.

Children as "Rescuers"

Children who suffer from secondary traumatization may or may not assume a "rescuer" role in relation to their fathers. The rescuer role may be assumed by another child in the family who takes it upon himself to help make the father happy (Rosenheck 1986; Rosenheck and Nathan 1985).

One child, Ben, did assume the rescuer role and, when he wasn't playing sports or war games, he spent most of his time with his father, who was not only his father but his best, if not only, friend. At the age of fourteen, however, Ben, began to want to separate from his father. Also, he became interested in girls, most of whom frowned on his interest in violence. Ben felt guilty about experiencing the normal adolescent process of separating and becoming an adult, as if by growing up he was abandoning his father.

At the same time, Ben's father was experiencing his son's growing up—and away—as still another loss, rekindling feelings of betrayal and abandonment associated with his wartime experiences. In an effort to hold onto his son, who had been not only a son, but an admiring companion, Ben's father began to impose unnecessary restrictions on his son's activities and to criticize him for minor imperfections, which led to further conflict between father and son, and, to more guilt on Ben's part.

Ben's father needed counseling to see that punishments and negative remarks were not bringing his son closer to him, but driving him farther away. Ben's father needed to be repeatedly told by his therapist, and by his friends who were parents, that losing children to their own growth is a normal part of parenthood, not a personal rejection.

Yet it still felt like a rejection to Ben's father and for a while he considered emotionally divorcing himself from his son and not interacting with him at all. "You don't have to disappear from your son's life. You only have to recede gradually," his therapist advised him.

"Your son still needs you and will continue to need you for the rest of his life. You are no longer in the forefront of his life as you were when he was younger, but this doesn't mean he doesn't love you. You need to learn to let go, a little bit at a time."

The therapist's advice sounded easy, but Ben's father had difficulty tolerating the wrenching pain involved with allowing his son to develop his own interests and activities. Losing people is hard for anyone, but especially for trauma survivors like combat veterans who have already experienced many losses and because it threatens their sense of control. It highlights their powerlessness over people, even their own children.

Yet this veteran was finally able to see that, by not demanding so much of his son's attention and by not creating friction over minor matters, his son showed him more respect and talked to him more often.

The ultimate compliment came when, after a week of reining in his criticisms, Ben's father heard Ben say, "Gee, Dad. You haven't bugged me for a whole week. That makes me feel real good. Like I have a real Dad."

On a day-to-day basis, however, it was usually difficult for Ben's father not to be jealous when his son rushed through dinner and then left to be with his friends. The pain of realizing that his son was growing up, and in small but real ways, progressively leaving him, filled him with anger and despair.

"What my son is doing is all so normal. I'm glad he doesn't want to listen to my war stories anymore and is interested in other things," he told his therapist. "Why can't I adjust?"

The therapist responded, "Turn the situation around and look at the positive. Isn't your son's growth beautiful? Even though you over-loaded your son with your war stories, you also played a part in pro-ducing a mentally and physically healthy child. Would you really want your son to have no friends and be glued to you all the time? What if all your son did was hang around with you and ask to listen to your war stories over and over again? Then you really would have a problem."

Dennis presents another case of secondary traumatization. Like Ben, Dennis listened attentively to his father's war stories but, more importantly, he was present while his father grieved and expressed great remorse for having been involved in the killing of women and children. (Some of these women and children had been warriors in disguise; some had been innocents.)

Dennis took on his father's guilt, as well as his sorrow, and at age fifteen, he began to drink heavily. Although there were various reasons for his drinking problem, the internalization of his father's anguish and guilt was a major factor.

Dennis was hospitalized several times for alcoholism. After each hospitalization he attended AA meetings. However, all his dedication to recovery did not seem to help him to maintain sobriety. At age twenty-five, he achieved sobriety when he met and married an impoverished Vietnamese refugee woman who had been brutalized during the war. He adopted not only her children, but also her three siblings, one of whom had lost both legs during the war.

"I've never been happier in my life," says Dennis. "And alcohol no longer calls my name. There are people who need me now. I can't afford to drink."

Advanced training in psychology is not required to see that in caring for the traumatized Vietnamese refugees, Dennis found a reason to stay sober and a means of making restitution for the actions over which his father had carried such tremendous guilt, grief, and shame.

Loretta's mother is an incest survivor. When Loretta's mother became a teenager, she ran away from home and lived on the streets until she met and married Loretta's father. From a young age, Loretta was told details about the incest and about her mother's life as a runaway, during which time her mother had engaged in prostitution, drug addiction and other criminal activities, and had been frequently raped. Loretta's mother also described some individuals who had shown her kindness during her difficult years. She told Loretta that only physically handicapped men and women had ever helped her without trying to exploit her. In particular, a blind man was heavily praised for having provided Loretta's mother shelter and protection when she really had needed help.

Loretta was constantly "on guard," afraid that unsavory people from her mother's unhappy past would track her down and try to harm her and others in the family. When adult males came to the home or telephoned, Loretta wondered if any of these men had ever raped or paid for sex with her mother. As a teenager, Loretta harbored great resentment and animosity toward young boys who seemed similar to the boys and men who had harmed her mother. For example, Loretta's mother had described in great detail how she had been gang-raped by members of a wrestling team who were all blue-eyed. As a result, Loretta would have nothing to do with men with blue eyes or men on sports teams. She generalized that aversion from her mother's experience.

In college, Loretta met a blind student and had sex with him, even though she was not attracted to him. She felt "obligated" to have sex with him because, in the past, a blind man had helped her mother. Loretta majored in special education and she has devoted her life to helping physically handicapped children, mostly because when her mother was desperate, people with physical handicaps had come to her aid.

Exercise: Identifying Secondary Traumatization

In your journal, answer the following questions as completely and honestly as possible. Use a separate sheet of paper for each child.

Before you answer the questions, review the symptoms of posttraumatic stress disorder and depression that are described in appendix B. Then take some time to think about each of your children in detail. Before you begin writing, mentally review the following points:

- What is your child's current daily routine? What are his/her interests? Who are his/her friends? What kinds of games does your child like to play? How is your child similar to, or different from, other children that age, or other children in the family?

- Over the years, how has your child changed? Have there been any abrupt changes in your child's attitude, appearance, or behavior that are not the result of normal growth processes?

- What have others observed or stated about your child? Consider the feedback you've received from teachers, neighbors, relatives, your partner, and your children other than the child you are writing about. Eliminate any comments about your child that were ill-founded or based on malicious gossip.

You are now better prepared to answer the following questions in your journal.

1. Do any of your children evidence PTSD or other traumatic reactions similar to yours?

2. If you have shared part, or all, of your traumatic history with your child, have you asked your child how he/she feels about what was shared? You might want to ask your child to tell you what he/she remembers about what you shared, to see if there are discrepancies between what you told the child and what the child understands as having been your trauma.

3. Are any of your children preoccupied with parts of your trauma or your traumatic issues?

4. Do you treat any of your children like your therapist or best friend in that you frequently tell that child about the trauma and turn to that child for emotional support?

5. If one of your children is evidencing signs of secondary traumatization, would you consider discussing the situation with a trained professional or taking your child for an evaluation?

Helping Children Cope with Parental Trauma

Based on his studies of World War II and Vietnam War veterans with PTSD, Robert Rosenheck suggests that children who are extensively and repeatedly exposed to detailed descriptions of their father's war experiences are more likely to develop secondary traumatization than children who are given little or no information about their father's war experiences. He notes that secondary traumatization did not occur in those World War II families where the father deliberately kept his war experiences a secret so as not to negatively affect his children (Rosenheck 1986; Rosenheck and Nathan 1985).

This finding, however, should not imply that trauma cannot be openly discussed in the family. There is a profound difference between exposing a child to excessive descriptions of traumatic events and giving that child certain basic information about a parent's trauma and the potentially devastating effects of trauma on the human psyche. Furthermore, children from homes in which there are "no-talk rules" often hunger to understand the traumatized parent. In addition, if they are educated about PTSD, clinical depression, addiction, and other traumatic reactions and the effects of these reactions on the family, they are less likely to blame themselves for their parent's problems. They will also feel less alienated from the traumatized parent.

Helping Young Children

Although it is difficult, if not impossible, for young children to understand the nature of many kinds of traumas or to comprehend the meaning of trauma in an adult's life, even children as young as four or five can understand some of the basic feelings associated with trauma. While a young child will certainly not profit from gory descriptions of an accident, rape, criminal assault, or battle, he or she can usually understand anger and sadness. "Mommy (or Daddy) is sad (or mad) because somebody she (or he) loved died (or got sick, hurt, or lost) when she was hurt." Perhaps an analogy can be made between the traumatized parent's feelings and the child's feelings when a toy or precious object is stolen or damaged or upon watching a pet die.

Fight-flight-freeze reactions can also be explained to children in terms of animals' reactions to danger. If children have ever seen their pets or other animals go into an attack mode, run away frantically, or withdraw or hide when they are afraid or hurting, these experiences can be used to explain how the trauma survivor felt during the trauma, or feels today when triggered in the present. The trauma survivor's limitations, in terms of activities, emotional expressiveness, and triggers, can be explained in terms of a medical condition, such as diabetes, a heart condition, or the loss of a limb. Although I hesitate to draw a parallel between someone who has been traumatized and someone who is crippled due to the loss of a limb, sometimes this kind of analogy is more concrete and understandable to young children than that of a physical illness, such as heart disease or diabetes.

The purpose in drawing such an analogy is to explain to the children that the illness, or crippled condition, is real; but it is also limited. People with heart problems or diabetes can't do everything someone who doesn't have such problems can. They have to be careful about certain activities or foods, for example. But that doesn't mean they are invalids and can't function. Similarly, someone without a leg or an arm can't do everything that a noninjured person can do, but there is plenty that even a double amputee can do.

Using Physical Analogies

The traumatized parent's difficulties or inability to feel certain emotional responses or engage in certain activities can be explained in terms of a physical problem the child understands. It is also important to emphasize those aspects of the parent's situation that may be permanent and those that might improve over time. For example, if you are a car-accident survivor, who is unable to drive without being triggered, you may feel that you may never be able to drive in the geographical area where the accident occurred. However, with time and help, you may be able to resume driving in other parts of town. Therefore, you can tell your child that while you may never be able to drive downtown again, you think you will be able to drive to a certain mall or movie theater in a while. An analogy can be made with someone who lost a foot. Such a person may be able to walk again, but not run. Or such a person might be able to walk quickly on smooth ground, but would have to walk very slowly on rough terrain.

In addition, parents need to acknowledge to their children when the trauma survivor is behaving unusually or inappropriately. It is not necessary for the nontraumatized parent to ridicule or denigrate the traumatized parent. But factual statements can be made about the behavior of the traumatized parent that may help the child to understand. A father can say, "When Mommy was hurt as a child, she learned that knocking on the door meant something bad was going to happen. That is why she jumps when you make noises that sound like a knock on the door," or "In the war, Daddy learned to be afraid of strangers and new places. That is why he likes to sit near the door," or "When Mommy was in the car accident, it was raining. That is why she can't drive you places when it rains."

Often children, especially young children, cannot identify their feelings, especially when they are coping with several emotions at once. A parent can help a child get in touch with various emotions by asking, "How do you feel when Mommy needs to leave the dinner table early?" or "How did you feel when Daddy punched a hole in the wall?" or "How do you feel when Mommy/Daddy is so grouchy?"

If the children cannot articulate their feelings, a parent can suggest feelings to them. A parent can say, "If I were a little boy (or girl) and my Daddy/Mommy was angry a lot, I would be scared that she/he would start hitting someone and forget about taking care of me. I would be mad at my Mommy/Daddy too. I would want to stop her/him from being so mad or sad but I wouldn't know how to do that. Do you ever feel any of these ways?"

Instead of pretending that the traumatized parent's moods or absence or sudden departure from the home doesn't matter or should not be talked about, the remaining parent can acknowledge the reality of the other parent's absence. "When Daddy/Mommy leaves like that, I worry a lot. I wonder if she/he is going to be alright and if she/he is safe and I am scared she/he might be hurt. But I'm also mad at him/her for leaving without saying where she/he is going. Sometimes I get so mad at him/her I wish she/he would never come back. But then I'm sorry for thinking like that. It sounds funny, but I can be mad at him/her and love him/her at the same time. Do you ever feel like me?" or "How do you feel when Mommy/Daddy is gone?"

Depending on the particular family situation, a parent can encourage the children to share their feelings about their family life with him or her and with the other parent. In addition, unacceptable behavior must not be denied or minimized. If there is violence in the home, it is important that it be stated that violence is wrong and dangerous. Similarly, if the traumatized parent still has an alcohol or drug problem or an eating disorder, it is important that the problem be acknowledged.

Regardless of their ages, children need to be told repeatedly that they are not the cause of the turmoil evidenced by the traumatized parent. Even if the children never indicate that they feel they are to blame for the trauma survivor's pain, anxiety, or depression, they need to be told over and over again that they are not the cause of the parent's anguish. Even if they were the best little boys or girls in the whole world every single minute they couldn't make Mommy or Daddy happy all the time. This kind of message cannot be stated often enough. You know when you have succeeded in communicating this point when your children tell you, "Don't say it. I know. I'm not to blame. I've heard it a million times."

Helping Disturbed Children

Self-mutilating children, depressed, or suicidal children, or children who manifest other psychological symptoms need professional help, such as that provided by a private psychologist, psychiatrist, or social worker. It should go without saying, but it must be said that physical or sexual abuse of children is both illegal and immoral. The children's physical safety must be the top priority, regardless of the circumstances. Either the abuser, or the children, must be removed from the home and appropriate help sought for each. Child abuse is not only a moral offense—it is a crime. All states have mandatory child-abuse reporting laws for professionals and others who come into contact with children. In some states, however, the mandatory child-abuse reporting laws apply to all persons, including family members. Therefore a parent may be in violation of the child abuse laws of the state if he or she permits the children to be abused by the other parent without reporting that parent.

The Child as the Parent's Helper

In homes where one of the parents is exceptionally stressed and lonely, that parent may turn in desperation to one of the children for excessive emotional or other forms of support. Although this is technically not child abuse, turning to a child to assuage one's emotional pain is an insidious form of abuse that can cause lifelong emotional damage to a child. This tendency must be avoided at all costs.

In this section, an example follows of how the significant other of a trauma survivor can turn to a child for emotional support in an extreme and inappropriate manner. The significant other was not getting her needs met in her relationship with her trauma survivor and turned to one of her children to meet some of her needs. Although the example is of a significant other turning to a child to be a substitute partner/friend/therapist, the same story could be told about the trauma survivor as the parent who turned to a child for emotional help. This is especially likely to occur if the parent is a trauma survivor who has not been able to form supportive relationships with other adults or who is alienated from his/her partner. In general, women more often turn to daughters than to sons for help with housework or child care, which can set the stage for talking intimately and emotional sharing.

In marriages where one partner (or both) has a trauma history and that trauma history interferes with good marital communication and support, it is possible that one (or both) parents will turn to a child for companionship and help. Sometimes one parent "takes" one child and the other parent claims another child, which can lead to numerous divisions and rivalries in the home.

Marge and Jim's family is typical of this type of excessive use of a child for emotional support. Jim is a survivor of child abuse. Although he was able to marry, he was ambivalent about having children. When his wife wanted children, he agreed. Their first child was a girl named Carol. When his wife, Marge, had their fourth child, the birth precipitated a panic attack in Jim, who found himself having flashbacks and periods of being unable to concentrate at his management job. He resigned from his position as vice-president and found a job in sales. However, the pay was less and because his depression had worsened, he was unable to muster the enthusiasm and commitment necessary to be successful as a salesperson. As a result, Marge had to help him with his selling as well as taking a part-time job to make up for Jim's lower salary. Meanwhile, her fourth child was still an infant. Marge then began to turn to Carol, her eldest daughter for help.

"It started when I found Mom crying in the kitchen, sobbing 'God help me. I can't do it all. I just can't do it all," said Carol.

"'I'll help you Mommy,' I said, and from that day on I helped with all the dishwashing and dinner preparations and cleanup. I felt proud to help my Mom and when the new baby got old enough for me to hold, I took over being Mom to him, too.

"I didn't mind not being able to watch television after school, but I did mind having to quit Girl Scouts. But Mom needed me more and more and I had to help her so she could help Daddy, so our family wouldn't be poor and have to move."

It was not Marge's turning to Carol for household help that was destructive, rather it was Marge's sharing of her marital secrets and emotional pain with her daughter that was so damaging. As Marge instructed her daughter in certain chores, or when they did them together, Marge often would graphically describe to Carol how Jim shut her out emotionally and how disappointed she was in her marriage. She also warned Carol never to marry someone who had been abused as a child or who had ever been in any kind of trauma.

At the age of seven, Carol was not old enough to hear her mother's secrets about her father. But she also felt privileged that her mother had confided in her. Since her father was usually emotionally distant from her and had often disappointed her, Carol quickly sided with her mother. Still, as with any child, she wanted and needed to believe that her father was a good man.

Surely her Daddy wasn't bad. And if he was so horrible, didn't that make her, as his daughter, horrible too? Carol also felt disloyal listening to her mother criticize her father. But how, at the age of seven, could she tell her poor overworked Mommy to stop talking to her in that manner?

As a child, Carol had few defenses against her mother's feelings. She was easily overpowered by them and they became a part of her personality. Instead of developing along her own lines and having her own feelings, Carol became emotionally "enmeshed" with her mother and took on aspects of her mother's personality.

For example, she felt her mother's pain and sorrow as if they were her own and intuitively knew when her mother was unhappy. Often she spent her entire allowance to buy her mother perfume or flowers, which she would give to her mother saying, "Someday Daddy will love you the way you like and buy you presents. Meanwhile you have me."

Starved for love and affection, Marge accepted the gifts. By the age of ten, Carol was not only buying her mother gifts, but giving her mother pep talks and advice on how to handle her husband and the other children. She could not imagine life without her mother and processed life through her mother's eyes. Furthermore, she dared not be different from her mother, lest her mother crumble.

Needless to say, Carol's peer relationships suffered. Additionally, at the age of eleven or twelve, when children normally begin to separate from their parents, Carol's natural separation process was stunted.

When Carol, at age thirteen, developed an ulcer, Marge went for help. "I know it wasn't fair of me to put Carol between her father and me," Marge told her therapist. "But before I came here, I had no one to turn to. I was so alone and afraid. Without Carol, I might have never been able to keep my sanity. And I needed her, I really needed her help. But I should have never had her take emotional care of me."

To reverse the unhealthy direction that Carol's growth was taking, Marge stopped confiding her marital problems to her daughter and she asked her other children and Jim to assume some of Carol's chores. She also started Carol in therapy.

According to Carol's therapist, Carol suffered from depression, as well as nightmares due to repressed anger and fear surrounding the rift between her parents and her enmeshment with her mother. In one recurring nightmare, her mother's hairbrush and her father's belt flew together from room to room of the house, sometimes attacking each other, sometimes chasing Carol, and sometimes destroying furniture. The hairbrush was interpreted as symbolizing her mother's anger, the belt, her father's, in that her father had described to Carol how he had been beaten with a belt as a child.

The dream showed that Carol was afraid of her parents' arguments, symbolized by the hairbrush and the belt attacking each other and destroying property, as well as her mother and father's individual anger toward her, symbolized by the hairbrush and the belt chasing her. Carol believed that if she did not help and comfort her mother sufficiently, her mother would go mad. She also was afraid that by sympathizing with her mother, she was incurring her father's wrath.

In another dream, Carol saw herself as a mummy glued to her mother's leg. She asked her mother to release her, but her mother refused. This dream depicted the symbiotic nature of the mother-daughter relationship and Carol's desire to be her own person. It also represented Carol's awareness of the fact that if she remained an obedient "mother's helper" and caretaker, she would never have a life of her own. Instead, she would remain a reflection of her mother's emotions and problems.

Depression and conflicts like Carol's are not unique to families where a parent was traumatized as a child. In many families where the mother is overwrought, either because she is struggling with trauma-related issues and has an inadequate support system, or because she is married to a trauma survivor who is emotionally unavailable to her, it is not uncommon for a daughter to become a little adult and take emotional care of the mother.

The same process can take place between fathers and daughters. If the father is stressed by his traumatized wife's emotional distancing or upheavals or her inability to function as a housekeeper or mother to his children, he may turn to a daughter to serve as a "little wife" in the family and to take emotional care of him. The resulting depression in the daughter has been observed among daughters of combat veterans and refugee camp survivors, as well as daughters of other trauma survivors (Sigal and Rakoff 1971, 253; Sigal 1976).

References

Albeck, J., M. Armsworth, N. Auerhaln, C. Figley, J. Kudler, D. Lamb, K. Nader, L. Pearlman, K. James. 1994. "The Intergenerational Effects of Trauma," Audiotapes 12, 13, 14, and 15 of the panel discussion Trauma, Memory, and Dissociation presented at the 12th Annual Convention of the International Society for Traumatic Stress Studies. Chicago. November.

Armsworth, Mary. 1994. "Integrating the Effects of Trauma." Audiotape 941ISTSS–12 of lecture presented at the 10th Annual Meeting of the International Society for Traumatic Stress Studies. Chicago. November.

Epstein, J. 1979. *Children of the Holocaust*. New York, Putnam's.

Matsakis, A. 1996. *Vietnam Wives; Women and Children Living with Veterans with Posttraumatic Stress Disorder*. Lutherville, MD: The Sidran Foundation.

Rosenheck, Robert. 1986. "Impact of Posttraumatic Stress Disorder of WWII on the Next Generation." *The Journal of Nervous and Mental Disease* 174 (6) 319–327, Serial No. 1243.

Rosenheck, Robert and P. Nathan. 1985. "Secondary Traumatization in the Children of Vietnam Veterans with Posttraumatic Stress Disorder." *Hospital and Community Psychiatry* 36(5):538–539.

Sigal, John J. 1976. "The Effects of Paternal Exposure to Prolonged Stress on the Mental Health of the Spouse and Children." *Canadian Psychiatric Association Journal* 21:169–172.

Sigal, John and Vivian Rakoff. 1971. "Concentration Camp Survival, A Pilot Study of Effects on the Second Generation." *Canadian Psychiatric Association Journal* 16:393–397.

Silverman, Joel. 1989. "Post Traumatic Stress Disorder." *Advanced Psychosomatic Medicine* 16:115–140.

14

To Significant Others

In your bitterness and sorrow
All you see is the dark side of life.
In all your trials,
Only pain has been your friend.

Your heart is empty
But you won't let me in.
Your dreams are lost
But you won't let me in.

I want to help you carry the pain
But you won't let me in.
No matter how much I love you
You won't let me in.

—Greek folk song

To Those Who Care

To be the husband, wife, partner, sister, brother, parent, child, or significant other of a trauma survivor requires an enormous amount of patience and sensitivity. It is easy to become discouraged (and angry) when your loved one does not seem to respond to your love and to your efforts to be supportive. This is especially so if you are in an intimate relationship with a trauma survivor and you have become frustrated in achieving the kind of emotional and sexual intimacy you envisioned in a partnership.

Whether you are a parent, spouse, or child of a trauma survivor, at times the survivor may ignore your efforts to provide help and even interpret those efforts in a negative way because of his or her distorted thinking patterns. These mistrustful and cynical thinking patterns are not the result of your actions (unless you have emotionally or physically attacked or otherwise severely hurt the survivor) but rather the result of the survivor's devastating history of trauma.

Your hopes of being close with the trauma survivor are dashed when she/he withdraws from you at the very moment you try to share your feelings. The more intense your emotions are, the more threatening they may seem to the trauma survivor, who may avoid you or, alternatively, respond with sarcasm or other forms of anger (Johnson, Feldman, and Lubin 1995). Such responses can leave you feeling alone and abandoned because you have just taken the risk of being emotionally honest and made yourself emotionally vulnerable to him or her. You need assurance and affirmation but they may not be forthcoming, not because you don't deserve an attentive response or because you "said something wrong," but because emotional interactions and deep feelings can set off a survivor's triggers and diminish his/her ability to respond appropriately. The more the survivor is aware of not responding "normally" or appropriately, the more ashamed, guilty, and inferior he or she will feel, which creates even more stress, and further increases the difficulty in responding to you in a caring way.

Why Trauma Survivors Seem Emotionally Inaccessible

Your trauma survivor's ability to listen to your emotions, or the emotions of others, and to respond on an emotional level is a function of his or her current levels of anxiety, depression, and stress. Research indicates that as people become less depressed and anxious and as they make progress in healing, they become more receptive to the love and support others offer and more able to risk sharing on an emotional level (Coffman and Jacobson 1996). Before you blame yourself for the lack of emotional closeness in your relationship, keep in mind that your survivor's difficulties in responding to your attempts to be intimate are probably more a function of his or her internal state than any inadequacies of yours.

If your loved one has suffered repeated or chronic trauma, it is very likely that he/she has less energy available for relating. Dr. Nancy Cole, a therapist who has worked with many survivors, thinks of available energy in units of ten. She frames the problem as one of "nine-tenths." People who have been severely or repeatedly traumatized spend nine of their ten units of energy trying to feel safe. They must be constantly vigilant about their environments; and, in their relationships, they must manage anxiety, depression, and emotional pain, while sorting out present-day from past realities. This means they have less energy available to think, work, have fun, or relate to others (Cole 1995).

For some trauma survivors, relationships with any emotional content feel more like threats than sources of comfort. If this is the case, then your survivor is responding more to being in a relationship where emotional sharing is required (or expected) than to you personally. In other words, he/she would be very likely to react the same way to someone else.

On the other hand, if you criticize and reject the survivor, press him/her to relate in ways that set off triggers, or inadvertently retraumatize the survivor because, unconsciously, you remind him or her of someone associated with the traumatic past, then you may be contributing to the survivor's distress. For these reasons, it is important that at some point you become part of your survivor's therapy program, so that the unintentional ways you might be triggering your loved one can be identified and dealt with and so that the problems that originate in the survivor because of the trauma can be identified and not blamed on you.

The Rewards of Perseverance

Despite such major difficulties, if you are committed to your relationship with the trauma survivor, the rewards can be enormous. At the end of all of your struggles to understand each others' needs, you and your trauma survivor will be closely bonded, like comrades in arms. Indeed, you will have fought a kind of war together; a war against the ghosts of the past and against ignorance, misperceptions, selfishness, and selflessness (which can be a "psychological enemy" in its own right); and a war against the capacity of a debilitating mental disorder to destroy human connections.

Even if you are deeply committed to your trauma survivor, it would be highly unusual if you never became so exasperated that you didn't think of leaving or curtailing your relationship with him or her. This does not mean you are a disloyal or unloving child, partner, relative, or friend. It means that you are a normal person who, understandably, wants to be cared about, appreciated, and respected on a consistent basis by the person to whom you are committed.

When your trauma survivor needs to withdraw, is "hyper," or puts limits on the kind and type of sharing that can take place in your relationship, you may feel discouraged, abandoned, and alone. These are miserable feelings and when your disappointment with the relationship is intense, it is normal to think about limiting your relationship, or even saying good-bye. Although you may try to be rational and understanding, when your needs aren't being met, your frustration and sense of rejection can be very hard to bear.

Your trauma survivor is important, but so are you. His or her feelings matter, but so do yours. In fact, your feelings and mental and physical health matter as much as those of the trauma survivor. Just because you haven't been traumatized, doesn't mean you are a less important member of the relationship than your trauma survivor. (In a parallel manner, just because the trauma survivor was traumatized doesn't mean he or she is less important than you either.) Furthermore, you are entitled to some measure of happiness, pleasure, and power, despite the enormity of your trauma survivor's pain.

Do Not Tolerate Abuse of Any Kind

If you are being consistently hurt, neglected, or confined in your relationship with the trauma survivor, you may be struggling with the issue of whether to leave the relationship or to curtail it in other ways. This chapter, however, does not address these issues. It is assumed that those who are reading this chapter are committed to the relationship and are seeking to find ways to support their trauma survivor while at the same time preserve and promote their own mental health.

Under no circumstances should your trauma survivor's difficulties be used to excuse emotional, physical, sexual, or economic abuse of you or anyone else. Neither you, nor anyone else the trauma survivor knows, need tolerate any form of exploitation in the name of being supportive. Abuse of any kind helps no one, not you, nor the trauma survivor, not any children involved. If you are being hurt and are told to accept certain kinds of pain and deprivation in the name of the trauma, this is a misuse of the survivor's history. Engaging in emotional, physical, economic, and sexual abuse, lying, stealing, or destroying other people's property are not symptoms of post-traumatic stress disorder, depression, or any other traumatic reactions.

Abuse can occur when the survivor is in a dissociated or hyperalert state. For example, combat veterans with PTSD sometimes attack their girlfriends as the result of nightmares or flashbacks. Childhood victims of sexual assault have been known to attack their own children when they have been triggered into a state of terror. But when such attacks are trauma-related, and not based in other problems, they are predictably followed by remorse and attempts to avoid their repetition.

For example, Joe attacked his wife one night in the midst of a high anxiety state because he thought she was an enemy soldier. Afterwards, he felt guilty and ashamed and slept in a separate bedroom for fear of losing control again. The next day he sought professional help. In contrast, there are veterans who blame their wives for their problems, deny or minimize the fact that they are violent, take little responsibility for their behavior, and take no corrective steps or go to therapy only because their wives threaten to leave them or because they are court-ordered to do so. In this latter group, combat trauma is an insufficient explanation for the degree of violence and other forms of abuse in their homes.

Similarly, some incest survivors who find themselves sexually attracted to their children go running to their pediatricians or to therapists for help. Other sexual abuse survivors use their history of abuse as an excuse to continue the pattern of child molestation.

If your survivor is abusive only on occasion, takes responsibility for his or her behavior, and seeks help, it is likely that the abuse is related to traumatic reaction symptoms and can be stopped. On the other hand, if there are frequent outbursts of anger and destructive behavior or any kind of a consistent pattern of abuse, then most likely the survivor has problems in addition to those caused by the trauma.

You need to be safe and if you feel you are in danger, you need to seek professional medical, psychiatric, legal, or police services to ensure your safety. You cannot help your trauma survivor heal from his or her trauma by allowing yourself to be traumatized.

Although abuse is unacceptable because it does not promote your life or the trauma survivor's, in most cases, it is also illegal. While you may have no problem deciding that you will not tolerate abuse, there also may be other behaviors that you find intolerable or destructive to your mental, emotional, or physical health. Only you can decide what behavior you will accept from your trauma survivor and what behavior you will not. You can make such decisions without necessarily divorcing or formally separating from the trauma survivor.

For example, Roberta's husband was extremely possessive and protective. He called her when she got to work, before she went to lunch, after she returned from lunch, and right before she returned home. If she was even ten minutes late, he would become highly anxious. Although he was never abusive to her, the fact that he feared she would be victimized, as other members of his family had been, dominated his existence, as well as hers.

Roberta found her husband's overprotectiveness confining and infuriating. She did not want to divorce him, but in order to stay with him she had to create some breathing room for herself. Over time, she learned to assert herself. She began by limiting her husband's phone calls to her at work. Then she registered for music lessons. She continued to pursue other interests in spite of her husband's protests that he wanted her near him as much as possible to be assured of her safety. It was hard work, but eventually Roberta's husband learned to accept the independent life she created for herself.

Educate Yourself

Knowledge is power. Learn all you can about post-traumatic stress disorder, clinical depression, dissociation, addiction, or whatever type of traumatic reactions and symptoms your loved one suffers. You will also want to learn about the kind of trauma your loved one experienced. There are now many excellent books on the effects of physical and sexual abuse, rape, combat, suicide, murder, and crime. Information is your first line of defense against the damaging assumption that you are responsible for your loved one's distress. It is also critical to understanding his or her behavior, emotions, and responses to you (see appendix A).

If, after you have made some attempt to learn about trauma, you still feel that your trauma survivor was to blame, or if you are still severely critical about how your trauma survivor behaved during the trauma, you probably need to read and learn more about trauma, as well as talk to someone about your disbelieving and blaming feelings. If, on any level, you don't believe your significant other and condemn him/her for the trauma or some aspects of his/her behavior during the trauma, your attitude eventually will reveal itself. When it does, the trauma survivor's guilt, shame, sense of inferiority, and anger, will increase and plunge him or her into a state of anxiety, depression, increased symptoms, or some form of relapse.

If you simply cannot accept that the trauma happened and that your significant other was trapped in a situation over which he/she had very little control, then you may not be able to be a suitable partner for, or companion to, the survivor. It may be that you cannot relate well to people who have a trauma history, in which case, you may want to consider very carefully whether it makes sense for you to try to sustain a close relationship with someone who has been traumatized.

Negative Cycles

Your acceptance of the trauma survivor's pain is critical. If acceptance and understanding cannot be gained through education and discussion, then it is highly unlikely that either your needs or the trauma survivor's need for love and acceptance can be met in the relationship. Criticism and rejection by family members has been found to be a major cause of relapse among individuals suffering from a variety of psychiatric problems, including schizophrenia, depression, and post-traumatic stress disorder (van der Kolk, McFarlane, and Weisaeth 1996; Keitner, Miller, Epstein, et al. 1990).

In Keitner et. al. it was found that depressed persons who were criticized by their family members were three times as likely to relapse as those who were not criticized (1990). Although it can be argued those who were so criticized by their families deserved the criticism because of their difficult behaviors and attitudes, the situation is not clear-cut. All families are different. Gross generalities cannot be made about which comes first: the criticism or the behavior that evokes criticism. What is fairly clear, however, is that there is an interactive effect. Negative family responses can worsen a trauma survivor's condition. The survivor's worsened condition then creates further stress on the family.

Once a negative cycle has begun, it tends to reinforce and repeat itself. For example, suppose your trauma survivor forgets an important appointment. She/he may have forgotten because memory problems are a frequent post-trauma stress symptom. Yet you may wonder if she/he forgot because of irresponsibility or not valuing her/his promises to you, which are legitimate concerns. You may confront the survivor in a critical manner and she/he, in turn, will retaliate either by criticizing or withdrawing from you. You may both wind up feeling alone, abandoned, and unloved. Neither you nor your loved one is getting your needs met and the resulting sense of deprivation can make both of you more irritable and hostile with each other, which sets the stage for still more criticism.

In cases where such a negative interaction pattern has begun, it can take on a life of its own. Action is needed to stop the vicious cycle. It doesn't matter whether you, or the trauma survivor, began the negative interaction. Once such a destructive exchange has begun it has the potential to damage both of you. The survivor's symptoms are aggravated by the tension in your relationship and you run the risk of developing stress symptoms yourself, or even a clinical depression. In such situations, professional assistance is needed to help break the cycle.

Develop a Support System for Yourself

It is a given that there will be times your trauma survivor will not be emotionally or physically available to you. Because of that fact it is critical that he/she not be your only source of affection, companionship, or affirmation. You need other people to turn to when you are hurting because your trauma survivor is not going to be available to you every time you have an emotional need. Even if your survivor had not been traumatized, he/she would not be available each time you needed him or her. No one can be available *all* the time. Are you?

Therefore, you must have other people with whom to talk and relax and have fun. Just because your survivor may need to isolate at times (or much of the time) does not mean that you too must lead an isolated life. If she/he needs time alone due to a trauma anniversary, a depressive episode, or an emotional shutdown, you need a plan so that your needs for companionship and human contact can be met, at least, in part. Of course, there will be times you will have to sacrifice some of your plans and personal needs to be supportive of your trauma survivor, but you cannot sacrifice your life for him or her.

Popular thinking in our society tends to emphasize putting oneself first and focusing on one's own needs. Yet the hard truth is that *all* relationships, whether at home or at work, require some kind of compromise. The issue is not whether you will have to compromise—for you will—as will the trauma survivor, but how much to compromise and on what issues.

Neither you, nor the survivor, can sustain yourself on a steady diet of self-sacrifice. Although putting aside some of your own agenda is necessary and unavoidable, you also need to take care of yourself or there will be no self left to support the survivor. It bears repeating that taking care of yourself is just as important as helping to take care of the survivor.

When to Talk

Balancing your needs with your survivor's needs may seem easy in theory but it is difficult in practice. Nevertheless, it can be done. The first step is to have an open discussion and work out a plan with your loved one to help meet both sets of your needs. For example, if you are in an intimate relationship and you like to socialize more than your traumatized partner does, you can make an effort to avoid unfounded jealousies and unnecessary misunderstandings by discussing all the relevant issues *before* a crisis erupts.

For example, if your trauma survivor is in the midst of the confusion, terror, and emotional pain of a trigger or an anniversary reaction, he/she may cling to you like a terrified child clings to its mother and simultaneously yell at you to make you go away. This would not be the time to rehash old conflicts or issues, even if they are relevant to the present crisis. Also, this is probably the worst time to announce to him/her that you are going to make *your* needs your priority, and that no matter how she/he is feeling, you are going to do what you need to do for yourself.

You may be correct in feeling that you are entitled to bring up past issues and the importance of your needs; however, bringing up such concerns when your trauma survivor is struggling to hold on to his or her sanity may be the least effective course you can take. Your attempt to discuss these important matters probably will be futile because your survivor will be minimally receptive to listening, or to giving. In such situations survivors may wish to respond in an empathic and rational manner; but they may simply be unable to do so. As a result, they may become ashamed of their obvious inability to respond the way they feel that they should; i.e., reasonably and lovingly. Their shame can easily become transformed into anger at you for "pressuring" them for a response just when they feel unable to handle the issues you are raising. Part of the anger may be directed at you, but part is also directed at themselves for not being a "good enough" partner, parent, friend, or child.

On the one hand, he/she may feel guilty because of being unable to meet your needs and want you to do what you must do to be happy.

On the other hand, she/he may be jealous and resentful that you are capable of socializing or even of having something you want to do while she/he is trapped in the emotions and physical states of a traumatic past. She/he may feel out of control and try hard to control his/her mind and emotional reactions and not to explode; or try hard to muster the energy to get out of bed. In contrast, you may seem like the picture of health.

At such times, survivors' awareness of the toll their symptoms take on their lives is made especially vivid by the contrast between their lives and their significant others'. To them, it seems as if they do not have lives and their partners do. You, on the other hand, may feel that enough of your life has been taken by your survivor's trauma

If the survivor is aware of and grateful for your sacrifices and efforts, she/he may also feel guilty about "being a burden" and fear that you will leave if she/he has yet another panic attack, dissociative episode, bout of depression, or flashback.

It's always hard to talk about such issues, but the best time to discuss your feelings and needs is during a relatively peaceful time. The best time to agree to talk is when you are getting along, not when you are both strained to the max. When things are calm, you can discuss what to do when you need to be with people and she/he needs to be alone. Is it possible that the two of you, together, can work out a plan?

You can talk about the conflict you might be feeling between wanting to be supportive, yet needing to do something else. If you discuss these issues together, calmly, in advance, you will minimize the possibility that your partner will feel rejected simply because you have social or other needs.

Support Systems

You don't have to wait until your trauma survivor is "all better" to enjoy your life, talk about yourself, or build a support system. You need a support system now, independent of your loved one's situation. Your support system can include members of your nuclear and extended family, neighbors, members of an organization of your choice, or your own therapist or therapy group. Just as the trauma survivor can't do it alone, neither can you. You need supportive others to help you cope with the crises imposed by your loved one's tragic history, as well as to give you support when your loved one is not available to you emotionally.

It may be hard to find and maintain a supportive network of friends and caring others. Those who are members of churches or twelve-step programs have an easier time meeting others than persons for whom church attendance or twelve-step meetings are not appropriate, suitable, or desirable. Building a network of supportive friends takes time, effort, and commitment. If you are working and have many responsibilities, it may be difficult to make those efforts, but it is critical that you do so. If you have children, it is important that they, too, develop and maintain friendships and social and other involvements.

If you or your children sacrifice your other relationships, your social and leisure time involvements, and your other sources of growth and satisfaction, it will not help your trauma survivor heal. The better you take care of yourself, the more you will have to give him/her on a daily basis, especially during times of stress.

Know and Anticipate Triggers and Anniversary Reactions

If your trauma survivor has done his/her homework, he/she has written a list of triggers and anniversary dates (see chapter 4). Most likely this list will be incomplete in that many trauma survivors are constantly discovering their triggers and anniversaries. However, the list is a starting point for a discussion on how to manage trigger and anniversary times. One part of the list should include ways the trauma survivor thinks that others might be able to help. After you look at the list, decide whether you are willing to do any of the actions on that part of the list.

Just because your survivor wishes someone would do these things, doesn't mean that you must be the one. If you can, terrific! For those items on the list that you can't help with, you might be able to help find other people who can. You might have suggestions to add to the list. Together, you and your trauma survivor can create a plan for handling difficult triggers or anniversary times.

Again, it is far more productive to discuss how to handle trigger and anniversary times when your trauma survivor is relatively calm. The plan may need to be revised when the actual trigger or anniversary arrives, but it is important to have a plan with which to start. Remember, you are not a saint and the purpose of your life is not to be there one-hundred percent of the time in every way possible for your survivor.

You may or may not be able to go along with what the survivor thinks would be the most desirable assistance on your part. Or, you may be able to help out with only part of the request. If the survivor knows this in advance, then she/he can seek out others to provide the additional needed support. Also, you might want to ask your loved one what she or he would like from you when going through an emotional shutdown, anniversary or trigger time, hyperalert stage, or time of depression. Doess she/he want you around? If so, how much? Is it necessary for you to be there the entire time?

It is quite possible that your trauma survivor may not know what she/he would like from you. One part of her/him may want to be left alone entirely. Another part may want you nearby. She/he may feel rejected if you proceed with your plans. Yet if you gave up your plans to be with her/him, she/he may feel guilty about depriving you. And, even though your survivor may want you to stay home, she/he may not feel like communicating or doing anything with you. This may seem very unfair since you are a person, too, with legitimate needs for human contact. However, if there are solitary activities you can pursue in a "side by side" manner while the trauma survivor does whatever she/he needs to do to calm down, you may not mind giving up your plans to stay nearby, although not necessarily together.

When you tell your trauma survivor that you want to be helpful during difficult times and you ask for directions on how to best be supportive, you should also have a clear view of what you need to do for yourself. Although you might be able to put some of your needs aside some of the time, you cannot do that all of the time. You need to have as clear an idea as possible as to what your limits are. If you don't know what your limits are, perhaps you can find out by trying out a plan and then evaluating it.

During a crisis, such as an anniversary date, the survivor tends to be frightened and confused because of feeling out of control of his or her feelings, thoughts, and physical condition. He or she may want you to stay home for support, but, as stated above, that doesn't mean that he or she will be available to you. What can you do that will be nurturing or rewarding for you? Are there activities you like to pursue on your own? Can you contact friends by phone? If you give up your plans, how resentful will you be? If the trauma survivor is aware that you are giving up something important for him/her, how much guilt will that create in him/her?

Is there a way to compromise? For example, could you go out for only a few hours, or could your friends come to your home? Could you alternate—one anniversary date you will stay home and the next one, you will be free to pursue your personal plans?

Flexibility Is the Key

Keep in mind that trigger events, anniversaries, emotional shutdowns, and depressions vary in intensity. Sometimes the trauma survivor may need you more than other times. Although you must have a plan, the plan needs to be flexible. The trauma survivor may be surprised to find that he/she needs you more than anticipated and he/she should be able to state that without being chastised or rejected.

Similarly, you may agree to do something to support your survivor, but find that when the time comes, you have a pressing need of your own, which may have priority. Given that neither you, nor the trauma survivor, can predict the intensity of the emotions and needs of one another, and given that life is full of unexpected crises, it is essential that both you and the survivor have a supportive network of friends, relatives, and professionals to whom you can turn (if you cannot turn to one another).

No matter how much you love your trauma survivor, you cannot make him or her your entire life. To the extent that your trauma survivor is embroiled in the past and in his/her therapy, you will have a relatively lonely life if you restrict your life according to his/her needs. If your trauma survivor makes progress in recovery, he/she may have more to give you emotionally down the line. But this may or may not occur, and the speed of this kind of progress is unpredictable.

You too may have a trigger and anniversary list that should be discussed. Although your triggers and anniversaries may not be linked to traumatic experiences, there may be situations and times of the year that cause you predictable stress. Your partner should be aware of these emotional facts about you, just as you must be aware of his or her emotional realities. Your triggers, too, need to be respected. Part of your planning should include details about how your survivor can help you through your difficult times and how you plan to take care of yourself, which may mean that temporarily you will not be as available as you usually are to your trauma survivor.

Additionally, there may be words and actions of the survivor that trigger you. These kinds of triggers also need to be discussed. If you cannot discuss these triggers without the discussion becoming a hostile exchange or an otherwise unproductive endeavor, you may want to seek the help of a professional counselor or clergyperson.

The Importance and Limits of Being Supportive

There are some basic ways to support your trauma survivor. These are

- Respecting trigger and anniversary dates
- Going to therapy with your survivor
- Respecting his or her need to disclose or not disclose aspects of the trauma to you
- Understanding that he/she will not always be as available to you as you (or he/she) would like
- Not tolerating abuse of yourself or self-abuse on the part of the survivor

Although you may want to be as supportive as you can, you cannot be all things to your trauma survivor. No matter how much you love him or her, your love cannot "fix" the past or "make right" all the injustices he/she has experienced. If you exhaust yourself trying to nurture your loved one, you may end up full of resentment when he/she does not heal as rapidly or as thoroughly as you would have hoped.

The Al-Anon acronym "C-C-C" applies here. C-C-C stands for Cause, Cure, and Control. *You didn't cause the trauma survivor's problems. You can't control him or her and you can't cure him or her.* While you definitely can be supportive, you can't undo the past, no matter how much he or she might like you to and how much you might wish to do so. You will be wonderfully supportive if you do the following:

- Refrain from criticizing the survivor for his or her symptoms

- Don't blame all the family's problems on the survivor's trauma or traumatic symptom reactions

- Respect his or her need to withdraw or be alone

- Make the effort not to needlessly (or heedlessly) trigger him or her

Although you can't control the healing process of your loved one, when you are supportive in the ways outlined above, you will facilitate the process as much as is humanly possible.

Backing Off

If the trauma survivor says, "Back off! I can't deal with this now," consider dropping the subject and not pressing the survivor at that time. Backing off in this way will not "cure" him/her, but it helps in that you won't be setting off triggers, deeper depression, rage reactions, or a dissociated state. At a later time, you can bring up the subject left unattended to; but to force a discussion when a survivor is having a traumatic reaction is never productive.

He or she is emotionally shut down or hyperalert and therefore is in a "no-think" zone unable to properly attend to whatever the issue may be. In either zone, rational thinking about the issue is very difficult if not impossible. The trauma survivor is preoccupied with managing the symptoms and intrusive memories of the trauma. His or her ability to attend to you is minimal, especially if she/he feels inadequate because of not being able to respond to you. The survivor may feel like a failure because she/he cannot deal with an issue that is obviously important to you and that she/he may acknowledge is important in its own right.

If there is an emergency to be addressed and the survivor does not wish to discuss it, you may need to take action and make a decision on your own. However, if your survivor *always* tells you to back off and refuses to discuss *any* issues with you at all, ever, not just during difficult times, then you have a problem of a deeper and more serious nature. It is difficult, if not impossible, to live with a partner who evades all issues and confrontations. In such a situation, you probably need to seek professional consultation.

Suicidal Thoughts and Other Dangers

Part of your trigger and anniversary planning must consider what action to take if the survivor becomes severely depressed or suicidal, begins to self-mutilate, has strong urges to return to an addiction such as drinking or drugging, becomes violent, or begins to hallucinate or dissociate in an extreme manner. You need to have a plan of action for these potentially dangerous situations that includes a list of medical and mental health professionals, emergency room phone numbers and addresses, and supportive friends and relatives. When you are the significant other, you, not the therapist, will be the most likely person to notice if the survivor begins to self-mutilate or use alcohol or illegal drugs. You need to be prepared with a plan of action in advance of such an event.

Suicide is not restricted to any particular social class, age, race, or religious background. In fact, there is no one type of suicidal person. However, the following characteristics have been found to correlate with suicide:

1. A family history of suicide or depression, or, a recent suicide of a friend, relative, or fellow survivor

2. A prior suicide attempt

3. Lack of strong affiliative bonds to another person or group, or feelings of not belonging to anyone or to any group

4. Social isolation—lack of a support system or inability to use available supports

5. Alcohol or drug use

6. Reckless behavior

7. Conflicts with authority

8. Depression, with possible irritability or agitation

9. Feelings of hopelessness, helplessness, worthlessness, or humiliation

10. Feelings of being trapped, stuck, or sinful

11. Suppressed rage or free-floating hostility

12. Negative thinking: negative view of past, present, and future; black-and-white thinking; irrational beliefs (Berman 1987; Victoroff 1983; Smith and Bope 1986; Bhatia and Sharma, 1986)

Signals that suicide is a possibility include the following:

1. Announcements of suicidal thoughts or intentions, such as, "I'm going to kill myself," "I won't be here for the holidays," "You won't have to worry about me anymore," "This might be the last time you see me," or "This is my last day"

2. Suicidal writings or drawings or notes written as if already dead

3. Termination behaviors (giving away prized possessions, writing a will, cleaning up unfinished business, saying good-bye to friends and relatives, purchasing a burial plot, writing one's own eulogy, designing one's tombstone, purchasing a one-way ticket to a potential suicide location)

4. Noticeable withdrawal from family or friends or previously attended therapy

5. Any dramatic changes in mood or emotional state

6. Changes in eating habits that result in significant weight gain or loss

7. Changes in sleeping habits (increased sleeping, fitful sleep, insomnia)

8. Loss of interest in friends and formerly pleasurable activities such as sex, music, or sports

9. Difficulties with concentration

10. Recent interpersonal loss (death in the family, rejection by a significant person)

11. Increased alcohol, drug, or food usage

12. Decreased functioning at work or in school

13. Preoccupation with fanatical or cult material

14. Outbursts of violent or rebellious behavior (especially if out of character)

15. Psychomotor retardation—slumped posture, slow movements, repetitious behavior and statements

16. Any evidence of loss of touch with reality

17. Excessive or inappropriate guilt (Berman 1987; Smith and Bope 1986)

Although you should not try to assess your loved one's suicidal potential on your own, you need to be aware of the factors that increase the likelihood of suicide and share any information about your loved one's suicidal intentions with an appropriate mental health professional, clergyperson, or some other authority, such as the police.

Upon the mere mention of the word "suicide," or upon the emergence of any of the suicidal indicators listed above, your trauma survivor should be encouraged to seek professional help. Even if he or she is only thinking suicidal thoughts and has made no definite plan, he/she needs to discuss the suicidal thoughts openly. If your survivor is already in treatment, he/she needs to be encouraged to share the suicidal thoughts with the therapist. Left unaired, such negative thoughts grow and develop into a full-blown suicide crisis.

Assessing the Probability of Suicide

In general, the probability of suicide is increased if the trauma survivor has a well thought-out, definite plan for suicide rather than a vague wish to die. For example, people who say they are planning to kill themselves with an overdose of pills, but do not know which pills they would take, or in what quantities, and do not have a specific date established for their suicide are less likely to kill themselves than people who have spent weeks researching various types of medication, have already purchased the pills, and have a definite date in mind. Similarly, people who say they will shoot themselves, but do not own a gun, and have no plans to purchase a gun are less likely to kill themselves than people who have one or more guns at their immediate disposal and who spend a lot of time at rifle ranges.

This does not mean that people who talk about suicide but do not have a plan are not capable of suicide. They are, and their suicidal wishes need to be acknowledged and openly discussed.

If the trauma survivor feels compelled to act on an impulse to self-destruct, it is a sign that suicide is imminent (Berman 1987; Schutz 1982). Statements like, "I'm afraid to be alone," or "I don't know if I can stop myself," or "There's a voice in my head that says, 'Do it. Do it, now'" or 'Hide the rat poison, I'm afraid I'll take some'" warrant an immediate response. Even if your loved one has powerful deterrents to suicide (such as a strong commitment to work, family, or certain friends, or strong religious beliefs against suicide), if there are any signs that your loved one is unable to control his or her impulses, you should not leave him or her alone. She/he may need hospitalization or at least the intervention of a therapist or clergyperson. If your loved one states that God, voices, people who died in the trauma, or some outside force is "ordering" the suicide, psychiatric hospitalization is almost always needed.

Another important clue that suicide is imminent is if the survivor, after having communicated a suicidal wish or plan, is unable to discuss that wish or plan. As long as someone can talk about suicidal feelings and maintain an emotional connection with at least one person, whether it be a partner, relative, friend, or therapist, there is hope.

Basically, you should ask your survivor the following questions:

- Do you plan to kill yourself?

- Do you have a plan?

- What is your plan?

- On a scale of one to twenty, what is the probability you will put the plan into effect? How much do you want to die? How much do you want to live?

- Do you feel there is someone trying to kill you? (For survivors with paranoid tendencies.)

- Is there someone or something telling you to kill yourself? (For survivors with histories of psychoses or paranoia.)

- Are you willing to give me the pills, the gun, the keys to the car (or whatever is the designated means of suicide)?

- Can you promise me you won't kill yourself until you talk to a therapist (the family doctor, a clergyperson, or some other trained professional)?

Seeking Help

Your survivor's responses to these questions can help you identify the possibility that your loved one might hurt himself/herself. If he/she has a plan, a date, and a means, and is unwilling to relinquish the means of self-destruction, or is unable to promise not to commit suicide for a short period of time, you must not hesitate to act. In addition to any of the observable signs or disturbing answers to the questions above, you must trust your own gut reaction.

If, for any reason, you feel your loved one might possibly hurt himself/herself or is not in control of himself/herself, you must try to get control over whatever the survivor has identified as the means of self-destruction and seek outside help immediately. You can call your local emergency line, or any local suicide crisis hotline for help. The police or a rescue squad could also be called for information and assistance. In an emergency, you can take your loved one to the emergency room of any hospital offering psychiatric care.

If there are signs of impending suicide and you must leave, a relative, friend, or neighbor should be called to your home to stay with the survivor. Your survivor might welcome the protective presence of another human being, or she/he might yell at you that a baby-sitter isn't needed and argue with you about the necessity for outside help. Similarly in other situations where suicide seems imminent and you insist on finding help, sometimes the survivor will resist your efforts. He or she may call you names, yell at you, or try to flee your presence. He or she may say you are "overreacting" or that you are acting from personal, selfish motives.

If you meet with such resistance, firmly say, "I am afraid. You just indicated to me that you are thinking about killing yourself. I care about you too much to take the chance that you might act on your impulse. Even if the chances of you killing yourself are one in a million, you mean too much to me to give you the opportunity to end your life. I would rather be safe than sorry."

The suicidal person needs to be told, "When you say you are going to kill yourself, I believe you," not "Oh, you can't mean it," "You'll get over it soon enough," or "Nothing is that bad." The latter responses can convey to the survivor one of the following messages:

- Suicide is so socially unacceptable or morally repugnant to me, I don't want to discuss it.

- There's something wrong with you if you're talking that way.

- I'm sick and tired of hearing you complain.

- You aren't entitled to feel that bad.

- I don't care enough about you to listen.

Providing Help

But you probably do care, deeply so. Yet even you, at least initially, may shrug off your loved one's suicidal statements and discourage him/her from sharing freely. You may fear death or be struggling with your own suicidal feelings. You may feel inadequate to handle the situation or emotionally exhausted. Yet you may be the one who saves your loved one's life.

In our culture, there is an overreliance on professionals. People often feel inadequate when dealing with a suicidal significant other. Yet you may have learned a great deal of wisdom and may be able to support your loved one on a day-to-day basis with a depth of heart and commitment that far exceeds what can be found in a therapist's office. You should not limit yourself to the suggestions presented in this chapter in trying to save your loved one's life. Furthermore, you should discard any ideas presented in this chapter that you feel would not be effective with your particular loved one.

How to Tell If Your Loved One Is Getting Better

What is the meaning of "healing" or "recovery" from trauma? How can you tell if your loved trauma survivor is indeed healing or recovering?

Today, in our society, there are two popular concepts of what it means to be "healed" or "recovered" from trauma. The first holds that recovery means a person is in a constant state of positive thinking and positive action; the second holds that recovery means a drastic reduction or total elimination of post-traumatic stress syndrome or other traumatic reaction symptoms (Harvey 1995). Using these standards, you can consider your loved one "normal" when he/she no longer thinks about the trauma or no longer has nightmares, anxiety attacks, fear attacks, paranoid thoughts, suicidal feelings, homicidal urges, or powerful desires to enter oblivion through the use of alcohol, drugs, or food.

Both of these concepts are unrealistic. Unfortunately, they are held not only by the general public, but by many mental health and other trained professionals, as well as by trauma survivors themselves. Yet if these are the true standards of recovery, then no trauma survivor, even if he/she spent forty hours a week in therapy for several years, could ever be considered "healed." Why is this so?

First of all, no human being alive constantly acts and thinks in a positive way (Harvey 1995). Second, it is impossible for all the symptoms to disappear because PTSD and other traumatic reactions are constantly being triggered by anniversary dates, current losses and disappointments, and by therapy and counseling itself. Being in therapy means at least a temporary increase in PTSD or other symptoms, hopefully, for the purpose of better understanding. Also, since the world is full of traumas such as wars, crimes, auto accidents, violence, and natural disasters, people who have traumas in their past are constantly being retraumatized in the present. It is therefore not possible to hold up the absence of symptoms as a standard of mental health, because by the very nature of PTSD and other traumatic reactions, such as clinical depression, such a standard cannot be met (Harvey 1995).

What Does It Mean to Be Healed?

Your loved one may think, dream, or suffer because of the trauma every day of his or her life. But this does not mean that all is hopeless. Rather it means that different ways of measuring "progress" are needed. Consider the following questions:

1. Does your loved one try to structure and arrange her/his life so that she/he is not unnecessarily triggered?

2. Since no one has the power to arrange the universe so that he or she is never triggered, can your loved one live in a non-self-harming way and in a way that does not harm others, even during attacks of PTSD, bouts of depression, or periods of high anxiety?

3. Is your loved one increasingly able to find ways to soothe and comfort himself/herself that are not destructive to himself/herself or to others, for example, you?

4. Is your loved one better able to cope with and manage symptoms that are not preventable in ways that do not hurt himself/herself or others? For example, is it possible for the survivor to go through a terrible anniversary without some kind of suffering? The question is not, "Will he or she remember and hurt," but rather, "Can he/she go through that period without damaging himself/herself or others?"

If you can answer "yes" to the questions above, then your loved one is well on the path to recovery.

Harvey (1995) points out eight other ways of measuring progress: increased power or authority over memories; memory with manageable emotions; increased ability to manage overwhelming emotion or symptoms; greater control over behavior; increased self-care; growth in self-respect;

the formation of safe, human relationships; and the desire and increasing ability to extract meaning out of the trauma.

Power or Authority Over Memories

If you were asked to remember the most delicious dessert your mother ever made, you could probably remember it, talk about it, and then put it away in the back of your mind and not think about it anymore. This means that you have power over your memories. Trauma survivors lose power over their memories. They remember the trauma when they don't want to and once they remember it, they cannot "put it away."

The opposite is also true. Sometimes trauma survivors want to remember certain events, but cannot. They try to recall the specifics of what happened during the traumatic event and literally "draw a blank." They do not have the power to recall what happened to them during the trauma, or they have only a partial memory.

"Getting better" involves having increased power over traumatic memories. This doesn't mean total power, but increased power to turn off memories when they are intrusive and increased ability to remember what happened. If intrusive thoughts become less frequent, or last for shorter durations, if nightmares become less frequent and less violent, this is wonderful progress. To ask that all intrusive thoughts disappear forever is to ask for the impossible (Harvey 1995).

Memory with Manageable Emotions

Survivors who are not engaged in the healing process tend to remember with overwhelming emotions (hyperarousal) or with no emotions at all (numbness). When remembering is accompanied by overwhelming emotions, the survivor feels disoriented and confused by his or her feelings and there is a tendency for all of the different emotions—anger, grief, guilt—to mingle together and to feel like some kind of internal bomb, which, when it explodes, will propel the survivor into the realm of insanity.

When the survivor is in the reexperiencing or hyperaroused state, everything that happens to him/her feels as if the trauma is happening again. Small events in the present can feel traumatic and the intensity of the feelings can be unbearable. The survivor becomes so overstimulated emotionally that he or she does not feel safe.

When the survivor is in the numbed-out state, he or she does not feel safe either, because of feeling "dead" inside, and not being able to recognize or identify danger.

Healing means being able to remember with emotions that are manageable, or being able to remember without experiencing a debilitating arousal of the body and emotions, or without experiencing or a debilitating state of numbness (Harvey 1995).

Managing Symptoms

If the absence of symptoms or strong traumatic reactions is a measure of recovery, then the survivor gets no credit for being able to manage his or her symptoms when they are strong and inescapable (Harvey 1995). Some credit must be given to your loved one who tries to manage his/her symptoms in ways that work.

These ways include, but are not limited to, working hard, using relaxation techniques, listening to music, calling up friends, exercising, helping others, writing, engaging in artistic projects, visiting family members or friends, getting involved in political or social actions to help other survivors, taking care of pets, taking care of sick or elderly relatives, taking showers, cleaning the house, going to the movies, or reading. The fact that your loved one can manage or at least make an honest attempt to manage his or her intense emotions needs to be honored.

Control Over Behavior

Can your loved one control his or her behavior? If he or she is enraged, does he or she have the choice of how to express that anger? Or does he or she automatically act on a violent or destructive impulse? If your loved one can control his or her destructive or other problem emotions and act appropriately, this is recovery. To ask that he or she never feel destructive is not realistic.

Self-Care

Healing means increased willingness to take care of oneself, emotionally, physically, and spiritually, if, indeed, your loved one has a spiritual side (Harvey 1995). Is your loved one able to do things for himself or herself even when he/she feels as if they aren't worth the trouble? Does he/she stay away from destructive people and from addictive substances and behavior, even when extremely depressed or suicidal?

Self-Respect

Is your survivor growing in self-respect? Is more and more of his or her life free from secrecy, duplicity, and the effects of the trauma? Is he/she becoming increasingly consistent across various areas of his or her life?

Safe Human Relationships

Is your survivor avoiding destructive relationships? Is she or he selecting friends or intimates who are not harmful to her or him? Can she or he negotiate in a relationship, including your relationship, so that some of her/his needs are met (Harvey 1995)? Can she or he compromise in a way that doesn't make it impossible for you, or her/him to survive in the relationship?

Extracting Meaning from the Trauma

Another way to measure healing is the ability to make meaning of the trauma (Harvey 1995). No therapist or doctor can do this for the survivor. Neither can you. Only the survivor can figure out what the trauma meant in his or her life. Like the survivor's doctors and therapists, however, you need to believe that the survivor *can* figure out what the trauma means to him/her and provide support as he or she struggles with the issue of the meaning of the trauma.

Slips

You might ask, "But what if my loved one begins to drink or use drugs or abuse food again? Is this the beginning of a slip or the beginning of a downhill descent into addiction?" The issue of "slips" is quite confused. Although some people manage to maintain almost perfect abstinence from alcohol, drugs, or food abuse after joining a twelve-step or other recovery program, it is not uncommon for even the best-intentioned person to slip back on occasion. Such slips, however, do not necessarily mean that your loved one is in total irreversible relapse or that he or she is not in recovery.

Only you can decide how many slips you will tolerate. However, for a greater understanding of your loved one's slips, you may want to discuss your survivor's behavior with his or her therapist or another qualified counselor. There are also several questions to consider:

- Does your loved one admit to the slips or try to hide them? After a slip, does he or she attempt to resume efforts to get help? Over time, are the slips shorter in duration and do they involve less and less of the abused substance? Or do the slips get longer every time, involving larger and larger quantities of alcohol, drugs, or food?

- Does he or she attend counseling sessions or twelve-step meetings regularly? Regular attendance is a positive sign. It is not, however, a guarantee of permanent abstinence from substance abuse.

- What is her or his attitude toward counseling? Has she/he been able to establish a trusting relationship with the therapist, counselor, or group leader? If she/he is in a group, has she/he been able to identify with, or make friends with, some of the other members? Or is your survivor almost always negative and contemptuous of the counseling program, therapist, and other survivors?

If your loved one is able to maintain an open-minded trusting attitude towards treatment and is able to emerge from social and emotional isolation by forming some kind of emotional bond, either with the therapist or the other survivors in the group, this is another positive sign. Recovery from trauma doesn't mean forgetting about the trauma as much as it means being reintegrated into society and being able to emotionally connect and trust others again. For some survivors, this process begins in group or individual therapy when the survivor forms ties with the therapist or other group members.

- Are there any consistent signs of positive change, either in behavior or attitude, however small? The important word in this question is "consistent." Most people can display good behavior for a short time, but the changes need to be long-lasting and able to endure the inevitable stresses of life.

- Is your loved one beginning to assume responsibility for his or her moods, emotions, and behavior or does he or she blame others?

The survivor who shows increased awareness of his or her traumatic reactions and who is making progress in therapy will have an increased ability to recognize his/her emotional, physical, or other needs and have less need to blame others. He or she may say, "Something happened today at work that reminded me of the trauma. I didn't think it would bother me, but, apparently, it did. That makes me feel like not being with you tonight. Usually, I would start a fight with you just so I could be alone. But this time I can just tell you that I need to be by myself." Or the survivor might say, "You picked a terrible time to ask me for help. I feel awful, but it's not your fault. I'm just really angry about _____ . Maybe I'll feel better in an hour or two."

- Was your loved one previously unable to talk about the trauma, but is now able to discuss some aspects of the experience with you? Alternatively, if your loved one was previously obsessed with the trauma, has his or her preoccupation with the trauma lessened somewhat?

"Yes" responses to any of the bulleted questions above indicate some movement toward resolving the trauma. Your next question might be, "How long do I wait and how many signs of change do I have to have before I can be sure that my loved one is really improved and going to stay that way?" Unfortunately, once again, there are no pat answers to such questions. These issues must be addressed on an individual basis, taking into account the full complexity of your loved one's experiences and the full complexities of your relationship.

Some Do's and Don'ts

1. Don't tell the trauma survivor to "let go," or "forget the past," or "get a life" or "get over it."

2. Don't call the trauma survivor a "cry baby," a "psycho case," "a sicko" or a "whiner."

3. Don't blame relationship problems on the trauma or traumatic reactions. For example, don't say, "We can't have a good relationship
because you have all these triggers," or "You and your damned
rape history," or "I can never have fun with you because you freak
out all the time."

4. Don't interpret emotional coolness on the part of your trauma survivor as a sign of disinterest.

5. Don't expect your trauma survivor to respond to a death or illness
in the family or another important loss as others do.

6. Don't press the trauma survivor for details of the trauma or for
details of his or her therapy. Respect the trauma survivor's need
not to disclose certain aspects of his or her past and his/her treatment.

7. Don't press the trauma survivor to solve a problem or do something
if she/he clearly indicates that she/he has reached her or his limit
and feels like exploding or is starting to shut down.

8. Don't tolerate emotional, physical, or sexual abuse of yourself or
others.

9. Don't try to be your survivor's therapist or magic rescuer. You can
be supportive without making your survivor your "project" or your
entire life.

10. Expect that there will be times the survivor doesn't trust you and
needs to be distant from you.

11. Don't mock him or her for his or her symptoms.

12. Develop a support system for yourself.

13. Work together with the trauma survivor to create a plan for handling
predictable difficult times, such as anniversary dates of the trauma.

14. Work together with the trauma survivor for an "emergency plan"
for unpredictable times when the survivor may feel out of control,
extremely depressed, or about to relapse into addiction. This emergency plan should include the names and phone numbers of doctors,
therapists, hospitals, friends, and family members.

15. Know the signs of impending suicide and take action immediately.

16. Find a balance between taking care of yourself and the needs of
your trauma survivor.

17. Be honest with yourself and the trauma survivor.

You and Your Survivor Can Make It

Much of this chapter has focused on the difficulties inherent in forging
a relationship with someone who has been traumatized. Yet having a

fulfilling relationship with a trauma survivor is possible. In fact, once some of the initial hurdles have been crossed, your survivor and you may have an even more rewarding and long-lasting relationship than many others because you will have taken the time to communicate your feelings, values, and personal limitations to each other.

Also, in those instances where trauma survivors have been able to accept their pain and grow from it, their loving feelings toward family members, friends, romantic partners, and others are usually intensified. Having been traumatized has taught them the value and necessity of human connection and human love. For such survivors, relationships, not work or external forms of success have top priority, and their relationships are helped, not hurt, by the realization that life is full of loss and pain and that past events affect the present.

The reason this chapter emphasizes the various difficulties involved in forming and sustaining a relationship with a trauma survivor is to make it clear to you that making a few minor adjustments or having a few brief discussions would be woefully inadequate.

You—and the survivor—will need as much information about trauma and its effects as you can acquire, as much open communication as you both can tolerate, and as much patience and ability to compromise as you can muster. You will also need tenacity. However, maintaining the relationship will not require as much effort as overcoming the initial hurdles.

The Initial Hurdles

What are these initial hurdles? They involve overcoming certain myths, such as through sufficient willpower, love, or self-sacrifice you can erase the scars of the trauma, i.e., that you can be the survivor's magic rescuer. Not only you, but your survivor too, must disregard this myth. Your caring can help, but you cannot heal your survivor or make the trauma go away.

Another initial hurdle is accepting the fact that your survivor has real limits on what he/she can and cannot do; limits that were imposed by the trauma. Similarly, you have real limits on what you can tolerate and what you are willing and able or not willing and able to do with or for the survivor. Once you accept the survivor's limitations and your own, you will have come a long way to establishing an enduring relationship with the survivor.

Additionally, the survivor must be able to respect and meet some of your needs and not to confuse you with the negative people encountered during the trauma. The survivor must realize that you, too, are entitled to happiness, despite the magnitude of his/her pain and the fact that if he/she has certain limitations, that does not mean you must constrict your life.

You are to be *in* each other's lives, not to *be* each other's life. For example, a mother whose child has been sexually abused initially might focus all of her energies on that child, while the child is an acute state of distress. But that mother cannot devote her entire life to that child. Similarly, although it is appropriate for the child to turn to, if not cling to, the mother at first, eventually, the child will have to face the world with the scars of the abuse. The mother can help and be there as support; she may need to give more to that child than to her other children; but she cannot allow the child's needs to suffocate her, nor can she disregard her obligations to other family members, including her obligations to herself. The same principle holds true in other situations, whether the relationship is between siblings, friends, parent and child, or romantic pairs.

Positive Aspects of a Relationship with a Trauma Survivor

A relationship with a trauma survivor is not only possible, it can be just as fulfilling as a relationship with someone who has never been traumatized. Survivors who are aware of their limitations and the strain that their symptoms impose on relationships may be grateful for your acceptance and therefore be less demanding and judgmental than people who see themselves as "perfect" and expect all others to live up to their high standards.

A survivor might put it this way: "She/he stuck with me when I was so hard to live with, when I didn't know what was happening to me and even when, in my confusion and pain, I was very mean to her/him. She/he must have really cared to put up with me. Others would have left, but she/he stood right by me. I can never forget that. I owe her/him so much for loving me when I didn't love myself. I will always honor her/him for that and do what I can to make her/him happy." In my practice, I have heard such sentiments from dozens of survivors.

Such survivors, who have felt close to losing their sanity or who have lost control of their minds and bodies during anxiety attacks, deep depressions, or dissociative episodes, are hardly in a position to demand that their loved ones be without flaws. Given the understanding that many trauma survivors have of human suffering, social and political problems, the importance of loyalty and honesty, and the fragility of life, relationships with them can be very profound and provide the deepest kind of compassion when you need it.

A relationship with a trauma survivor can survive and flourish if it is limited to three: you, the survivor, and the trauma. But the relationship cannot survive if you include certain other elements, namely, critics. The trauma can almost always be handled (unless the survivor is addicted or psychotic). What can destroy a relationship, or keep one from developing, is not so much the trauma itself, as the critical judgments that trauma survivors and their significant others have about the trauma and the survivor's traumatic stress reactions. If either you or your survivor have strong internal critics or if either of you tend to be highly critical of the other, it isn't the trauma that will undercut your relationship, but one of these deadly critics.

If you criticize the survivor for actions or characteristics that are clearly part of the involuntary aftermath of the trauma, or, if you criticize yourself for not "doing enough" for the survivor and see yourself as a "failure" because the survivor's symptoms continue to manifest, much of your energy is being directed toward unattainable goals. Criticizing the survivor for being depressed, having flashbacks, or needing to isolate is fruitless. Your criticism will not make these symptoms go away, it will only make them worse. Similarly, criticizing yourself for not being able to heal your loved one won't help you or your loved one. It will only make you irritable and depressed and, eventually, resentful of having spent your energies in vain.

If the survivor's self-criticism could erase the symptoms or problem behaviors, then self-loathing would be a recommended therapeutic technique. Thus far, however, self-hate has not proven effective in solving the problems of hyperarousal, numbing, nightmares, or anxiety attacks.

Keep in mind the fact that all relationships have their issues and all people have their histories and limitations. You may be disappointed that your survivor cannot participate in certain activities you enjoy, for example, boating trips. But there are many nontrauma survivors who do not enjoy or cannot tolerate boating trips. If you love to go boating, then you need to go boating, with or without the survivor. And the survivor will need to set aside feelings of overprotectiveness, possessiveness, and jealousy and not create conflicts or anxiety for you when you choose to pursue activities that bring you happiness, growth, and fulfillment.

Similarly, you need to set aside your feelings of possessiveness and jealousy when the survivor wishes to share certain secrets with other survivors, but not with you, or needs to keep aspects of himself/herself a secret from everyone. Perhaps someday he/she will share with you, but pushing him/her before he/she is ready, will probably not produce the intended results.

If you are willing to talk openly about your feelings, to compromise without significantly diminishing your own life goals, and to explore new, creative, but nontraditional ways of relating, you can have a relationship with a trauma survivor where you both feel loved, cared about, and important. There can be great joy in facing the challenge of dealing with some of the symptoms of PTSD or other trauma reactions and succeeding. But you must throw away old ideas about how relationships *should* be and view the problems in an emotionally neutral manner.

For example, if your survivor is having an anxiety attack, the attitude you—and the survivor—need to have is that it is a problem to be managed, not a sign of deformity or inferiority, or a cause for shame and guilt. If the temperature suddenly dropped and you and the survivor felt cold, you would get wraps and sweaters. You wouldn't accuse each other of being or causing a problem, of "overreacting," of being "weak-willed," or a "mental case." You would do what you needed to do to ward off the cold and then go on with your lives.

When an anxiety or panic attack is going on, the same problem-solving, accepting focus needs to be adopted. You can't wonder what you did to cause the attack and the survivor can't wonder why she/he is so weak or deficient as to be in a state of panic. The only concerns should be what helps and what doesn't.

It is a truism that spiritual love is born of sorrow. In going through difficult times together and in facing the sorrows inherent in having been traumatized, you and your survivor can know a closeness that transcends relationships based on superficialities. Your commitment to each other will be real and substantial. Not only in your relationship with your survivor, but in all the parts of your life, you will have acquired an invaluable ability: You will have learned how to make positive use of your frustration, fear, anger, and pain. In this and in many other ways, you and your survivor will be able to consider yourselves truly victorious.

I hope that I have not presented any simplistic or stereotypical thinking about trauma survivors and their loved ones in this book. As I have repeatedly stressed, each trauma survivor and each survivor's loved ones are unique. Our knowledge of trauma and its effects on survivors and their families is only beginning to unfold and I view my observations as preliminary and limited in nature. I offer them in hopes of assuring those who are troubled that they are not alone and that with effort and guidance, important human relationships need not be yet another casualty of whatever trauma was endured. Indeed, after trauma, relationships cannot only survive, they can help heal the effects of the trauma and contribute to the development and courage of all involved. For those trauma survivors who lost relationships as a result of their trauma, current relationships may be especially valued and lovingly cherished.

References

Berman, A. L. 1987. "Suicide." Staff Development Seminar. Counseling Center, University of Maryland, College Park, MD, April, 17.

Bhatia, S., M. Khan, and A. Sharma. 1986. "Suicide Risk: Evaluation and Management." *American Family Physician* 34 (3), September. 167–174.

Coffman, Sandra and Neil Jacobson. 1996. "Social Learning-Based Marital Therapy and Cognitive Therapy as a Combined Treatment for Depression." In *Depression and Families: Impact and Treatment*. G. I. Keitner, Ed. Washington, D.C.: American Psychiatric Press. 137–156.

Cole, Nancy. 1995. "Effective Treatment of Dissociative Disorders." Audiotape P3-1055-95A of lecture presented at the Seventh Annual Regional Conference on Abuse and Multiple Personality, Training in Treatment. Alexandria, VA. June.

Harvey, Claire. 1995. "Stores of Resilience in Trauma Survivors." Audiotape 95ISTSS of lecture presented at the Annual Conference of the International Society for Traumatic Stress Studies. Boston. November.

G. Keitner, I. Miller, N. Epstein, and D. Bishop, 1990. "Family Process and the Course of Depressive Illness" In *Depression and Families; Impact and Treatment*. G. Keitner, Ed. Washington, D.C.: American Psychiatric Press, Inc. 1–30.

Johnson, David, Susan Feldman, and Hadar Lubin. 1995. "Critical Interaction Therapy: Couples Therapy in Combat-Related Posttraumatic Stress Disorder." *Family Process*. 401–412.

Reynolds, D. K. and N. L. Farberow.1976. *Suicide Inside And Out*. Berkeley, CA: University of California Press.

Schutz, Ben. 1982. *"The Suicidal Patient."* Staff Development Seminar. Department of Veteran's Affairs, May 12, 1982.

Smith, C. W., and E. T. Bope. 1986. "The Suicidal Patient: The Primary-Care Physician's Role in Evaluation and Treatment." *Postgraduate Medicine*. 79(8) 195–199, 202 June.

van der Kolk, B. A. McFarlane, and Lars Weisaeth, Eds. 1996. *Traumatic Stress: The Effects, Experience on Mind, Body, and Society*. New York: Guilford Press.

Victoroff, V. M. 1983. *The Suicidal Patient; Recognition, Intervention, Management*. Oradell, NJ: Medical Economics Books.

Appendix A: Books on Trauma

Adams, Caren and Jennifer Fay. 1989. *Free of the Shadows: Recovering from Sexual Violence*. Oakland, CA: New Harbinger Publications.

Bard, Morton and Daw Sangry. 1986. *The Crime Victim's Book*: Second Edition. Secaucas, NJ: Citadel Press.

Barrett, Terrence. 1989. *Life After Suicide: A Survivor's Grief Experience*. Fargo, ND: Prairie House.

Bass, Ellen and Laura Davis. 1988. *The Courage to Heal*. New York: Harper and Row.

Bradshaw, John. 1981. *Healing the Shame That Binds You*. Deerfield Beach, FL: Health Communications.

Brende, Joel Osler. 1991. *Trauma Recovery for Victims and Survivors: A Twelve-Step Recovery Workbook for Group Leaders and Participants*. P. O. Box 6689, Columbus, GA 31907: Trauma Recovery Publications. 404-563-9893.

Burns, David. Feeling Good: *The New Mood Therapy*. New York: Signet Books.

Copeland, Mary Ellen. 1992. *The Depression Workbook*. Oakland, CA: New Harbinger Publications.

Courtois, Christine. 1993. *Adult Survivors of Child Sexual Abuse*. 117 West Lake Drive, Park Place, Milwaukee, WI 53224: Family Service America.

Crook, Marion. 1988. *Teenagers Talk About Suicide*. Checktowaga, NY: University of Toronto Press.

Crook, Marion. 1992. *Please Listen to Me: Your Guide to Understanding Teenagers and Suicide*. Second Edition. Bellingham, WA: Self-Counsel Press.

Davis, Laura. 1990. *The Courage to Heal Workbook*. New York: Harper and Row.

Engle, Beverly. 1989. *The Right to Innocence: Healing the Trauma of Sexual Abuse*. New York: Ivy.

Farmer, Steven. 1989. *Adult Children of Abusive Parents*. Los Angeles: Lowell House.

Gil, Eliana. 1992. *Outgrowing the Pain Together: A Book for Spouses and Partners of Adults Abused as Children*. New York: Dell Publishing.

Hansel, Sarah, Anne Steidle, Grace Zaczek, and Ron Zaczek. 1995. *Soldier's Heart: A Survivor's View of Combat Trauma*. Lutherville, MD: Sidran Press.

Heckler, Richard. 1994. *Waking Up Alive: The Descent, the Suicide Attempt, and the Return to Life*. New York: Grosset-Putnam Books.

Herman, Judith. 1994. *Trauma and Recovery: The Aftermath of Violence*. New York: Basic Books.

Kunzman, Kristin. 1990. *The Healing Way—Adult Recovery from Childhood Sexual Abuse*. Center City, MN: Hazeldon Educational Materials.

Ledray, Linda. 1986. *Recovering from Rape*. New York: Owl Books, Henry Holt and Company.

Lew, Mike. 1989. *Victims No Longer: Men Recovering from Incest and Other Sexual Abuse*. New York: Nevramont Publishing Company.

Lewis, Michael. 1992. *Shame: The Exposed Self*. New York: The Free Press.

MacPherson, Myra. 1984. *Long Time Passing: Viet Nam: The Haunted Generation*. Garden City, NY: Doubleday and Colk, Inc.

Martin, Del. 1981. *Battered Wives*. San Francisco: Volcano Press.

Mason, Patricia. 1990. *Recovering from the War: A Woman's Guide to Helping Your Vietnam Vet, Your Family, and Yourself*. New York: Penguin Books.

Matsakis, Aphrodite. 1996. *I Can't Get Over It*, Second Edition. Oakland, CA: New Harbinger Publications.

Matsakis, Aphrodite. 1996. *Vietnam Wives: Women and Children Surviving Life with Veterans with PTSD*. Second Edition. Lutherville, MD: Sidran Press.

Matsakis, Aphrodite. 1991. *When the Bough Breaks: A Helping Guide for Parents of Sexually Abused Children*. Oakland, CA: New Harbinger Publications.

Nathanson, Donald. 1992. *Shame and Pride: Affect, Sex and the Birth of the Self*. New York: W. W. Norton.

Nice, Suzanne and Russell Forest. 1990. *Childhood Sexual Abuse: A Survivor's Guide for Men*. Center City, MN: Hazelden Educational Materials.

Presnal, Louis. 1985. *First Aid for Depression*. Center City, MN: Hazeldon Educational Materials.

Ratner, Ellen. 1990. *The Other Side of the Family: A Book of Recovery from Abuse, Incest, and Neglect*. Deerfield Beach, FL: Health Communications.

Robbins, Christopher. 1987. *The Ravens*. New York: Crown Publishers, Inc. (This describes the experiences and feelings of a combat veteran.)

Robinson, Rita. 1992. *Survivors of Suicide*. North Hollywood, CA: Newcastle Publishing.

Ross, Eleanora. 1990. *After Suicide—A Ray of Hope*. Iowa City, IA: Lynn Publications. To order: Contact Ray of Hope, P.O. Box 2323 Iowa City, IA 52244.

Schneider, Carl D. 1977. *Shame, Exposure and Privacy*. New York: W. W. Norton and Company.

Walker, Lenore. 1979. *The Battered Woman*. New York: Harper and Row.

Warshaw, R. 1988. *I Never Called It Rape*. New York: Harper and Row.

Wertheimer, Allison. 1991. *A Special Star: The Experiences of People Bereaved by Suicide*. New York: Routledge.

White, Evelyn. 1985. *Chain Gang Change: For Black Women Dealing with Physical and Emotional Abuse*. Seattle, WA: Seal Press.

Zambrano, Myrna. 1985. *Major Sola Que Mal Sacompanada: Para La Mujer Golopeada* Seattle, WA: Seal Press. (This was written for the Latina in an abusive relationship.)

Where to Buy Tapes

Tapes of lectures from the conferences of the International Society for the Study of Dissociation can be ordered from Audio Transcripts, Ltd. 3660-B Wheeler Avenue, Alexandria, VA 22304. Phone: 703-370 TAPE (8273). Fax: 703-370-5162. The International Society for the Study of Dissociation is located at 4700 West Lake Avenue, Glenview, IL 60025-1485.

Tapes of lectures from the conferences of the International Society for Traumatic Stress Studies can be obtained through Professional Programs Audio Cassettes, P. O. Box 221466, Santa Clarita, CA 91322-1466. Phone: 805-255-7774. Fax: 805-254-4774. The International Society for Traumatic Stress Studies is at 60 Revere Drive, Suite 500, Northbrook, IL 60062. Phone: 847-480-9028. Fax: 847-480-9282.

Appendix B: Reactions to Traumatic Stress

What Is Trauma?

Events that are usually considered traumatic are (1) man-made traumas such as war, family violence, crime, technological disasters, and vehicular accidents and (2) natural catastrophes such as fires, floods, earthquakes, and hurricanes. Traumatic events involve death or the threat of death; injury or the threat of injury. It is not just the events themselves but the *experience* of those events that makes them traumatic.

In this sense, trauma involves three elements: being afraid, feeling overwhelmed, and being or feeling helpless. If you are afraid, but not feeling overwhelmed and can take decisive action on your own behalf, this may be very stressful, but it doesn't necessarily constitute trauma. Similarly, you may be in a situation where you are overwhelmed and feeling helpless, but if you are not afraid of possible loss of life or injury to yourself or others about you, this is not technically considered trauma.

Common Reactions to Trauma

Post-traumatic stress disorder, or PTSD, is just one of several possible reactions to trauma. As Doctor Judith Herman points out in her book, *Trauma and Recovery: The Aftermath of Violence—From Domestic Abuse to Political Terror* (1944), other common reactions include depression, somatization, and dissociation (see definitions below).

Trauma can also trigger episodes of manic depressive illness, paranoia, panic attacks, and other disorders, especially if there is a family history of such problems. In addition, trauma can trigger medical problems, which, in turn, can induce clinical depression.

Many illnesses are known to be stress-related, for example, respiratory illnesses including asthma and bronchitis, certain allergies, anxiety-induced heart conditions, skin problems, and urinary or bladder infections. Although it is not clear that stress causes these problems, repeated trauma and unrelenting stress do break down the immune system, leaving the individual more vulnerable to illness. If the stress continues, the survivor will have difficulty finding the rest and peace of mind necessary for recovery. In addition, almost any medical problem can be aggravated by psychological or economic stress.

Post-Traumatic Stress Disorder

Post-traumatic stress disorder occurs when people react to traumatic stress by dissociating or by experiencing extreme feelings of helplessness and terror and then, subsequently, experiencing periods of emotional numbing and hyperalertness, as well as periods when they re-experience the trauma in the form of nightmares, flashbacks, intrusive thoughts, or other types of "re-living" experiences. *Emotional numbing* refers to a shutdown of emotions, and to difficulties in feeling close to others. *Hyperalertness* refers to being constantly on guard, sleep difficulties, and difficulties managing irritability and anger.

Depression

What happens to a car that is driven cross-country many times without a tune-up, oil change, or tire rotation? What happens to a car that is well-maintained but is driven coast to coast 1,000 times? Would some parts start to wear out? Perhaps the car would eventually cease to function.

Clearly, people are not cars. However, what happens to a car because of overuse or inadequate care is similar to what happens to people when they undergo repeated traumas or prolonged severe stress, and they do not have the time, money, or ability to take care of themselves. Under such conditions, their emotional and physical reserves become taxed to the point where they develop clinical depression all too easily.

The term *depression,* as used here, does not refer to the normal "down" periods experienced by almost everyone, that is, to temporary feelings of sadness, more commonly known as "the blues." Rather, depression refers to biologically based clinical depression, which usually needs to be treated with psychiatric medication, as well as with psychotherapy.

Symptoms of depression include feelings of worthlessness, hopelessness, and fatigue; irritability and anxiety; falling or staying asleep at inappropriate times; and the loss of the ability to feel pleasure.

Somatization

Somatization occurs when the body expresses the pain, anger, and other feelings associated with the trauma in the form of physical pain or impairment. As Herman (1994) points out, somatization tends to occur more commonly in situations where speaking up is dangerous and may be punished or cause for social ostracism or rejection.

Somatization does not mean that the sufferer is mentally deficient or a manipulator trying to "pull a fast one." It also does not mean that the pain is not real or that it "is all in the head." The pain is true bodily pain. The illness is genuine. But the body is also expressing the feelings and memories that cannot be easily or sufficiently put into words because, if expressed, they will put the individual into jeopardy.

In trauma survivors, somatization can take the form of physical pain or an increase in the pain of injuries experienced during the trauma. For example, Martha lost her arm in a car accident on October 5, 1990. Martha has phantom pains in her shoulder. "I don't like to complain about the fact that I still have to deal with infections, bleeding, and other problems because of my missing arm," says Martha. "But I guess the phantom pains do the complaining for me."

Dissociation

Have you ever driven to a familiar place and missed the exit on the highway because your mind was somewhere else? Have you ever left your keys or wallet somewhere by accident because you were stressed out or on "overload"?

Such experiences of forgetting are common to everyone. They are minor forms of "dissociation," or a problem with memory where certain parts of reality are overlooked and other parts are focused on intently.

Without the ability to dissociate, we could not drive or even watch a movie because any concentrated activity requires paying attention to one part of reality, and blocking out the other parts. Many survivors probably wish that they could "dissociate" from their families and other problems so they could simply enjoy a quiet walk or an afternoon to themselves. To truly dissociate, however, they would have to not only temporarily forget or dim some of their memories, they would also have to weaken or nearly obliterate their feelings about those memories.

True dissociation can involve not only the blocking of information or memories, but a numbing of the emotions associated with that information or those memories. Hence, a combat veteran may not recall a firefight or may be confused or vague about the specifics of a battle, but also report that he cannot remember his feelings at the time and has few or no feelings about the event today.

Like many symptoms, dissociation varies in severity and in the amount of havoc it can create in someone's life. Yet dissociation can also help lessen the emotional pain of living in a horrendous situation. For example, the ability to dissociate helps abused children to do their homework and abused women to bear unbearable conditions. However, when dissociation is extreme, it can make keeping a job and maintaining good communication with others almost impossible.

For more complete discussions of the above-defined reactions to trauma, see *I Can't Get Over It* (Matsakis 1996).

Resources

CIVITAS Child Trauma Programs
Baylor College of Medicine
http:// www.bcm.tmc.edu/civitas/index.html

Incest Survivors Resource Manual
International Friends Meeting House
15 Rutherford Place
NY, NY 10003
P.O. Box 7375, Las Cruces, NM 88006-7375
505-521-4260
Fax 505-521-3723
http://zianet.com/ISRNI/
email ISRNI@zianet.com

Many Voices (a newsletter for people recovering from trauma)
P.O. Box 2639
Cincinnati, OH 45201-2639
513-531-5415

Mental Health Net—Self-Help for Trauma, PTSD, and Stress Resources
http:// www.cmhc.com/guide/trauma.html

National Center for PTSD
U.S. Dept. of Veterans' Affairs
http://www.dartmouth.edu/dms/ptsd/

Rape, Abuse, and Incest National Network (RAINN)
24-hour national hotline
http://www.cs.utk.edu/~bartley/other/RAINN.html

Tapes of lectures from the conferences of International Society for the Study of Dissociation can be ordered from Audio Transcripts, Ltd., 3660-B Wheeler Avenue, Alexandria, VA 22304. Or call 703-370-RAPE (8273) Fax: 703-370-5162. The International Society for the Study of Dissociation is located at 4700 West Lake Avenue, Glenview, IL 60025-1485.

Tapes from lectures from the conferences of the International Study for Traumatic Stress can be obtained through Professioanl Programs Audio Cassettes, PO Box 221466, Santa Clarita, CA 91322-1466, 805-255-7774 or Fax: 805-254-4774. The International Society for Traumatic Stress Studies is at 60 Revere Drive, Suite 500, Northbrook, IL 60062. Phone: 847-480-9028 Fax: 847-480-9282.

Some Other
New Harbinger Titles

Surviving Your Borderline Parent, Item 3287 $14.95

When Anger Hurts, second edition, Item 3449 $16.95

Calming Your Anxious Mind, Item 3384 $12.95

Ending the Depression Cycle, Item 3333 $17.95

Your Surviving Spirit, Item 3570 $18.95

Coping with Anxiety, Item 3201 $10.95

The Agoraphobia Workbook, Item 3236 $19.95

Loving the Self-Absorbed, Item 3546 $14.95

Transforming Anger, Item 352X $10.95

Don't Let Your Emotions Run Your Life, Item 3090 $17.95

Why Can't I Ever Be Good Enough, Item 3147 $13.95

Your Depression Map, Item 3007 $19.95

Successful Problem Solving, Item 3023 $17.95

Working with the Self-Absorbed, Item 2922 $14.95

The Procrastination Workbook, Item 2957 $17.95

Coping with Uncertainty, Item 2965 $11.95

The BDD Workbook, Item 2930 $18.95

You, Your Relationship, and Your ADD, Item 299X $17.95

The Stop Walking on Eggshells Workbook, Item 2760 $18.95

Conquer Your Critical Inner Voice, Item 2876 $15.95

The PTSD Workbook, Item 2825 $17.95

Hypnotize Yourself Out of Pain Now!, Item 2809 $14.95

The Depression Workbook, 2nd edition, Item 268X $19.95

Beating the Senior Blues, Item 2728 $17.95

Call **toll free, 1-800-748-6273,** or log on to our online bookstore at **www.newharbinger.com** to order. Have your Visa or Mastercard number ready. Or send a check for the titles you want to New Harbinger Publications, Inc., 5674 Shattuck Ave., Oakland, CA 94609. Include $4.50 for the first book and 75¢ for each additional book, to cover shipping and handling. (California residents please include appropriate sales tax.) Allow two to five weeks for delivery.

Prices subject to change without notice.